The Global Predicament

The Global Predicament

Ecological Perspectives on World Order

Edited by
David W. Orr and Marvin S. Soroos

Foreword by
Richard A. Falk

The University of North Carolina Press
Chapel Hill

© 1979 The University of North Carolina Press
All rights reserved
Manufactured in the United States of America
Cloth edition, ISBN 0-8078-1346-X
Paper edition, ISBN 0-8078-1349-4
Library of Congress Catalog Card Number 78-10207
First printing, May 1979
Second printing, February 1980

Library of Congress Cataloging in Publication Data

Main entry under title:

The Global Predicament.

    Bibliography: p.
    Includes index.
    1. Natural resources—Addresses, essays, lectures.
2. Human ecology—Addresses, essays, lectures.
3. International organization—Addresses, essays,
lectures.   4. World politics—1965-   —Addresses,
essays, lectures.   I. Orr, David W., 1944–
II. Soroos, Marvin S., 1945–
HC55.G56   330.9'04   78-10207
ISBN 0-8078-1346-X
ISBN 0-8078-1349-4 pbk.

34,050

To Michael, Daniel, Joel, and Valerie

Contents

Foreword

When, how, and under what circumstances will a new global political order emerge? What will be its attributes? Will its operation embody values associated with peace, equity, human dignity, and ecological balance? These questions arise at a particular moment in world history when it is increasingly evident that we are in the midst of a transition from one world order system (based on state power) to another (based on interdependence, humane scales of governance, and some variety of central guidance). Such a transitional process could continue for centuries; it could evolve badly, stabilizing around some type of tyranny, empire, or chaos. The early forms of planetary order might not prove sustainable for very long, that is, whatever structures of coordination and administration do evolve may go through long periods of trial and error before a relatively stable or desirable planetary order takes definitive, although never static, shape.

Despite these uncertainties, it seems correct to associate the cumulative drift of historical process with political integration at the global level and partial disintegration at the state level, these opposing movements being expressions of *will*, *capability*, and *necessity*. At the same time, certain contradictory tendencies suggest the continuing potency and durability of the state as the dominant organizing reality in world society. Decolonialization, followed by the diffusion of technology and by the rise of national consciousness, has contributed to a rapidly expanding role for the state in all regions of the Third World. Economic nationalism is everywhere evident and has given a group of Third World countries, especially oil producers, greatly increased leverage and stature in the world as now organized. States have in recent years extended the traditional scope of their authority outward to encompass new domains of sea and space as well as inward to provide for the basic needs of their people and, above all, to exert effective control over potentially hostile populations. Also, most governments are eager to safeguard their domestic arenas, as best they can, from adverse encroachments by multinational corporations and international financial institutions. These various tendencies have naturally led to the steady growth of state power, expressed through the increasing size of government and by the growing share of gross national product appropriated in one form or another by the public sector.

More fundamental even than these statist trends are, I believe, the integrative trends associated with the many global dimensions of an emergent ecological reality. The appreciation of limits and interrelations on a global scale is giving rise to various forms of planetary consciousness. More and more people everywhere realize that the boundaries of sovereign states are artificial, whereas the unity of the planet is natural. As a consequence, many people who do not know or will not acknowledge the words, or are bothered by their rootless cosmopolitan resonance, are beginning to feel and act as if they are "planetary citizens." More and more, such people question inequities in the distribution of wealth and income within and among countries and they are beginning to doubt whether the war system brings security to their own society or to the peoples of the world. Naturally, such people also experience a deepening conflict between their loyalties to the state and their feelings of human and planetary identity.

Of course, at the same time, any prudent political analysis would argue the futility of mounting this kind of world order challenge. Militarism is rampant everywhere. Governments in all parts of the world, reflecting each major culture and ideology, seem entrapped in the logic and assumptions of the war system. Population pressure, rising demands for equity, and growth-oriented, capital-intensive development strategies induce most governments to view the mass of their own population as a hostile social force to be pacified if possible, intimidated if necessary, but controlled in their aspirations and behavior by centralized bureaucratic and paramilitary techniques. Even affluent countries are being shaken to their foundations by terrorism, a form of desperate politics that automatically engenders a vicious cycle of violence and repression. The failure of moderate politics, given the goals of welfare and progress associated with the modern state, reveals the extent to which the character of national government is unable to satisfy fundamental human aspirations, especially if one assesses its viability by normative criteria of consent and well-being as well as administrative criteria of effectiveness. In essence, most governments lack the resources or will required to satisfy claims emanating from the various segments of their population, and they feel obliged to rely on coercion rather than consent to achieve stable rule. Often this reliance reflects an unwillingness on the part of presently privileged sectors of a social order to diminish their relative position so as to promote more equitable overall patterns.

In terms of adjusting to the new global context of ecological fragility, states are the main obstacles on the path. The international dynamic of governmental policy is the selfish pursuit of interests, oriented around maximizing economic growth, military power, and diplomatic stature. The largest states, the so-called superpowers, are alert to global challenges and seek to meet them by enlarging their own managerial role to encompass virtually all sectors of the planet. Such imperial designs on the future are severely constrained by the commitment and capability of a large number of governments to defend, by force if necessary, their political independence and territorial integrity against all outsiders. What is evident, however, in such critical areas as economic growth and arms policy is the persistence, and even the accentuation, of old, delegitimized, obsolescent attitudes and patterns of practice. It is not surprising that political actors with a declining capacity to carry out their traditional roles will actually intensify their standard operating procedures in a frantic effort to adapt themselves in a deteriorating situation. Hence, challenge induces persistence, even intensification, until it overwhelms the capacities of the actor, causing abrupt collapse. A slow decline in the role and pretensions of sovereign states is not, accordingly, to be expected at this time of mounting world order challenge. In fact, the fundamental character of the challenge places a premium on pretending it does not exist as there is no indication of a willingness to impose (on elite elements) the social costs that would be required to meet the challenge. Confirmatory of this interpretation of governmental behavior is the absence of any disposition in official Moscow or Washington (or in most other capitals) to consider reorienting their identities and roles through the adoption, or even serious contemplation of steady-state economics, disarmament, or global environmental guidelines. Furthermore, these governments disclose no willingness to strengthen the prestige and authority of the United Nations or to replace it with a more acceptable organizational framework that is assured the capabilities (resources and procedures) as well as the mandate to safeguard planetary interests.

Let's face it. As long as leading governments persist in their old patterns and maintain traditional convictions about stability, security, and order, it would be naive to expect the elites of the world to shape the politics of transition in a beneficial direction. The deepest despair associated with these concerns is felt, I think, by those who understand both the madness of this persistence in old ways and the futility of appeals to governments, but fail to regard evidence of populist political and cultural ferment as hopeful.

Kurt Vonnegut, for instance, a bitter, ironic interpreter of our cosmic plight, describes the appropriate stance toward the future as one of "terminal pessimism." Vonnegut evidently believes that the death warrant for the human species has already been issued. Humanity is clearly doomed, and, what is more, deserves to be—"we are pollution." Indeed, Vonnegut, in the course of affirming the gloomy outlook of science-fiction writer Stanislaw Lem, acknowledges that he is "appalled by all that an insane humanity may yet survive to do." There is no doubt about the ending of history, merely about its precise form. Vonnegut quotes a letter from his son, a medical student: "We're destroying the planet, there's not a damn thing that can be done about it. It's going to be very slow, drawn-out and ugly or so fast it doesn't make any difference."[1] Such deep despair stems from a disappointed rational secularism. Its outlook is completely cut off from vitalizing populist and spiritual movements that provide a vision of renewal and affirmation within the present setting.

A quite different manifestation of secular rationalism is prevalent in the Third World where many spokespeople believe that everything will be all right if benevolent people get into power with a mandate to build a just society, and thereafter frame official policy in enlightened terms, directing their energies outward to combat imperialism and inward to eliminate class privilege. Such analysis seems persuasive with respect to the formation and content of social policy at the national level in many countries. We have available increasingly rigorous demonstrations—for instance, in the world model of the Bariloche Foundation—that ample resources exist in all parts of the world for development strategies designed to achieve the satisfaction of the basic needs of everyone. In effect, poverty is a consequence of political will and societal structures, not an inevitable result of resource scarcity.[2] Such demonstrations unmask the reactionary ideological underpinnings of metaphors such as "lifeboat ethics" or "triage" which remain modish in Western elite circles. Neither population pressure nor resource scarcity provide any persuasive empirical ethical foundation for global policies that divide the human race into those who can be "saved" and those whose misery and death is unavoidable.

Fernando Henrique Cardoso, a widely admired Brazilian social scientist, contends that *"everyone knows that the utopia of our century is materially possible"* (italics in original). For this reason, Cardoso believes it imperative "without disguise" to focus all attention "on the question of power."[3] Cardoso, in a manner characteristic of many neo-Marxist thinkers, implies that planetary malaise, with its generalized anguish, has the effect, whether deliberate or not, of diluting the pressures building up against existing imperial and domestic structures of inequity and exploitation. For Cardoso, as for many others in the Third World, national structures of distorted priorities are partially caused by the transnational use of power to maintain the economic interests of ruling classes in rich and poor countries alike. These structures are created and sustained by power and can only be transformed by power; any more timid approach to reform must be dismissed as either naive or insincere.

Anyone concerned with world-order values must, of course, be sensitive not only to the gross disparities within and among states but also to the importance of acting urgently to reduce and eliminate those disparities. The political premise for such action rests on the universal acceptance of human rights as an essential precondition for minimally acceptable forms of social, political, economic, and cultural order. Unfortunately, even this intense struggle for distributive justice on a global scale does not exhaust the array of dangerous challenges.

It is strange that so many advocates of social and economic justice in human relations ignore the special problems posed by the existence and evolution of nuclear weaponry, including the tendency of this weaponry to put the largest states on a permanent prewar footing of military readiness; the possibility of genuine peace no longer exists even in the minimal sense of a demobilizing pause between wars. Also, strategic doctrines associated with nuclear deterrence flagrantly violate standards of restraint implicit in the "just" war tradition, especially the obligation to refrain from indiscriminate targeting of the civilian population. Furthermore, the process of technological transfer and sales of arms has made every substantial country in the world the possessor of sophisticated military capabilities. As a result almost every state has become a potential nuclear weapons state; that is, by a determined effort, almost any country with some advanced technology can arrange to have some bombs fabricated as well as acquire an effective system for their delivery.

The crowding of the planet in a setting of continuously accelerating industrialization has caused a variety of distinctive and uncertain hazards that are quite independent of distributive injustice. The nature of mass production—of mature industrialization—is posing a series of acute physical and psychic symptoms of severe distress, ranging from cancer to terrorism. Population growth in poorer countries, especially, is increasing the work force at a much faster rate than can be absorbed by the domestic economy, producing escalating unemployment and deep discontent. In addition, resource constraints by way of cropland and energy at unacceptable costs may impinge upon the capacity of even a reformed distributive system to satisfy human needs for the indefinite future; a physically confined ecosystem like the earth, even allowing for the extension of operating room via space exploits, has limits of optimal and sustainable population and industrialization. The failure to adjust the scale of human activity within these limits causes unnecessary suffering and danger, and it deteriorates both the life experience of individuals and groups and endangers life prospects for future generations.

In other words, the agenda for global activists is far longer than a preoccupation with power shifts would imply. The experience in the more industrialized countries, whether organized as market or command economies, suggests that fairer distribution brings no assurance of even minimally humane governance, let alone utopia. It is necessary to emphasize the complementary, rather than the competitive, nature of these observations, whose intention is to link the struggle for equity to the broader agenda of global reform.

Especially in the rich countries, this broader agenda will be taken seriously only after the cultural indictment upon which it ultimately rests is coupled with a positive vision of viable and attainable economic, political, and cultural alternatives. Demonstrating the reality of viable alternatives also helps us reject both the apocalyptic forebodings of those who proclaim an irreversible collision course and the technophilic manifestos of those who assure us that a new era of leisure-laden abundance is on its way.

It is also crucial to avoid shallow optimism about the future that overlooks the kind of evidence that induces either terminal pessimism or radical politics. The technophilic optimism of those who continue to regard technology as the ground from which a new utopia will rise is not only mindless, it is dangerously irresponsible. Perhaps the most absurd exponent of this outlook is F. M. Esfandiary, who in a series of books has set forth the outlines of his Up-Wing (as distinct from left and right wing, dismissed as outmoded categories) ideology of incredible optimism: "Limits to growth? What limits? The only limits are in some people's imagination and vision. How ridiculous to emphasize limits at this very moment when we are expanding into a limitless Universe of limitless resources, limitless space, limitless potentials, limitless growth." Esfandiary is completely conditioned by an electronic vision. He looks forward to a variety of drastic changes in the human situation including the opportunity to "deanimalize": "Replace our animal organs and body parts with durable painfree nonflesh implants." He also thinks positively about becoming "telehuman" as "the next stage in the evolution of humans. A linkup of the human mind and durable versatile telebodies. Our fragile animal parts as eyes-ears-lungs-hearts-kidneys-livers-etc. . . . are replaced by implanted microcomputers-microtelevision-microantennae-microcassettes-microrecycling units and so on."[4] Tendencies that George Orwell and Aldous Huxley envisioned in the most dysutopian terms are revisioned by Esfandiary in a wildly utopian frenzy. At the same time, Esfandiary's future is ice-cold when it comes to the present victimization of billions of people or on the matter, even, of how the structures of secular power are to be transcended by the emergent generations of telehumans. Reading Esfandiary makes one want to mount the nearest barricade, although, in one sense, his vision of the future is only an unabashed version of what passes for wisdom and common sense in most centers of First World power. For instance, Herman Kahn, with his milder endorsement of the same scenario, is actually taken seriously as a cultural interpreter.

A more compelling form of optimism is associated with the countercultural repudiation of the technological path. This repudiation is expressed in many different forms, all converging around the need to revive the spiritual center of human experience and emphasizing what has been called "voluntary simplicity." E. F. Schumacher's emphasis on self-reliance, religiosity, and the virtues of smallness has been widely accepted by proliferating groups of countercultural advocates of lifestyle revolution. This movement remains underappreciated as a new force for change, and yet one still wonders how it will ever crack the hard institutions of the state or overcome the managerial/manipulative reality of large-scale economic enterprise, whether in the form of corporate or state ownership. How can the counterculture stimulate a "politics" that is sustainable in the face of determined opposition?

Joined to this growing receptivity to change on a personal level, especially in the most advanced countries, is a slowly growing movement to reshape world order. Undertakings like the World Order Models Project draw support from participants in all parts of the world and seek to mobilize intellectual energies and moral passions around "the next ideology," a rationale for political life on a planetary scale, as well as a program of intermediate tactics and strategies. Its strength and appeal arise from its insight into the deteriorating historical situation. The increasingly evident bankruptcy of existing institutions manifest in their failure to organize stabilizing responses even to such obvious menaces as weapons of mass destruction or processes of ecological decay reinforces the argument that global reform depends on a social movement of global dimension.

This book of essays is in the best spirit of a new enlightenment that uses reason and understanding to discover what kinds of adjustments are possible and necessary to facilitate a humane transition to the emergent planetary culture we will inevitably possess in the next century. The authors gathered here exhibit new modes of thinking, feeling, and acting that hold out the promise of improving our capacity to cope with a personal and collective situation that is laden with both danger and opportunity. In its essence, I believe, this book receives its editorial inspiration from what Teilhard de Chardin more than fifty years ago expressed as "the cry of a world trembling with the desire for unity."[5]

Richard A. Falk

The Global Predicament

Introduction

Throughout history nature has been regarded by most societies as a forbidding and hostile antagonist. By comparison with the awesome dimensions of the natural world, man's achievements and artifacts seemed to be insignificant. It is no mystery why many assumed that civilization could expand only as the uncontrolled parts of nature diminished. But whether civilization in fact expanded as man's technological control over nature increased is at least questionable. What is certain, however, is that man's often haphazard interventions in nature in the industrial-technological era have progressively undermined the stability of the same natural systems on which his life and well-being depend. No longer can we assume the abundance of natural resources, the stability of climate, or the purity of air and water. Given the increase in man's numbers and in the power of his technology, the nature that once appeared so awesome is now known to be fragile and limited. The speed with which this revolution occurred is remarkable. Even a hundred years ago, nature, though not uncontested, was clearly dominant. Although this is no longer the case, many of our habits, attitudes, and institutions are still grounded in the belief that man plays only an insignificant role in the processes and cycles of the biosphere.

If any one symbol captures the essence of this change, it is the photograph of the earth taken from the Apollo spacecraft in 1969. What is striking is the background of space, which appears as a vast, dark void against which the earth is only a small, green and blue oasis. From Apollo, the earth had neither boundaries nor divisions, only oceans, deserts, polar caps, mountains, forests, and drifting clouds blended in a unique mosaic of life. There could be no clearer demonstration of what Adlai Stevenson once called "spaceship earth," and no more stark evidence that earth is the only possible habitat for man. Destroy or degrade that home, and we must surely destroy or degrade ourselves.

From this perspective, it is instructive to note that the term *ecology*, first used by the German biologist Ernst Haeckel in 1869, is based on the Greek root *oikos*, meaning *house*. Literally, ecology signifies the study of life forms "at home." Since Haeckel, ecology has emerged as the science of "interrelationships between living organisms and their environment."[1] These interrelationships are described by contemporary ecologists in terms of energy flows, food chains, patterns of diversity, nutrient cycles, evolution, and cybernetics. The principle of interrelatedness is implicit in the concept of "ecosystem," which describes any natural community, and the concept of "biosphere," which denotes the global envelope of air, water, and land necessary to life.

The emphasis on relationships or "holism" has led some to suggest that ecology is subversive of contemporary science, which prospered by fragmenting, dissecting, and reducing reality to its physicochemical properties. In this regard science bears resemblance to the modern international system and the division of the earth into competing, antagonistic, political units. Ecological deterioration not only requires alternative ways of scientific knowing but, more directly, confronts mankind with its first truly global crisis, for whose resolution there are as yet no effective global institutions. The web of ecology is intricate, complex, and inclusive, yet we have only a rudimentary ability to perceive and think holistically. Although environmental problems are evident in the now familiar agenda of pollution, over-population, resource and energy shortages, and land abuses, we have scarcely begun to consider what meaningful solutions will imply for a world sharply divided between rich and poor. Some have argued that we can avoid substantial value or behavioral changes through the beneficent march of technology—particularly those forms that are complex, expensive, and centralized—so that within a century or two mankind would be "everywhere rich and in control of the forces of nature."[2] Whether a technological utopia is either feasible or desirable is not our immediate concern. At least in the foreseeable future, there are no technical fixes that can quickly erase the ecological crisis. Were we to assume the contrary, we still might prudently wonder what other unwanted and unanticipated side effects would be generated in the process.

The impossibility of any near-term technological solution to the crisis raises a number of questions. The most pressing of these concerns the distribution of wealth in a world characterized by enormous disparities of income. If wealth is either fixed or created at rates well below those of recent decades, how can the affluent justify their advantage? In the past the rich took refuge behind the ideas of inherent virtue, divine election, or societal efficiency. But these have lost their power to enchant. More recently they have resorted to statistics to demonstrate that the poor need not worry about wealth because the ongoing miracle of compound growth and consequent trickle-down would make everyone rich. But if we are now entering an age of scarcity in which growth is either impossible or possible only at great environmental risk, large disparities of income may become overwhelmingly oppressive, undermining social stability both within and between nations.

The unlikelihood of any near-term technical fix raises other, and larger, questions concerning the interface between human and purely natural systems. Decisions made in the political arena affecting society and the economy ought to be made with a greater understanding of ecology. To fail to do so will eventually jeopardize the stability of ecosystems and ultimately society itself. If we envision the political system as a resource allocation mechanism, we can begin to see the outlines of a new area of inquiry where man and nature interact. The ecological perspective encourages us to extend our vision to see ourselves as a dependent component of the biosphere against the span of geologic time. If in this larger perspective man's function is to be other than that of a global plague or a means to recirculate stored carbon, he must learn to live within natural constraints.

For those interested in the relationship between politics and ecology, this implies the need to develop new perspectives, concepts, theories, and research priorities. Scholars need to explore the effects of government policies on the ecosystem, and the ways in which ecological factors in turn influence political development. The ecological perspective suggests that we give serious attention to the international political system and those environmental issues that transcend political boundaries.[3] There are an increasing number of global issues for which there are no purely national solutions.

Problems of oceanic pollution, international river management, climate disruption, protection of atmospheric ozone levels, and resource depletion will require the emergence of new forms of institutions and radical changes in the prevailing concept of national sovereignty.

II

Despite the intensification of ecological problems in the past two decades, it is evident that environmental mismanagement was also characteristic of previous civilizations. The early development of agriculture led to permanent and frequently adverse alterations of ecosystems, including deforestation and eroded and salinated soils, notably in the Middle East. Homer, for instance, once poetically described the wooded hills of Thrace, hills that now support little but weeds. Similarly, biblical references to the cedars of Lebanon stand in marked contrast to the barren and eroded land of contemporary Lebanon. North Africa, once the granary of the Roman Empire, is now capable of supporting only marginally productive agriculture.[4] Given adequate rainfall, ecosystems may recover but not in humanly meaningful time.

Issues of global ecology have recently assumed heightened importance for a number of reasons. First, the demands placed on the ecosystem have grown in pace with the rapid increase in both world population and the gross world product. As these multiply further, we can expect to see signs of even greater environmental stress. Many of these signs are quite visible in polluted air and water, eroded land, and denuded hills, so that even the most indifferent are aware of a crisis. Second, the emerging knowledge of resource limits has kindled an intense debate about equity and justice in a number of international conferences. It is apparent to many observers that ecological issues, including scarcity, will intensify international conflict unless resolved by farsighted statesmanship and by a redefinition of our notions of progress. Third, issues of ecology are closely intertwined with issues of technology. There is a growing opposition to some forms of "high" technology, such as SST's nuclear power, supertankers, and even that ultimate symbol of mobility, the automobile. Fourth, the emergence of a system of global communications has led to the wide diffusion of information about ecological issues and the spread of influential books such as Rachel Carson's *Silent Spring* and the MIT study, *The Limits to Growth*.

Attention has also been focused on global ecological problems because of the series of United Nations conferences dating back to the 1948 Conference on the Conservation and Utilization of Resources at Lake Success and the 1957–58 geophysical year. More recent conferences have been held on the biosphere at Paris in 1968, environment at Stockholm in 1972, population at Bucharest in 1974, human settlements at Vancouver in 1976, and water at Buenos Aires in 1977. Environmental issues were also implicit at the United Nations Conference on the Law of the Sea, which began in 1974 and at the special sessions of the General Assembly on raw materials in the spring of 1974 and in the fall of 1975.

The development of an international response to environmental affairs can also be traced through the formation of international organizations, including the Food and Agriculture Organization (1945), the International Meteorological Organization (1951), the United Nations Scientific Committee on the Effects of Radiation (1955), the Intergovernmental Maritime Consultative Organization (1958), and the United Nations Environmental Program (1972). Some degree of international response is also evident in the growing number of treaties that directly or indirectly affect the environment, including the test ban of 1963, prohibitions on ocean dumping in 1972 and 1975, as well as agreements to control pollution in the Baltic and the Mediterranean. To date however, none of these organizations or agreements taken singly or collectively has done more than nibble at the fringe of the larger crisis of planetary ecology.

III

As problems of "ecological scarcity" intensify in coming decades, we can expect far-reaching changes in the substance of international politics. Issues of resource management and equity will become more acute, creating incentives for both conflict and cooperation. The probability of ecological disasters will increase with the spread of "high" technologies and with the large-scale alteration of ecosystems such as those contemplated in the Soviet plan to divert fresh water supplies from the Arctic, or the Brazilian plan to develop the Amazon Basin. Similar, if less dramatic, threats to the stability of the international system will arise from the slower processes of soil erosion, climate changes caused by thermal disruptions or carbon dioxide, and the despoliation of oceans. Moreover, these disruptions will occur against the background of increasing demands exerted by a growing world population that is expected to increase by 50 percent by the year 2000. The competition for food, energy, and resources will create new linkages and relationships between international actors. We have recently witnessed the creation of resource cartels (OPEC), the International Energy Agency (IEA), and increasing militancy among the less developed states in UNCTAD (United Nations Conference on Trade and Development) and in the United Nations General Assembly.

Since no state can insulate itself, the ecological crisis will also create opportunities to transcend the state-centric, conflict-oriented paradigm of power politics. The rationale for cooperation and altruism grows with the likelihood of mutual self-destruction. But whether the crisis will lead to cooperation or conflict depends in part upon our ability to reconceptualize the study of international relations and to create a model of political behavior that accords with ecological realities. For the discipline of international relations, this suggests changes in (1) perspectives and methods of inquiry; (2) concepts; (3) central issues and problems; (4) policies; and (5) the design of political institutions.

Perspectives and Methods

Garrett Hardin once observed that "you can never do just one thing," yet the conduct of most academic research is premised on the assumption that we can. Science has progressed by fragmenting reality into manageable bits and pieces but in the process has tended to ignore the larger questions of meaning. To supplement "normal" science, we now urgently need broad visions to tell us what the bits and pieces mean. The ecological crisis transcends the relatively fixed boundaries between academic disciplines. To respond to this crisis, we must surmount reductionism and narrow academic specialization in order to perceive the complex functioning of whole systems. The perceptions of the generalist and the specialist must be integrated to create interdisciplinary modes of thought and inquiry.

The ecological perspective also suggests a different orientation toward time and values. As change quickens in pace and becomes

more abrupt, there is more need for anticipation of future problems
having historically unique attributes. This implies the adoption of
future-oriented methods of inquiry, including technique both for
forecasting probable futures and for designing more desirable alternative futures that are possible but not necessary probable. Such
future-oriented inquiry will require a relating of empirical research on
questions of *what is* to normative concerns for *what ought to be*. The
role of the "value-free" social scientist who observes but remains
intellectually and morally detached is no longer adequate to a world
of rapidly multiplying human needs.

Concepts

At the heart of any field is its unique set of concepts. In addition to
providing a means for communication of ideas, this basic language
guides perceptions of problems and issues and becomes the building
blocks for the construction of theory. The evolution of human
understanding is in part dependent on the process of continual
revision of the conceptual underpinnings of knowledge.

Social scientists concerned with environmental matters have
adopted a number of the concepts from the fields of ecology and
systems theory, including *ecosystem*, *biosphere*, *carrying capacity*, and
overshoot. The application of these concepts to social phenomena,
however, is often difficult. The level of economic development, for
example, can have an important bearing on definitions of "carrying
capacity." Poverty and malnutrition are to some observers signs of
overshoot, whereas to others they are indicative of basic inequities in
the distribution of the world's wealth.

The conjunction between ecological concepts and traditional disciplines has led some to propose radical changes in our approach to
reality. Nicholas Georgescu-Roegen and Herman Daly have proposed
that economists adopt the perspective of physics, which would
suggest the necessity of steady states where net growth must eventually stop. Economists have developed elaborate theories of the
economic process as if it were independent of physical constraints
and of itself magically conjured up the wealth produced by economic
activity. Perhaps no less absurd are theories of development and
modernization that assume a continual abundance of energy and
resources. The essays in this volume suggest revision in a number of
concepts of long-established acceptance: "development" needs to be

redefined for an era of scarcity; "conflict" and "peace" should be interpreted more broadly to take into account the impact of present generations on the welfare of future generations; definitions of "crisis" and "catastrophe" normally applied to social interactions need to be supplemented with the idea of man/nature interactions; new ideas of dependence and interdependence are needed to describe relations on a planet where resources are unevenly distributed.

Issues and Problems

As the demands on a depleted planet increase with rapid growth in population and industrialization, we can expect that changes will occur in the predominant patterns of conflict in the global political system. Although conflict over resources is not new, the form it has taken is changing rapidly. Colonialism, for example, is a thing of the past, but politically independent states of Africa, Asia, and Latin America must still struggle to gain control of their natural resources from multinational corporations based in the developed world. Competition among petroleum-exporting nations has given way to competition between importing nations. The interests of resource-producing and resource-consuming nations are in conflict over both the level and the stability of prices, while the interests of present and future generations collide over issues of intergenerational equity. As land-based resources become more scarce, conflict over ocean resources will sharpen. International disputes have already emerged over the control of fishing rights, offshore oil, and resources of the seabed. Similar conflicts are possible over the control of resources in Antarctica and eventually in outer space.

   All of these conflicts are intimately tied to perceptions of distribution and equity that the less affluent states understandably argue must take priority over ecological considerations. From this perspective, the squalor of poverty is regarded as a more pressing environmental problem than industrial pollution. The text of environmental principles adopted at the Stockholm Conference illustrates this view: "The environmental policies of all states should enhance and not adversely affect the present or future development potential of developing countries, nor should they hamper the attainment of better living conditions for all, and appropriate steps should be taken by states and international organizations with a view to reaching

agreement on meeting the possible national and international economic consequences resulting from the application of environmental
measures." The prospect of economic growth has made inequalities
easier to accept by the disadvantaged in the belief that all would
become wealthier. In an era of ecological scarcity, however, conflict
over distribution will assume zero-sum qualities. Demands for redistribution will become increasingly strident, a trend already evident
in the program for a "new international economic order."

Policies

Modern states operate closer to ecological limits with much less
margin for error than ever before. This implies that greater attention
ought to be given to the design of policies governing energy,
technology, resources, and population. Particular care must be taken
in the growing number of decisions where there is a possibility of
large-scale, irreversible consequences. New decision strategies that
go beyond incrementalism are clearly in order, not only on the
national level but also at the global level, where the separate decisions
of governments, corporations, and intergovernmental actors inter-
sect. This implies not only the restructuring of the decision process
but also the creation of new forms of institutions capable of anticipating and responding to potential crises so as to avoid an era of
ecological brinksmanship.

Ecological scarcity also implies the reconsideration of the substance
of policies governing exchange relationships between nations. In the
past, policies of trade and aid were conducted on the basis of
advantage and power, with the result that the have-nots were often
locked into a descending cycle of poverty. In the foreseeable future,
with the possibility of mutually disastrous outcomes increasing, the
gap between altruism and self-interest may narrow appreciably.
"Realists" advocating policies of "triage" or "lifeboat ethics," which
would withhold food from the hungry, might consider the consequences of the application of a similar logic to our own consumption
of imported energy and resources. There are, moreover, substantial
questions about the relationship between one nation's choice of a life
style and its effects on another nation. The choice, for instance, of a
high meat diet in the United States substantially reduces the world
supply of cheap protein.

There is an increasing number of policy trade-offs between energy production and food production, between "high" and "intermediate" technology, and between industrial growth and the stability of ecosystems. In these circumstances, we need to enhance the capacity to weigh policy choices on a long-term basis. Moreover, we need to identify those leverage points where policies can have the maximum effect. There is a good case for the use of depletion quotas, severance taxes, and birth licenses to encourage movement toward a sustainable society. But for underdeveloped societies that still need to grow there are other questions concerning the balance between agriculture and industry, the choice of an energy supply system, the type and scale of technology, and the desirable level of population.

We cannot assume that policy choices will become easier in the future. The current energy debate demonstrates that we face increasingly complex questions about technology and also about the type of economy and society we will have and the level of risk we are willing to accept. The possibilities of resolving energy and resource dilemmas by reaching into outer space, as suggested by the L-5 Society, or into the depths of the atom suggest something about the range of choices we face.

Design of Political Institutions

It is now a truism to suggest that we live in an increasingly interdependent world. It is equally obvious to most observers that the global system is becoming more sensitive to perturbations from a growing number of sources. In recent years, system-wide tremors have been caused by monetary crises, terrorism, and increases in the price of energy. We may expect that these and other sources of disturbances, including a range of ecological issues, will become more disruptive in the future. There are some problems that states can "resolve" unilaterally, as in the U.S. creation of a 200-mile fishing zone. Many issues are not, however, susceptible to such an approach. This is particularly true of ecological problems where pollutants can migrate across political boundaries or where large parts of the ecosystem are involved, such as climate, or in issues concerning the use of mineral resources that are not uniformly distributed throughout the earth's crust.

Given the increasing potential for system-wide breakdown, one option is to reduce the "hyperactivity" of the system by reducing the

frequency of certain types of interactions to levels consonant with
system capacity. This view coincides with the approach taken by E. F.
Schumacher and others who propose a more disaggregated social
system with relatively self-sufficient components. Others recommend
a "one-world" approach to environmental management requiring the
creation of international institutions to coordinate international behavior.

Each of these approaches has merit, and we will undoubtedly see
movement in both directions over the next several decades. It will be
important to identify the source of ecological problems and the
appropriate level at which remedy can be applied. Efforts to control
population, for instance, will be best undertaken at the national level,
while resource management may require international action to
stabilize supply and price and to guarantee equity. The potential
consequences of a mismatch between problem and response are
evident in the current deliberations on the law of the sea. Without
agreement on an ocean regime, we can reasonably expect a chaotic
race to exploit the seabed that only the rich can win, but at the
inevitable price of increasing international tensions, ecological damage to the oceans, and a widening gap between the rich and the poor.

Despite the potential for conflict, there are a growing number of
equally important cases where environmental disputes have been
resolved by treaties or by the creation of permanent organizations.
The United States and Canada have a history of joint action on
problems of water pollution beginning with the Boundary Waters
Treaty of 1909 and continuing through the agreement on water quality
in the Great Lakes in 1972. The Soviet Union and Iran have also taken
bilateral action to protect the Caspian Sea. European nations have
reached agreements on the use of the North Sea, and efforts are being
made to alleviate severe problems in the Mediterranean. At the global
level, the creation of the United Nations Environmental Program may
represent the beginning of a meaningful response to ecological
problems. The UNEP "earthwatch" program will provide, for the
first time, base-line data and early warning on serious problems.

In sum, the ecological crisis will result in major changes in the
substance of international politics and in the structure of the international system. Issues relating to resources, population, food, oceans,
development, pollution, and climate change are rapidly growing in
salience. At present we still tend to see these issues through the prism
of the state-centric paradigm of power politics. Mutual dependence

on a common biosphere will become the rationale for a more cooperative model of international politics. In any event, to make effective responses to new challenges and realities we need to develop new approaches, concepts, and theories that explicitly recognize ecological variables.

The essays that follow are exploratory, speculative, and future oriented. Collectively they suggest something of the breadth of political aspects of ecological issues at the global level. In selecting topics for inclusion, the editors tried to maintain a balance between those that are primarily conceptual, as in parts 1, 2, and 6, and those that deal with specific issues of long-term importance, as in parts 3, 4, and 5. In this respect the volume is necessarily schizophrenic, poised betweeen abstraction and concrete issues. There is a long list of other important topics that might have been included: the world order implications of climate change, North-South conflicts, the ecological effects of global militarization, and so forth. That these topics are slighted or omitted altogether reflects both the constraints of space and the judgment of the editors that these areas could be more substantively considered elsewhere.

Anticipating the Future

It is frequently asserted that one of the primary qualities that sets man apart from other forms of life is the capacity to plan for the future. If true on an individual level, such an observation seems less warranted for societies whose collective behavior is often ecologically destructive. In the past, societies seldom planned the future but more often simply reacted to the flow of events. As problems of environmental deterioration and technological growth proceed, however, ad hoc approaches to the future are unacceptable.

The first essay, by Jørgen Randers and William Behrens, attempts to lay out the "terrain" that man will be traversing in the coming decades by applying the technique of trend projection. The environmental problems that we have begun to encounter are metaphorically seen as foothills, the crossing of which will offer us a foretaste of the more strenuous journey that must be taken across high mountains as growth trends in population and economic production bring us closer to the carrying capacity of the planet. A more gradual, less traumatic transition to an ecological equilibrium may be possible if anticipatory action is taken on a global basis.

In the second essay, Marvin Soroos argues that we must become more conscious of the future; in particular, we need to be more alert both to the problems that may jeopardize our welfare and to whatever opportunities there may be for coping with them.

1

In offering an overview of some of the
more general types of future-oriented inquiry,
Soroos explains how forecasting directed toward
understanding the most probable futures differs
in fundamental ways from the designing
of alternative futures that are possible and
desirable but not necessarily probable. Scholars
must become active participants in designing
and constructing alternative futures for our
complex, rapidly changing societies, which are
operating with a much smaller margin for error
than did those of the past.

Watch for the Foothills: Signaling the End to Growth in a Finite World

Jørgen Randers and William Behrens

Introduction: Anticipatory Action

The world, for the most part, behaves in a regular and predictable manner from the perspective of a physicist. Thanks to years of observation, experiment, and scientific inquiry, a body of physical laws now exists to describe the path of falling meteorites, the melting of icebergs, or the expansion of gases. There are still many physical phenomena that remain unexplained, but at least the macroscopic world can be described with a fair degree of confidence that the descriptions will be accurate and consistent through time. Under such conditions, anticipatory action to avoid a problem that has not yet occurred is rational, meaningful behavior, because one can be confident that nonaction will lead to the hypothesized problem. An example of anticipatory action is to reduce engine speed to avoid overheating.

For a social scientist, the situation is more uncertain. Extant social theories cannot yet be depended upon to be either accurate or consistent through time. Perhaps the social world will at some time be described by a set of behavioral "laws"; economists have been developing some such laws over the past century. Rarely is there agreement that available social laws authoritatively tell what future developments may be. Presently, pleas for anticipatory social action must be based on imperfectly validated hypotheses about the future effects of action and nonaction. There are cases where decision can be postponed until further study has satisfactorily established the hypotheses, but in most cases it is necessary to take positive action before one has ultimate proof of the validity of the underlying theses.

The working hypothesis of social science for decades was that population growth and material growth were unblemished benefits to any society. Since then, an alternative hypothesis, that population growth should be controlled, has won its way into dominance. Although population control is now widely accepted as necessary, the need for population control was never rigorously proven in the way a new hypothesis in physics can be. Twenty years ago, despite its wide acceptance, no one could vigorously validate the hypothesis that population growth was an untainted good. And today one cannot prove that population growth is wholly undesirable.

The gradual shift toward acceptance of the need for population control was not the result of some unambiguous, controlled experiment but the outcome of extensive public consideration of the hypotheses in the form of discussion, observation, and induction. The hypothesis that unchecked population growth is problematic was established by becoming more widely known and less threatening and by proving capable of making sense out of various bits of real-world information. No experimental validation of the hypothesis, accompanied by appropriate statistics, was involved.

In many cases it appears desirable to hasten social acceptance of an unverified hypothesis of the above type because of fear that the problem will grow out of hand while final verification is being performed. Presentation of the hypothesis and the world view from which it stems may speed up the process. So may clear demonstration of the expected consequences of action and nonaction, indicating the relative advantage of various approaches.

We are presenting here the social hypothesis that the current rapid growth in both population and industrial activity will come to an end and that the transition to slow growth can be made less traumatic through conscious, anticipatory action by global society. This is a case where we believe action must be taken before the ultimate validity of the underlying hypothesis can be established. To hasten such acceptance or, for that matter, agreement on the *in*validity of the theses, we explored aspects of the hypothesis in a mathematical model described in *The Limits to Growth*.[1] In this paper we pursue the good of widespread acceptance—seeking to increase the plausibility of our hypothesis and the attractiveness of anticipatory action. In so doing we are fully aware that the final validity of our hypothesis can only be established through future real-world experience, which may well be affected by societal consideration and reaction to the hypothesis itself.

Below, we first outline the world view that leads to the hypothesis that the current rapid material growth cannot be sustained. The world view puts the 200-year time period described by the *Limits to Growth* model in a larger perspective; the model emerges as an account of the end to an abnormal era remarkably free from growth-impeding constraints. Our world view indicates that the problems accompanying the transition to a slower rate of growth may be alleviated by anticipatory social change to values more compatible with life on a finite globe. The second part of the paper describes current signs of the proximity of the transition, indicating additional urgency. In the third part, we describe the formal *Limits to Growth* model and show how its conclusions supplement intuitive reasoning in earlier sections regarding the proximity of the transition and the desirability of social value change ahead of time. The last section looks at the transition process and the slow growth situation in more detail.

Both the qualitative world view and the formal model are seen as tools for increasing the plausibility of our hypothesis. The accentuation of urgency and desirability of a slow growth situation are intended to increase the attractiveness of anticipatory action. The overall objective is to help others decide whether to accept or reject the view that man will be better off trying to control material growth *before* nature forces a decline in human activity on earth.

A World View: Rapid Growth Will Stop

In this section we present our qualitative basis for expecting that the current period of rapid expansion of population and industrial activity will come to an end.

Carrying Capacity

The root of our social hypothesis, our world view, lies in the concept of a carrying capacity—the level of activity that can be sustained through time by an ecosystem without damage to the system. For any ecosystem, its carrying capacity is defined by its endowment of physical capabilities, such as its food productivity and its mineral resources; by the life style adopted by the resident population, specifically the way in which the population chooses to exploit the ecosystem's endowment; and by the time period over which the ecosystem is required to support activity.

Animal populations in general have no control over the carrying capacity of their ecosystem. Human populations can exercise control. They can increase their ecosystem's carrying capacity by adopting a more frugal life style, requiring fewer amenities, and thus lowering the ecological input per person. Or they can shorten their time horizon and require that their ecosystem support them for a century rather than forever. Or they can apply their ingenuity and develop means whereby fewer ecological inputs are needed to provide the same amenities—in a word, technology.

A Historical View: Growth Pressing against the Carrying Capacity

In our world view, history is seen as a continuing expansion of physical and social constraints through ingenuity. Man has been able to repeatedly increase the globe's carrying capacity without having to adopt a more frugal life style and without—at least in most cases—jeopardizing the opportunities of future generations. Until recent centuries, the rate of increase in the carrying capacity was very slow, occurring through minor and infrequent technical and social innovations. The capacity of much quicker expansion of human activity, particularly of the number of people, insured that human activity was always at or very near the maximum sustainable level as defined by the then current technology and life style. In short, throughout history society continually pressed against the most serious, or active, constraint. How human activity catches up with new and wider limits is well illustrated by the stepwise expansions in the global population subsequent to new discoveries in agricultural techniques. In our view, the normal condition of man appears to be one where the level of human activity increases rather slowly, always in near-perfect balance with the slowly increasing carrying capacity. We will refer to the slow growth situation as "the state of equilibrium."

A somewhat anomalous stage in the historical process seems to have occurred over the last few centuries. Through the historically simultaneous breakthroughs in many different fields—the birth of modern science, the opening up of new continents, the discovery of printing, the spread of literacy, and the development of new theories and practices in human social organization—man proved able to increase significantly and rapidly the carrying capacity of his world. The recent accelerating surge in human activity can be seen as an expansion into the void that was created between the new carrying capacity and the existing load on the system. The current high rate of exponential growth in people and industrial activity is possible because almost all constraints—disease, energy supply, food supply, coordinating capability—were pushed back so far and so quickly that man was essentially expanding into a constraint-free vacuum. Naturally, minor problems or constraints were met, but they were generally successfully overcome by technology before they limited the general expansion in any serious way. For example, paved roads were introduced to make possible continued expansion of road traffic upon discovery of the automobile, and steel was substituted for wood to facilitate further concentration of people in large building complexes.

Growth in the Future

This recent explosive expansion of human activity is clearly abnormal from a historical perspective, and it is reasonable to ask whether the rapid growth will continue indefinitely. Our firm belief is that it will not, that mankind will return sooner or later to the historically normal situation where the level of human activity is pressing against the carrying capacity of the globe and the rate of expansion is controlled by a slow but steady lifting of the globe's physical and social constraints through sporadic, hard-won discoveries.

The important limits to expansion were not *eliminated* by the breakthrough of the past few hundred years. The many constraints still exist, although they are not currently as evident as they were in the past. People still die—though at age seventy instead of age thirty. Sustainable land yields per hectare are still finite—although often 3,000-kilogram crops per hectare per year rather than 700. There still is a limit to the size of cities that can be managed—though it may now be 8 million people rather than 1 million. The available potentially arable land is still limited—although there are now 3.2 billion hectares as compared to roughly 1 billion in the "old world." Currently, human society is enjoying a relatively easy and very rapid expansion toward the higher carrying capacity inherited from the past. All available ingenuity can be used to remove the sporadic constraints uncovered in the growth process. Once this abnormal gap between carrying capacity and load has been covered, new constraints will start appearing at a much quicker pace than today, and they will be harder to overcome. There will be more and more difficult problems to solve, and it appears that maintaining the same rapid rate of expansion will be impossible.

Future rates of expansion will be lower because of the

1. unavoidable onset of diminishing returns in a finite world
   —where there are no new places to look for minerals and no new
   elements to discover
2. strong interconnections among problems in a crowded and
   complex society—where a noisy, air-polluting power source is
   not an acceptable method of providing power
3. tendency for many problems to appear simultaneously in a
   closely coupled system—where a power failure not only
   removes light and cooling but also makes most stored food
   inedible
4. implementation delays for new solutions are much longer in a
   society where a large number of people are affected by
   decisions—where fanatic proponents and opponents to any
   conceivable suggestion are guaranteed

The rate of expansion in human activity will slow down to a more
normal rate from a historical perspective, say, to doubling times of the
order of a century rather than doubling times of the order of a decade
as are found in the current era. We have chosen to call this future
situation a state of equilibrium because change on a hundred-year
horizon seems slow from the vantage point of today's exploding
societies.

How Growth Might Slow Down: Natural Forces

The end of the current period of rapid expansion might be brought
about through a variety of mechanisms. One possibility would be to
allow expansion to continue until it approaches the carrying capacity
and allow natural forces—lack of resources, polluted water supplies,
inadequate food supplies—to slow down the rate of growth. This
option seems undesirable, since it will result in a society kept stable
by strong, unpleasant, negative pressures on birth rate and capacity
for industrial expansion.

A second possibility is that the uncontrolled, rapid expansion of the
environmental and social load may build up a momentum too great to
be overcome before societal activity has exceeded a level that can be
sustained for long. And once the sustainable limits are surpassed, the
result will be a reduction of the carrying capacity (for instance,

destruction of soil fertility from overly intensive agriculture, depletion of nonrenewable resources faster than substitutes can be developed), eventually forcing not only stabilization of but even reduction in the level of human activity. The slower one is in observing and responding to such overruns, the larger the overshoot will be and the more drastic the subsequent contraction. Overshoots associated with letting natural forces build up until they halt present growth are particularly worrisome, because the erodibility of the carrying capacity does not seem to be amenable to technological repairs. Once land is eroded, it is essentially unavailable for future use; once fuels are consumed, they are gone; once species are extinct from overconsumption, they are impossible to rejuvenate.

How Growth Might Slow Down: Social Change

Another mechanism whereby the current rapid growth might be ended would be a conscious human choice to slow down expansion before the strict constraints of the carrying capacity were encountered. This second and seemingly more desirable option would require a societal value change away from the value structure of growth, even *without* the impetus of imminent limits. Such a change may occur spontaneously—for instance, by all people becoming so rich that material expansion is no longer viewed as the most rewarding activity—or it may have to be induced by active education in order to be completed before the constraints are reached. The spontaneous social change is feasible only if sufficient time is available before the natural constraints are reached. If that time is unavailable—if the natural constraints are reached before all people become sufficiently affluent to automatically abandon rapid material growth—then a societal value change must be actively initiated in advance. Such a value change could make possible a smooth adjustment to the next period of equilibrium with the carrying capacity, but it would require great foresight and a considerable measure of voluntary restraint.

The Current Situation: Foothills Signal
Imminent Transition to Equilibrium

In this section we discuss some real-world phenomena indicating that
the current period of rapid expansion is *already* coming to an end.

Our social hypothesis foresees a change from rapid to slow growth
in material activity on earth, in short, a transition to equilibrium. But
when? If it is 1,000 years away, certainly man can better spend his
time by pondering the problems of today's poverty-ridden and
warring populations than by considering whether to emphasize the
need for value change. However, there seems to be in society today a
multitude of signs indicating not only that the transition is near but
that it has actually begun. Because the state of equilibrium will find
society again pressing against the carrying capacity, the transition
from growth to equilibrium will be characterized by the resurgence of
major constraints to human activity. They will first appear as minor
inconveniences, foothills signaling the massive mountain chain of
constraints further ahead. The obstacles hindering expansion over the
last couple of centuries have been minor rocks that could easily be
moved out of the way. After the transition, expansion will again be
limited by the speed at which one can manage to bulldoze the
mountains themselves.

What are the foothills that can already be perceived by the social
observer? What are the constraints appearing now that have the
potential for seriously limiting human material activity? There is the
continuing large-scale starvation in most parts of the world and the
need for industrialized countries to take an increasing fraction of their
resource supplies from poorer countries that have not yet had the
time to consume those resources. The contamination of the
environment—of air, food, and water—is another obvious example.
Others are the increasing inability to cultivate new land due to lack of
fresh water; the emergence of heat islands around large cities caused
by intensive consumption of energy; the difficulty involved in implementing a large reactor program because of the lack of suitable
dumping grounds for the radioactive wastes; the increasing difficulty
of taking a vacation without hearing the sound of running engines;
the rise in the price of Maine lobster or Peruvian anchovies. It is not
difficult to find examples of emerging, purely physical constraints on
human activity.

By looking around one can also sense the emergence of major social constraints, which surprisingly often can be traced back to physical constraints. One obvious example is the friction between Iceland and Great Britain caused by Iceland's expansion of its fishing territories—in our view, a social constraint to peaceful relations arising from the approaching limits to annual fishing catches. The human suffering in Bangladesh and other poverty-stricken areas can be viewed as the result of land shortages forcing people to live in areas normally flooded at regular intervals. The appearing constraint to rapid inflow of foreign oil to the U.S. by the organization of oil-producing countries is a seemingly political constraint precipitated by the critical lack of oil in this country.

Even cursory inspection of today's reality reveals a large number of physical and social constraints, none of which seems likely to decrease in importance as human society increases in size, complexity, and impact on the ecosystem. From these observations, it appears that the transition from rapid growth to equilibrium, far from being a remote possibility, is to the contrary already happening. It would seem prudent to assume that the automatic value change, occurring when all of the world's people are abundantly wealthy, will not occur in time to halt the expansion before the natural constraints become operational, increasingly reducing man's ability to act. It seems of paramount importance to do what is possible now to spread understanding of the potential for crisis, hoping thereby to induce the value change to occur earlier than it might come automatically.

A Global Simulation Model: Transition through Overshoot Is Likely in Current System

We came to hold the above world view during the years we spent constructing a mathematical simulation model of global population and industrial growth. In this section we describe how our view of the world as expanding out toward finite limits is represented in the formal computer model World3. We also discuss the conclusion resulting from refinement and study of World3: that adherence to current social policies will lead to overshoot and decline during the adjustment of human activity to the global carrying capacity. In short, a model conclusion is that the extant societal organization is unstable.

It may be needless to point out that one can agree with our world view without accepting our mathematical model. But as formal models are recent elements in discussion of social issues, we start by clarifying the role of models in the public debate.

Models as Instruments for Social Value Change

Over the past decades a wide variety of models have been made about social systems. These models have ranged from verbal, intuitive descriptions of the behavior of a small group of factory workers to elaborate, year-by-year, mathematical predictions of a nation's unemployment rate or its rate of inflation. Existing social models cover the entire spectrum, from imprecise guesswork to statistical measurements, over all time spans from a few weeks to 100 years. All of these models are attempting to simplify the real world in order to understand it better. They all rest on assumptions about how man, his institutions, and his artifacts interact to produce the trends observed in the real world.

No model can predict the future. To be able to tell exactly what the future condition of a social system—for example, the world—will be, the model would have to assume that man is a purely reactive, predictable creature, whose actions and decisions and values can be foretold. Over some very short period of time, say, one year, and with large aggregations of people to confine individual behavior by group behavior, this assumption might be justifiable. But over any extended period of time, man is creative, even collectively. The way he reacts to and changes his environment is continually responding to shifts in his values, norms, and surrounding social goals. Modelers whose objective is to be able to tell precisely what the 1980 national budget will be, or how much wheat the United States will sell to the Soviet Union in 1995, are going to be disappointed. Striving for predictive accuracy over the long term is a waste of time. In fact, detailed prediction should not be the goal of a descriptive model of the future. Not only is it impossible, but prediction also seems undesirable if it has to rest on some mechanistic concept of man.

The goal of a descriptive model should be to stimulate social change. A model's unique capability, particularly in mathematical modeling, is its proficiency in drawing the logical conclusions from a set of assumptions. Assumptions might deal with how a population's desired family size decreases with increasing wealth, or how the yield of an acre of land increases as the amount of farm machinery increases. A descriptive model, if well formulated, can tell, if the way in which decisions are currently made and the way actions are taken were to remain unchanged, what the consequences would be over future years. For example, if families continue to have on the average 2.4 children, what would be the population in twenty years? Such a "conditional forecast" serves a very different purpose than a prediction—a conditional forecast alerts the social system to what would probably happen if no changes were made, thus pointing to changes that might be desirable. If the population reached over twenty years by a model with a constant birth rate is for some reason judged undesirable, then one should look in the corresponding real system for ways in which the birth rate might be changed.

Often one's tendency is to look at the output of a model, to look at the picture of the future that the model presents and reject the model because its conditional forecast does not match one's own expectations about the future. That mismatch usually arises because one assumes that man will adapt, that he will change his way of doing things when faced with undesirable conditions. The change is usually expected to be automatic, immediate, and above all, successful. The model, on the other hand, does not make such an assumption. The model rather points to the consequences of continued adherence to current decision rules, thereby accentuating the discrepancy between the conditional model forecast and the hopes of an observer. The goal is to stimulate action to eliminate the discrepancy. If the changes needed to match the conditional forecast with the hopes would not have otherwise been forthcoming, then the model certainly performs a useful service. If it happens that the adaptation would have indeed occurred automatically, without the aid of the model, then it can hardly be said that the model has done a disservice. Social change requires a catalyst, often an anticipatory catalyst, and social models of the future can fill that need.

A mathematical model is in general more useful in highlighting the need for change than an intuitive model. Particularly when combined with a graphic presentation technique, such as flow diagraming, a mathematical model serves as a facile device for communicating a conditional forecast of a social system. Its advantages over an imprecise intuitive description are many. Diverse disciplines and information sources can be combined through a single language to allow for informative debate. Diverging perceptions of how a system operates can be implemented in the model, and their impact on the social system can be seen quickly. Most importantly, the assumptions

on which the model is based are more clearly exposed for careful
scrutiny. Usually the assumptions of a verbal description are too
obscure to evaluate (it may even occur that conclusions do not follow
from assumptions in a verbal model). In a mathematical model,
logical consistency is assured.

The World Model: Assumptions

The formal World3 model was constructed to illuminate the transition
from material growth to material equilibrium in a system with several
constraints. More specifically, it is a model made to study the
question of how the current rapid expansion of human material
activity will ultimately adjust to the finiteness of the physical world.

Of the basis of information from the real world, explicit
assumptions were included about the processes that cause the
growth in population, the growth in industrial machinery, the
availability of food and resources, and the creation of pollution.[2] The
second set of essential assumptions in World3 are those outlining the
physical environment. We assumed: (1) a finite stock of land; (2) a
finite stock of nonrenewable resources (minerals and fuels); (3) an
upper bound on the sustainable agricultural yield—that is, on the
crop that can be obtained each year from each hectare of cultivated
land; and (4) an upper bound on the amount of pollution that can be
absorbed each year by the ecosystem.

Our objective was to explore the time pattern of material growth in
a finite world over a time span of a century. We deliberately excluded
from our model many social interactions, not because we felt them to
be unimportant but because we felt that a study of the physical
aspects might indicate what would result in an ideal, well-organized
world without conflict—in a world without any active social
constraints. The inclusion of social interactions and constraints (that
is, representation of man's inability to manage a rational and optimal
use of the globe's resources on a long-term basis) would essentially
be effected by a reduction of the physical limits assumed in the
model. Roughly speaking, the imperfect real world is "smaller" than
the one portrayed in World3, where physical and biological
interactions dominate.

We thus assumed a finite world, an environment with fixed
physical constraints. These assumptions are of course consistent with
the world view described above: over a hundred-year period, the

"normal" slow change in the carrying capacity is so small that it is acceptable to approximate it with constant constraints. The current rapid expansion of human activity was modeled in the form of two growth processes: population growth and growth in material production. We did not assume fixed rates of growth but tried to model explicitly how the growth rates depend on other factors—for example, desired family size, birth-control effectiveness, desire for more products—in the real world.

It is intuitively easy to see what one outcome of our model will be. Within the assumed physical constraints, the physical growth in population and material output cannot continue indefinitely. The growing population and material output will at some point in time reach the physical limits and be forced to stop growing. The computer outputs recorded in *The Limits to Growth* exhibit the general behavior. Thus the computer output confirms one intuitive conclusion that follows from the model assumptions. Everlasting growth in population and material production is impossible in World3 because of the assumptions made about physical limitations. World3 does not *prove* that material limits exist in the real world; rather, we created a model in which physical limits were *assumed to be fixed* in order to examine their consequences for a growing system during its transition to equilibrium.

The World Model: How Growth Stops

Our basic assumptions of physical limits tell us that growth in the model must cease. But they do not tell us *how* growth will stop. Will the rapid expansion of population and material production come to an orderly end at the carrying capacity, or will some instability be associated with that end? What are the consequences of trying to avoid the limits? How can potential instabilities be reduced? World3 offers some observations on these questions, which should be seen as the real conclusions of the model.

World3 often shows behavior in which the population and material production stop growing and then exhibit a rather steep decline. In fact, this type of behavior, which we call overshoot and decline, is more prevalent in the various model runs than a gradual slowing down of population and production growth, although this second type of behavior is possible. Why does the model exhibit this overshoot and decline, when a priori one would hope that gradual slowing down is more likely? If population and material production reacted immediately to impending food or resource shortages or pollution overloads, the growth in the model would stop without overshoot. But reaction delays exist in reality, allowing time for problems to grow supercritical before a solution can be implemented. Several delays were included in World3 and lie at the root of the unstable behavior.

The delay in reacting to emerging, ambiguous problems, like the proximity of limits, is a conspicuous characteristic of the real world. The reaction arises from the entire string of decisions and actions that lead from a perception of a problem to the implementation of an attempt at its solution. A ten-year reaction delay is probably optimistic. Over ten years elapsed between the early realization of the possible harmful effects of DDT and the implementation of a partial ban on its use. At least ten years went by before arguments for the legalization of abortion led to the Supreme Court decision in favor of this issue. This delay is not likely to become shorter in a more complex society, nor is it likely that any conceivable technology could circumvent the social delays inherent in obtaining agreement on the reality of a problem and on the appropriate response.

The delay essentially decouples the growth in population and material production from the negative pressures of an approaching global carrying capacity, thereby making overshoot possible. Even if a constraint indicates that growth should cease—for example, because current activity already generates the maximum rate of pollution that can be tolerated in the long run—growth continues until the constraint has become operational, say, for the time it takes for pollutants to appear in their harmful form and for society to react to the threat. If the resulting overshoot causes erosion of the carrying capacity—for example, through the supercritical load of pollutants actually poisoning and destroying the self-cleaning capacity of the ecosystem—the result will be a subsequent abrupt, involuntary decline in human activity to a level low enough to be sustained by the impaired ecosystem.

There are many other delays in the model that reinforce this type of behavior: the delay inherent in the momentum of a growing population; the delay between the generation of a waste product and its appearance at the point where it adversely affects man; and the delay required to shift productive capital from one type of output to another. The presence of multiple delays makes it much more likely that the population and material production of the model will grow past the long-term carrying capacity and then fall back. In this respect World3 is a vivid demonstration of one of the basic tenets of our world view, namely, the inherent undesirability of letting the transition from growth to equilibrium occur "on its own."

The World Model: Avoiding Overshoot

Can the overshoot behavior be avoided? One way to avoid it might be to relieve the constraints to growth as they are encountered. We included four different constraints to growth in World3: availability of land, availability of nonrenewable resources, productivity of each piece of land, and ability to absorb pollution. Usually, in World3, the population and material production encounter one of these limits alone. For example, growth may be halted by a lack of nonrenewable resources. If we try to relieve that constraint, population and material production will grow for a little longer until another constraint is reached, perhaps a lack of land. This new constraint induces another decline, and if the land constraint is removed, a third decline results. Each time we try to raise a successive limit, growth eventually runs up against one of the other limits. This observation is a key to understanding growth within a world of many constraints. If the objective is to allow growth to continue, then efforts designed to relieve one constraint only guarantee that pressures to stop growth will rise even higher from some other constraint. There is little long-term effectiveness in relieving one constraint; in the long run society will always be pressing against the carrying capacity— manifested in the constraint that is currently active. At that point the rate of expansion is determined essentially by the gradual increase in the global carrying capacity that we call material equilibrium.

Another approach one might try to avoid overshoot and decline in the model is to introduce into World3 representations of forces that will actually work to stop the population and material growth even in the face of unapparent limits. One such force is value change; another might be a law, enforced by some central power. Such forces do not simply react to the proximity of constraints but slow down growth before serious constraints are encountered. To be effective in World3, such forces must take into account the multiplicity of limits and recognize the delays that encourage overshoot. They can effect an orderly transition from growth to equilibrium by anticipating the approach of limits and deliberately stopping population and material growth well before human activity surpasses the carrying capacity of the world.

In summary, "overshoot and decline" is a robust characteristic of World3 established through computer simulation. Yet this unstable behavior could also have been foreseen by a careful mental examination of the relationships we put into the model. Indeed, the conclusions have been offered by others before us. The computer simulation aids in bringing out these conclusions, but certainly we would not accept them as valid consequences of the model assumptions if they were not also logically derivable without the aid of a computer. The function of computer simulation is not to replace all logical deduction but to point to unfamiliar behavior patterns and to provide a guide and a check against which one's intuitive conclusions can be evaluated.

The World Model: When Will Growth Stop?

Thus, World3 is quite a useful model for studying the general behavior modes of importance in the transition from growth to equilibrium. In addition, the model can be of some help in indicating the immediacy of the impending transition. By choosing the parameters of the model to represent the real world as closely as possible and by initializing it in the year 1900, it is possible to make the model retrace the historical evolution as it occurred over the ensuing seventy years. The model re-creates a picture of the rapid expansion into an essentially constraint-free vacuum. But by running the model further into the future, one can investigate the question of how many years will pass before expansion starts running up against the assumed constraints. On the basis of real-world data, we made the following choice for the sizes of the four model constraints:

1. That the arable land can be increased to 2.5 times the acreage cultivated in 1970
2. that there are sufficient nonrenewable resources left in 1970 to sustain 250 years of consumption at the 1970 rate
3. that the average agricultural yield (annual output per hectare) can be increased to 3.5 times the yield in 1970
4. that the maximum rate at which pollution can be absorbed is 25 times the rate at which pollution was generated in 1970

Even with these seemingly wide constraints, World3 overshoots and erodes its carrying capacity within one hundred years after 1970.

Raising the constraints—for example, by quadrupling the stock of nonrenewable resources—seems to have little effect on the timing of the overshoot. The power of exponential expansion is astonishing, quickly overtaking any finite increase in carrying capacity. Further, the indicated proximity of the carrying capacity is not so surprising when we consider the many current signs of transition to equilibrium.

Elaboration: The State of Material Equilibrium

In this section we present some further thoughts on the transition period ahead and on the goal of equilibrium.

The Process of Transition

We see societal value change, a nontechnological fix, as necessary to achieve an acceptable transition from growth to equilibrium. We are cognizant of the noted tendency of technologists to ask for non-technological solutions to problems while stating that no technological fix will be found, and the similar tendency among social scientists to assert that the technological fix is the most appropriate response to difficult problems. In our view, however, a smooth, orderly transition cannot be obtained through purely technological means—for example, through lifting of constraints or reduction of ecological impact. On the other hand, the change toward no-growth values—self-realization, community—appears to have already begun, with isolated developments of antiexpansionist values appearing at the grass-roots level in the rich societies. Pockets of people exist who have a general uneasiness toward the continuing growth mania in their societies, along with a firm conviction that man has much more to gain by growing in all other dimensions save the one representing material production and consumption. These values could spread if their importance could be emphasized.

The undesirable impact on society of the transition can be substantially reduced by anticipatory, voluntary action, by decisions to halt the current wave of expansion before natural forces are allowed to do so. But there is an element of chance involved, because the possibility still exists that the transition is so far away that stabilization through natural value change will occur in time. For most of the world's poor, continued expansion seems to hold smaller risks than joining the rich in their attempt to control growth. Current conditions in many countries of the Third World are so intolerable that further material growth, except in population, must be pursued even at the risk of environmental damage. Global inequities are currently so serious that a freeze without some form of redistribution seems unrealistic. The more feasible alternative is to limit growth only among the currently wealthy. If successful, this approach would result in control over a significant part of the expansionary forces in the world and would work toward a more just distribution of global material wealth.

World3 illustrates behavior in which the whole world simultaneously encounters a single constraint if material expansion continues. We believe that in the real world a more likely future is a situation where different regions reach different limits to growth at different points in time. Some regions may suffer food constraints; others might suffer resource constraints. Extended international trade exploiting comparative advantages, plus large international mutual relief actions intended to forestall local declines, will perhaps soften the impact of regional limits, at the same time masking the proximity of global limits. In our view, such local crises should be seen as symptoms of the general problems of growth approaching the global carrying capacity.

The implications of the finite world and the resulting need for material equilibrium are very different for the industrialized regions than for the less industrialized regions. It is our feeling that the conclusion for the rich countries must be to stabilize their material consumption, preferably below current levels, and that the poor regions should continue to develop materially until their physical needs are satisfied. The questions of intra- and international distribution of material wealth must be faced simultaneously. We believe that the feasibility and stability of a material equilibrium system will depend in large measure on an equitable distribution of material wealth. Redistribution can be defended either for ethical reasons or, more pragmatically, because it reduces some of the pressures for growth provided by interpersonal and international envy. Finally, in material equilibrium the tensions of inequity cannot be relieved by promises of further growth.

But the mechanisms of redistribution are still not clear, and the problems of maintaining a fair system are even less so. The most serious deficiency of World3 is probably its exclusion of these and other social constraints. Social breakdowns, whether caused by maldistribution of wealth or resources or by some other trigger, are probably more likely to constrain growth in the real world than physical breakdowns. In addition, there are certainly the same kinds of trade-offs between social and physical constraints as World3 has illustrated among the purely physical constraints. Efforts to relieve physical constraints may create increased social pressures against growth, pressures that society is perhaps even less able to handle without serious damage.

In Equilibrium

It is likely that the state of equilibrium in many ways will be more desirable than the current rapid expansion, once the basic physical needs of all persons are satisfied. The state of equilibrium is characterized by very slow changes in its physical aspects—the population is fairly stable, the size of cities changes at a slow rate, the amount of wilderness does not decrease at alarming rates, and the number of artifacts and the material wealth remain essentially constant. The level of human activity is at all times in balance with the long-term carrying capacity, greatly reducing the risk of sudden overshoot and erosion of the global support system.

Given man's current potential for causing irreversible erosion of the carrying capacity through short-term abuse, it seems clear that the general acceptance of a long time horizon is necessary to make equilibrium sustainable for a large, technologically powerful society. This dedication to long-run sustainability implies anticipation of possible problems rather than mere reaction to current crisis. It will no longer be acceptable to put an untested insecticide on the market and postpone its withdrawal until *after* it has been proven through large-scale damage that the chemical has harmful side effects. To the extent that the market mechanism is used to distribute goods and services, the new societal values will be incorporated in a more inclusive formulation of prices. Not only will price tend to include the cost of all *current* externalities of production and consumption, but the price of a product will also include the *anticipated* cost to future generations of the current consumption of the product.

Material equilibrium is not stagnation but redirection of growth to dimensions of less material impact. We perceive in equilibrium the potential for emphasizing those aspects of human activity that enhance the quality of life at little material expense to the ecosystem. Quality of life is not found in unlimited material consumption; yet the current growth society provides only that single dimension for personal and societal development. There are many other dimensions that offer great rewards and yet are currently ignored because of the preoccupation with material growth. Losing that preoccupation means that man must face knotty problems, to be sure; the most critical is probably the distribution of the limited material wealth. But in restoring an emphasis on personal growth in directions other than material, man could achieve even greater advancement in its total sense.

Material equilibrium is not utopia. In material equilibrium, social problems would not be avoided, but perhaps more effort could be devoted to solving social ills because less effort is utilized in the pursuit of unlimited material expansion. Material equilibrium may at least offer a structure where the opportunity for rapid cultural development exists, where technological development is in response to real social needs rather than to artificially created demands, and where the sustainability of the human social system is a clear objective.

Epilogue: Watch for the Foothills

In this paper we have presented our world view as it has evolved over a two-year effort to model global physical growth. The historical position of the current rapid growth seems to be as a 300-year interlude between two much longer periods of relative material equilibrium. We think that the world is now approaching a transition from the interlude of rapid material growth to a period of slow material growth. The transition appears to be beginning today, as signs of physical constraints are becoming increasingly manifest in the industrialized regions of the globe.

The mathematical model made during those two years was instrumental in forming this world view and provided an analytical tool to test and examine the tenets of that view. The process of making and running the model has enforced an internal logical consistency that perhaps would have otherwise been lacking and pointed to the inherent instability of the system. The conditional forecasts of the model seem to indicate a rather urgent need to begin the value changes necessary to achieve an orderly transition to equilibrium, particularly in view of the tendency for overshoot and decline that seems to be a characteristic of current society. Attempting to achieve too rapid social change would be counterproductive if all of current culture collapsed under the strain. But we feel that it would be prudent to initiate, at least in the industrialized world, a process of social change that would extend over the next twenty to fifty years, bringing to a controlled end the current period of rapid material expansion.

Such corporate action will not be taken, however, until our social hypothesis of an approaching transition to relative material equilibrium has become widely accepted in the population about to take the step. There is, however, no way to establish a priori the "objective validity" of our hypothesis. Only the credibility obtained from enduring success of our world view in giving consistent meaning to seemingly independent real-world events will cause general acceptance of the view. That process is lengthy, and there is need to begin evaluation of our social hypothesis in terms of currently observable events.

We hope that others will make rigorous efforts to decide whether to accept or reject the view that those foothills are indeed the true precursors of an imminent transition to equilibrium.

Exploring Global Ecological Futures

Marvin S. Soroos

The Imperative for Future Consciousness

Even most critics of the reports to the Club of Rome, upon which the preceding essay by Jørgen Randers and William Behrens was based, concede that some very basic changes are in the offing for mankind as growth trends in population and resource consumption reach points at which natural limitations begin to take effect. There is reason for hope that these changes can evolve gradually, guided by conscious human design, rather than taking the form of an abrupt, cataclysmic series of events, as is often feared.

During eras of little change, insights from past experiences can be a sufficient basis for coping with future situations. As major changes become imminent, however, problems bearing little resemblance to past experiences may emerge with increasing frequency. Adapting to rapidly changing circumstances requires a capacity to anticipate the future implications of present trends as well as an ability to visualize and create desirable future possibilities.

Some sensitivity to the future would appear to be a universal human trait. Most decisions are based upon an implicit forecast of the probable consequences of an action being considered. The depth and scope of thought about the future may, however, vary considerably from one individual to another or, in a broader sense, across cultures. The depth of future consciousness may vary from a tendency to think almost exclusively in terms of the next day, week, or year to a much more extended outlook that takes into account decades or even lifetimes of descendants. The scope may vary from a narrowly focused concern with personal and family affairs to a far more diffuse interest in the future of one's national society or even in that of the entire human race.

Granted that some degree of future consciousness is a universal human trait, can it be further assumed that contemporary man is sufficiently foresighted to successfully adjust to the looming ecological challenges? Several reasons for anxiety have been expressed. Kenneth Boulding warns that concern about future problems is subject to "time-discounting"—the greater the time between the present and the future implications of a problem, the less the level of concern—and to "uncertainty-discounting," a tendency for concern to be inversely proportional to the degree of uncertainty about the future.[1] There may also be a tendency toward less thought about the future for large social units, such as mankind in general. To the extent these theories are valid, it may be anticipated that concern about the global ecological problems discussed in this volume will be limited.

Declining confidence in the "technological fixes" has led to increasing interest in social policies as solutions to a wide range of future problems. Thus far, social thought and research directed toward the anticipation and creation of the future, particularly at global levels, have been sparse, as social scientists have been perhaps too content to describe and explain patterns of past phenomena that may not bear much resemblance to future worlds. It is not that the empirical research methods cannot be of considerable utility in future-oriented inquiry but that their potential has not been very fully realized.

It is imperative that social scientists become more future-conscious and adopt strategies of inquiry that identify potential problems in time for plans to be designed and implemented that will avert ecologically related catastrophies and contribute to a world order that more fully satisfies human needs and aspirations. Bertrand de Jouvenel has argued that political scientists should seek to be "coordinators of anticipations"—including forward-looking views of experts in other fields—as well as "detectors of trouble to come."[2] Johan Galtung maintains that science should be "an activity that brings about a new world more similar to our values—not only [one that] produce[s] theory more similar to old data."[3]

The essay that follows is a digression into the intellectual challenges posed by the ecological problems that face mankind. Rather than describing concrete implications of environmental factors for world politics, I have raised questions about how the problems at hand may be analyzed. Examples of some of the types of future-oriented inquiry that are discussed can be found in the other essays in this volume.

The Future as a Subject of Inquiry

In what ways does the study of the future differ from research on the past? The latter is generally directed toward answering the questions of *what has been*. The product may be a history that re-creates past happenings chronologically or a theory that describes and explains patterns of events that have recurred in a variety of contexts. These histories and theories can normally be verified by comparing them to empirical data. In contrast, future-oriented inquiry is undertaken in response to questions of *what probably will be, what could be, what should be*, and *how what should be could be*, resulting in visions of what is probable, possible, desirable, and feasible. In an immediate sense, these images of the future can only be speculative in that no comparisons can be made with an existing reality.

As a subject for study, the future also differs from the past in the number of alternative sets of phenomena that must be considered. Research on a past time and place is limited to a single set of historically fixed phenomena. This single set of phenomena may be very rich in observable detail, complicating the task of description and analysis. In contrast, an almost limitless variety of alternative futures could come to pass, given the potential for human intervention. As time passes, each of the original alternatives branches out into a succeeding set of possibilities. The task of the futurist is to envision and analyze a variety of potential futures, prior to selecting those that are most probable or desirable. Thus, what complicates future-oriented inquiry is not the richness of the details of any one set of phenomena but the necessity of analyzing multiple futures simul-taneously.

What occurred in the past is not subject to modification, except in the way in which it is described or interpreted. Thus, a study limited to a consideration of past phenomena is inherently a spectator activity. In contrast, many features of the future are yet to unfold, pending human decisions and actions. Those who envision the future may, but do not always, adopt an interventionist stance in which they seek to influence future events.

Despite inherent differences in the study of the past and future, it should not be assumed that the theory and method of the two types of inquiry are mutually exclusive. In fact, most conceptions of the future are developed from experiences and empirical observations of the past. The objectives of the futurist dictate what features of the past merit observation and analysis. Some of the specific ways theory and data on past events and trends can be used in future-oriented inquiry will be discussed later in this essay.

Types of Inquiry on the Future

In the most general sense, future-oriented inquiry refers to any disciplined effort to formulate images of phenomena that could come to pass. In surveying types of futures research, a fundamental distinction can be drawn between forecasting the future and designing alternative futures. In forecasting, the most probable alternative is selected from the range of possible futures. In designing alternative futures, a preferred future is selected from a range of possibilities, and a strategy is formulated for bringing it into reality.

Forecasters tend to play a passive role in relation to that which they predict. This does not preclude, however, the possibility of forecasts having an important impact on future developments, particularly in stimulating adaptive responsives. Purposeful modification of the predicted future conditions goes beyond the role of the forecaster and into the realm of the designer who seeks to intervene in the course of history.

Forecasters and designers typically approach a future span of time in different ways. Forecasters usually begin with the present and plot a sequence of probable future developments. As forecasters probe further into the future, there is an increased likelihood that unanticipated occurrences will alter the probabilities of potential later happenings. Thus, less confidence can normally be placed in forecasts of the more distant future. Moreover, as time passes and events begin to diverge from the forecast, it soon becomes obsolete and requires updating. In contrast, designers of alternative futures typically skip the immediate future and select a more distant period as a reference point. Alternative possibilities for that future time are considered until an attractive possibility is singled out for implementation. Only then does the designer return to the present to plot policies that would lead to a world similar to the one that has been designed. A longer time dimension generally works to the advantage of the designer in that the range of what is feasible is greater. As with forecasts, however, intervening future developments may render a design obsolete if these events alter the range of future possibilities.

Both forecasting and designing the future require an integration of objective and subjective modes of analysis. Objective methods, such as those employed in empirical social science, generally play, however, a more central role in forecasts. Many forecasts are based almost exclusively on a statistical projection or an analysis of empirical data, in which case the forecast could be replicated by others, with similar forecasts resulting. The design of alternative future worlds draws more heavily upon creative skills similar to those applied by an artist, architect, composer, or novelist. This is not to the exclusion, however, of the use of scientific methods of inquiry at several stages of the design process.

It should not be assumed that these two basic types of future-oriented inquiry are generally used in isolation from one another. A later section will describe the integral role forecasts play in the process of designing alternative futures.

Forecasting Probable Future Developments

Types of Forecasts

A forecast is a statement that identifies a probable set of future developments. Forecasts may take a variety of forms, reflecting the specific objectives of the forecaster.

Some forecasts are simply a best estimate of what will probably happen. Alternatively, preconditions may be assumed, in which case a foreseen turn of events is contingent upon some intermediate developments. The precondition may simply be the implicit assumption that present trends will continue uninterrupted. In some cases, a forecaster may believe that intervening events are likely in the form of adaptive responses, yet purposely exclude them in order to demonstrate the consequences of inaction. A failure to take note of such an objective accounts for some of the criticisms of the Club of Rome studies. In policy making, forecasts are made of the probable consequences of manipulatable courses of action. This type of forecast is integral to the process of designing alternative futures, as will be discussed later.

Many predictions are estimated changes in the values of variables that have been continuously recorded over time, such as statistics on gross national product figures or world population. Others call attention to the possibility of events that are aberrations in an estimated flow of events, such as technological innovations, famines,

environmental catastrophies, political or economic crises, and out-
breaks of war. Barry Commoner warns that ecological processes,
because of their inherent complexity, often lead to "sudden, qualitative changes in response to gradual quantitative ones."[4] Noncontinuous events may be historical turning points, as was the case with the
oil price rises in 1973–74. The specific nature and timing of these
developments is often not as foreseeable as their eventual occurrence
in some form. Forecasting them is generally a less scientific and more
speculative exercise than projecting trends. Nevertheless, a forewarn-
ing of possible abrupt events, particularly those of potentially
calamitous nature, is often more useful information than forecasts of
very gradual changes of little consequence regardless of their scientific qualities.

Approaches to Forecasting

The task of a forecaster is, first, to select and gather information
offering insights into future developments and, second, to integrate
this information into sketches of probable futures. Let us briefly
consider a few of the principal approaches that may be used in social
forecasting.

Forecasts may simply be a projection of trends continuing from the
past into the future. Trend projection is implicitly based upon what de
Jouvenel describes as the "postulates of unchanging change"—
values of a variable will move in the same direction and the same rate
in the future as in the past; or the "postulate of periodic
variations"—the patterned fluctuations in a trend that have been
observed in the past will continue into the future.[5] These assumptions may not always be warranted, especially if little is known about
the conditions that have sustained the regular patterns of change in
the past. Eventually, growth trends will level off or even reverse
directions for the reason that infinite growth is impossible. The more
immediate the limiting factors, the more important it is that they be
taken into account by forecasters. In this regard, the message of the
Club of Rome studies is not that growth in population and industrial
production will eventually cease but that the limitations on growth
will probably have a major impact sooner than expected.[6] In certain
cases, some form of breakthrough may make it possible to surmount
obstacles to growth. Such is the faith of technological optimists, such
as Herman Kahn who foresees in 200 years a world population of
fifteen billion and a per capita product of $20,000.[7] Unanticipated

advances in agricultural production explain in part why Malthus's predictions of severe food shortages did not come to pass during the nineteenth century.

In trend projection, future values of a variable are estimated from the previous values of the same variable. Alternatively, forecasts may be based on theories that identify conditions that in the past have preceded the type of developments being forecast. Predictive theories may be grounded in a subjective interpretation of a few past cases, the technique of historical analogy, or on a systematic, empirical investigation of a large number of cases, the method of social scientific prediction. Usually more confidence can be placed in forecasts based on theories that have been well verified in a variety of contexts. Moreover, a large empirical base allows the forecaster to assign relative probabilities to a range of possible futures. The adequacy of the theory-based approach to forecasting is diminished by historical changes that may alter the relationship between predictor conditions and forecast occurrences.

A number of forecasts in the field of social ecology have been based on computer simulation models, including the first two reports to the Club of Rome and the United Nations–sponsored study of Wassily Leontief.[8] This approach to forecasting merges the methods of trend projection and theory-based prediction. A model is constructed containing preprogrammed relationships among variables that are either being forecast or in some way predict to them. Initial values of what are known in the vernacular as exogenous variables are set using actual data or assumed values in the case of some conditional forecasts. In ecological studies, these may include figures on population size and growth rates, levels of industrial production, and known reserves of petroleum and mineral resources. The model is then run through a series of operations that represent the forecast period. During the run, forecasts may be periodically generated from the ongoing calculations.

Simulation models incorporating human participants have also been used for some types of social forecasting.[9] Human decisions are fed back into the operating model to generate new situations to which the participants will later respond. In the field of global social ecology, human simulations, or "games" as they are sometimes labeled, have been used almost exclusively as educational tools.

Any forecast is at least in part a product of intuitive speculation. The intuitive element is sometimes limited to the implicit assumptions that underlie the use of scientific methods of prediction. At the other extreme, some forecasts are based almost exclusively on intuition and are aptly described as educated guesses. While most intuitive forecasts are the informal and undisciplined speculation of one prognosticator, some structured group procedures have been developed and refined. The Delphi technique, for example, allows a selected group of "experts" to anonymously critique each other's forecasts. Each participant is then invited to modify his initial forecast if persuaded by the reasoning of others. Ideally, the predictions of the group converge toward the best-informed forecasts.[10]

Intuitive forecasting can be criticized for reflecting the idiosyncracies of the experts, as well as for generally lacking scientific qualities. Despite the serious inherent shortcomings of the intuitive approach, it may be of value in making certain types of forecasts, particularly those of potential noncontinuous developments, such as technological advances. Intuitive forecasting may also serve a brainstorming function in which attention is drawn to previously unperceived future possibilities that may later be given closer scrutiny by more disciplined methods of forecasting. Interactive types of group forecasting may also be an effective medium for interdisciplinary communication from which a more holistic vision of the future may emerge.

Evaluating Forecasts

The criteria that are appropriate for evaluating the quality of a forecast depend to a large extent upon how it is to be used. The question that comes immediately to mind is that of how closely a prediction corresponds to actual future developments. Unfortunately, such an evaluation can be made only at the completion of the period being forecast. If some form of cataclysmic future is predicated, as is the case with many of the global ecological forecasts, action is necessary before a judgment can be made on whether the prediction has come to pass. The forecaster may expect, or at least hope, that the predictions will stimulate action toward the creation of a very different type of future. There is the danger, however, that future problems may seem overwhelming and trigger inappropriate responses that further complicate the problem, such as panic, inaction, crime, hoarding, or violence. For these reasons, otherwise excellent and useful forecasts may ultimately prove to have little resemblance to what actually transpires.

Some qualities of forecasts can be assessed before the forecast period transpires. For example, is the forecast specific enough to allow for an unambiguous determination of whether a predicted turn of events has come to pass? How adequate and reliable are the data upon which it is based? Are the underlying assumptions and theories sound? Questions may also be asked about the replicability of a forecast; in particular, are the procedures that were used sufficiently explicit to allow other forecasters to derive similar predictions? Also, is the forecast consistent with those developed using different methods? Is it compatible with the predictions of scholars from other disciplines?[11]

The Designing of Alternative Futures

As with forecasting, the design of alternative futures involves an examination of a range of future possibilities. Rather than identifying what appear to be the most probable futures, the designer narrows the realm of possibilities to those that appear to be the most attractive and devises strategies for increasing the likelihood that the preferred futures will become realities.

The design of alternative futures can be described as a multistage process that includes (a) clarification of values, (b) problem identification, (c) envisioning of desirable future alternatives, (d) selection of a preferred future, and (e) formulation of transition strategies. These stages should not be looked upon as self-contained units that are completed in the order indicated. Normally, there is an interplay between stages, or efforts are directed toward only one or two stages in the overall design process.

Value Clarification

Values are the raison d'être of the design process. They are the criteria for identifying problems, and they guide the design of desired futures. Analysis of values may be directed toward the welfare of individual human beings, such as satisfaction of material needs, security, education, freedom, and other aspects of human happiness and fulfillment.[12] At a more macro level, consideration may be given to societal or global values, such as economic development, the absence of wars, and environmental preservation. Reconciling individual, societal, and global values can be a very difficult task.[13]

Among the more prominent contemporary expressions of goals for mankind is the charter of the United Nations, which calls for international peace and security, friendly relations among states, and cooperation in solving international economic, social, cultural, and humanitarian problems. These generally stated goals have been given more specific interpretations in countless resolutions, notable examples of which are the Universal Declaration of Human Rights of 1948 and the Charter of Economic Duties and Rights of States of 1974. Guidelines for international ecological policy have been set forth in declarations adopted at Stockholm in 1972 and at succeeding conferences on more specific environmental problems.

Value questions have also been addressed within academic circles. For example, in peace research, questions pertaining to values underlie discussions of the meaning of peace, in particular the issue of whether the concept should be used to refer only to the absense of physical violence or be extended to include the realization of social justice. Concern over ecological problems prompted the issuance of "The Humanist Manifesto II," a statement of values and goals by the editors of the journal *Humanist* in 1973.[14] Ervin Laszlo's recently published *Goals for Mankind*, the fourth in the series of reports to the Club of Rome, is an elaborate effort to analyze and integrate national goals into a set of global priorities.

Values are not always fully compatible, a realization that is at the heart of environment consciousness. One of the key challenges facing global designers is the problem of reconciling the aspirations of the Third World for economic development with environmental values that are of concern to ecologists. This issue is discussed in depth in Lawrence Juda's article, chapter 5 of this volume.

Problem Identification

The values specified in the preceding step become criteria for identifying present and future problems. The greater the discrepancy between the desired and actual or probable conditions, the more important it is that the design process continue. Even when there is general awareness of serious problems, a systematic evaluation may more convincingly demonstrate the need to consider possible alternative futures.

A comprehensive effort to identify world problems has been undertaken jointly by Mankind 2000 and the Union of International

Associations. More than two thousand problems are briefly elaborated in their 1976 *Yearbook*, many of which are ecologically related.
Statistical series can be helpful for identifying present or future
problems.[15] The yearbook of the Stockholm International Peace
Research Institute traces arms races over time. Numerous statistical
series of the United Nations also provide an extensive data base for
assessing social and economic conditions in most nations. Projection
of trends may reveal serious long-range problems that do not yet
have readily observable manifestations. Such is the nature of ecological problems related to population growth, resource consumption
and depletion, and pollution identified in the Club of Rome studies.

Integral to the second stage is an analysis of causes of past
problems as well as factors that account for desirable features of the
contemporary order. Particularly relevant are causal factors that can
be altered by human design. A broad range of findings from behavioral research may be of interest to the designer at this stage. The
contributions of much of contemporary peace research on such topics
as the causes of wars and arms races are best seen in this context, as
well as efforts to understand the origins of the environmental crisis.[16]
These explanatory theories may be of considerable assistance in the
next stage, in which models are drawn up to alleviate present or
foreseen problems.

Future Alternatives

The heart of the design process is the third stage, in which models are
drawn up of possible futures that hold promise of more fully
actualizing the guiding values. Envisioning alternative futures, particularly those with elements that have never existed previously,
requires creative skills akin to those of an artist or architect. At this
stage, the designs should be viewed not as rigid models but as
tentative images of the future that may be discarded, modified, or
combined with other designs on the basis of further evaluation.
Given the enormity of the task of designing global futures, most
efforts are only partial designs. Some are radical departures from the
present; others specify only a few relatively minor changes. A design
may be a "snapshot" vision of the future on a given date or describe a
process evolving indefinitely into the future.

There is a long tradition in the design of international systems that
would reduce, if not eliminate, the possibility of the devastating types

of wars that have occurred in the first half of the twentieth century.[17] Among recent efforts is the World Order Models Project of the Institute for World Order in which designers from eight regions of the world drew up preferred futures for the 1990s.[18]

Social ecology is rich in designs of alternative futures. Among them is the "equilibrium model" of the original Meadows *Limits to Growth* study in which population and capital formulation are held constant.[19] An elaborate design has been developed by Jan Tinbergen entitled *Reshaping the International Order*, also commissioned by the Club of Rome. Mention should also be made of the numerous efforts that have been made to design steady-state economic systems and technological alternatives to the energy-intensive Western model of industrial development that projects an increasing reliance on nuclear power.[20] There is considerable disagreement in the field about whether highly centralized systems of national and global scope are needed or whether it is better to encourage relatively small, self-sustaining, and self-governing communities. This issue is more fully discussed in the articles by Andrew Scott and by David Orr and Stuart Hill in the concluding part of this volume.

Selection of a Preferred Future

The next step is to critically review the designs roughed out in the preceding stage in order to narrow the range of alternatives to a preferred possibility. It is also quite possible that none of the designs will be found to warrant further consideration.

A variety of questions may guide the review process, the following being examples of some of the important ones that may be asked. To what extent would the design realize the values specified in the first stage? Are the components of the design logically consistent? Are there any critical factors, such as natural resource limitations, that have not been taken into account? What is the likelihood that the design could be successfully implemented? Are there risks of undesirable, unintended consequences?

Several techniques for evaluating the potential futures may be employed at this stage. Intuitive assessments may be made of the design to identify its more apparent strengths and weaknesses. Some of the premises incorporated into the design may be expressed and tested as empirical propositions. Computer simulations may be used to project the outcomes of a complex set of interacting variables to ascertain how a design would work out over time. It may be possible to field test certain aspects of a design, as has been done in a number of experimental, self-sustaining communities. Occasionally, an examination can be made of instances in which some of the features of a design are already operational on a regional basis, such as in the European community.

Transition Strategies

For the design to have a potential for being more than an intellectual exercise, it is necessary to formulate a transition strategy through which the preferred future would evolve. In essence, transition strategies are policy proposals based on forecasts of what will probably follow from a given course of action.

Although transition planning must be adapted to the unique attributes of a design of a preferred future, some questions are generally pertinent. For example, the timing and order of changes can be critical factors in the success of a transition process. The Club of Rome studies conclude that ecological problems are converging so rapidly that any response will be inadequate unless initiated in the very near future. Questions may also arise regarding the sequence of changes. In one of the more richly elaborated transition strategies, Richard Falk proposes concentrating on value changes and heightened political awareness in the national publics during the 1970s, on a mobilization for action through transnational activities during the 1980s, and on a transformation of institutions at the global level during the 1990s.[21]

In contrast to the construction of a building, the creation of a preferred social order takes place not on a cleared patch of ground but in highly complex social systems. Major modifications in the existing order invariably have their costs in the disruption of established institutions and patterns of behavior. It is also quite possible that the strategy would provoke a backlash from groups threatened by the changes, with the result of reversing whatever progress was being made. Unanticipated developments may cause the plan to go awry with disastrous, unintended consequences. Questions may also arise over whether the strategy violates basic human values, such as by significantly reducing the freedom of individuals. These potential costs and dangers of implementing a design strategy must be weighed against the probable benefits of the changes and the consequences of inaction.

The ultimate success of a transition process is in large part dependent upon whether a widespread commitment to its implementation is forthcoming. In general, strategies that encourage promising tendencies that are already emerging in the existing world would appear to be more feasible than those that would directly confront established organizations and institutions that are working at cross-purposes with the designer.

Concluding Considerations

It may be concluded from the preceding analysis that the design of alternative futures has become the principal intellectual challenge as ecological problems become increasingly salient in world politics. The design paradigm can offer a sense of direction and integrative framework for empirical research on the past as well as for the forecasting of future developments.

A question that has not been asked thus far pertains to who should be called upon to participate in the design of future worlds. One school of thought would encourage a democratic procedure or what Arthur Waskow describes as "participatory futurism."[22] In a similar vein, Gerald Feinberg has proposed what he calls a Prometheus Project that would engage a sizable portion of the human race in setting goals for mankind.[23] In addition to ethical reasons to include those who would be affected by a created future world order, it may be argued that the successful implementation of a design requires a broad base of support that can be established only by widespread consultation in drawing up the preferred future.

Alternatively, it may be argued that most people, even those who are highly educated, have far too limited a perspective to comprehend the complexities of the problems facing mankind. Moreover, the general population has values and perceptions that are shaped to a large extent by existing institutions and, therefore, is not a very fertile source of ideas on how to transcend inadequate contemporary policies and practices. It would follow, then, that the task of designing future world orders is better left to a broadly representative elite, including scholars and specialists in the humanistic fields and the natural and social sciences as well as leaders of national governments, subnational groups, including minorities, the transnational corporate world, and international governmental and nongovernmental organizations. Widespread acceptance of a resulting design could then be fostered through education and consciousness raising.

Relatively broad-scale social designing has become a generally accepted dimension of a number of disciplines and subfields in the academic world, such as in urban transportation and land-use planning and in national economic planning. Following a flourish of world order thinking in the interwar period, there has been a general reluctance in recent decades to design systems of international and global scope. This reluctance can perhaps be attributed in part to the hugeness of the task, given the immense proportions and great complexity of global systems as well as the difficulties that would be encountered in gaining the acceptance and commitment of the leaders and peoples of very diverse cultures.

It should be recognized that a failure to design and seek to create a more desirable global system is as much a decision as to undertake such an endeavor. Regardless of whether efforts are made to design at a macrolevel, a multitude of actors in global political arenas will plan and seek to implement their narrower visions of a preferred future. The failure to effectively coordinate these micro-level designs could be a chaotic breakdown of the complex network of global social systems. National and international economic and political systems have collapsed in the past; the world wars and the Great Depression are notable examples. Although it has been possible to rebuild after these breakdowns of the past, future breakdowns could be far more disastrous, given the huge arsenals of nuclear weapons and their imminent proliferation. Recovery may be far more difficult in a world in which natural resources are no longer bountiful. The imperative for the future is to anticipate potential future problems and make the necessary adjustments before a disastrous series of developments unfolds.

There are encouraging signs of a renewed commitment to the design of alternative futures within academic circles, as evidenced by many of the studies that have been mentioned above. Of potentially greater significance has been the series of United Nations–sponsored conferences on environmental problems. It is quite possible that these conferences will mark the beginning of a process by which a more promising alternative future world will be designed and created.

Growth and Development in Ecological Perspective

Economic growth and development have been universally accepted as the highest priority goals for any society. Ecological realities, however, dictate a reevaluation of the cluster of traits we refer to as "development" and "modernization," two concepts that have been used almost interchangeably in the comparative study of political systems. To Richard Clinton, the explosive population growth rates in many less developed regions point up a major failure of the Western model of development, which is based on capital intensive industrialization: social advancement with its accompanying incentives for smaller family size tends to be concentrated in a relatively small, "modernized" sector of a population. The mounting frustrations of those who are bypassed by the process, many of whom join the mass migration to squalid urban centers, pose a threat to the political stability of many countries. The Chinese experience of the past thirty years can possibly offer insights into how the fruits of development can be spread more widely with less damage to the environment.

David Orr argues that from an ecological perspective the conventional model of "modernity" is obsolete, that its applicability was limited to little more than a temporary, if exciting, interlude of human history, during which resources were available in abundance. What is needed is a paradigm shift to an environmentally based model that will offer a new sense of direction to man's creative tendencies, one that will take into account the finitude of the natural resources of the planet, yet allow for a greater measure of human fulfillment.

2

A frontal attack on global environmental problems will require a global commitment, including nations of the Third World, which account for three-fourths of world population. In the final essay in this section, Lawrence Juda explains why the environmental activism that has surfaced in the industrial world has been received with indifference, suspicion, and even hostility by representatives from the less developed regions in forums such as the United Nations Conference on the Human Environment of 1972. Their concerns are, first, that environmental standards may require expenditures of their very limited economic resources and reduce their exports and, second, that environmentalism may be used as a rationalization for neglecting their aspirations for development.

3

Population Dynamics and Future Prospects for Development

Richard L. Clinton

The generation pouring
From times of endless date
. . . .
And humanity is growing
Toward the fullness of her fate.
Herman Melville

The primary purpose of this chapter is to focus on the population factor in the complex equation that yields the future. Because that equation is so complex, with so many variables and coefficients of unknown value, it is helpful to expand the one term—the demographic one—that is relatively well specified so far as the next few decades are concerned, for it can enable us to estimate the parameters of the possible and even to suggest what seems more or less probable under varying assumptions.[1]

Population History and Population Dynamics

The problem of adjusting to the limitations of his environment has been a perennial challenge to man and one that he has responded to with varying degrees of success at different times and places. There have been population explosions many times throughout human prehistory as new areas of abundance were encountered or improved means for extracting food from the environment were devised and diffused.[2] In some cases, these prehistorical population explosions resulted in the overshooting of local environmental carrying capacities and the dieback of human populations. Often, however, as long as unoccupied space existed, the increasing strains of the tightening fit between man and his environment produced the "budding-off of colonizing groups,"[3] which accounts for the migratory movements that eventually peopled practically every habitable area of the planet.

On the whole, however, the trend of ever-increasing global population expansion that commenced some ten thousand years ago with the shift from hunting and gathering to agriculture represents a sharp break with the demographic pattern dominant during man's evolutionary past. That dominant pattern was one of extremely low, essentially unmeasurable rates of net increase, in spite of local and temporary fluctuations.[4]

To understand why this *had* to have been the case, one need only consider the unimaginable potential for growth inherent in even the smallest rates of increase when the mode of that increase is exponential—as it is in all reproducing organisms—and the equally mind-boggling period of time implied by the phrase "man's evolutionary past."

A quantity is said to increase exponentially when it grows by a *percentage* of the whole (that is, of itself) in a constant time period. This is in contrast to linear growth, which is growth by a constant *amount* in a constant time period.[5] Superexponential growth, the pattern of recent population increase, occurs when the percentage rate of growth itself is also increasing (for example, 1.5 percent in the first period, 1.8 percent in the second, 2.1 percent in the third, and so on). Only a pattern of minuscule annual net increase could possibly have prevailed over the more than three-million-year period since the genus *Homo* emerged,[6] therefore, for almost any perceptible positive rate of increase for such a span of time would have resulted in astronomical population sizes by the time recorded history began some five thousand years ago. This assertion remains valid even if we choose to consider only the approximately 200,000-year species history of *Homo sapiens*.[7]

To grasp the magnitudes involved, these 200,000 years can be made proportional to a single calendar year. On such a basis, with January 1 representing 200,000 years in the past, the agricultural revolution of around 8000 B.C. occurs on December 13, the dawning of civilization and recorded history five millennia ago begins on December 22, and

the Industrial Revolution of 200 years ago takes place at 3:00 in the afternoon of December 31.

With mathematical rigor, then, it can be inferred that during the long sweep of man's evolutionary history (or prehistory) annual population growth rates were, on the average, negligible. Because the population growth rate is the resultant of the interplay of birth rates (natality) and death rates (mortality)—that is, BR − DR = GR—there are only two alternative explanations for how this minimal rate of net increase came about. Either birth rates and death rates were both high, the many births slightly more than compensating for the many deaths, or else humankind was able somehow to regulate its numbers in relation to a varying death rate. In view of the high fecundity (biological capacity to bear offspring) of the human female, the high birth rate–high death rate explanation has long been accepted, along with the picture of primitive man's estate as "solitary, poor, nasty, brutish, and short." Hobbes's famous phrase was a logical device and was never intended to describe the state of nature that actually existed in primordial times, but certainly most moderns seem to have an image of their forebears' past existence largely congruent with this formulation. The assumption that mortality was high requires that we assume that fertility was also high. Otherwise, the human population would have disappeared.

Recent anthropological research, however, has tended to undermine the high birth rate–high death rate explanation and to support the self-regulating alternative. Ethnographic studies of extant hunting and gathering societies have produced empirical findings that have led to surprising revisions in the conventional anthropological wisdom concerning early man.[8] For example, (1) while infant mortality was high, life expectancies actually compared favorably with those of "many subsistence agriculturalists and impoverished urbanized people of the tropics today";[9] (2) total fertility (total number of children born to a woman throughout her reproductive period) appears to have been approximately half that which normally would occur (four instead of eight);[10] (3) infanticide, abortion, and various mechanisms to ensure spacing of offspring three to four years apart were regularly practiced;[11] (4) the nutritional levels of hunters and gatherers were impressively high,[12] starvation was exceedingly rare,[13] and diseases and parasites were much less of a scourge than had previously been thought;[14] and, perhaps most remarkable of all, (5) not only were populations maintained well below the carrying capacity of their environments,[15] but the effort required for insuring adequate subsistence amounted to less than three days per week per adult,[16] with a significant proportion of the population contributing little or nothing to the group's food supply.[17]

The picture of primitive life emerging from these research findings evokes an image more reminiscent of Rousseau's noble savage than of Hobbes's deprived and depraved brute. Marshall Sahlins has offered a persuasive explanation of why Western man has found the Hobbesian view of the past so compelling:

Scarcity is the peculiar obsession of a business economy, the calculable condition of all who participate in it. The market makes freely available a dazzling array of products; all these "good things" within a man's reach— but never his grasp, for one never has enough to buy everything. . . . We stand sentenced to life at hard labor. It is from this anxious vantage that we look back on the [past]. . . . Having equipped the hunter with bourgeois impulses and Paleolithic tools, we judge his situation hopeless in advance.

Scarcity is not [however] an intrinsic property of technical means. It is a relation between means and ends. We might entertain the empirical possibility that hunters are in business for their health, a finite objective, and bow and arrow are adequate to that end.[18]

Yet all this changed with the shift from food gathering and hunting to food production. With agriculture, the possibility of accumulating a surplus appeared for the first time, a possibility that became a reality through such innovations as increased division of labor and the development of improved seeds and techniques, particularly irrigation. These innovations, however, required extensive social adaptations, one of the major ones being the abandonment of a mobile in favor of a sedentary existence. As productivity and the need for more coordination increased, villages became towns and towns grew into cities. The early role divisions of priest, warrior, and farmer proliferated as specialization and urbanization gave rise to the complex social stratification of civilized states.

All this involved a movement on the part of man away from his former intimacy with nature. Although still depending on nature more directly than we seem to today, early agricultural man clearly represented the decisive step from adjustment to and cooperation with nature to domination and manipulation of it. As a consequence of this new orientation toward nature, many of the mechanisms that man had evolved to maintain his numbers in balance with his environment were lost, and the human population began the expansion evident up to the present. This expansion was not without its setbacks, however, for with increased dependence on agriculture, populations became more vulnerable to massive famines when unfavorable weather conditions persisted, erosion or salinization of soils reduced yields, or the silting of canals disrupted irrigation. Moreover, epidemics became vastly more virulent as more people lived in closer contact with one another and as sanitation around areas of permanent habitation became more of a problem. Even nutrition seems to have deteriorated for many, compared to the wider variety and higher quality of the hunters' and gatherers' diet. In response both to high death rates and to the need for labor in the fields, therefore, it seems that agricultural societies evolved strong pronatalist norms encouraging large families. With temporary and usually local interruptions, then, the population of the human race began steadily increasing.

Drawing on recorded history and our own limited observations, we have tended to think that high fertility and large families were always characteristic of human populations. It appears, however, that these demographic tendencies were concomitants of the agricultural mode of life, which had interrupted the steadystate existence that predominated during approximately 95 percent of man's species history. Once the homeostatic (self-regulating) mechanisms that had enabled man to maintain a balance between his population and the carrying capacity of his environment were replaced by pronatalist cultural norms, however, the latter tended to persist even after declining death rates and changing modes of production made them less and less necessary. Thus, for the postprimitive, premodern period of human history, the high birth rate–high death rate hypothesis seems reasonably sound.

As the process of modernization occurred in Europe, the English-speaking countries, and Japan, death rates in these areas experienced marked declines, and the combination of high birth rates and lowered death rates gave rise to rapid rates of population increase. Fairly quickly, however, birth rates in these areas also began declining, and in consequence the differential between birth rates and death rates was again narrowed. The resulting return to low rates of population growth differed from earlier historical periods of low population increase in that it was now maintained by low birth rates and low death rates rather than by high ones. This shift is known as the *demographic transition*, that is, the three-stage movement from a condition of low population growth maintained by high birth rates and high death rates, through a period of rapid growth based on continued high birth rates but lowered death rates, and culminating in a new period of low population growth derived from low birth and death rates (see figure 1).

The exact mechanisms by which the demographic transition came about—that is, how the modernization process resulted in strong motivations on the part of individual parents for smaller families— and indeed whether the theory of the demographic transition is a valid way of explaining what occurred in the presently modernized countries are the subject of continuing controversy among population specialists.[19] What is clear, however, is that medical-scientific advances and public health programs have succeeded in reducing death rates all around the globe, whereas the forces associated with the modernization process that depress fertility have in many places not yet come into play. The result is the unsustainable imbalance between high fertility and low mortality that has been characterized aptly enough as "the population bomb."[20]

The general pattern of recent population growth is shown in table 1. That this unprecedented rate of population expansion cannot continue indefinitely or even for finite periods such as the next century is certain. Equally certain are the two, and only two, alternative means for bringing this growth rate down to sustainable levels, which eventually means zero population growth (ZPG): either birth rates will come down or death rates will go up. (Of course, some mix of the two could occur simultaneously.) Barring nuclear holocaust or some other global catastrophe, however, the trend of world population during the remaining decades of this century and well into the next will unavoidably be one of continued growth. The only

Figure 1. The Demographic Transition

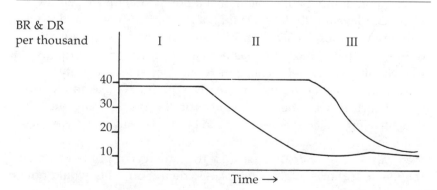

Table 1. World Population Growth

Date (A.D.)	Estimated World Population	Doubling Time
0	250 million	
1650	500 million	1,650 years
1850	1,000 million	200 years
1930	2,000 million	80 years
1975	4,000 million	45 years
2010	(8,000 million)	(35 years)
2040	(16,000 million)	(30 years)

Source: Annabelle Desmond, "How Many People Have Ever Lived on Earth?" p. 12.

essential question, therefore, is whether the population increase of the next several decades will be very rapid or only moderately rapid.

It is clear that most of this increase will occur in the low-income countries where, because of very rapid growth in recent decades, populations are extraordinarily young—often with nearly 50 percent below the age of fifteen. Young populations have continued growth literally built into them because of the increasing numbers of women who will be entering, and remaining for thirty years in, the reproductive age period as the younger cohorts (birth groups) mature. Thus, under the most optimistic possible assumptions—and even under such completely impossible ones as a replacement level of fertility (Net Reproduction Rate = 1) being achieved tomorrow (each couple having only enough children to replace themselves, or an average of one daughter for each mother)—these populations will continue to expand in size for many decades to come (see table 2). This is what is meant by the "momentum" or "inertia" of population growth.

This momentum is the reason that a population may reach replacement level fertility, as has that of the United States, and still be sixty years or more away from ZPG. Because of the large young cohorts in a population that has been experiencing rapid growth, the number of new mothers will be increasing for at least twenty to twenty-five years as young girls reach reproductive age and marry. Even if each new mother were to bear on the average only one daughter (for which it is necessary to bear on the average two children), the total number of births each year would be greater than the total number of deaths, because the latter occur primarily among the smaller cohorts of older people. By definition, ZPG would not be

**Table 2. Total World Population (in Millions)
and Indices of Population Size (1970 = 100),
1975–2075 Linear Decline of Fertility to NRR Level of 1.0**

| Year | Period in Which Net Reproduction Rate of One Is Reached | | | | |
	1970–75	1980–85	2000–2005	2020–25	2040–45
1975	3771.9	3953.2	4007.0	4022.2	4029.6
	103	108	109	110	110
1980	3932.7	4212.8	4387.1	4436.3	4460.4
	107	115	120	121	122
1985	4126.7	4403.5	4782.5	4889.6	4941.9
	113	120	131	134	135
1990	4344.9	4628.0	5182.3	5377.5	5473.0
	119	126	142	147	150
1995	4560.2	4873.1	5570.5	5893.3	6051.9
	125	133	152	161	166
2000	4746.1	5115.6	5922.5	6422.1	6669.8
	130	140	162	176	182
2010	5031.4	5522.6	6523.6	7473.2	8003.5
	138	151	178	205	219
2020	5270.1	5831.8	7116.0	8426.0	9418.1
	144	159	195	231	258
2030	5441.6	6077.8	7599.2	9216.0	10813.3
	149	166	208	252	296
2040	5505.8	6215.7	7942.1	9930.5	12038.7
	151	170	217	272	330
2050	5591.6	6286.2	8172.2	10473.2	13024.7
	153	172	224	287	357
2075	5674.9	6399.8	8357.3	11084.7	14660.6
	155	175	229	304	402

Source: Tomas Frejka, reference tables to *The Future of Population Growth*, p. 18.

reached until the total number of births equaled the total number of deaths, and this could not occur until the large young cohorts had aged and the number of deaths they were contributing each year was sizable enough to offset the number of births their children were by then having.

Given, therefore, that most cultures have evolved powerful pronatalist tendencies in response to high death rates or to heavy demands for labor, plus the fact that in subsistence farming situations there are rational economic incentives for couples to have large families, the outlook for rapid acceptance of the idea of family-size limitation in low-income countries is not encouraging, particularly in the absence of marked declines in infant mortality rates. It is some- times argued that simply making modern means of contraception freely available will suffice to reduce population growth rates in these countries, but the evidence seems to support the position that motivations for smaller families are the crucial variable.[21] Moreover, because of the momentum of population growth, the real question is not whether population growth rates can simply be reduced but whether they can be reduced quite drastically, within as short a period of time as possible, and through means that improve the lot of those born rather than worsen it.

A Demographic Perspective on Development

The prospects for rapid and substantial declines in population growth rates in the low-income countries are made even more unlikely by the fact that in the absence of structural changes that provide functional equivalents for the services traditionally performed by children for their parents—status requirements, supplementary labor or income, protection against aggression, disability and old age insurance, a sense of meaningful accomplishment, and a source of hope for the future—there is little reason to expect the motivations of couples regarding family size to change in anything approaching the degree necessary. Pessimism on this point seems unavoidable considering the multiple sources of resistance to effecting structural changes of the required nature and magnitude. Moreover, it should be recalled that the myriad decisions that combine into demographic trends are made by individual couples, not by government bureaucrats or national leaders. These countless couples reach their decisions on these matters through processes that are still far from well under- stood. That fertility behavior, in particular, is in large part a rational process, however, is shown by the fact that hardly anywhere does human fertility approach the biological maximum of some fifty-five births per thousand people per year. The best-known exception merely confirms that rational control is operative, for the elaborate subculture of the Hutterite religious sect places a premium on high fertility.[22] The point to be made is simply that fertility behavior is a response to the total milieu in which a couple is embedded—both in a cultural, economic, and political sense and along the time dimension of past, present, and expected future. Consequently, population policies often prove less significant in influencing demographic variables than do other aspects of a government's program or of a culture's values. Antinatalist policies in a pronatalist cultural setting are therefore unlikely to have a wide impact, unless the conditions within which people live are such that delaying marriage or having smaller families makes sound economic sense to them personally. Coercive antinatalist policies might theoretically be more effective than the voluntaristic, propagandistic, or incentive-based approaches currently employed in most countries, but, on the other hand, few Third World "soft states"[23] could efficiently enforce or administer such policies, and as one experienced population specialist has remarked, any attempt to impose them "could cause a nation's government to fall much faster than its birth rate."[24]

The considerations just reviewed lend credence to the oft-heard formula, "Take care of people, and population will take care of itself." Taking care of people, however—or, more accurately, creating conditions within which people can take care of themselves—is what development is supposedly all about. Yet what has been called development has rarely made this its primary goal, and what has actually been promoted—industrial growth and modernization—is creating its own distinctive problems, which are no less serious than those associated with rapid population growth, for example, environmental degradation, resource depletion, arms races, environmentally induced cancer, alienation, and assorted social pathologies.[25] Moreover, the feasibility of what has been thought of as development—constant per capita increase in GNP through capital-intensive industrialization—has been called into question by man's growing recognition of the limits of nonrenewable resources, ecological life-support systems, and human capacity to administer and to function effectively within large and complex organizations. Clearly, new concepts of development are needed so that what gets promoted is an arrangement of production and consumption that leaves a population in a healthy and *sustainable* relationship with the ecosystem of which it is a part. This type of arrangement has been labeled by various authors as "ecodevelopment."[26]

Seen in this context, the often acrimonious debate between those advocating immediate efforts at population limitation and those arguing for "development first" seems a sterile enterprise. Prescribing development as the cure for a low-income country's population growth rate of more than 3 percent per annum is like urging the emaciated host of a tapeworm and sundry amoebas to eat heartily and build up his strength. Vicious circles are involved in both cases. Perhaps, however, guided by new concepts of development that emphasize utilization of the resources available to them and that focus directly on providing the most basic needs of the neediest, the low-income countries can break the vicious circle of unemployment-poverty-malnutrition-fatalism-high fertility-unemployment and establish a viable form of life for their populations.[27]

At any rate, although industrialization and modernization were the primary generators of motivations for smaller families in the Western experience, the outlook is not bright for a repeat of this performance in non-Western cultural milieus under radically altered historical and ecological conditions.[28] In addition to the fact that present low-income countries are constrained by the influences on them emanating from already modernized countries, the era of cheap energy, rich ore deposits exploitable through relatively simple technologies, and wide environmental tolerances during which Western countries modernized has now ended, thus significantly increasing the start-up costs of modernization through industrialization in present-day low-income countries and probably limiting its overall potential decisively.

As the mainland Chinese have demonstrated, however, political mobilization can in many ways be made to substitute for modernization. Organizing rural people into relatively self-sufficient communes and production brigades has apparently made it possible to provide many of the functional equivalents for the services of offspring and thus to lay the groundwork for receptivity to massive propaganda campaigns in favor of delayed marriage and a two-child family norm. Equally as important has been the way this form of social organization has been able to utilize peer pressure in enforcing the prescriptions of its propaganda.[29]

Not unrelated to these and other accomplishments of the Communist Chinese has been their success in providing employment for everyone, thus making use of the resource that currently is most abundant yet most wasted in practically every low-income country—man- and womanpower. There is a lesson here of inestimable significance for whatever sort of development model other low-income countries hope to pursue, for just as the momentum of a young population insures continued growth, it also guarantees a continuous flood of entrants into the labor force for many years to come. Whether these new members of the labor force are productively employed or not will have profound implications not only for the economy of the particular country and the stability of its political structures but, in an interdependent world with proliferating nuclear capabilities, for the future international system as well.

The employment aspect of the Chinese example merits emulation by other low-income countries, for, where capital is scarce and populations are young, the inevitable waves of new unskilled workers will have to be employed in labor-intensive processes, primarily agriculture and infrastructural projects such as roads, bridges, irrigation, drainage, reforestation, and erosion abatement. In addition to the direct contributions of these activities, a coordinated approach to development along these lines could reduce the current exodus from the countryside into cities that plagues most low-income countries at the same time that the potential of the countryside for adequately feeding both its own and the swelling urban populations is enhanced. If these two goals are not approached simultaneously and rapidly, the prospects for famine, turmoil, and opportunistic attempts to benefit therefrom are very likely to have extensive international repercussions.

Let us briefly recapitulate the reasoning underlying this dire assessment. Medical-scientific advances and extensive public health measures have resulted in a marked lowering of mortality rates throughout the world. In the low-income countries, however, death control without birth control has produced an imbalance between births and deaths that has given rise to the currently unsustainable rate of population expansion. Rapid population growth has, in turn, contributed to fast-expanding labor forces in all low-income countries. In most of these countries, land tenure arrangements or the scarcity of arable land have made it impossible for the agricultural sector to absorb these increases in the labor supply. Massive unemployment, underemployment, and cityward migration have resulted. Because capital is scarce and investors are daunted by the risks involved, because the prices of needed resources—particularly fuels—continue to move upward as supplies dwindle, and because many needed skills as well as sufficient purchasing power among the masses to constitute a market are lacking, there is no possibility of the industrial sector absorbing very substantial portions of the swelling labor force; only labor-intensive activities can possibly do so. Labor-intensive activities, especially with a largely unskilled labor force, are most easily created in rural areas in infrastructural types of projects. These types of projects are urgently needed in most low-income countries and could significantly expand agricultural production. This, in turn, if better nutrition results, could improve overall productivity and could strengthen a country's foreign exchange position by reducing food imports and augmenting agricultural exports, with significant collateral effects on world commodity prices. Of equal importance, such a strategy could perhaps deflect a substantial portion of the rural migrants away from the burgeoning urban areas, where the superexponential increase of population in recent years has severely overloaded the capacities of many Third World cities to provide even minimum levels of public services. This lessening of pressure on the water, sewerage, and waste removal systems of urban centers, combined with an increased food-producing capacity in the rural areas, might prevent the epidemics, worsening food shortages, and civil unrest that otherwise would render the political situation of these countries so vulnerable to disruption that rival power contenders could hardly resist the temptation to try their luck—a situation in which foreign powers might feel constrained to intervene or from which threatened power holders might seek to distract attention by some form of foreign adventure.

A political system that has achieved sufficient levels of political mobilization to carry out the suggested strategy of massive infrastructural development through labor-intensive means should also be capable of providing basic—albeit perhaps very basic—health services, in the context of which family-planning methods could be disseminated to the population (again the Chinese example, with their "barefoot doctor" paramedics, seems germane). The availability of modern methods of contraception, abortion, and sterilization would enable those couples who had already reached their desired family size to cease reproduction, a valuable first step toward eventual movement in the direction of replacement-level fertility. If propaganda programs aimed at delayed marriage, wider spacing of siblings, and reduced overall family size were politically feasible, as doubtless they would be in a mobilization regime, this goal could be approached even more rapidly.

The principal point, however, is that by providing productive and remunerative employment for everyone able to work—"jobs and justice," as this approach is often labeled—the political system would be preparing the way for lower family-size norms. It seems axiomatic that people who cannot plan ahead to their next meal are unlikely to consider planning their families, and for the jobless the next meal often becomes an all-consuming preoccupation. Employment, therefore, with the material and psychological rewards it provides the individual, is, if not the sine qua non of, certainly a sound first step toward effective population growth limitation. And without population growth limitation there can be no viable form of development.

I have painted here with broad strokes, purposely omitting mention of the precise mechanisms through which low-income government might attempt to mobilize and organize their unemployed masses. A variety of mechanisms exist,[30] each with its advantages and drawbacks, and some better suited to the particular circumstances of a given country than others. My principal aim has *not* been to urge replication of the Chinese experience but only to make a case for the plausibility and potentially salutary effects of a rural-oriented, labor-intensive approach to development. I hope the logic of the foregoing argument has made it obvious that the only alternative to achieving these effects involves disasters and dislocations of potentially international proportions.

The Probable Future

Having seen what *could* be done, let us now discuss what seems most likely *will* be done and what implications this more probable train of events might have for future prospects for development.

Although it is conceivable that the worsening conditions created by archaic land tenure patterns, skewed distributions of wealth and influence, widespread unemployment, massive urban migration, and deteriorating urban and rural environments will provoke a more viable developmental strategy than has been pursued in the past, the factors inhibiting such a response in most low-income countries are formidable and are likely to prove as decisive in the near future as they have in the past.

The first of the factors, of course, is that the governments of most of these countries are primarily concerned not with the welfare of their people but with maintaining and enhancing the trappings of national identity and the privileges of the classes and individuals that in fact they represent. This indictment derives from no prior ideological commitment but rests on the universally observed tendency for political power to accrue to those who already control some other power resource—be it wealth, social status, official position, or whatever—and for this accretion of power to be used to protect and advance the interests of the groups who wield it. Moreover, it offers the only satisfactory way of explaining why so few Third World governments have even attempted to push through the kinds of reforms so obviously required for the benefit of the masses— sweeping agrarian reforms, steeply progressive tax laws, massive training and employment programs and so forth.

In addition to the self-serving nature of most political regimes, there are, of course, the myriad bottlenecks and obstacles to effective action that characterize all low-income countries' administrative establishments and political cultures. Bureaucratic politics and the politics of scarcity make effective implementation of even well-conceived programs almost impossible under present structures. Furthermore, the political clout of well-organized government workers and of the unionized urban industrial and commercial work force in general protects these key sectors from the drastic reorganization they need to become efficient, as well as making them powerful forces to reckon with for any government that might wish to institute policies favoring rural areas and the worst-off segments of society. It has also been repeatedly demonstrated that the political power of the urban middle sectors, both in the capital and in the provincial cities, is a significant bulwark against thoroughgoing reforms, even where a government seeks to implement them.

In short, only revolutionary regimes would be very likely to attempt, or have much chance of succeeding in, the sorts of programs that could mobilize the masses and channel both their muscle power and their brain power into productive pursuits, thereby laying the basis for defusing the population bomb as well as for "development." Yet, in addition to the oft-repeated tendency for the new regime to become the old regime, the prospects for staging a successful revolution have declined steadily as the military in Third World countries has become better equipped, better trained, and more sophisticated in counterinsurgency tactics. The alternative of a revolution from above under the direction or with the cooperation of the military remains a possibility theoretically but has, thus far at least, failed to yield very encouraging results in the few places it has been tried.

Realistically, therefore, the outlook is for a worsening of the trends already so prominent in practically every city of the Third World. Congestion, crowding, squalor, disease, unemployment, pollution, crime, violence, and unconscionable disparities between elites and masses are likely to increase, while the adequacy of public services and the quality of life even for the better-off will steadily decline.

Urban migration specialists endlessly debate the effects these conditions have on the political attitudes and behavior of the migrants themselves. Whether they are increasingly frustrated and alienated and therefore potentially rebellious or whether they perceive themselves as so much better off in their new surroundings, however wretched, than they were in their rural homelands that they are supportive of the system in which they feel they are "making it" is still disputed.[31] However this may be, three almost certain results of this worsening state of affairs within the Third World can be foreseen: (1) increased emigration of the better educated and more highly skilled workers ("brain drain"); (2) increased incidences of repressive authoritarian regimes; (3) increased numbers of deaths due to disease, undernutrition, and malnutrition, if not to outright starvation. The present decade has already witnessed a marked acceleration in all these trends.

The distinction being drawn between the Third and Fourth Worlds since the so-called energy crisis of 1973–74 seems relevant here. The Fourth World is that unhappy group of low-income countries which lacks oil or any other highly marketable resource. It is they who have suffered most from the quintupling of petroleum prices by the OPEC countries, for their inability to augment their foreign exchange earnings has left them with severe balance-of-payment shortfalls and forced them to cut back on petroleum imports, with a consequent decline in all their fossil fuel–based productive activities, including agriculture. The Third World nations should take warning from this example, for many of them will be in a similar position long before the end of the century as petroleum reserves decline and the high-income countries outbid them for what is being produced (assuming that the high-income countries haven't already taken more drastic action to secure their foreign oil supplies by that time).

Obviously, the most severe dislocations and the most devastating famines will occur first in the Fourth World countries. Some of these countries will probably disappear as separate sovereign nations and be absorbed by their neighbors or reestablished as protectorates of the United Nations or of some high-income country. While the potential for destabilizing the global economy and the international system is certainly present in these events, it is relatively low compared to that inherent in the situation of many Third World nations. Some of these countries have quite sophisticated industrial and scientific capabilities, and several of them already possess or are acquiring nuclear reactors—for "peaceful purposes," of course. The increasing cost and imminent exhaustion of petroleum have accelerated these countries' nuclear energy programs, which can only augur ill for the world as a whole as increasing amounts of plutonium 239 and other high-level materials are accumulated. Even were these radioactive fuels and wastes to prove inadequately fissionable for use in nuclear devices, many of them are such potent poisons that their release in populated areas could result in massive loss of life.

Although nuclear blackmail between nation-states is not at all unimaginable, it is vastly more likely to occur through the agency of terrorist groups or criminal elements. And, once it has happened for the first time, the world will be worse off by several orders of magnitude, not necessarily because of actual deaths, destruction, or released radioactivity but as a result of the measures most people everywhere will accept in order to prevent a recurrence of such an eventuality. The example of airplane hijacking is instructive here, although the preventive measures taken in that instance scarcely begin to foreshadow the kinds of controls, regulations, and invasions of privacy that would be required to guard against nuclear, chemical, viral, or bacteriological blackmail.

Again, let us pause to review the argument being presented. Because of the lack of political vision and the disproportionate power of vested interests opposed to sweeping change, it is unlikely that most low-income countries will take the necessary actions to ameliorate the disastrous trends already clearly discernible both in their cities and in their hinterlands. In consequence, these trends will steadily worsen, reducing the quality of life even for the relatively well-off and contributing to a declining capacity to respond to the challenges as the brain drain accelerates, authoritarian governments increasingly predominate, and the vigor and spirit of the people are eroded by uncontrollable inflation, increasing scarcities, sporadic labor stoppages, poorer nutrition, environmental contamination, contagious diseases, and the spectacle of societal inability to cope with the problems facing it. Couple all this with the strikes, riots, epidemics, famines, and periodic collapse of public order certain to occur in the neediest countries, and the stage is set for the desperate measures sure to be taken by some individuals or groups among the increasing numbers of people—not all of them among the poverty-stricken masses—with little or nothing to lose. And the counter-measures employed to try to anticipate and prevent these desperate measures will very likely prove to be a remedy as ultimately debilitating as the disease itself.

Some version of this appalling scenario appears all too likely to become reality by the end of this century, given man's oft-proved inability, particularly at the national level, to act generously, compassionately, wisely, and with foresight. The international system, with its structure firmly based on the outmoded concept of national sovereignty—and, at a deeper level, on hierarchy and competition,[32]—resembles nothing so much as a sandbox filled with selfish, unsocialized toddlers whose playthings are hand grenades and fragile flasks of deadly germs. Although this somewhat trite analogy may seem overdrawn, it is hard to see how anyone could disagree with the assertion that mankind's technological cleverness has far outstripped both his moral and his social development, and the disequilibrium has begun to reach unsustainable proportions. For almost any problem area one cares to examine, a comparison of what clearly needs to be done with what in fact is being done leads to the conclusion that events have slipped out of human control—or, more probably, have reached such magnitude and complexity that we can no longer maintain our illusion of controlling them.

Yet, as the second part of this essay sought to show, solutions are possible. As dismaying as the prospects are, there may still be time to prevent their materializing or at least to alleviate their worst effects. The hope for the future lies paradoxically in the unparalleled perversity of our present situation, for our current attitudes and actions are so demonstrably unsustainable, so suicidal, that the task of discrediting them might be more easily accomplished than is usually thought. Moreover, the scale of the initial task is often exaggerated. Not everyone has to be convinced of the need for new directions in order for new directions to be taken. Dedicated minorities have produced major changes in society many times in the past.

If the folly of continuing to increase the gap between the rich countries and the poor can be grasped, self-interest can perhaps be aligned with altruism (or more cynically, with the psychic gratification to be found in self-abnegation and submersion in a noble cause) in effecting drastic alterations of values, life styles, consumption patterns, recreational preferences, modes of transportation, diets, and all the other aspects of our lives that will have to undergo radical change if the resources are to be made available and the example set where they must be—in the rich countries—before the problems of the poor countries can begin to be resolved.[33] If more people, especially in the rich countries, were to demand political leaders with demonstrated breadth of vision and reasonable proposals for a saner, more just, and sustainable world order, and if the means now employed to promote consumerism, competition, waste, and war were directed instead toward inculcating "earthmanship" values,[34] the prospects of the future need not be as dismal as they currently are.[35]

Admittedly, the problems that would have to be overcome in the poor countries, even assuming the near-miraculous turnaround within the rich countries just described, would be of mind-boggling difficulty. But so too will be the problems that will have to be confronted as a result of our failure to make the sorts of changes suggested above. If the argument presented here is correct, there is only one alternative to willing sacrifice and service on behalf of a decent existence for all mankind in an ecologically sustainable relationship to our life-support system, and that is increasing fear, frustration, and futile struggling to secure our own comfort and safety in a world characterized by monstrous suffering, inhumanity, and ecological destruction.

In my view, the responsibility for making these alternatives clear to political leaders and the mass public in the rich countries lies primarily with their better-educated citizens, particularly the intellectuals, the scholars, the scientists, and the students of those countries. Ill suited though we are—overprofessionalized; overspecialized; overwhelmed, if we are honest, with how little we can know—it falls to us to respond to this historic challenge as best we can. If we do not, very probably it will not be done, and the future will inexorably unfold not through foresight but by default.

Modernization and the Ecological Perspective

David W. Orr

Thomas Kuhn, in his classic *Structure of Scientific Revolutions*, suggests that scientific knowledge grows in two distinct ways. The first of these, which he labels "normal science," expands like an inkblot around an accepted "paradigm" of shared values, methods, rules of evidence, and not the least, problems. Normal science works well until "anomalies" occur that cannot be solved and may even go unrecognized or be purposely ignored.[1] When this happens, some scientists may deviate from orthodoxy, creating an alternative paradigm to solve otherwise insuperable problems.

Kuhn does not deal specifically with the social sciences, but it is plausible that social knowledge similarly grows both incrementally and through revolutionary paradigm changes in which methods, values, and perceptions are radically altered. The differences between the natural and the social sciences arise because paradigm changes in the latter are somewhat more subject to shifts in societal values and situations, knowledge is less obviously cumulative, and there is less consensus regarding methods of verification. The obsolescence of paradigms, however, likely occurs for similar reasons, including a growing vagueness owing to the burden of unexplained anomalies, increasing remoteness from reality, and the resultant difficulty in commanding the loyalties of new generations of scholars.

Perhaps no paradigm in the social sciences has been subjected to more thorough analysis and criticism than that of modernization. Early critics, including Marx, Weber, Durkheim, and Freud, regarded modernization as a mixed blessing, but all assumed its inevitability. To some degree, the essence of their criticisms has been met by

alteration of the cruder aspects of early industrial society. Evidence
has accumulated, however, that shows that the ecological basis of
modern society is being undermined by the very means that led to its
creation. By questioning the capacity of modern systems to effect
their own survival, environmentalists have made the most radical
assault yet. Given what is already known about environmental
deterioration, it remains to be seen whether modern systems can
successfully solve environmental problems within the context of the
present social paradigm or, alternatively, whether it will become
necessary to create a new social paradigm.

This is a complex question that cannot be answered until we know
more about both the dimensions of the "ecological crisis" and the
adaptability of modern society. In the pages that follow, I intend, first,
to describe the paradigm of modernity; second, to present the
essence of the environmental critique; and third, to sketch an
alternative paradigm.

Modernity

There is general agreement among sociologists and political scientists
that the complex set of changes comprising the process of modernization resulted from the rapid increase in knowledge.[2] The development of science and technology has had profound effects upon the
way modern man related to other men and to nature. Modernity is
characterized by "rational" modes of thought in which decisions tend
to be based on secular, goal-oriented, and universal criteria. Primitive
man, while not necessarily irrational, had no obvious counterpart to
modern science. For interpersonal relations, modernity meant a
value shift from ascriptive, specific, and universal criteria to achievement, diffuse, and particular criteria.[3] At the societal level the
emphasis on personal efficiency was matched by the stress on
bureaucratic routine governed by explicit secular rules.

There also occurred a simultaneous increase in the range of
phenomena open to human intervention and control. Previous
taboos, dissolved by the expansion of science, were replaced by a
new ethic in which the search for knowledge, profit, or the "need for
change" abolished the notion of taboo itself. In this atmosphere, the
only enduring certainty became the lack of certainty. Modern

societies thus came to be distinguished chiefly by their superior ability to initiate and to accommodate change. In contrast to primitive and transitional societies that operated little above subsistence levels, modern societies have developed elaborate mechanisms for promoting economic growth through planned saving and investment. In addition, modern societies are increasingly dominated by corporations sufficiently large to exploit economies of scale and sufficiently dispersed functionally and geographically to insure greater stability and access to labor and raw materials. Modern economies are also undergirded by substantial normative support for increased productivity, so that economic growth has become the most widely used indicator of system performance. Thus, although individual accumulation is no longer regarded as a sign of divine election, economic productivity is universally thought to indicate election to the divine condition of modernity.

Finally, modern societies are characterized by complex social patterns in which the imperatives of efficiency have led to a division of labor based on narrowly defined role systems. Modern societies are thus characterized by "structural differentiation" and "role specificity" as opposed to the more generalized patterns of primitive social systems. Moreover, modernization has altered the scale of human relations. Whereas primitive and transitional man lives in small villages and towns, modern man is predominantly urban. The link between these two stages involves what Karl Deutsch has described as social mobilization, which entails the uprooting of old values and commitments and the acceptance of new ones.[4]

Implicit in the theory of modernization are at least two underlying assumptions. The first of these refers to the basic irreversibility of the process in which systems evolve toward higher and more complex forms. Gabriel Almond and Bingham Powell, for example, have argued that "the pervasive nature of the changes and enormous incentives they offer to individual [sic] and society have made them unidirectional. It would seem that only a worldwide catastrophe, such as a nuclear war, could possibly reverse the process."[5] Similarly, Marion Levy argues that modernization exerts a magnetic pull on less developed peoples such that "All of the present relatively non-modernized societies will change in the direction of greater modernization . . . regardless of whether their members wish it."[6] Linearity, however, does not imply that modernization is necessarily unidirectional in all systems. Rather, although they still assume the irreversibility of the process, modernists admit the possibility of localized setbacks.[7]

A second assumption of the theorists of modernization is that modern systems have progressively risen above natural constraints. Indeed, the extent of the triumph over nature is the yardstick of modernity. Modern man has risen above constraint, whereas primitive man was bound by environmental constraints over which he possessed little mastery. Thus, Levy defines modernity as the ratio of inanimate to animate sources of power; the higher the ratio, the greater the degree of modernization.[8] Cyril Black defines modernization more broadly as "the process by which historically evolved institutions are adapted to the rapidly changing functions that reflect the unprecedented increase in man's knowledge, permitting control over his environment."[9] For the modernists, the only limits to the domination of nature are those inherent in human ingenuity and organization.

The more orthodox theorists of modern society, including Herman Kahn and Daniel Bell, see the future as essentially a further elaboration of economic and technological trends.[10] Bell's "postindustrial society" is little more than an expansion of the present social paradigm with a somewhat greater role for what he calls "theoretical knowledge."[11] If there are problems, they will be solved with the application of technology; if there are limits, technology will expand them; if there is social unrest, sociologists will write very long books about it. The ethos of postindustrial society is that of science, and its problems are those of the management of information, time, and resources.

The Environmental Critique

Despite differences, the array of thinkers that we can describe as environmentalists share a common view of the world as a finite ecosystem whose stability is jeopardized by population, economic, and technological growth. Modernists, while not necessarily disagreeing with the proposition, have been less inclined to regard it as fundamental. They assume that environmental limits can be expanded by technology, which in turn would be socially benign. The environmentalist's rebuttal can be better appraised when regarded as a set of six related propositions.

Modern Society Is Based on the Belief That the World Is without Limit

If there is any single belief that unites environmentalists, it is that the biosphere is finite and that economic growth can only speed the entropic process described by the second law of thermodynamics.[12] While this seems self-evident in the abstract, there is room for disagreement on specifics. Exactly what is "finite?" What limits exist on which activities? How close are we to these limits? Thomas Malthus was one of the first to suggest limits inherent in the fact that population increased geometrically while food supply grew arithmetically.

Malthus fell into disrepute for a century or more, but his logic was revived by the authors of *The Limits to Growth*,[13] who purported to show that global carrying capacity would be exceeded within the next hundred years by the exponential growth of population, resource use, industrialization, land use, and pollution. Critics responded by pointing out the crudeness of the model and the overly restrictive notion of a fixed carrying capacity.[14] Resources, for example, are not simply given but depend on both the level of technology and the effect of prices. Moreover, demand may not continue at past rates, so that simple extrapolation can be misleading. Critics further contend that the use of aggregate data in *The Limits* concealed significant local and regional variations and thus distorted reality. But the second report to the Club of Rome, *Mankind at the Turning Point*, which divided the global model into ten regions, reached only marginally different and even slightly more drastic conclusions.[15]

More recent studies, including the third report to the Club of Rome, coordinated by Jan Tinbergen, and *The Future of the World Economy* by Wassily Leontief, have argued that growth can and should continue for the next twenty-five years.[16] Although these studies are regarded as optimistic, their conclusions (if not emphases) do not necessarily conflict with those of *The Limits* and *Mankind at the Turning Point*. We can be euphoric because growth is theoretically possible for twenty-five years or gloomy because they suggest that it will only occur with increasing difficulty and may not be possible much beyond the year 2000.

But these questions aside for the moment, if the world is in fact finite in some meaningful sense, how could we have so grossly misconceived it? One answer, provided by the MIT group, suggests that the problem is the deceptive speed of exponential growth. Most of what we have come to associate with the ecological crisis occurred as the gross world product more than doubled in the last thirty years. Barry Commoner attributes the problem to recent changes in industry that favored the production and use of synthetics, chemicals, automobiles, and similar energy-intensive and ecologically disruptive technologies.[17] Lewis Mumford and William Leiss argue that the roots of the crisis can be found in the origins of science and in the legacy of Bacon, Galileo, and Descartes, who encouraged the fragmentation of reality and the devaluation of those aspects not subject to empirical verification and in the process left us with a "humpty-dumpty" problem of creating meaningful wholes from thoroughly researched bits and pieces.[18]

Modern Society Is Based on an Incomplete Model of Man

The first proposition suggested that there are flaws in our model of the world; the second proposition suggests that there are flaws in our view of man. According to the environmental critique, modernization is based upon a faulty model of man that overemphasizes his malleability, rationality, and economic needs at the expense of equally important traits of humaneness, creativity, and compassion. The process of modernization dehumanizes, creating, in Mumford's words, "a type [of person] unable to react directly to sights or sounds, to patterns or concrete objects, unable to function in any capacity without anxiety, indeed, unable to feel alive, except by permission or command."[19]

The economist portrays man as little more than a compulsive producer and consumer with little thought for either his deeper needs or ecological constraints. The purpose of the producing system, Mumford suggests, "is not primarily to satisfy human needs . . . but to multiply the number of needs."[20] The emphasis on production leads to the ever greater use of ever more scarce resources in order to conserve labor that has become abundant. According to E. F. Schumacher, growing levels of consumption are also morally degenerative and can lead only to a "collapse of intelligence."[21]

Theodore Roszak goes beyond this to argue that science and

technology, the principal agents of modernization, are antithetical to the spiritual nature of man and have eroded his "transcendent energies" to the detriment of creativity and spiritual awareness.[22] The triumph of the scientific, rational model of man led to the denial of those portions of human nature not quantifiable, easily observable, or narrowly functional. The result is a world in which men respond only to the alien imperatives of technique and are no longer aware of their potential for transcendence.

Modernization Has Destroyed the Unity between Man and Nature

Environmentalists since George Perkins Marsh have argued that industrialization and modernization have jeopardized the necessary relationship between man and nature. The awareness of membership in a natural community has been dimmed by layers of concrete, steel, asphalt, and glass and an ethic that stresses conquest. But the question remains as to why man should regard nature as anything other than subject to his domination.

One answer is that nature must be protected and its laws understood so that it can serve man more efficiently. Modern techniques of high-yield forestry, sea farming, and agribusiness, based on the concept of "maximum sustainable yield," reflect this instrumental view. But from the environmental perspective, it is not clear what the management (conquest?) of nature means and precisely who manages what and why. C. S. Lewis provided one answer by suggesting that the conquest of nature was one way for some men to use nature to control other men.[23] But in the end the "conquest" proves to be illusory, with nature in the form of uncontrolled human nature subduing man. Aldo Leopold reached a similarly ironic conclusion that nature can serve man instrumentally only if "people really believe that Nature is something which exists and has value for its own sake."[24]

Modernization Jeopardizes "Social Carrying Capacity"

As a fourth proposition, environmentalists tend to agree that there is a limit prior to planetary finiteness in the capacity of social, political, and economic institutions to adapt to growing ecological stress. As we approach physical limits, with increasing scarcities and environmental deterioration, the capacity of society to manage strain will likewise deteriorate. Harold and Margaret Sprout suggest that complexity has led to "multiple vulnerabilities" that have radically increased the prospects for social breakdown. Vulnerability rises with the standard of living, the size and density of populations, the degree of interdependence, and the level of technological development.[25] In general, the higher the level of these factors, the greater the economic and social effort necessary to keep society going. Disruption can originate from a variety of sources, including sabotage, cataclysmic accidents, simple failure, loss of community morale, conflict over distribution, and a host of external causes.

In a different vein, Fred Hirsch has presented an argument that modern societies are reaching what he describes as the "social limits to growth." Economic growth, according to Hirsch, is like everyone in a crowd standing on tiptoe, so that despite the effort no one is relatively better off. Moreover, the conflict for limited or what he calls "positional" goods places potentially fatal strains on the capitalist social order and "threatens to displace Smithian harmony by Hobbesian strife."[26]

Although Hirsch is concerned with the logic of growth and not ecological issues, his argument nonetheless lends substantial support to those made by the Sprouts and Roberto Vacca. Should production of material goods be restricted by scarcity, as described in *The Limits to Growth*, the effect would be to intensify the increasing social fragility described by Hirsch.

Modernization Has Led to the Loss of Control over Science and Technology

Skepticism about science and technology is certainly not new, but environmentalists tend to regard them with a special hostility. This attitude is not directed, as some have charged, to all technology but, rather, is directed toward a particular form that is variously described as "compulsive," "maniacal," and "imbalanced."[27] It is this loss of balance that has led society to submit to any technological possibility or what Jacques Ellul calls "technique" without seriously appraising the consequences. Indeed, the ability to critically evaluate technology and to occasionally say "no" is limited by the pervasiveness of the technical mentality itself.

Environmentalists further charge that science and technology have contributed to a variety of problems, including the loss of human scale, social instability, and severe environmental stress. Equally dangerous is the extent to which science has become the equivalent of a religion in which scientists have assumed the role of a new priesthood.[28] Having discarded religion, modern man "transfers his sense of the sacred to the very thing which has destroyed its former object: to technique itself."[29] By ruling out important but nonquantifiable phenomena, however, science cannot lay claim to genuine objectivity. Moreover, science, having separated objective knowledge from subjective values, has lost the means of determining questions of ethics and perhaps the possibility of control as well.[30]

Modernization Will Lead to Political Instability

In contrast to the widely held belief that modernization would promote both domestic and international tranquillity, environmentalists argue that it may lead to the rise of authoritarian governments and to the possibility of international conflict. Economic growth in conditions of resource scarcity and ecological stress will become increasingly difficult and political turmoil more likely.

The potential for instability is compounded by the bias toward the short term implicit in both the political and economic sectors. "Government," in the words of John Quarles, "does not begin to attack a problem until that problem has become severe."[31] But given the long lead time necessary for some solutions, the prospect for remedy may be dim by the time government is ready to act. According to Robert Heilbroner, scarcity with the incremental bias of democratic politics will lead to the end of democratic systems.[32]

At the international level, the combination of technological dynamism, population growth, and the perception of resource shortages, will lead to the exertion of "lateral pressure" and to increased conflict.[33] The implications of more and more struggling for the control of less and less in an already fragile international order are hardly reassuring. This recognition suggests the need for a global strategy that would reduce conflict, control population growth, lower the demand for scarce resources, and limit environmental abuse.[34] The problem is compounded by the intimate ties between the vehicle of modernization, the nation-state, and war, economic growth, and the development of high technology. The state as an institution has evolved in large measure through its success in these areas, so we cannot assume that it will relinquish its position easily.

Toward an Environmental Alternative

The environmental critique argues that the modern emphasis on
growth and technology is neither physically sustainable nor socially
desirable. But what alternative paradigm have environmentalists
offered? Only if we loosen somewhat the criteria defining "paradigm" can we discern the outline of a common world view based on
the general notions of finiteness, quality, man-in-nature, and holism.
The creation of such a paradigm will involve, in Mumford's words,
replacing "megatechnics" with "biotechnics" based upon our
knowledge of living organisms and complex ecosystems. The most
obvious feature of such models is the fact that they describe a closed
system of flows and cycles oriented to some level of overall stability.

Steady-State Economics

The core of an environmental paradigm is the concept of a steady-
state economy in which a constant stock of wealth and population is
maintained by equalizing inputs and outputs.[35] The level of energy
and resource flows required to maintain any given level should be as
low as possible, thus converting our conception of gross national
product from a "good" into a cost required to support a particular
level of wealth. The emphases in such a system necessarily shift from
quantity to quality and from production to distribution.

In a steady-state system, only the factors of population and capital
need to be held constant. In order to accomplish the first, Kenneth
Boulding has proposed a system that would give each person at birth
a license to procreate so many units of new life. Capital stocks might
similarly be held constant through a system of depletion quotas
for both renewable and nonrenewable resources, which would be
periodically auctioned off by the government. As depletion occurred,
prices would be driven higher, thus encouraging both conservation
and the development of substitutes. The logic of a steady-state
system suggests a ceiling and a floor on incomes and the redistribution of wealth within and between nations without which there
would be little hope of maintaining public order.

Even more revolutionary is the idea partially embodied in Herman
Daly's resource depletion quotas that we ought to extend our sense
of obligation to future generations. For a generation uncertain of its
own future and of its obligation to those coexisting in time, the
revolutionary implications of this proposal can hardly be overstated.

Ecological Man

Although there is not yet an ecological alternative to models of economic or rational man, there is consensus that "ecological man," however defined, would be less materialistic and less dominance oriented. Consumption and production would lose their priority in favor of creative activities of intellect and culture. A less hierarchical society would permit, as Marx once envisioned, the development of a wider range of skills and abilities conducive to human fulfillment and would allow greater social and cultural diversity. The adoption of a "new image of man" would require men to identify as "one with the vast community" of life and to act in partnership with nature.[36] The nature ecological man would conquer would be his own; his triumphs would be those of culture, self-knowledge, and interpersonal relations; and his behavior would be more finely tuned to the cycles of nature, and to his own biological rhythms.

Man and Nature

The environmental view of nature is a mixture of four different but related elements. First, nature is portrayed as a set of constraints or boundary conditions to which society must adapt. Although technology can extend some of these, it inevitably encounters unmovable natural limits. Nicholas Georgescu-Roegen, for example, describes the economic process as "entropic: it neither creates nor consumes matter or energy, but only transforms low entropy into high entropy." To speed the pace of economic development is also to hasten the creation of high entropy and social disorder.[37]

A second view portrays nature as the source of materials and food and man as a manager. In order to utilize nature efficiently, it is necessary to understand its laws and for man, in Sterling Brubacker's words, to become a "restrained and benevolent leader."[38] But there is much that we do not know, and may never know, about the effects of human actions in ecosystems, so it becomes prudent to leave a large margin for error. From this recognition it is only a small step to proposals for a "religion of nature" or to granting natural objects legal standing.[39]

A third view stresses the possibility that man needs nature on its terms for his own sake. In contrast to the second view, which stressed the manipulation of nature for utilitarian reasons, this position suggests that man is the object acted upon by a nature that sustains his inner being. Although modern life has severed the close bond that once existed between man and nature, man "is still of the earth" and carries the indelible imprint of nature.

There is finally the possibility that nature might provide a source of insight for understanding social systems. Human ecologist William Catton, for example, has proposed the use of ecological concepts such as competition, community, succession, and climax as analogies to help explain social evolution. Industrial civilization might be compared with detritus life forms (for example, yeast cells in a wine vat) or possibly with pioneer successional systems that render themselves obsolete, or even with catastrophe climax systems (for example, chaparral in California, which is a climax system but is also highly vulnerable to fire).[40]

Social Organization and Finiteness

Social life in the modern paradigm is increasingly dominated by large structures (the megalopolis, the corporation, the university) and by narrow role definitions. Citizens of modern societies find themselves playing ever smaller parts in ever larger and more complex settings. But these tendencies are conducive neither to human fulfillment nor to efficiency in the largest sense. The answer, according to Murray Bookchin, is the creation of small cities of 50,000, where agriculture and industry might be combined to meet a large percentage of local needs.[41] In place of huge, unstable urban conglomerations, there would be smaller, more self-sufficient units. The authors of *Blueprint for Survival* similarly favor the creation of a network of small villages of 500 and cities of not more than 50,000, combined into regions of approximately 500,000.[42]

Science and Technology

The basis of smaller, more self-sufficient communities would require a radical shift in technology toward what E. F. Schumacher has called intermediate technology. The term has since come to mean a variety of things—small-scale, participatory, environmentally benign, safe, labor-intensive, reversible, and relatively less expensive per workplace. It represents an attempt to meet human needs with "appropriately" matched technological responses and is intended to restore human scale to modern societies dominated by technological giantism.

Implicit in Schumacher's thought is a radically different perspective on the relationship between society and technology that is rooted in the philosophies of Jefferson, Gandhi, and perhaps Mao. The choice of intermediate or soft technologies that are less pervasive and more "forgiving" would serve as a basis for a more humane society, allowing human imperatives to reassert themselves. Such changes, however, would also require changes in science toward what Eugene Odum and others have called holism. The Cartesian emphasis of contemporary science that tends to fragment reality would give way to the model of science once proposed by Leibniz that stressed the study of wholes and interrelationships.

The Politics of Finiteness

There is general agreement among environmentalists that the politics of "spaceship earth" will be more "problem oriented than interest oriented" and that solutions to environmental abuses must be framed by central governments.[43] Consensus, however, disappears over questions about the size, scope, and power of centralized institutions. One side suggests that the ecological crisis will inevitably lead to authoritarian governments and the end of representative democracy.[44]

There is, however, another view that emphasizes a "bottom-up" form of societal transformation occurring outside governments and large organizations. Mumford, for one, argues that "The changes that have so far been effective, and that give promise of further success, are those that have been initiated by animated individual minds, small groups, and local communities nibbling at the edges of the power structure by breaking routines and defying regulations."[45] In contrast to the thinking of Heilbroner and William Ophuls, Mumford, Schumacher, Edward Goldsmith, and Bookchin emphasize noncoercive and nonhierarchical political structures that place much greater reliance upon small-scale organization and decentralized power. Although proponents of both positions agree about the urgency and scope of the crisis, they differ about the ability of a highly centralized government to plan for the long term, to make accurate forecasts, and to maintain its flexibility without succumbing to the pathologies of large scale. It is not always easy, as Davis Bobrow reminds us, to distinguish a leviathan from a dinosaur.[46] The contrary position, however, raises other problems of determining which structures and

functions must be decentralized and with what effects. Some proponents of decentralization, moreover, go further to argue that solutions
to ecological problems will require the devolution not only of power
but of wealth also. Michael Best and William Connolly, for example,
state that "inequality combines with the system of corporate power
and the weakness of communal ties to encourage the growth of
ecologically devastating support systems. . . . A more egalitarian
society would not necessarily maintain rational ecological policies,
but it would be more likely to do so."[47]

Conclusion

Both the modern and the environmental paradigm represent different
ways of perceiving the world, and each has radically different
implications for personal behavior and for public policy. If, as
environmentalists charge, the affluent societies are nearing the end of
the era of abundance and rapid growth, many of our present
institutions, policies, and behaviors will need to be altered or eliminated altogether. We will have to live more modestly, with greater
frugality, and place controls on our technological capacity to manipu-
late nature. This view is not unchallenged, however. Some maintain
that this course represents a loss of nerve precisely at the time when
the further expansion of technology could give us complete command
of nature and make all of us rich in the process. For the same ends,
others propose "Faustian bargains" between scientists and society to
create an inexhaustible supply of energy[48] and frontal assaults on the
second law of thermodynamics.[49] Surely we suffer from no deficiency
of technological imagination. But imagination is not the same as
wisdom, and so the questions remain as to which course to choose
and how to decide.

While I am fully persuaded by the ecological point of view, I confess
that it is difficult to "prove" conclusively that the modern paradigm is
at the point of collapse. Even if we could, there are a variety of ways
societies and individuals have to dismiss such evidence. But for those
who are open to reason and persuasion, the issues are complex and
the solutions are uncertain and debatable. If indeed we were to
experience what the authors of *The Limits to Growth* called overshoot,
how would we know it? The breakdown of life-support systems
would be experienced as inflation, disease, social instability, hunger,

and conflict. But these can occur from other causes as well. In sum, the interaction and causal relationships between natural and social systems are intricate and poorly understood. Some would muddy the water further by asserting that we can make no valid distinction between these systems, because man himself is a part of nature and all his acts, presumably including the destruction of nature, are thereby "natural." This view, however, ignores the unique role of human consciousness that (as far as we know) is found nowhere else in nature and leaves our better judgment bound, gagged, and at the mercy of our less civilized and discriminating instincts.

In large measure, however, our plight is one of perception and intellect and, some would add, spirit. We have grown accustomed to seeing the world in fragments and now must learn to see it whole, as systems, cycles, and dependency relationships. This will also require the development of a sense of empathy with future generations. Kenneth Boulding once facetiously asked, "What has posterity done for me lately?" Is there any reason to include questions of altruism and intergenerational equity in the ecological perspective? Since our individual welfare is in part dependent upon a common biosphere, there is at least some reason to include those now living. But it is less clear what this relationship means when we think of posterity. Boulding answered his own question by suggesting that civilizations that become indifferent to the welfare of future generations tended to do a bad job managing their own affairs. Indifference, according to Boulding, is an easily transferable posture, applicable to one's fellows as easily as to posterity.

Finally, assuming that we could agree on the merits of the ecological critique and an ecological paradigm, the problem remains of what to do then. The process of paradigm change in science described by Kuhn occurred through the application of intellect and logic, but social change customarily occurs in war, revolution, and social upheaval. Could the environmental paradigm be adopted in advance of the disasters environmentalists predict? To do so will require the creation of a strategy of change and the identification of those social leverage points where small exertions can yield large results. This suggests the translation of environmental issues into a realistic political program for change and the creation of coalitions with other groups open to change.

International Environmental Concern: Perspectives of and Implications for Developing States

Lawrence Juda

During the 1960s and 1970s widespread concern with the progressive destruction of various ecological balances developed within the industrialized world. A veritable revolution had occurred in the quantity and nature of the waste introduced into the natural environment. Modern economic activity, through its development and use of synthetic substances and its tremendous demands for raw materials and energy, had created very considerable problems both within states and for the international community. Ecological problems were the focus of the 1972 United Nations Conference on the Human Environment.

The Stockholm Conference almost failed to convene because of the apathy and even hostility of many developing countries. These states saw ecological concern of the type displayed by the industrialized countries as irrelevant and, at some points, even detrimental to their own interests. They had only limited concern for problems of "pollution," the seriousness of which seems to correlate with what is generally regarded as economic well-being. Environmental degradation is in a broader sense, though, a global problem that manifests itself differently in the developed and the less developed states.

Preparations for the Stockholm Conference

As it began its work preparatory to the conference, the UN Secretariat was faced with the problem that neither in the discussions before UN organs nor in the General Assembly resolution calling for the conference did the term *human environment* receive any precise definition. It was thus left to the Secretariat to attempt some delineation of the scope of the conference. In his first report to the General Assembly on this subject, the secretary-general observed that the term could be interpreted as meaning the physical and biological environment resulting from natural processes or human activities. An alternative view would extend beyond such factors and give prominence to socioeconomic and sociocultural considerations. In the early formulation of conference scope, the Secretariat leaned heavily toward the first interpretation, indicating that matters such as fiscal policy, international trade, and pricing agreements should not be considered by the Stockholm Conference.

In light of this perspective, it is not surprising that the less developed states were not overly impressed with the forthcoming conference. Maurice Strong, secretary-general of the UN Conference on the Human Environment, quickly perceived that interest on the part of these states was quite low. Strong believed that if the conference were to be a success the developing states would have to be encouraged to play an active role in both the planning for the conference and the conference itself.

Increasingly, Strong stressed that the environmental crisis was not limited to industrial pollution but involved also the environmental problems of poverty. This latter problem was said to be at least as significant and widespread as that of industrial pollution.[1] Protection of the environment and economic development were not at all necessarily antagonistic objectives. Indeed, he maintained that there was an essential harmony between developmental and environmental considerations. He noted that in economic terms the failure to consider the costs of environmental damage would result in long-term harm, because correcting such damage was far more costly than taking timely preventive measures. He urged that the Stockholm Conference constructively consider the relationship between development and the environment. To that end, Strong convened a panel of experts in June of 1971. The resulting Founex report[2] was strongly endorsed by representatives of developing countries, for it indicated that development was the cure for the type of environmental problems suffered in those countries. The report urged the developing states to explain their apprehensions and suggested that, in fact, there might well be tangible benefits that would accrue to them as a result of the enforcement of stricter environmental standards in the industrialized countries.

To further assuage the misgivings of the developing states and win their support for the conference, a series of regional meetings of experts was arranged in the less developed world. At these meetings, in discussions within the UN, and at the Stockholm Conference itself, the fears and the desires of these states were expressed.

Their concerns included, first, *the impact of higher environmental standards on international trade*. In this category at least four problem areas were envisaged. First, there was a widespread belief that new environmental standards in the developed countries would lead to a decline in the terms of trade of the developing states. From their perspective, the goods they must import, industrial and capital goods, in particular, would become more expensive as factories in the industrialized states were required to meet new environmental standards and as they passed along to their customers the attendant increases in production costs. If the goods of the developed states became more expensive while the primary products of the less developed countries did not gain higher prices, the terms of trade of the LDCs would deteriorate. In fact, such an erosion in the terms of trade has occurred, though environmental factors are seen, at most, as a marginal cause.

Second, it was feared that the cause of ecological protection could be used to mask a trade policy of neoprotectionism. Products from LDCs might be forbidden entry to markets because they would not meet new environmental regulations in receiving states. Such regulations might provide opportunities for domestic producers to restrict imports of competitive goods. There was also concern that higher production costs in developed states would lead producers to demand tariff or nontariff barriers against rival producers in other states who were not subject to similar environmental regulation. A 1971 study prepared by the General Agreement on Tariffs and Trade (GATT) indicated, however, that protection based on a factor of higher production costs would be in basic contradiction to the principles of GATT.[3]

Third, recycling, a practice that environmental concern had encouraged, was spreading. Recycling provides an important response to the desire to conserve nonrenewable resources, and at the same time it aids in alleviating the growing problem of waste disposal. A study conducted by the United Nations Conference on Trade and Development (UNCTAD) and released just prior to the Stockholm Conference warned that "In the long run, the recycling of raw materials and natural resources will have a depressing effect on the volume of exports from developing countries."[4] Spokesmen for some Third World states saw a political motive in the increased use of recycling. According to them, the developed states were obviously attempting to reduce dependence upon the LDCs for primary goods.

Fourth, interest in environmental matters and the establishment of new standards and regulations added a new variable to international trade matters. A new cause for product substitution was being added to an already uncertain economic picture. During the early 1970s, to take only one example, the United States, and later other industrialized states, began to set limits upon the sulfur content of fuels used in urban areas. Such regulations were damaging to Venezuela whose oil contained high levels of sulfur. To retain market access, Venezuelan oil would have to be cleaned, an operation that would cut into profits.

Another concern of the developing countries was *the impact of higher environmental standards upon development prospects.* Aside from the possible influence on trade, as discussed above, a number of states feared that the need to incorporate strict environmental safeguards would delay and increase the cost of development projects. The developing countries began to work for the adoption of the principle of "additionality," in accordance with which the developed states would make available an increased amount of aid to compensate for extra project expenses.[5]

Concern was also expressed that the granting of aid would now be conditioned upon the inclusion in projects of costly environmental surveys and safeguards. This apprehension was aggravated when, in 1970, Robert McNamara, president of the World Bank, informed the Economic and Social Council that the bank had established an environmental unit to "enable it and other developmental financing agencies to consider the environmental factors of development programmes in some kind of cost-benefit framework."[6] Some developing states saw such action as a threat to their sovereignty, declaring that the establishment of environmental policies was within the exclusive jurisdiction of the individual states. The World Bank action in this view was inadmissible.

Many representatives of less developed countries feared that the preoccupation with ecological problems of the economically advanced states would result in a shift of funds from foreign aid to domestic programs of environmental protection. According to UNCTAD, estimates indicated that approximately 1.5 to 2.0 percent of the GNP of developed states might be diverted in the near future from present uses to ecological protection measures.[7] A decrease in financial assistance, were it to occur, was viewed as yet another blow to development prospects.

The belief that too much attention was devoted to pollution and not enough to the different environmental problems of the developing states was a third concern. The point was frequently made by LDC representatives that international environmental contamination was caused by the industrialized states; the developing countries were said to contribute insignificantly, if at all, to such problems. The difficulties of the LDCs stemmed from underdevelopment; rapid economic growth was the required solution. It was in the realm of aid and trade that the developed countries could make a meaningful contribution to the betterment of the environment in Third World areas.

Greater attention, it was asserted, had to be given to the causes of environmental problems in the less developed world. Third World spokesmen strongly maintained that the present structure of world trade contributed to the degradation of the environment of developing countries. Such states were forced to increase their exports of agricultural goods and raw materials to pay constantly rising prices for the goods they purchased in developed states. The pressure to export more contributed to soil erosion and excessive exploitation of agricultural and mineral resources, which in turn created a danger to the rural environment. Consequently, it was fair, and even necessary, for international trade to be scrutinized at the Stockholm Conference.

Reflecting the general views of the LDCs, the General Assembly approved on 7 December 1970 resolution 2657(XXV), recommending that the Preparatory Committee for the Stockholm Conference include in its agenda specific items "relating to economic and social aspects in order to safeguard and promote the interests of developing countries with a view to reconciling the national environmental policies with their national development plans and priorities."

Fourth, the less developed countries believed *that Western concern with the environment was motivated in part by limits-to-growth analyses, which implied that the LDCs would have to forego rapid economic development and take measures to limit population growth*. This general issue was not as openly discussed as the others, though in various ways it affected the thinking of a number of governments. *The Limits to Growth*, the influential study prepared for the Club of Rome, came under strong attack from spokesmen of the LDCs. The representative of Brazil, for example, emphatically rejected any policy that implied an exclusion of economic growth. Needed resources, he stated, would not be exhausted because technological advances would provide solutions to problems caused by scarcities of particular goods. The problem faced by LDCs, he argued, was not a lack of natural resources but rather the need for suitable markets in which fair prices could be obtained for such resources.[8]

There was broad agreement among the developing countries that the answer to their environmental problems was to be found through a process of rapid economic development, the occurrence of which should not be hampered by an unreasonable concern for the physical environment. In this view the environment had to be evaluated in terms of how it could best serve human interests rather than in terms of some abstract ecological balance. There was in evidence some belief on the part of the LDCs that the despoliation of the natural environment in the industrialized states had engendered in those states the desire to keep less developed portions of the world in a more natural state and, in effect, to maintain them, at the expense of development and the consequent well-being of the inhabitants, as "nature reserves."

Specifically addressed by some states in the preparations for Stockholm was the matter of "overpopulation," which, according to an American spokesman, would certainly result in continued poverty in the Third World.[9] A representative of Brazil strongly lashed out at such thinking remarking that the "Plans for the Stockholm Conference are marked by what might be called the 'Calvinistic' attitude that the developed countries have demonstrated, by their development, a special right to salvation and perpetuation, thus passing on to the more numerous underdeveloped peoples the responsibility for creating the necessary space on earth."[10] In most parts of Latin America and Africa, it was asserted, population densities were, in fact, below the levels required for efficient economic development, and limiting population growth would thus be harmful to development prospects. A meeting of Latin American experts concluded that because of the different conditions in various states it should be left up to each state to determine its own population policies. At another meeting, Asian experts were considerably more alarmed at the possible negative effects of high population growth rates on development prospects and environmental conditions.

Under pressure from the less developed states, and with the support of the conference Secretariat, the agenda for Stockholm was expanded; a new item entitled "Development and Environment" was added. Correspondingly, the level of support for the conference among such countries rose. As the possible implications of enhanced environmental interest in the developed world were evaluated, some potentially beneficial consequences for developing states were identified:

1. *Primary commodities from developing countries might regain the importance they had lost to synthetic goods, the manufacture of which contributed to pollution problems in the developed states.* UNCTAD, for example, speculated that it might be economically worthwhile for everyone to promote the use and improvement of natural products rather than spend additional funds to decrease the level of pollution associated with the production of synthetics. A group of experts drawn almost exclusively from the developed states concluded in the summer of 1971, however, that there was little likelihood that natural products would replace synthetics. It noted that the manufacture of most synthetics was cheaper than the exploitation of the natural resources and wondered if, indeed, the harm to the environment caused by the manufacture of synthetics was greater than that caused by the utilization of natural resources.[11]

2. *The relocation of industries from the developed countries to the less developed countries would be encouraged.* An increase in production costs due to the need to meet rising environmental standards would serve to make less developed states more attractive as production sites. Developing states, because of the lack of industrial concentration, could tolerate a rise in pollutant levels and could thus afford to maintain lower environmental standards. Lower standards implied lower costs and, so the argument goes, would give such states a competitive advantage in attracting industry. In this scenario, environmental concern in the developed states could result in an acceleration of the economic development of the LDCs. The interests of both the developed and the developing states would be served. According to a pre-Stockholm UNCTAD report, such a movement of industry, though on a small scale, was already occurring between Japan and some of the states of Southeast Asia.[12]

3. *The developing states could learn from the experience of the now-developed countries and thus avoid costly environmental mistakes and achieve*

greater economic benefits. It was necessary that in the process of development a state take into account the ecological implications of its choices. To do otherwise, it was asserted, would prove to be very costly and would ultimately set back development efforts.

The less developed states were concerned with all of these possibilities, and the UNCTAD Secretariat reflected this interest in calling upon the Stockholm Conference to "take fully into account the trade and development aspects of measures for the protection of the environment."[13]

The Stockholm Conference

It was in the context described above that the United Nations Conference on the Human Environment met in Stockholm from 5 June to 12 June 1972. The deliberations resulted in a declaration, an action plan, and five resolutions.[14]

A comparison of the declaration approved by the conference and the first draft of that document drawn up by the preparatory commission shows a substantial shift in the direction of accommodating LDC views. The Stockholm declaration, for example, specifically states that the environmental problems of developing states are due to underdevelopment and indicates an awareness that environmental standards that were valid for economically advanced states might well be inappropriate or even dysfunctional when applied to developing states.

Further, the declaration began to delve into specific economic relationships that the LDCs felt were to blame for the poor state of the human environment in their countries. Stable commodity prices were said to be an essential condition for a well-managed environment; in a general sense, economic patterns, as well as ecological processes, were seen as affecting the nature of the environment. This point was developed in the action plan, a stipulation of which indicated that economic factors, such as the inadequate payment for the agricultural produce of developing states, contributed to soil degradation. Farmers could ill afford the investments needed for soil regeneration and conservation. In this view higher and more stable prices for agricultural commodities would make possible the necessary conservation actions. This recommendation was unsuccessfully opposed by the United States, which felt that the relation of commodity prices to soil improvement was distant and that there was no guarantee, in fact, that price stabilization would lead to improved soil regeneration.

In the realm of international trade, the Stockholm Conference urged that environmental concerns not be employed as a rationale for discriminatory trade policies or the limiting of market access. At the behest of the developing states, the action plan called for compensation in those cases in which environmental considerations led to new standards that, in turn, had negative impact upon exports of the LDCs. This particular provision was strongly and unsuccessfully contested by the United States. While the United States expressed a readiness to discuss its environmental actions relative to its GATT obligations, American representatives expressed the view that "many forces affect export earnings and to single out any of these, such as environmental actions, for compensatory treatment would be wrong in principle and a disincentive to environmental responsibility."[15] Reflecting the concern of many states, the Stockholm action plan called upon UNCTAD and GATT to maintain a continuing review of new tariff and nontariff trade barriers resulting from changes in environmental policies.

With regard to technology transfer, Algeria and the People's Republic of China called upon the developed states to make available to the LDCs, at no cost, advanced technology for environmental protection and improvement. The final formulation of the conference on this subject, however, merely indicated that such technology should be made available to the developing states "on terms which would encourage their wide dissemination without constituting an economic burden on the developing countries."

At the conference the developing countries pushed hard for some recognition of "additionality." Principle 12 of the Stockholm declaration gave recognition to this need. LDC opposition to international agencies' consideration of environmental implications of development projects in the making of assistance decisions was not apparent at Stockholm. There is little doubt that a better understanding of the far-reaching consequences of environmental damage was taking hold among developing states.

At the same time there was apparent, on the part of the developed states, a new awareness of the economic fears of the LDCs. The clear message from developing states was that a drop in economic growth rate was unacceptable; the only responsibility of the developing countries was to harmonize their development policies with the needs of environmental protection. Further, they insisted that the costs of new environmental policies in the developed countries not be passed on, directly or indirectly, to the developing states.

Finally, on the controversial question of population a split was evident in LDC ranks. Some states felt that this was a subject the conference ought not to treat, whereas others, most particularly those in southern Asia, felt that the problem of rapid population growth deserved specific attention. The action plan, as finally approved, called upon the World Health Organization to intensify research on human reproduction, but the Stockholm declaration made it clear that it was up to the government of each state to decide upon "appropriate" demographic policies.

The developing countries' evaluation of the results of the Stockholm Conference was mixed. Representatives of some states believed that too much attention had been paid to the special problems of the developed states. Others were of the opinion that the conference had accepted as fact that underdevelopment was the main environmental problem for the majority of mankind. In the view of this second group, the relationship between environmental damage and the inequitable international distribution of wealth had been demonstrated.

To the extent that the LDCs had shifted the focus of the Stockholm Conference from issues of "pollution" to the more pertinent (for the developing states) questions of economic development, they had achieved some success.

Post-Stockholm

What has happened to the fears and to the hopes raised among the developing states by the Stockholm Conference on the Human Environment? Preoccupation with the possible effects on trade and the transfer of industry due to the enactment of new environmental policies has been largely replaced by concern for increased energy costs, a basic questioning of the validity of the international market mechanism, and demands for a new international economic order.

In dealing with trade and industry relocation impacts, we must consider the distinction made by Charles Pearson and Ingo Walter between process pollution, that which is detrimental to the environment of the producing state, and product pollution, that which is harmful to the environment of the consuming state.[16] Attempts to control the former will result in higher costs of production and will serve to change the competitive positions of producer states. Control of the latter will typically be in the form of product standards and, consequently, will affect access to markets.

Richard Blackhurst and others have observed that states vary as to their waste assimilative capacities.[17] In regard to process pollution, the developed states have overutilized that capacity while the less developed states, for the most part, retain an abundance of it. In this sense the LDCs may have a comparative advantage in productive processes that generate considerable pollution as a by-product. A transfer of such production to the LDCs would seem to be beneficial to both developed and developing countries.

This suggestion, however, raises the matter of "exporting pollution." Blackhurst attacks the use of this term as misleading and harmful. The export of industry is usually welcomed by the receiving state, and the point is stressed by Blackhurst that similar activities have varying environmental impacts in different locations due to the variances in waste assimilative capacities. On the other hand, in developing states with a great proportion of people dependent upon agriculture or fishing and lacking basic services such as water treatment plants, even limited increases in pollution levels may have severe impact.

Among economists there are diverging opinions as to the significance of the cost of controlling process pollution as a factor motivating international industrial relocation. Some feel that the magnitude of potential shifts in investment resulting from environmental protection costs may be considerable. Others believe that, with some exception, such costs will be marginal in nature and lead to little in the way of international locational shifts of industry.

In this regard an UNCTAD study has found, for the most part, that environmental controls so far adopted in the developed states have led to the development and employment of technological solutions to pollution problems rather than to wide-scale international industrial relocation. Cost increases occasioned by environmental measures have been, on the average, only marginal in nature, though in some instances, such as in metal processing, the paper industry, and chemical works, they have been significant.[18]

Some industrial relocation based, at least in part, upon ecologically related grounds has occurred. This is evident in Japan, a small country with a great concentration of heavy and chemical industries. In that country one estimate is that 15–20 percent of the total of new capital investment is in pollution control.[19] This is the result of public pressure for environmental restoration and new laws and regulations. The solution to the problems associated with environmental damage, according to the Japanese government, is to move polluting industry abroad and to restructure the Japanese economy toward "clean" and "knowledge-intensive" industries. Environmental protection costs and regulations are clearly encouraging the Japanese petrochemical industry to place new plant capacity overseas. This development is expected to lead to a huge increase in Japanese investment in the Middle East and complements the desire of the oil-producing states to get more involved in the processing of crude oil.

Environmental expenditures, though, are but one of many costs considered in the decision as to where plants should be built. In Japan wages and other costs are rising and provide incentive to an overseas move of industry, as does the desire to skirt the protectionist trade policies of other states. The construction by Kawasaki of a motorcycle plant in Lincoln, Nebraska, for example, is due to such nonenvironmentally related factors.

Assuming that direct foreign investment is being encouraged by environmentally related concerns in states such as Japan, where are investments likely to be made? Are LDCs apt to be the recipients of such investment? To the extent that these states possess a comparative advantage due to unemployed waste assimilative capacity and to the extent that environmentally related costs are significantly important relative to the total cost of production, logic would suggest that the answer would be in the affirmative. Political instability and a lack of investment security, though, may offset the advantage of lower operating expenses associated with lower environmental standards in many developing states. It has been noticed, for instance, that there is now a reluctance among the Japanese to invest in Southeast Asia and a preference for investment in Brazil, Canada, Australia, New Zealand, Europe, and parts of the Middle East. One Japanese observer detects as a recent trend an increasing flow of investment in manufacturing going to the advanced countries, notably the United States.[20] According to a report in the *New York Times*, there seems now to be a general turning away by multinational corporations from conducting business in Third World states because of the belief that the risks of operating there are too great and the problems too many.[21] In such a context, the higher costs of operating in developed states may well be deemed as an acceptable trade-off for security of investment.

The impact of environmental forces on trade will be manifested largely through product standards. Goods not meeting such standards will be forbidden access to the markets of developed states, or consumers will be encouraged to use those products or raw materials identified with lower levels of pollution. Some effect on trade will be felt, though it is not yet discernible how significant it will be. In his study of the environmental product standards imposed by the United States government, Pearson has found no indication that American regulations are being employed as covert restrictions on international trade. He asserts that at this point the most serious problem is one of information, that is, making known in a timely fashion applicable environmental standards so that adjustments can be made in the production process. International organizations such as UNCTAD and GATT can play a very significant role in this regard, serving as a clearinghouse with respect to environmental regulations and also encouraging, where possible, uniform standards so as to ease the production and marketing tasks of countries producing for export. In 1972 GATT did establish a Group on Environmental Measures and International Trade, but it has remained dormant despite the hope of the Stockholm Conference that this GATT body would actively examine and act upon trade problems. The vitalization of this group is overdue.

Not surprisingly, UNCTAD has been more active than GATT in the study of the consequences of environmental concern for the LDCs. A study by UNCTAD observes a basic link between environmental degradation and the pricing and market mechanism for natural resources and commodities. It points out that many of the producers of primary resources have economies highly dependent upon a given commodity and are thus in the position where they must sell their products irrespective of price. In this view the operation of the free market has resulted in an underpricing of commodities and raw materials. This, in turn, has been an important contributing factor to wasteful consumptive patterns and industries with attendant environmental damage in the wealthy countries. At the same time, the continuing poverty in the LDCs encourages excessive exploitation of the environment there, as in the example of the farming of marginal land at great risk of soil erosion and with consequent migration to already overcrowded cities. The adoption of an integrated program for commodities is seen as an appropriate response to these problems. Such a program would treat a basic structural problem in the world economy, a problem perceived to be a fundamental cause of widespread environmental damage and also an important factor that helps to explain the failure of the LDCs to develop at a faster rate.[22]

In its assessment of environmental regulations as nontariff barriers to international trade, another UNCTAD study indicates that such barriers are of greatest importance in relation to the trade among the developed states and particularly in their trade of semimanufactured and manufactured products, automobiles, and chemical products. Only a limited part of LDC exports has been affected by such regulations, and the research division of UNCTAD concluded that "this problem does not in the present circumstances seem to be as acute as it was previously expected to be."[23]

With regard to the possible substitution of natural goods from the LDCs for synthetics manufactured in the developed states, several international agencies, most significantly UNCTAD and the United Nations Industrial Development Organization (UNIDO), have undertaken relevant studies. Whereas in 1972 the mitigation of environmental damage was seen as a possible motivating force for such substitution, in the present post-oil-embargo era, high prices for petroleum, an important ingredient of many synthetic goods, are seen as a new, more pressing and immediate incentive.

In September of 1974 an expert group met in Vienna under UNIDO auspices, with the cooperation of the United Nations Environmental Program (UNEP), to evaluate the situation of natural rubber as compared to synthetic rubber. This conference was seen as an initial undertaking that would encourage further examination of the advantages of natural and synthetic products. The conclusions of the rubber study were that from both environmental and economic perspectives natural rubber production had several advantages over synthetic rubber. The production of one ton of the synthetic product required about 3.5 tons of crude oil or its equivalent as compared to 0.3 tons of crude oil equivalent for the same amount of natural rubber. According to UNIDO the economic advantage of natural rubber will continue to increase as petroleum prices rise and as more efficient methods of farming natural rubber are widely deployed. A further bonus is the fact that natural rubber production is labor intensive and, thus, can create many employment opportunities in LDCs. The UNIDO study, consequently, suggested that natural rubber cultivation be maximized.[24] There may be other natural goods that have ecological and economic advantages over their synthetic counterparts, and UNIDO and the Permanent Group on Synthetics and Substitutes of UNCTAD are continuing their work in this area.

As to the impact of environmental concern on the flow of foreign aid, an UNCTAD study notes that the cost of environmental maintenance and cleanup has been largely financed by price adjustment rather than from general taxation. Thus, it is believed that "environmental issues have not generally led to any diversion of funds from aid flows to developing countries."[25] Disappointment has been expressed, however, at the failure of the principle of additionality to gain widespread support among the developed states.

The issue of World Bank evaluation of projects from an environmental perspective has faded since 1972. Although the bank and its affiliates have made the incorporation of environmental safeguard measures a condition for the granting of loans, these institutions have adopted the practice of providing within project financing funds to cover costs occasioned by the inclusion of such safeguards. At least to this extent, the concept of additionality has been accepted. Dr. James Lee, director of the Office of Environmental and Health Affairs of the World Bank, notes that there have been no protests lodged with the World Bank group because of the imposition of environmental protection measures.[26]

In 1975 several environmental organizations brought suit in federal court to force the Agency for International Development (AID) to prepare environmental impact statements (EIS) in connection with its pesticide export program. The suit was settled out of court with AID agreeing to prepare an EIS pursuant to the National Environmental Policy Act.[27] According to information received from an attorney for the Center of Law and Social Policy, one of the plaintiff organizations, the desire is not to export American environmental standards but rather to insure that recipient states are aware of the risks as well as the benefits of proposed projects. The point is made that environmental impact statements are of particular importance to developing states that may well lack the capability to undertake such studies themselves. In his environmental message of 23 May 1977, President Carter indicated that the secretary of state and the administrator of AID had been instructed to give full consideration to the environmental impacts of development projects under review for possible assistance and to make available to LDCs assistance in environmental and resource management.[28]

Although agreeing that there is a continuous need for the LDCs to industrialize, a 1976 report by UNEP's executive director indicates disappointment over the limited attention paid to environmental concerns by development programs and conferences. Criticized in this vein are the *International Development Strategy for the Second United Nations Development Decade*, issued in 1970 and revised in 1973 and 1975; the Second General Conference of UNIDO (the Lima Conference), which called for the LDCs to increase their share of world industrial production from less than 7 percent to at least 25 percent by the year 2000; and the Seventh Special Session of the UN General Assembly. The report warns of the grave danger inherent in a major relocation of polluting industries to developing states and observes that industrialization that is too rapid may result in unexpected economic and environmental dislocation.[29]

UNEP has given a considerable amount of attention and study to what its first executive director, Maurice Strong, has referred to as ecodevelopment, that is, ecologically sound development. This concept, the adoption of which UNEP has strongly advocated, stresses the need for concerted planning in agricultural, industrial, urban, and rural systems.[30] It involves careful evaluation of socio-economic facts and practices, biophysical resources, and the impact of the employment of various technologies. A variety of projects are being undertaken by UNEP in the implementation of the ecodevelopment concept.

Conclusions

For the LDCs the environment and the concern for its well-being have implications in at least two major areas: first, in terms of possible effect upon international trade and investment; and second, in terms of the influence of environmental considerations upon development patterns and choices.[31]

At this point in time, the overall significance of worldwide interest in environmental matters for LDCs remains unclear. This is a subject that merits further attention from international agencies such as UNCTAD, GATT, UNIDO, and UNEP. Certainly, in a world in which each state determines the environmental standards for products used within its territory, there is a need for some organization to provide up-to-date information on such standards so that foreign producers can take timely action to maintain access to present markets. The economic effect of LDC actions to meet higher environmental standards in the developed states to which they export must be monitored to see if it contributes to a further increase in North-South economic inequality.

Numerous questions have yet to be resolved. Has the under-employed environmental assimilative capacity, in the LDCs that possess such capacity, served to attract industry from the developed states, and if so, with what effects? When international plant relocation occurs, which states are the beneficiaries, and why? How significant is environmental assimilative capacity as a factor of production in various industries, and will its importance increase relative to other factors of production as more stringent environmental regulations go into effect in the developed states? Are there natural substances in LDCs, such as rubber, the production of which can be identified as being less harmful to the environment and less dependent upon the use of nonrenewable resources than the production of synthetic counterparts?

To date, the area in which environmental concern seems to have had most impact upon developing countries is development planning. As a consequence of the work of agencies such as UNEP and the World Bank and as a result of the Stockholm Conference, the 1974 World Population Conference in Bucharest, the 1976 Habitat Conference in Vancouver, the 1977 United Nations Water Conference in Mar del Plata, Argentina, the 1977 Desertification Conference in Nairobi, various expert meetings, and a growing body of practical experience in the development process, there is without doubt a greater understanding of the need for ecologically sound development. Comprehension of environmental impacts and limitations is a matter of central, and not peripheral, importance if the LDCs are to fulfill the basic needs of their populations. The Aswân Dam in Egypt might be used as a case study to illustrate the difficulties that can result from the failure to undertake proper environmental assessment in the planning of development projects.

The shift away from the narrow, pollution-oriented interpretation of environmental problems has made ecological concern highly relevant to the LDCs and has presented a new perspective on questions of inequality of wealth between the developed and the developing states. The Stockholm Conference underscored the split between the North and the South by emphasizing the different kinds of problems faced by each. Most basically, the states of the developed North were increasingly victimized by pollution, whereas the states of the South were suffering from chronic underdevelopment and poverty. The Stockholm Conference can be seen as one of several conferences that worked to develop and reinforce solidarity among the LDCs.

For the developing states, the problems of the environment provide further ammunition in support of a new international economic order. Within UNCTAD and among representatives of many developing states, there is the strongly held view that the world's environmental woes are largely rooted in the existence of North-South economic inequality. This imbalance encourages a tremendous waste of resources with attendant pollution in the developed countries, while in developing states it permits widespread poverty and over-exploitation of natural resources and the environment. In this view, environmental well-being and a more equitable international distribution of economic benefits are intimately related. Environmental problems are only in part technologically based; essentially, they stem from socioeconomic patterns, patterns that LDCs believe must be altered for a variety of reasons.

Global Food Alternatives

Remarkable increases in agricultural yields over the past quarter-century are based on the intensive use of fertilizers, chemicals, and energy and the introduction of the high-yield strains of wheat and rice referred to as the "green revolution." In spite of these accomplishments, the number of people experiencing hunger and malnutrition continues to increase, a trend caused by rapid population growth, particularly in the less developed regions, and by inequalities of food distribution. In recent years, periods of drought in key food-producing regions and disruptions in the supplies of petroleum and fertilizers have compounded food problems, particularly for the highly vulnerable countries referred to as the Fourth World. For these nations in particular, the outlook for the remainder of the century is ominous; many experts anticipate that food production will level off while population growth will continue into the twenty-first century.

In the essay that follows, Thomas Sloan calls attention to the range of policy options that may be exercised by the United States in its capacity as the predominant food exporter. During eras of food scarcity, American policy makers may be unable to avoid difficult decisions that will have life-or-death consequences for those in need of food assistance. Whether food will be used as a coercive instrument of foreign policy is one issue that remains to be resolved. There is also the larger question of whether nations possessing an abundance of food or other scarce, vital natural resources have a responsibility to share with resource-poor countries.

The second essay, by Marvin Soroos, explores the logic underlying Garrett Hardin's policy of "lifeboat ethics" that would restrict food assistance to the poor in order to allow nature to "prune" excessive population growth in less developed countries. The logic of Hardin's argument can be illustrated by suggesting a parallel scenario in which the oil-producing states would withhold petroleum from the developed countries under the guise of discouraging excessive, wasteful energy consumption. Given increasing resource interdependence of nations, it appears that "one-worldism," proceeding from the belief that the destiny of mankind is indivisible, may offer a more rational and humane approach to food and resource issues.

The Soviet Union has recently made several huge purchases of wheat on the international market that depleted the world grain reserves. In the concluding chapter of this section, Ole Holsti calls attention to the failure of Soviet agriculture to keep pace with the performance of Western countries, a lag he attributes to an ideological commitment to social institutions that fail to encourage personal initiative. In an era of food scarcity, Holsti asks whether the Soviet Union has an ethical responsibility to implement whatever social changes are needed to encourage greater productivity, regardless of the political embarrassments that may result.

A Look at America's Potential Roles in a Global Food Crisis

Thomas J. Sloan

Introduction

The struggle to provide adequate world food supplies may become a problem of overarching priority, especially for the United States, in the decades before us. The momentum of global population growth, especially in the Third World, is so rapid that serious and concerted efforts to reduce fertility would not halt the rapid growth of the world's population for decades. Thus, many nations face the prospect of massively larger populations with the threat of domestic and international crises if their legitimate needs for survival and development are not met.

Three background conditions about the world in 1977 need to be kept in mind as we consider world food shortages. First, world population will continue to increase at a rate of a little less than 2 percent per year until the end of the century, with a near doubling of world population between now and then. Much of the increase in world population will come in less developed regions of the world where use and acceptance of family planning have only recently begun. Population growth rates in less developed nations average about 2.5 percent as compared to 1.0 percent in developed nations, and population numbers are what largely determine food needs.[1] In 1970, the less developed nations together contained approximately 70 percent of total world population, and this percentage will continue to increase as the birth rates of the developed nations continue to decline. The nations with the most rapidly growing populations are concentrated in Asia (including the People's Republic of China, India, Pakistan, Bangladesh, and Indonesia), although

Africa (Egypt, Nigeria) and Latin America (Brazil, Mexico) also are experiencing rapid population growth.

Second, the world is rapidly and increasingly becoming inter-dependent in food supply. Prior to World War II, only Western Europe was dependent on the rest of the world for the importation of grain; in recent years Western Europe, the USSR, Eastern Europe, Japan, and many other countries in Asia, Africa, and Latin America have become at least partially dependent on grain imports. The major grain-exporting nations are relatively few in number, principally including the United States, Canada, Australia, New Zealand, and France.

The third consideration is the great variety of food consumption–need situations facing the developing nations of Asia, Africa, and Latin America. Several food-deficit nations, (such as Iran, Saudi Arabia, and Libya) are now high per-capita-income nations because of their large foreign exchange earnings from oil or other resource exports. These nations are able to purchase all the food they need from the world's producers, whereas other nations with equal or greater food deficits do not have the funds to make similar pur-chases. The United Nations has identified forty-three "food-priority countries" with especially low incomes, inadequate diets and large projected cereal-grain deficits. This situation is particularly acute in South and Southeast Asia and in central Africa.

It is estimated that malnutrition currently affects some 400 million people in the developing world. If food resources are not utilized more effectively, starvation and famine in some areas of the world could become a recurrent disaster in the next two decades. During the 1950s and 1960s, global food production was consistently high with per capita output expanding even in the food-deficit nations. During those two decades, the world's total food output increased by more than half. In the 1970s a new pattern has developed. Inclement weather, which affected several subcontinents, simultaneously combined with uncontrolled population growth to contribute to widespread food shortages, with famine and massive starvation in some regions. In the 1971–74 period, world cereal production fell sharply—down 33 million tons from 1.2 billion tons; reserve stocks dropped to the point where further significant crop failures could result in a major disaster—a minimum level of 100 million tons of grain stocks represents only 8 percent of the world's annual consumption; and related problems of fertilizer shortages and rampant inflation have been compounded by the rapid rise in oil prices. Each of these developments has contributed to the raising of fundamental questions about the world's capacity to meet even its basic food needs. The record global crop yields for 1975–76 have at least temporarily alleviated the "food crisis" but have done little to change the world's predilection to "hunger."[2]

Food shortages in low-income nations are caused by natural disasters with resulting famines, or the lack of significant progress in food production per capita. Major famines or near famines caused by natural disasters have occurred three times in the last fifteen years. Two of these crop failures caused large numbers of deaths. The largest food shortage occurred in India during 1964 and 1965 as a result of very low rainfall during the major drought.

However, 10 million metric tons of food aid were shipped in two successive years to India, largely from the United States under the Public Law 480 Food for Peace program. These very large food shipments reduced the food shortage in India sufficiently so that relatively few deaths occurred from starvation. A second major famine occurred during the years 1970 through 1975, when a famine of disastrous proportions spread in the region of Africa just south of the Sahara known as the Sahal. This area extends from West Africa to Ethiopia. Due to much lower than usual rainfall for a number of years, several hundred thousand persons perished. The third famine occurred in Bangladesh in the fall of 1974 after a disastrous summer flood. An estimated 100,000 Bengalis died of starvation that fall. As we are surrounded by the bounty of life in the United States, it is often hard for us to realize that death by starvation still stalks the low-income nations of the world due to major natural disasters.

Chronic malnutrition is a predominant kind of food shortage in poor nations. It occurs year-in and year-out, even if there are no natural crop failures. Many poor people in these nations do not get enough calories of food energy for a full, active life; they have to compensate with lower levels of daily activity, including long periods of rest and sleep. Nor are minimum protein requirements reached by many people. The international nutritional standard is 70 grams or about 2½ ounces of protein per day; one-sixth of this protein should come from animal sources in order for full health to be assured. The recent average protein intake in the United States has been about 8 ounces per day of meat. In many low-income nations, the average intake of protein is estimated at around 60 grams per day on the

minimum standard.[3] This average, therefore, indicates that a large
proportion of the population in these nations does not reach this
level. It has recently been shown that lack of sufficient protein in
children's diets impairs the growth of the brain. Reduced IQ levels in
children who have suffered severe protein malnutrition have been
observed. Shortages of essential minerals and vitamins can have
equally serious consequences. One particularly horrible example is
lifelong blindness due to a lack of vitamin A in the diet of children.
This condition afflicts large numbers of children in certain tropical
nations. Malnutrition is estimated to be the major contributing factor
in more than half the deaths of children between the ages of one and
four in low-income developing nations.

The third type of food shortage results from a lack of significant
progress in increasing the amount of food produced per person.
Although many low-income, developing nations are increasing food
production at a rate of 2 to 3 percent per year, a very respectable rate
of growth in food production even for more developed nations, this
rate of increase in food production is not rapid enough because
population is also growing at these rates in these nations. The last
decade and one-half has shown little increase in food and agricultural
production per capita in less developed nations. Higher rates of
growth in food production will help reduce malnutrition and permit
greater stockpiling against the years of crop shortfalls.

The U.S. proposed to the World Food Conference a program of
action to meet this urgent problem. There are other programs, some
of which we will discuss, but the U.S. plan should indicate the degree
of urgency with which this problem should be approached.

Increased production by food exporters. As much as 150 percent more
food or a total annual global output of 3 billion tons of grain must be
produced even to maintain current inadequate levels of nutrition
in the face of the massive population increase predicted by the
year 2000.[4]

Accelerated production in developing countries. Currently, with 35 percent
more land in grain production than the developed nations, the
developing countries produce 20 percent less. By 1985 the gap
between what the developing nations produce and what they need
could rise from 25 million to as much as 85 million tons annually. The
international research network linking developing countries and
those more developed must be expanded.

Improved food distribution and financing. Food import requirements of the developing countries are likely to amount to 40 million tons a year by the mid-1980s or nearly twice the current level.[5] The traditional food donors and the new financial powers participating in the Consultative Group on Food Production and Investment should negotiate the funding of a minimum global quantity of food for food-deficient countries.

Enhanced food quality. A global nutrition surveillance system should be established under the auspices of the World Health Organization (WHO), the Food and Agriculture Organization (FAO), and the United Nations Children's Fund (UNICEF), which would be empowered to set priorities, identify appropriate research centers, and generate funds to improve the nutritional level of the diets of developing nations.

Security against food emergencies. A worldwide reserve of 60 million tons of food above present carry-over reserve levels may be necessary. An international system of nationally held grain reserves involving all major grain exporters and importers would exchange information on reserve levels and crop prospects and make decisions concerning the size of global reserves to protect against famine and price fluctuations.

Even a cursory review of the U.S. proposals must indicate the extraordinary amount of hard work and luck that will be necessary to prevent a global food crisis. The second part of this paper will be devoted to examining the possibilities and problems attendant to achieving this objective.

Limits to Survivability

Here, we will summarize the pessimistic outlook of many observers and prognosticators. Although many of these views may appear contradictory or mutually exclusive of one another, they all serve to define the severity with which the problem is viewed and to outline the prospects of countering the "root causes" of a global food problem.

The need for increased global production of foodstuffs calls for growing attention to the factors that may limit the ability of the world to increase production appreciably. Initially, the discussion will focus on the United States as the principal food-producing exporting nation in the world.

Under the provisions of the Public Law 480 program, the United States made large amounts of agricultural products available to Third World nations, either on easy, long-term credit terms or as outright gifts. These agricultural commodities were the result of U.S. domestic policies that had maintained high price supports, thereby encouraging U.S. farmers to produce as much food as possible. As the government guaranteed to purchase, at a previously established price, all grain that the farmers could not sell commercially on the open market, the United States developed a large surplus store of grain that was thus available for use in the foreign aid program. By 1972 most of this surplus was no longer available, due to changes in the regulations limiting the amount of acreage each farmer could plant, the success of the foreign aid programs, and the increase in the number of nations receiving grain shipments. The sudden massive entrance of the Soviet Union into the commercial market brought the declining U.S. surplus situation to a dramatic head; but rather than being the cause of a change in the international food situation, the Soviet purchases reflected the approaching world crisis.

The number of nations that have a surplus of grain to dispose of in the international market has been declining steadily over the last decade, accompanied by a smaller, but steady, increase in the number of nations importing grain. Even if a nation (for example, Mexico) does not import grain on a yearly basis, the shift from being an exporter to being a nonexporter and occasional importer puts a strain on the United States (as principal exporter) to pick up the market's needs previously met by Mexico and other countries.

A more significant shift than the entrance of additional nations into the "need to procure food aid" category concerns the ability and the willingness of the United States to produce and provide the necessary grains. From a strictly mechanistic perspective, there are limits to the amount of grain that can be produced. There is a limit to the amount of land that can be cultivated efficiently. Marginally productive land (for example, mountainous, arid, or poor soil) requires a much greater use of technology (fertilizer, terracing, irrigation) without returning the yields necessary to sustain profitable production. Thus, with relatively insignificant differences, the maximum amount of acreage possible is currently under cultivation.

Additional amounts of food will not come from increasing acreage under cultivation in the United States. In fact, a danger lies in the amount of acreage withdrawn from production each year. The effects of urban sprawl, public condemnation of roads and schools, inequitable tax laws, shrinking numbers of farm families, and the high cost of farming all contribute to the potential reduction in the amount of food available to ship abroad. Although more intensive agricultural production methods have proven successful in the past to maintain a large surplus of grain production relative to our consumption, the global demand may require the consideration of a national land-use law that would protect productive farm land from either the condemnation proceedings of government units or the speculative purchase for private development. Certainly, such actions would have to be coordinated with tax reform measures to insure that farm land is taxed as farm land and not on the basis of its value for commercial or residential development. Both of these measures represent courses of action that are unlikely to occur in the relatively near future. The future thus would appear to be a race between the withdrawal of the land from production and the technology necessary to maintain the same amount of total production from fewer acres. New hybrid strains, more effective herbicides, more fertilizers, and more efficient equipment have continued to appear, but it is not difficult to imagine a time when technology will no longer be able to offset the decreasing land under cultivation.

None of the above factors considers the vagaries of weather patterns. The presence or absence of rain or a late frost can destroy or severely reduce a grain crop. If a prolonged drought hit Kansas, U.S. wheat production could be cut in half that year. Such a drastic reduction would have wide implications for U.S. and foreign consumption patterns. Although large-scale irrigation of "western dry land" wheat farms is carried out, latest reports on water use indicate that water tables are falling (more water is being pumped out than is replaced through rainfall and return seepage during the irrigation process). The obvious long-term implication is that a day will come, probably within the next twenty or thirty years, when the water needed for irrigation will not be available and production will markedly decline. A fact to keep in mind throughout this discussion is that, as population and affluence continue to increase, food production must increase at the same or a faster rate just to maintain the same level of nutrition. If production even stagnates in the United

States, much less decreases, increased global hunger will result.

The above discussion has centered on the limits to U.S. production as they may be affected by the mechanical and unplanned growth of urbanization. However, there are other factors that limit the role this country can play in meeting the rising global needs.

As indicated above, the massive amounts of surplus grain owned by the U.S. government had disappeared by 1972. In late 1973, the price of oil rose dramatically, presenting the United States with a potentially large balance-of-payments deficit as our dependence on imported petroleum increased. As a practical matter, then, the sale of U.S. agricultural commodities took precedence over the donation of them. The practical result was a shift from employing grain as foreign aid to encouraging commercial sales to anyone who wanted to purchase grain and could afford to do so. Although this had little effect on our traditional large markets of Japan and Western Europe (except to raise the price per bushel), such nations as India, Bangladesh, and Pakistan had to shift to commercially purchasing the grain they had previously received on low-cost, long-term credits or as gifts. From the U.S. economic standpoint, the commercial sale of grain provides one of the means by which the dollar drain from petroleum imports can be offset. It also provides a market for surplus U.S. production so that the government does not have to subsidize U.S. agriculture by purchasing large amounts of grain. The result, although economically beneficial to the United States, does not help the Third World nations, because in addition to increased bills for petroleum and petroleum-based fertilizers, they are also confronted with large bills for grain. All of these import needs must be met from declining (relatively) foreign exchange holdings.

As shown above, there are limits to the ability of the United States to supply the food necessary to meet the rising demands for global consumption, and we can see why the price of such grain may continue to increase in a rough effort to keep pace with the rise in petroleum prices. It should be apparent that, if significant efforts are to be made to prevent mass famine or widespread malnutrition and the United States is producing at or near its peak capability, tremendous strides must be taken to rapidly increase the production within the Third World. The problems here are at least as severe as those already discussed regarding U.S. production capabilities.

The rapid increase in energy costs is an important problem, to which we have already alluded. Because energy constitutes a large share of the price of some types of fertilizers and much of the pesticides and herbicides used, the cost increase places a strain on the budget of many nations to pay for the modern "technology" needed to increase yields sufficiently to meet the demands of their rapidly increasing populations. The need to use scarce hard currency to pay for other imports for development, as well as for seeds, fertilizers, pesticides, herbicides, and other "technologies" of modern agriculture, means that less money can be devoted to agricultural development. The obvious exception to this last statement would be a policy decision to shift all available resources from other sectors (say, industrialization) to agriculture. This remains an extremely remote possibility, but it is an alternative. We will focus on suggestions to alleviate the problem of the lack of "hard" currency later in this discussion; for now, it is sufficient to recognize that the problem exists.

The cost of producing food in the Third World is another major problem. During the height of the U.S. surplus food distribution program, it was less expensive for the recipient nation to accept the low-cost U.S. food than to develop its own productive capability. Although the need for increased local production has increased, the cost factors have continued to mitigate against such development. Economies of scale plus the advantages of technology combined with the cost of that technology have continued to make imported grain more attractive than the alternative of massive investment in the agricultural sector of the Third World nations. Long-cherished dreams of industrialization and development might be postponed by such a shift in focus.

Even if the requisite political decisions are made to reorient the national focus, seemingly insurmountable problems remain (insurmountable, given the time available to find the answers to the expected food crisis). The preliminary steps necessary to increasing production have not been taken. Relatively little research on, for example, tropical production, with the objective of increased production of food grains, has been conducted. Few nations have developed experimental research centers for evaluating and improving the strains of native plants. Even the highly touted green revolution was based largely on research and development conducted in the United States. Corresponding efforts to develop plants compatible with local soil, weather conditions, and pest problems have not transpired among the Third World nations. Without such preliminary actions, major increases in production are not possible. Unfortunately, the lead time for major benefits of an active research program may extend for twenty years from the date an effective hybrid plant is developed to the time of its widespread growth by the farmers. Development of new plant strains is only the first step toward increasing production. Years can be spent in testing the hybrid for disease and pest resistance, nutrient needs, and reaction to adverse weather and soil conditions before enough seed is produced for initial dissemination to the farmers. Then the farmer must be taught how to grow the new plant variety for maximum production. The green revolution effort was often stymied or did not achieve maximum results possible, either because the peasants did not fully understand the intricacies of "modern" farming (for example, when and how much fertilizer, pesticide, or herbicide to use), because adverse weather or plant disease struck and the hybrids were not able to cope with the adversity, or because national governments were unable to make available the necessary seeds and production supplements (fertilizer, for example) in sufficient quantities. Often, costs of modern technology and inadequate transportation or storage capabilities were responsible for the gap between actual and potential production. In other instances, political and regional differences were responsible. Hybrid plants yield higher amounts of produce but also are usually much more sensitive to deficiencies in the soil and adverse weather or pests. The local varieties of rice, wheat, corn, and other grains that have been grown in the Third World have survived because of their hardiness and adaptability. Hybrids, with their greater sensitivity and needs, will often produce less than the native varieties when adversity strikes. This is yet another reason why plant research and development in the Third World must be increased without delay.

A related problem concerns the cultural-social problems of "modernization." Although volumes have been written about the "traumas" of modernizing and the need for such social redistribution programs as land reform, in this context a few observations are warranted. There are problems associated with "peasant" adaptability to new ideas and the lack of practical (though expensive) government application of technologies to the problems of food production (for example, desalinization of seawater for irrigation purposes). Foreign advice and aid are often geared to large production units (such as the American farm) so that ideas advanced are practical only if such social redistribution programs as land reform are halted and reversed. Large units of production that can efficiently employ the miracles of technology and the economies of scale are counter to the social-political development of the countries involved. Such incompatabilities must be faced and resolved in some manner (perhaps through increased development of cooperatives).

Population migration is another problem in the developing nations. In the United States, production per capita increased and the surplus agricultural workers moved to the urban areas, whereas in the Third World the peasants move to the urban areas seeking a better life without the corresponding prior productivity increases. This obviously additionally strains the production capability of the nation and limits its ability to respond to the developing food crisis. This is especially true when the inadequate transportation networks available for moving the food produced to the populated urban areas are considered. In many cases, this phenomenon was made possible by U.S. surplus grain shipments to the Third World countries during the 1950s and 1960s. The distribution of available foodstuffs is a two-way problem. Most developing nations have difficulty transporting food to the cities, but when natural disasters occur and the rural areas need relief, the inadequate transportation system will not carry relief supplies to those in need. The recent massive drought in the northernmost sub-Saharan nations pointed out their inability to transport food to those persons most desperately in need. Only massive airlifts by outside agencies and nations prevented more deaths from starvation. As the food crisis becomes more acute in the coming years, the inadequacy of transportation capacity will increase the difficulties governments experience in meeting the food needs of their people.

A final potential problem, which may actually constitute an "act of God," concerns the theory advanced by some climatologists (Dr. Reid Bryson of the University of Wisconsin, for one) that the world may be entering a "cold" period. These meteorologists speak in terms of a return within the next twenty years to the climate experienced during the nineteenth century. If this development were to occur, they envisage broad belts of excess and deficit rainfall in the middle latitudes; more frequent failure of the monsoons of the Indian subcontinent, South China, and western Africa; shorter growing seasons for Canada, the northern Soviet Union, and northern China; and a cooler, wetter Europe. If their projections are accurate, the shorter growing season would restrict production in high-latitude areas (such as Canada and the Soviet Union), and the southern shift of the monsoons away from the Indian subcontinent would significantly reduce grain output in those areas.

In addition to the climatological changes, other adverse results can be anticipated. Because most of the hybrids and "green revolution" strains were developed for the present warmth and moisture levels, significant shifts in temperature or precipitation patterns could negate these advances in yield. Although agronomists will develop new strains suitable for the new weather conditions, the delay in increasing production totals will adversely affect the ability of any program to increase the standard of living of the world's people.

The above is only a cursory examination of some of the problems associated with increasing food production in the world, but it is sufficient to indicate the magnitude of the problem.

A few brief observations about the validity of the arguments discussed above are in order. Major reductions in population growth rates are occurring through increasingly effective national government programs (for example, India's "compulsory" sterilization program). Success in such endeavors will do much to change the nature of the food problem to that of raising the standard of living level, which in itself will require large increases in available food supplies.

Climatological changes occur each year and favorably or adversely affect crop yields, yet present techniques of forecasting are inadequate to accurately predict what the next decade will experience. Consequently, alarmist reports of the approach of a "new ice age" are only subjective in nature, as there is inadequate information available to make accurate assessments of future climatological changes.

Efforts are being increased to redress the imbalance in agricultural research between developed and Third World nations. Joint, long-term collaborative efforts by U.S. land grant institutions and Third World governments and universities (for example, Kansas State University's College of Agriculture and the Philippines government) are steps in the right direction.

Finally, the question of the role of multinational corporations in the problem of global hunger has been increasingly raised.[6] Agribusiness has invested millions of dollars in the Third World with the assumption that this investment would return a profit. These firms have concentrated on developing the export market sectors (beef, poultry, cut flowers, strawberries, asparagus), which are then largely consumed in the United States and Europe. The increased flow of hard currency into these countries has gone not to the small farmer but rather to the agribusiness and the few wealthy landowners. The full implications of this evolving pattern of production shifts become apparent when the nutrition trends are examined. Land utilized for animal feed production provides approximately one-sixteenth the protein for human use that would be available if soybeans were grown for human consumption.[7]

Agribusinesses' concern for profit return will result in continued shifts in commodity production in the Third World countries away from protein for local consumption and toward the specialized, exotic, luxury export market. Many local business and political leaders are financially involved in such export activities and therefore do not seek to reverse the pattern. Global hunger is not "caused" by multinational corporation (MNC) policies, but these policies are not aimed at alleviating the world hunger problems. When combined with inefficient, misguided aid efforts by governments and international agencies, MNC policies compound the problems of technology, politics, and ignorance.

Even if progressive tendencies are continued, global food shortages and the potential for political instability will remain major factors in the daily conduct of international politics. Whether one accepts the "pessimistic" or the "optimistic" perspective, a detailed analysis of U.S. policy options is necessary. In this essay, the alternative futures can only be suggested. Other chapters of this volume and sources listed in the bibliography should be examined for more detailed analysis of these, and other, possibilities.

Alternative Futures

The role of U.S. agriculture in an increasingly interdependent world should be subject to searching debate from both the political and the philosophical perspective. The future international political system will be greatly influenced by the outcome of such debates, yet little public leadership has been generated on this complex issue. It is hoped that this essay—and this volume—will serve as a stimulus to such discussions.

The initial question that must be answered is, "What goals should America establish for itself?" Are we to narrowly define our objectives in terms of perceived self-interest, or do we espouse a broader, more humanist perspective? And what implications and consequences arise from the perspective selected? The first alternatives to be discussed involve the unilateral actions of the United States.

The first scenario is one that appeals to many Americans and concerns the use of American grain as a political weapon. In this plan the United States would exchange grain for political concessions, votes in the United Nations, favorable trade terms, or natural resources. The appeal of this plan is obvious; it would maximize U.S. influence and power in the world. As long as the other grain-exporting nations followed the U.S. initiative or were unable to replace the U.S. supply withheld from a particular nation, presumably U.S. political "strength" would continue to increase.

This scenario does little to resolve the problem of a world food shortage and in reality may do little to increase the "power" of the United States. Many of the nations that purchase U.S. grain are considered vital to U.S. interests and thus are relatively immune to U.S. pressures (for example, Japan, West Germany), whereas others import relatively small amounts of grain relative to that produced and consumed (for example, the USSR and Saudi Arabia). Nations with resources or strategic value to the U.S. may not be the nations most vulnerable to U.S. food pressure. Much of the U.S. agricultural aid in the mid-1970s has gone to aid such political allies as South Korea and Taiwan rather than nations that may have a higher need (Ethiopia, for instance). If the political-weapon scenario is followed, what are likely to be the implications? We may assume an increased polarization of the world between those who have enough food to adequately provide for their population requirements, those who have political or resource value to the exporting nations and who need agricultural assistance, and those who have no such political-economic value and who require aid. Those nations deemed not valuable, in the political-economic context, would not receive aid under this plan. Although the decision on worldwide grain allocations might be made in the councils of the developed agricultural nations, the leaders of those states excluded from U.S. (and other) grain suppliers may well determine the political stability of the world. It is unreasonable to expect the leaders of a nation excluded from the supplies necessary for national survival to quietly accept that decision. It is not difficult to imagine food wars between a nation the United States is aiding and one that is not receiving help.

A similar scenario involves the concept of *triage*. Again, there are three categories of states: those that are self-sufficient in grain (with or without exportable surplus); those in which conditions are such that immediate aid will make it possible for the recipient nation to feed its people and have the long-term possibility of self-sufficiency; and those for whom there is no possibility of any aid being successful in preventing long-term starvation. Efforts to serve this last group are doomed to fail because of the magnitude of the problem (high rate of population growth, lack of quality land, or logistical problems), regardless of what efforts are made. As in the previous scenario, political decisions largely determine the question of who should be aided. Although it can be argued that a more objective standard can be established empirically to determine levels of need and "savability" of nations, any standard is necessarily both arbitrary and political in nature. This system too would appear to be inherently unstable, because those nations that are consigned to the third category (left to their own devices) would presumably seek to change the conditions under which the allocative decisions are made. This might involve military or political actions against states in the first two categories, or it might mean increased threat to the stability of the international system. The inability of nations to satisfy the legitimate needs and aspirations of the local populations may well result in food riots, government instability, increased spending for development of military weaponry (including nuclear weapons), and perhaps an overall pervasive sense of desperation in which decision makers fail to perceive alternatives to violence. In an age where ideological differences remain important in interstate relations, any local instability may lead to the involvement of the superpowers, with all of the attendant risks.

An alternative scenario calls for food to be distributed on a per capita basis, rather than by the criteria suggested in the previous two scenarios. In this plan, each recipient nation would receive assistance in terms of the amount of its need as evidenced by the number of people involved. Each nation would receive a fixed amount of food per capita, and thus equality of aid would be achieved. The egalitarian nature of this idea may be applauded, but its practicality is questionable. Certainly, level of need for food aid may differ between two nations (due to such variable factors as climate, size of individual citizens, type of soil, local production level), even if they have approximately the same total population figures. Although this scenario is obviously unworkable from a pragmatic perspective, variants on it may have greater appeal. So that no politician need ever make the decision to exclude people from the opportunity to survive, it is more than likely that the United States (as principal world exporter) will attempt to provide some food to every nation in need. Obviously, if the total need increases with a growth in global population and affluence, the ability of the United States to meet the needs of the world may decline (that is, as the gap between each nation's ability to produce and the amounts of food necessary for consumption increases, the relative ability of the United States to provide the difference decreases). Such a policy of providing aid to all (presumably prorated according to "need") could conceivably result in no country receiving as much aid as it requires and all nations suffering from inadequate levels of food supply. Whether this system of distribution would minimize the problems of starvation and malnutrition is debatable. What is more likely is that more people would suffer and that once again political stability of the international system would be affected.

The final pessimistic scenario concerns "lifeboat ethics" (see the following chapter by Marvin Soroos) as advanced by Garrett Hardin. Briefly, this scenario involves excluding those nations in need from the American food stocks as a means of preserving the American standard of living for present and future generations. The rationale for this policy option is that the overpopulated nations of the world have the excess population to consume all of the surplus food available, with the result that both they and the altruistic Americans would suffer the consequences of an inadequate food supply. The anticipated consequences of this scenario closely resemble those of the triage scenario.

It has been suggested that denying food to nations in need may result in aggressive political-military behavior by those states against those that do receive food. If all nations in need of assistance receive only part of their requirements, it would appear more likely that greater efforts would be made to form regional or commodity political organizations in order to maximize the pressure the dependent states could bring to bear on the producing nations. This certainly would involve a minimal call for a reduction in the standard of living in the developed nations, which would presumably mean lower caloric intake by individuals and decreased feeding of grains to livestock. The situation might evolve into a struggle in which all Third World nations would attempt to influence the developed world to increase aid to the less affluent nations, perhaps by using the economic pressure available to those nations controlling natural resources (for example, oil). Such unanimity among the Third World states is highly unlikely, however. Their interests and perspectives are often radically different, and their political and historical differences serve to mitigate against such collaborative efforts. An example of the lack of coordination of policies can be drawn from the OPEC price increases. In order to gain political support from other Third World states, the Organization of Petroleum-Exporting Countries suggested possible benefits that might accrue to their supporters; these included a two-tiered pricing system in which developed nations would pay a higher price for petroleum than would Third World states; increased technical and financial aid from the oil-producing states to help defray the added costs of petroleum and related products (for example, fertilizers); and a series of refunds to accomplish the same goal. Unfortunately for the states without oil, most of these benefits have not been forthcoming in exchange for their political support, and the higher price of petroleum products is one reason that it is unlikely that agricultural production can be increased enough in those states to meet their needs. It is reasonable to expect increasing political conflict within the Third World as shortages of any commodity increase. It is also reasonable to expect increased domestic instability in nations undergoing the crisis of food shortages or facing the prospects of shortages due to an inability of national government to finance and manage the steps necessary to increase production.

An alternative approach to unilateral U.S. actions to provide food assistance is a multilateral effort, which, in addition to increasing the amount of resources available for assistance, would minimize many of the problems associated with bilateralism. The appearance of political, neocolonial, and racial or ethnic biases may largely be avoided by implementation of the following policy options.

The proposals recommended by the participants at the UN World Food Conference included calls for the establishment of (a) an early warning system for the exchange of information on projected global demand and supplies of grain; (b) an agricultural development fund;

(c) an international grain reserve system comprised of cereal producing, consuming, and trading nations to build up supplies for emergencies.

If such a program were successfully adopted immediately, the scenario of the future might be markedly different from those suggested above. The early warning system is the easiest part of the plan to implement; the U.S. Department of Agriculture, other developed countries, and the FAO routinely issue projections on production and consumption trends or needs. The development fund could be established by pooling the development aid provided by the individual developed nations and establishing a central administrative agency. The more difficult problems are related to the international grain reserve system. The initial obstacle revolves around the direct and indirect costs of the proposal. U.S. grain sales (and presumably the sales of most other grain exporters) are important to the maintenance of a surplus balance-of-payments situation. A large element of any program establishing a global grain reserve would necessarily involve a two-tiered price system. The poorer Third World nations are currently unable to purchase food in the commercial market, and it is unlikely that the situation will change radically in the foreseeable future. Nor is it likely that the United States will be in a position to donate large amounts of grain to such a project. The reserves accumulated by the U.S. government during the 1950s and 1960s have been distributed; and with the world market maintaining high prices at the farm level, it is unlikely that the government will intervene with tax dollars to make the necessary purchases. The popular discontent with any program that would raise the price of grain combined with the need for foreign exchange and the demand for grain from our traditional allies and customers strongly suggests only token U.S. participation.

Such an emergency reserve supply might well be inadequate to meet widespread famine. However, an even greater potential problem is related to the political aspects of the distribution system. There is not only the problem of deciding which nation's need is greater or more urgent than another's; of even more risk to a program that must be a cooperative effort is the threat that politics could determine which nations are "eligible" for assistance. Recent actions in the United Nations in which Taiwan was expelled, South Africa was expelled, and Israel was condemned indicate that other nations may also be vulnerable to the vagaries of democracy. In the context of humanitarian food aid, there is no reason to expect politics not to enter the decision-making process. It is conceivable that the decisions will involve having too little grain to distribute to too many people. Even with an acceptable criterion for deciding "need" and even if we ignore the problem of employing the grain as a political weapon, the logistical and economic problems remain. What means of funding will be utilized; and given the inadequate transportation systems in many developing countries, how does the grain get distributed to those most in need of it?

Conclusion

Among the most optimistic projections for the future are those of some U.S. Department of Agriculture experts and UN Food and Agriculture Organization specialists that net grain imports by the Third World nations will rise from an average of 15.5 million metric tons in the 1969–71 period to 40–45 million metric tons in 1985. They are assuming that production in these countries will rise by 2.6 percent per year with demand for food increasing by 3 percent a year. These projections imply no appreciable change in per capita consumption levels over this time period—181 kilograms per capita to 186.[8] Remember that this constitutes an optimistic view of the situation; even if local production meets this goal and consumption does not exceed the upper estimate (both occurrences being unlikely), no real improvement in nutrition levels for these people is foreseen. At best, the projected future will have millions more people at the same food-deficient levels as currently exist in much of the Third World (that is, nothing will have changed but the number of people who are ill fed; the problem will still be with us, though greatly magnified and more insoluble).

The more pessimistic forecasters point out that for most Third World nations the governing policy has been to promote industrial growth to the relative exclusion of agricultural development. The reversal, especially in the short run, of this policy would require enormous inputs of capital and skilled personnel, both of which are perennially in short supply in most Third World nations. Their absence severely restricts the ability of those nations to effectively utilize aid from donor countries.

The largely pessimistic view of the future has been deliberate in order to convey a feeling for the magnitude of the problem. Yet, the importance of this piece should not be viewed from the perspective that all is lost, though many of the authors included in the bibliography accept that position. Major progress is being made in slowing the rate of population growth in many parts of the world. India will perform approximately seven million sterilization operations in 1977; many developed countries have, or are approaching, zero population growth; and the People's Republic of China has had a major population control program in practice for several years. Although the world's total population continues to increase, education and changing government-social attitudes have slowed the birth rate. It will take many decades to achieve a stable world population, but the effort is now being made by the international community, not solely by a small group of "population alarmists."

The second aspect of this paper that should be noted is the call for a dialogue on future policy alternatives and the implications of those policies. Although Americans can choose to ignore the plight of the hungry abroad, fundamental changes in the conduct of daily American life may result. Not only does the threat to international political stability increase, which involves the risk of U.S. involvement abroad, but, more importantly, increased demands will be placed on the United States and each of its citizens. Another possibility is that the poor, hungry nations will attempt to blackmail the United States by threatening to employ inexpensive biological or chemical weapons against us unless we provide the assistance necessary to meet their needs. There would be literally no defense against such weapons.

How much food are we willing to share with the rest of the world? Will that food be sold to nations having the economic capability to purchase food, or will the American taxpayer help subsidize shipments to the poor and needy nations? Regardless of which option is selected, how will the American voter-consumer react to increased food sales abroad that result in high prices in U.S. supermarkets? Are we willing to eat less meat so that the grain fed to livestock can be sent abroad to aid those most in need? What levels of affluence and waste will we seek to maintain against the demands of the outside world? This last point applies equally to the United States and to other developed, affluent, consumer states. What is the collective "social conscience" of the relatively food-rich nations? What price are we willing to pay? Farmers are complaining that labor and consumer interests in this country serve to keep food prices too low for a proper return on the farmers' investment and labor. Will those same groups become concerned enough to act in support of the world's hungry at the expense of their own comfort and economic well-being?

The concept of "social responsibility" can be extended to all scarce resources—food, petroleum, copper, human dignity. Should these resources be made available to those in need, even when it is not in the long-term best interests of the producer (for instance, petroleum will be more valuable in five years than it is now, so why should OPEC members engage in unrestricted production in order to keep prices low in the United States?). Production of natural resources can be regulated, but food production fluctuates more widely depending on the vagaries of the weather. Increased global storage capabilities would enhance the ability of the world to avoid the feast-or-famine cycle of life.

Because of the vast complexity of the issues involved and the generally inadequate understanding between politics and the global life support systems, this discussion has been, of necessity, brief and in some areas superficial. The magnitude of the dilemma and the problems attendant to resolving the approaching global food crisis at times, and in some perspectives, appear nearly insurmountable. Even if all of the world's governments concertedly apply themselves to increasing the yield of grains, the logistical, political, social, and economic dimensions of the international political system will necessitate a long-term approach to solving this problem. The future will be determined by how the questions posed above are answered.

Lifeboat Ethics versus One-Worldism in International Food and Resource Policy

Marvin S. Soroos

Introduction

The question addressed in this essay is a slight variation of John Donne's often quoted aphorism, "No man is an island." Rather than asking whether an individual can stand alone, let us consider whether a nation-state can be an "island" in the last quarter of the twentieth century as food and resources become increasingly scarce.

Discussion of ecological problems in most academic and diplomatic circles proceeds from the premise that a modern nation cannot expect to maintain a completely independent stance. Mankind is often portrayed in a situation analogous to the crew of a spaceship, in which harmony and cooperation are essential to a safe flight whereas discord and isolation will usually lead to disaster. Similarly, it is assumed that the well-being, if not the survival, of mankind is dependent upon a coordinated global response to the ecological predicament that man faces. Advocates of this "one-world" approach generally concede that such a cooperative effort may require a far greater responsiveness on the part of the developed world to the demands from the less developed peoples for more equity in the distribution of the world's wealth.[1]

Biologist Garrett Hardin is a prominent advocate of an alternative school of thought that presumes that human welfare is divisible. Hardin encourages the residents of developed nations to be concerned with the survival and welfare of only themselves and their descendants. As cruel and insensitive as it may appear, it is argued that starvation must be allowed to reduce population in nations that fail to restrict its growth. Despite admirable intentions, food assistance to poor and hungry societies is counterproductive because it allows excess people to survive and multiply, thereby inevitably compounding future food problems for the rich as well as the poor of the world. Hardin's prescriptive theory has become widely known as "lifeboat ethics," in reference to an analogy he uses to present his theory, which will be explained in the following pages.[2]

This essay contains a critical analysis of Hardin's theories, followed by a brief examination of the one-world alternative. Some readers may ask whether such an effort is warranted given that food assistance has become inconsequential in relation to world population and food requirements. Moreover, as the "world food crisis" of 1972–74 has given way to abundance in most regions, the need for food assistance has declined. In response, it may be noted that Hardin raises questions about the wisdom of the efforts to establish an international food bank that grew out of the World Food Conference of 1974. Furthermore, with rapidly growing world population and inevitable climatic perturbations, the possibility of famines, appeals for emergency food assistance, and calls for the practice of lifeboat ethics cannot be discounted.

Lifeboat ethics may also be summarily dismissed for its ethical repulsiveness, even to those with the most tentative of humanist inclinations. Hardin directly challenges the wisdom of commitments to the welfare of all human beings as well as to social justice and equality, values that are central to such fields as peace research and world order inquiry. Ethics of the lifeboat genre will, however, undoubtedly continue to gain adherents in the developed world among those who believe that overpopulation in the less developed regions is the primary ecological peril of the times. In presenting a simple theory that offers moral rationale for the pursuit of narrowly construed self-interest, Hardin may further erode what limited concern there is for the plight of the poor of the world. Thus, it is important that the ethical challenges posed by lifeboat ethics be confronted rather than ignored.

There is also an intellectual reason for analyzing lifeboat ethics. It is an intriguing theory that is applicable not only to food but to the full range of other types of resources. In its extremeness, it is of assistance in plotting the terrain of policy alternatives for coping with conditions of scarcity.

The Hardin Thesis

Hardin contends that ecological problems typically arise when the narrowly defined self-interest of individuals is incompatible with the welfare of the larger community. In an earlier essay, Hardin explains this interest incompatability in terms of an analogy known as "the tragedy of the commons."[3]

It was once the custom in English villages to treat the community pasture as a commons on which the village herdsmen were permitted to graze their individually owned cattle for private gain. As long as the grass is abundant in relation to the size of the herd, restrictions on the number of cattle grazed by each herdsman are unnecessary. Problems arise, however, when the grazing capacity of the pasture is reached. An individual herdsman may at that time calculate that the supplementary income from adding a cow will accrue entirely to himself whereas the costs of overgrazing the pasture will be divided among all villagers. Even if he is aware of the need to practice conservation, he may fail to exercise restraints, anticipating that his sacrifice will be taken advantage of by less socially responsible neighbors who continue to add to their herds. Under these circumstances, the herdsman's personal interest is best served by adding to his herd not just one cow but as many as he can afford. Because this logic applies equally to all of the herdsmen of the village, Hardin concludes that the unregulated commons will inevitably be overgrazed to the point of ruin.

Several strategies may be used to avert the destruction of the pasture, two of which are of particular interest. First, the commons system can be retained if the number of cattle grazed on the pasture is strictly regulated by a village authority, a possibility that will be elaborated later in discussing the one-world alternative. Second, the commons system can be dropped in favor of an enclosure arrangement in which each herdsman is assigned a private section of the pasture on which he may exercise exclusive grazing rights. Not only would he reap all of the economic benefits that accrue from his section, but he would also bear all costs resulting from overgrazing. In this way, the herdsmen become "intrinsically responsible" for conserving their sections, which Hardin contends is the most effective type of incentive for restraint, as we shall see in reviewing his theory of lifeboat ethics.

If we apply the analogy to contemporary ecological problems, the village pasture can be compared to the natural resources of the planet, including those of an agricultural nature; the herdsmen to nation-states; and the cattle to the world's population. The natural resources of the planet can be treated as the common possession of mankind to be used by all nations. Alternatively, the resources may be regarded as private property to be exploited exclusively by the country in which they are located.

In presenting his theory of lifeboat ethics, Hardin extends the logic of his earlier essay.[4] The world's population is figuratively placed on a group of lifeboats afloat at sea. Americans are portrayed by fifty people occupying a lifeboat with an estimated capacity of sixty. One hundred swimmers who have been forced from other overcrowded lifeboats surround the American lifeboat, begging to be pulled aboard. Hardin suggests three options for the fortunate occupants of the American boat. First, all who desire to board the lifeboat may be permitted to do so. Unfortunately, the boat would become overloaded and sink, causing both the original and the newly boarded occupants to perish—as Hardin describes it, "complete justice, complete catastrophe."[5] Second, ten may be admitted to fill the lifeboat to its capacity of sixty. This option sacrifices the "safety factor" and poses the perplexing problem of how to make a nondiscriminatory decision on which ten swimmers will be taken aboard. The third alternative is to permit no additional persons to board. The swimmers are left to perish in the interests of the survival and comfort of the original occupants.

These policy options available to the occupants of the American lifeboat are analogous to three potential policy stances on food assistance. First, Americans can attempt to provide food assistance to all of the hungry of the world. Second, food assistance can be concentrated on a selected group of deserving countries while the needy populations of other countries are left to starve, as in the practice of triage, which was discussed in the preceding essay by Thomas Sloan.[6] The third alternative is to deny all requests for food assistance, thereby leaving the residents of each country to fend for themselves.

Hardin is concerned that food assistance, as provided for under the first two policy options, results in the food production systems of the donor countries taking on the attributes of an unregulated commons. With access to ample food aid, it is feared that societies will continue increasing their populations for reasons that parallel the rationale herdsmen have for adding cattle to the village pasture. The "tragedy" takes place when the population of the planet significantly overshoots world food production capabilities with widespread starvation resulting. Alternatively, if the third option of withholding assistance is adopted, societies become intrinsically responsible for the welfare of their population in the same way that each herdsman is responsible for the conservation of his private section of the pasture. Hardin concludes that the prospect or actuality of starvation "pruning luxuriant" population growth will provide a strong incentive for demographic responsibility that may avert even more serious ecological problems in the future.[7]

Space does not allow for a comprehensive overview of the questions that can be raised pertaining to Hardin's thesis. His assumption about the relationship between food availability and population growth is particularly questionable but will not be discussed here, given the treatment of the issue in Richard Clinton's chapter. The critique that follows will raise three questions. First, is overpopulation the primary cause of hunger in the world? Second, what are the implications of extending the logic of lifeboat ethics to its logical conclusion? Third, can Americans insulate themselves from the destiny of the poor and hungry of the world?

The Causes of Hunger and Malnutrition

Hardin is an advocate of "situational" ethics, the principal that the morality of an act is a function of the "state of the system at the time the act is performed."[8] He contends that what appears to be an ethically repugnant policy of ignoring the pleas of the desperate and hungry for assistance is justified, and even necessitated, by the increasingly serious difficulties of feeding a rapidly increasing world population. In this section, let us question whether this modern-day Malthusian analysis is a valid interpretation of the population and food situation.

That the world has food problems is beyond dispute. It is estimated that hundreds of millions, perhaps even more than one billion, of the planet's four billion human inhabitants suffer from hunger and malnutrition. The reason for such widespread hunger have been a subject of considerable dispute. Three types of explanations can be identified. The first claims that people are hungry because the planet is overpopulated; the second blames inequalities in wealth and the consumption of food; and the third attributes the problem to concentrated ownership of land and the means of agricultural production. Hardin clearly subscribes to the overpopulation school of thought. The mathematics of the lifeboat analogy implies that an overall condition of population is present inasmuch as the extra spaces on the American lifeboat are few in comparison to the number of swimmers dislodged from other boats.

The impression is left, although not explicitly stated by Hardin, that hunger is itself an indicator of overpopulation. This type of thinking is reinforced by the fact that the vast majority of the inadequately fed and nourished people of the world reside in less developed countries that generally have high population growth rates. On the surface, it seems logical to conclude that hunger results from a failure by some societies to limit their population in line with their capacity to provide food. Conversely, the well-nourished citizens of the developed countries are seen as benefiting from the foresight and restraint evidenced by low fertility rates. If food problems are interpreted in this way, it follows that food assistance from the demographically responsible to the irresponsible will allow the latter to continue multiplying and become an increasingly large proportion of the world's population while hopelessly overburdening the food-growing capacity of the planet.

The inequality theory of hunger does not assume that food is in short supply or will be in the foreseeable future. Hunger is attributed to the distribution of food consumption. From this perspective, a shortcoming of the lifeboat analogy is its failure to allow for differences in the size or weight of the occupants. Presumably, a raft would support a greater number of young children than adults, women than men, or thin as opposed to overweight people. Shouldn't provision also be made for the possibility that some occupants of the American boat brought along their belongings and household pets? Parallel questions can be asked about the carrying capacity of the planet. Shouldn't it be taken into account that some societies demand far more food and resources per capita than do others? Is the size of the world's population as important a variable as the aggregated impact of the human population on the natural endowments of the planet?

The more imbalanced the distribution of food consumption, the smaller the population that can be sustained by a given amount of food and natural resources. It has been estimated that on a worldwide basis roughly one-third of the population consumes two-thirds of the agricultural production. Average caloric intake varies from as little as 2,000 calories per day in South Asian countries to more than 3,500 among Europeans and North Americans.[9] This discrepancy does not indicate the substantial inequalities within countries. Nor does it reflect the fact that much of the food consumed in the developed world comes from livestock, which require as many as five to ten pounds of grain for every pound of meat produced. A United Nations study indicated that the grain necessary to feed the 460 million people suffering from malnutrition an additional allotment of 250 calories a day amounts to about 30 percent of the grain fed to livestock in the United States.[10]

Inequalities in food consumption can be explained in large part by imbalances in the distribution of wealth. The rich can use their higher incomes to outbid the poor for what food is available, not only to feed themselves but also to feed their livestock and household pets, who enjoy a more nutritious diet than many of the poor of the world. Continuing increases in the income gap have resulted in a substantial proportion of expanded world food output going to upgrade diets in the developed countries, as reflected in the rapid increases in beef consumption in the postwar period.[11]

If the food problem is inequality in income and consumption rather than overpopulation, it is hardly ethical for the United States and the industrial world to turn away from the problems of hunger. If necessary, steps should be taken to moderate increased demand for food by reducing the consumption of livestock products. Moreover, programs should be instituted to insure that food is available to the poor at prices they can afford.

A third explanation of hunger builds upon the inequality explanation that was just presented but is more specific in identifying concentration of land ownership and of the means of agricultural production as the primary cause of the problem. This theory has been developed at length in a recently published volume by Frances Lappé and Joseph Collins, the former being the author of the widely read book *Diet for a Small Planet*.[12]

Not only is it assumed that sufficient food is produced to feed the world's population, but it is further argued that all of the less developed countries, even the so-called basket cases, such as Bangladesh, have the potential for food self-reliance.[13] What keeps people hungry are the policies of governments and multinational agribusinesses that determine patterns of land ownership and the types of crops that are produced. On a worldwide basis, three-quarters of the agricultural land is controlled by the 2.5 percent of the landowners who own more than 100 hectares. Over half of the land is held by less than .25 percent of the owners. At the other end of the continuum, one-third of the rural agricultural population owns no land.[14]

Why is concentrated land ownership a problem? The general experience throughout the world has been that small, owner-operated farms are more productive on a per acre basis. Moreover, the food grown on subsistence farms by peasant owners goes to meet the basic food needs of the local rural population. Larger landhold-ings controlled by absentee owners or agribusinesses tend to be used for cash crops that are consumed by urban elites or exported, often to the industrial countries. Commercial growers have little incentive to produce food for the poor, who do not constitute a profitable market. Large operations also tend to be more mechanized and therefore have the effect of displacing agricultural laborers. The wages paid to those who are employed are often too low to allow them to purchase the very food they are producing.[15]

The net effect is that much of the best agricultural land, which could be used to meet the food needs of the poor of less developed countries, has since colonial days been appropriated to provide luxury foods, such as asparagus, strawberries, sugarcane, cocoa, bananas, and coffee, or fibers, such as cotton, for consumption in the industrial countries. In the Central American and the Caribbean regions, for example, more than half of the cultivable land is cash cropped. Ironically, large amounts of food were exported from the Sahal region of Africa even during the years of acute famine and starvation.[16]

Why do the governments of the less developed countries allow large areas of prime agricultural land to be used for export crops when it is needed to produce food for the local population? Export revenue is desired to pay for the imports that sustain the lifestyle of the relatively well-off, modernized classes. Unfortunately, the basic food needs of the poor population are ignored in the process.

Lappé and Collins concur with Hardin that self-reliance is a desired goal. Paradoxically, they see the obstacle not in demographic trends but in the way that prime agricultural land in the less developed countries is in effect appropriated to provide luxury foods and fibers for the rich. If this is so, the self-reliance of the less developed world would appear to be contingent on the industrial world living more within its own agricultural means. China presents an alternative example of how a less developed society can, if allowed to do so, use its agricultural potential to become food self-sufficient and eliminate hunger in its population.

A Logical Extension of Lifeboat Ethics

In this section, the analysis of lifeboat ethics will take the form of a reductio ad absurdum (challenging a proposition by demonstrating its absurdity when extended to its logical conclusions).

Central to Hardin's theory is the assumption that restraint can be most effectively encouraged by policies that incorporate intrinsic responsibility, an arrangement in which consequences of decisions fall most directly on their maker. Hardin would institute intrinsic responsibility in matters of population by requiring each society to be dependent upon itself for fulfilling its food requirements.

In the lifeboat analogy, the principle of intrinsic responsibility is applied quite narrowly. First, the analysis is limited to food with no mention being made of other types of demands a society places on planetary resources, such as for fossil fuels and minerals. Second, consideration is given only to food that is provided as a gift. Hardin's criticism of U.S. Public Law 480 for being a food "giveaway" program because loans are sometimes forgiven and of proposed world food banks for being one-way transfers of wealth from the rich to the poor leave the impression that the sale of food to foreign countries at market prices is not objectionable.[17] Let us consider these two limitations of Hardin's analysis in reverse order.

If it is assumed for the sake of argument that the logic underlying the principle of intrinsic responsibility is basically sound, is there justification for applying it to food assistance but not to food trade? What distinguishes aid from trade is the financial capacity of the importer to pay the international market price for food. To suggest that a policy of intrinsic responsibility is not applicable to cash imports would again seem to confuse the ecological carrying capacity of a country with its purchasing power. Indeed, the opportunity and the financial means to make purchases whenever desired can be even more potent disincentives for restraint than the unreliable prospect of foreign generosity. Thus, the logic of intrinsic responsibility would seem to dictate that a society be self-sufficient in the sense of not having to rely on either purchases or gifts of foreign food. In terms of the analogy, adding too many people to a lifeboat will sink it regardless of whether they pay their way aboard or are given a free ride.

The rationale for extending policies that incorporate intrinsic responsibility to commodities other than food, such as energy and mineral resources, also seems compelling. Although these nonfood resources are generally not as directly essential to human survival, they can be integral to the quality of life. More importantly, unlike food supplies that may be replenished, fossil fuels and mineral resources are generally nonrenewable. It follows from Hardin's ethic—"to be generous with one's own possessions is one thing; to be generous with posterity's is quite another"—that conservation of the finite reserves of nonrenewable resources should be a high priority consideration.[18] Moreover, as with food, it can be argued that international policies on nonrenewable resources that incorporate national self-sufficiency would serve as a strong incentive for conservation, while dependable foreign sources of raw materials at affordable prices would encourage high, wasteful rates of consumption that would rapidly deplete world reserves.

What are the implications of these extensions of Hardin's argument? First, questions may be raised about his singling out less developed nations for lacking "wise sovereigns" who can lead their populations to "equilibrate" below the carrying capacity of their countries.[19] Second, it becomes apparent that intrinsic responsibility is an impractical guide for food and resource policy in a highly interdependent world.

A quite different picture of relative degrees of self-reliance emerges if aid and trade are classified together as food inflows. Several developed countries are heavily dependent on foreign sources of food. Japan, the United Kingdom, Italy, and West Germany alone imported six times more grain than India and China between 1970 and 1974.[20] Japan, the leading food importer, relies on imports for more than 50 percent of its food requirements. If present trends continue into the mid-1980s, Japan's food deficit may approach the combined shortfall of all less developed countries.[21] Large purchases of food by the Soviet Union, which are discussed by Ole Holsti in the chapter that follows, were a major factor in exhausting grain reserves during the early 1970s. The United States is the leading food exporter, yet is third in food imports. America purchases approximately 40 percent of the beef entering into world trade, part of a pattern in which the developed world imports protein-rich foods in exchange for less nutritious grains.[22] It is also appropriate to note that industrialized nations with their technologically sophisticated factory ships have been the principal harvesters of fish taken in international waters.

The industrial countries consume a disproportionate share of energy and mineral resources. With only 5 percent of the world's population, the United States accounts for about one-fifth to one-third of the annual world consumption of these resources. The average American, European, or Japanese consumes as much as twenty times as much metallic ore as the average citizen in poor countries.[23] A substantial percentage of the resources consumed in the industrial world are imported, a proportion that will tend to increase as domestic reserves are depleted. Compared to most developed nations, the United States is relatively well endowed with resources, yet it became a net importer of minerals by the 1920s and is completely dependent on foreign mines for twenty-two of seventy-four nonenergy minerals important to an industrial society.[24] Moreover, the United States imports approximately 40 percent of its petroleum needs, a proportion that will continue to increase with rising energy demands and a decline in domestic petroleum production. Japan, which is in a far more vulnerable resource position, relies on foreign sources for nearly all of its iron ore and petroleum consumption, respectively. Most European countries are also quite heavily reliant on foreign sources for many key industrial raw materials.

The patterns of food and resource trade that have been noted undermine Hardin's characterization of the less developed societies as being the prime examples of ecological irresponsibility. Most developed countries would have to make major adjustments in their consumption practices if required to rely on their own natural resources.

What would be the implications of requiring all nations to live within the means of their resources? To pursue this question, let us slightly modify Hardin's lifeboat analogy, which, in its original version, makes no provision for interdependence or mutually beneficial cooperation. How many people would a group of three lifeboats support if we were to assume that one has the only containers of food, a second has the only containers of water, and the third has the only instrument that will open the containers? To require self-sufficiency would preclude the cooperation without which all would perish and the provisions go unused.

The modified analogy reflects the irregular distribution of natural resources on the planet. Interdependence is an inherent consequence of the fact that no country or region is completely self-sufficient in resources. Reserves of a number of vital natural resources are concentrated in a few countries, which are endowed with an abundance far greater than its residents can ever utilize, while other states have insufficient reserves, if any at all. Countries having an abundance of one type of natural resource may be deficient in almost all others. It is also possible that utilization of the resources of a country requires technologies or capital that are available only from foreign sources.

In regard to natural resources, the relationship of the developed to the less developed countries is not one of unidirectional dependency, as implied by Hardin's presentation of the lifeboat analogy. Most of the world's exportable reserves of such important resources as petroleum, copper, tin, cobalt, and bauxite are located in the Third World.[25] Overall, less developed countries account for an estimated 40 to 45 percent of the world reserves of major nonfuel minerals as compared to 35 percent in the Western industrial countries and 20 to 30 percent in the Communist states. Moreover, inasmuch as the less developed regions have not been as fully explored, it is quite probable that their undiscovered reserves of mineral resources are more extensive than those of the industrial regions.[26] For these reasons, it is unlikely that the developed countries with their high rates of resource consumption will be the first to seriously deplete their remaining domestic reserves.

Requiring self-sufficiency could hardly result in a very rational pattern of resource utilization. If the United States were to withhold food from foreign peoples in the interests of demographic responsibility, either surplus food would be wasted or large areas of land would have to be taken out of production. This would take place against the specter of substantial "dieback" of people in traditional food-importing countries. Conversely, Americans would for two reasons be unable to import commodities from abroad that they had grown accustomed to consuming: first, export earnings would be substantially reduced and, second, other nations would withhold commodities from the United States to force Americans to be self-reliant. Likewise, if the oil-producing countries were to withhold petroleum from world trade in the interests of energy conservation, the economies of the industrialized societies would collapse, with severe consequences for the entire international economic system. The OPEC members would have far more petroleum than could ever be consumed domestically, and they would not be permitted to import needed commodities that are unavailable within their countries. Additionally, many of the major mineral-exporting countries in the developing world would lose more than half of their foreign currency income under a system of enforced self-sufficiency.[27]

Resource interdependence dictates cooperative arrangements in which nations trade their surplus resources for those they lack domestically or for needed capital and technology. In doing so, the effective carrying capacity of the planet can be considerably increased. Conversely, a general practice of intrinsic responsibility, as logically extended to all types of natural resources whether traded or given in aid, would result in a very inefficient utilization of planetary resources and the sacrifice of many of the benefits of international trade currently being enjoyed by all nations.

The Vulnerability of the Industrial World

Let us return again to Hardin's more limited application of lifeboat ethics to food assistance. He offers no indication that the occupants of the American lifeboat could be seriously threatened by the swimmers who have been denied access. Would the analogy be more realistic, however, if it were possible for the desperate, frustrated swimmers to rock and capsize the American boat or to use a knife to slash and sink it?

Hostility in the Third World toward the rich in industrial societies has become increasingly pronounced, partly due to frustrations with the international economic order. It is widely perceived that the gross inequalities in the global distribution of income and wealth in the world are being perpetuated and even increased by exploitative relations between the rich and poor nations. This sense of alienation could sharply intensify if the United States and other developed countries adopted an overt policy of indifference to the plight of the disadvantaged of the world, especially after encouraging the expectation that the fruits of economic development can eventually be shared by all peoples.

Residents of the developed world should be concerned about these frustrations and hostilities for several reasons. Despite their overwhelming economic and military predominance, highly industrialized societies can be assailed by determined adversaries, even those with limited means. Let us briefly consider two such possibilities.

It has been hypothesized that the larger the quantity and variety of goods and services to which a population is accustomed, the greater will be their dependence upon external conditions and events and the more numerous will be their vulnerabilities.[28] Mention has been made previously of the growing importance of less developed countries as resource suppliers. Interruptions in the international flow of goods between nations, such as embargoes, sharp price increases, or cutbacks in production, can be very disruptive to the highly integrated economies of the developed world. Moreover, profitable investments by multinational corporations in the Third World could be jeopardized if North/South relations become seriously strained, particularly if political movements unsympathetic to foreign investment capitalize on the resentments toward the richer societies. Such developments would not only affect the economies of the parties directly involved but also reverberate throughout the highly integrated economic systems of the developed world.

Political extremists incensed by the magnitude of international injustices could cause considerable discomfort for rich, well-fed societies. A variety of forms of sabotage, terrorism, kidnapping, and blackmail could be used as part of a strategy to coercively redistribute world income. Foreign-based diplomats and corporate officials have already become targets for kidnapping and extortion. Chemical and biological weapons, which are relatively inexpensive to acquire, could have considerable nuisance potential if introduced into the water systems of large cities. It is not inconceivable that terrorist groups would acquire nuclear explosives and use them in attempts to extort concessions. Disrupters need not even be foreign based but may be domestic citizens who are strongly sympathetic to the plight of the less fortunate of the world.

High technology societies are particularly susceptible to sabotage.[29] Modern communication and transportation systems facilitate group formation among the radical fringes of societies. Recent experience with airline skyjacking reveals how difficult and costly protection against terrorists can be and how necessary international cooperation is toward this end. Saboteurs tend to have a tactical advantage over those working to maintain order. Even marginally adequate surveillance strategies require a sizable commitment of resources in the developed societies and necessitate the sacrifice of individual freedom and privacy.

A sensitivity to the needs of the poor and hungry of the world and a commitment to redress international economic injustice cannot insure that the vulnerabilities of the developed countries will not at times be exploited. Such a posture would, however, ameliorate some of the frustrations that give rise to terrorist activity and quite possibly prevent the potential problem from reaching unmanageable proportions.

The Alternative of a Regulated Global Commons

Discrediting lifeboat ethics as an approach to international policies on population, food, and resources does not alleviate the basic problem of political ecology identified by Hardin in his analogy of the village pasture. Unregulated, cooperative exchanges of natural resources between interdependent countries can rapidly deplete a number of resources if demand is heavy and producers are anxious to reap immediate payoffs. The challenge is to formulate alternatives to the lifeboat ethic that will insure a measure of ecological restraint while taking the realities of interdependence into account.

The many dimensions of international interdependence would appear to dictate a one-world strategy in which the entire planet is the basic unit of resource management. In the following pages, let us sketch a few characteristics of one such possibility, which will be referred to as the "regulated global commons" alternative.

In its purist form, a one-world design would incorporate features of the commons arrangement. Types of natural resources that are becoming scarce or are concentrated in only a few countries could be regarded as the common possessions of mankind. In effect, the "common heritage" principle that has been applied to certain ocean resources, as discussed in George Kent's essay herein, would be extended to some land-based resources.

If the resources of the planet are to be treated as a commons, some provisions must be made to avert the overshoot dynamic, or what Hardin refers to as the "tragedy of the commons." In the analogy, partitioning the village pasture into private sections, the approach adopted in lifeboat ethics, is not the only potential strategy for preventing an overshoot. As mentioned above, the commons system can be made ecologically viable if a village authority is established, empowered to institute and enforce regulations on the number of cattle each herdsman can graze, regardless of his financial means to purchase additional livestock. Implementing a regulated-commons system for world resource management would require an international regime authorized to limit the consumption of natural resources by each society, regardless of its economic capacity to purchase additional amounts.

Regulations pertaining to resource consumption could be designed to further any number of objectives in addition to conservation. For example, all societies could be guaranteed an equitable access to food and natural resources of the planet by making them available to poorer countries on a concessionary basis.

Decisions on the utilization of allocated resources could be left to the government of each state. In doing so, a modified system of intrinsic responsibility would be incorporated. But rather than having consumption limited to domestic resources, as in the lifeboat ethic, states would have to function with their assigned share of scarce natural resources, part of which would be from foreign sources. Thus, the restrictions could be expected to encourage population limitation and resource conservation. A variation on the regulated-commons arrangement would authorize an international regime to withhold some resources from nations that failed to limit population growth or to design their societies to be resource efficient.

Resistance to such an approach would probably be strongest among states that are rich in natural resources as well as among those that have become accustomed to high rates of resource consumption. The former would make two types of concessions under a regulated-commons approach. First, the resources located in their territories would no longer be regarded as their "private possession" but would become the common possession of mankind. Second, other states would be assured a share of these resources, thereby reducing opportunities to gain political leverage by threatening to withhold food or resources. Such a plan would not require that resource-rich states relinquish all rights of ownership. Revenues from the export of raw materials could continue to accrue to the producing state. Decisions on the development of the resources could be left to the producing states as long as they are consistent with the guidelines set to protect the interests of the broader community. Moreover, these concessions would to some extent be balanced by the benefits of a stable income from their primary commodities and secure access to the food or resources they must import.

Developed countries with the means to purchase immense quantities of resources would presumably resist the constraints on their consumption required by a regulated-commons arrangement. The trade-off for these countries would be a more secure access to somewhat smaller quantities of resources at more predictable prices. Reductions in resource consumption by industrial societies seem an inevitability, regardless of whether programs are undertaken to manage natural resources internationally. A regulated commons system would primarily affect the timing of these reductions. What's more, the transition to a steady-state economic system could be more orderly and gradual than would be likely if present trends in consumption are allowed to continue. Industrial states would also stand to benefit from less hostile relationships between developed and less developed nations that would probably follow from such an arrangement.

A dilemma is posed by industrial societies that have become accustomed to high levels of resource consumption. The perceived legitimacy of any resource allocation system depends in large part upon how equitable it appears to the participants. A complete equalization of per capita resource consumption would not, however, appear to be a realistic possibility, at least for a considerable period of time. To stand any chance of acceptance in the industrial world, allowances would have to be made for the resource inefficiencies built into their infrastructure that cannot be immediately altered. In recognition of this problem, provision should be made for encouraging industrial societies to gradually reduce their consumption of scarce natural resources. Equalizing levels of resource consumption up to those enjoyed in the developed world would result in a very rapid depletion of reserves of petroleum and some minerals at the expense of future generations. Third World countries could be compensated for lower allotments of resources by concerted international efforts to formulate development strategies that can provide an attractive quality of life on a relatively low level of natural resource consumption.[30]

One-World Tendencies

One-world approaches to resource management can be viewed as polar opposites to lifeboat ethics. As laid out in the previous section, the proposals for a regulated commons are as extreme a form of globalism as lifeboat ethics is a representative of nationalism. Admittedly, the full implementation of such an ideal type is probably an impossibility. It is conceivable, however, that some elements of the strategy may be incorporated to conserve some types of scarce resources.

In making his case for lifeboat ethics, Hardin tersely rejects the regulated-commons approach, advancing little more reason than his impression that the United Nations is a "toothless tiger."[31] Admittedly, the United Nations system in its present form is not equipped to play a strong, effective role in food and resource management. Inadequacies in the existing system are hardly sufficient cause, however, for dismissing the possibility of the design and implementation of international institutions and policies that could be potent instruments for confronting ecological problems in the future.

Developments over the past decade give reason to believe not only that some elements of a one-world approach to environmental management are a possibility but that there is even some international momentum in this direction. Despite a long history of environmental warnings, it has been little more than a decade since a UNESCO resolution was adopted that recognized the environment as an object of international policy and called for the convening of the Biosphere Conference in Paris in 1968.[32] The United Nations Conference on the Human Environment held in Stockholm in 1972 has been the most prominent manifestation of an emerging worldwide commitment to seek solutions to these problems through international cooperation. More specific international environmental problems have been considered at the subsequent United Nations conferences on population, food, raw materials and development, use of the seas, human settlements, water, desertification, and energy. Not only have these conferences drawn worldwide attention to ecological problems, but new international institutions, most notably the United Nations

Environmental Program and the World Food Council, have been established for implementing and coordinating international environmental policies.

Two perspectives can be taken on the recent international response to ecological problems. Focusing on what the conferences and institutions have failed to accomplish may lead one to conclude that little more has been done than to preserve national prerogatives on environmental affairs. A more optimistic inference may be drawn if the activities of the 1970s are viewed as the first stages in a transformation that may take decades to accomplish. Because environmental factors underlie so much of modern civilization, it is inevitable that ecological policies will have many significant, interrelated social implications. In view of these complexities of ecological problems and the fundamental nature of the societal changes they necessitate, it is to be expected that establishing the institutions and policies integral to an effective one-world response would be a lengthy transition process. From such a perspective, a broad-based recognition of planetary ecological problems, the formation of general principles to guide future discussions and policies, and the establishment of some international institutions and programs are as much as could be expected in less than a decade.

The preceding analysis has not been presented to establish either that tendencies toward a one-world response to ecological problems will continue to gain momentum or, if so, that the response will be equal to the formidable task of international resource management. Despite the apparent need for a coordinated international response and apparent movement in this direction, there are also tendencies toward a pursuit of narrowly defined national interests that may strengthen during times of imminent food and resource scarcities. The critical question is whether political leaders will come to a realization that national and global interests are not irreconcilable but complements to one another.

Global Food Problems and Soviet Agriculture

Ole R. Holsti

There is not one but many food problems,
and a surprisingly large number of them
are the result of human and governmental
decisions rather than of immutable forces.
Harry Walters

Introduction: The Problem

What obligations does a nation have toward the international
community? Few would disagree that it should refrain from attacking
or otherwise directly attempting to harm the legitimate interests of its
neighbors. There would be less agreement on the proposition that a
nation may also have obligations arising out of domestic institutions,
policies, and practices that contribute to or render more difficult the
solution of serious international problems, even indirectly. For
example, does a nation with a high population growth rate have any
obligations to undertake a serious birth control program? Unless it
does so, may it legitimately demand international assistance, citing
the economic plight of its citizens as the basis for its claim? Does a
nation that uses a disproportionate share of the world's nonrenewable fossil fuels have an obligation to reduce domestic consumption?
Unless it does so, may it legitimately demand access to foreign
sources at a congenial price?

A basic tenet of sovereignty holds that a nation's domestic
institutions are strictly a matter of internal rather than international
concern. Nevertheless, there has been a gradual, albeit uneven,
recognition that some domestic institutions and practices may have
sufficiently important international consequences that, claims of

sovereignty notwithstanding, they may become the concern of other nations. For example, French atmospheric nuclear tests in the South Pacific, although conducted on French possessions, elicited both official and unofficial protests from New Zealand, Canada, Peru, and other nations. The refusal of the Smith govenrment in Rhodesia to grant political equality to the black majority has aroused most members of the United Nations to place economic sanctions on Rhodesia. Although it is not difficult to find cases in which the international community has been less vigilant—for example, the genocidal policies of the present Khmer Rouge government in Cambodia have aroused few if any protests—there appears to be an unmistakable trend toward erosion of an absolute definition of sovereignty.

Thus, a few decades ago questions such as those on population or resource policies might have been found only in an abstract treatise on international ethics. Today they are increasingly likely to appear high on the agendas of foreign offices and international organizations.

This chapter focuses on an issue of this type: Does a nation have an obligation to organize its agricultural system in a way that enables it to contribute to rather than detract from the world's food supply? The specific proposition to be examined is this: The inability of the Soviet Union to produce consistent agricultural surpluses—and, more seriously, the Soviet policy of periodically importing large amounts of grains—constitutes a significant threat to the welfare of the international community.

By organizing the agricultural sector to satisfy its ideological preferences and political needs, the Soviet ruling class has prevented the USSR from being a consistent net contributor to the world's food supply. Worse yet, by periodically entering the international market to buy vast amounts of wheat and other cereals, the Soviet Union is contributing at least indirectly to malnutrition in many parts of the world, and it is creating a major barrier against establishment of the food reserves necessary to cope with future emergency situations arising from regional crop failures.[1]

In light of recent record grain crops in North America, food shortages may seem to be an unlikely candidate for any list of potential international catastrophes. A few decades ago, only Western Europe was unable to produce enough food to feed its population, and periodically the "agricultural problem" in North America has referred to the cost of coping with mounting surpluses.[2]

Recently, several analysts have published reports indicating that food supplies are likely to be quite ample in the future.[3] Optimistic appraisals of the future are based on the premise that increasing use of fertilizers, machines, and irrigation, combined with the opening up of new lands for agricultural production, will suffice to prevent malnutrition and starvation on a massive scale. Counterbalancing these views, however, are the recent estimate that 460 million persons are malnourished[4] and some rather pessimistic projections about the future of agriculture.

There are indications that merely increasing technological inputs may be insufficient to cope with the problem, may be too costly for most nations, or would entail side effects that are only slightly less unacceptable than widespread malnutrition. For example, the "green revolution" has resulted in higher crop yields in several parts of the world, but the high cost and scarcity of energy place this type of agriculture beyond the means of many nations. Although chemical fertilizers can significantly increase productivity, they are among the commodities whose prices have risen most dramatically in recent years. Prices aside, the environmental consequences of constantly increasing fertilizer usage may create other problems—for example, depletion of the ozone shield in the atmosphere that reduces harmful radiation.[5] Finally, although pesticides have contributed to dramatically better yields, there is also some evidence that insects are developing resistance to these chemical agents.[6] These may not all be insurmountable problems—for example, nonchemical forms of insect control may prove to be more effective and less potentially damaging to the environment—and some of the more dire warnings about the unintended effects of technology may well prove unfounded. Nevertheless, these examples suggest that perhaps one should err on the side of skepticism rather than complacency about the proposition that technology and/or high energy inputs into agriculture will suffice to make possible a nutritionally adequate diet for everyone.[7]

It may be possible to increase land under cultivation, but erosion, loss of irrigated land owing to waterlogging and salinity, and the spread of desert areas may offset much of the gain. Agricultural lands may be taken out of production by strip-mining, urbanization, and other demands related to population pressures and energy shortages. In the United States, rising grain prices and a period of unusually good weather have encouraged farmers to undertake "fence post to fence post" cultivation of marginal areas. If these lands are left fallow, grasses permit them to resist windstorms, but when they are plowed, droughts combined with high winds rip off the fertile topsoil in devastating dust storms. In 1974 the average loss of topsoil in these newly sown lands was 27 tons per hectare, more than twice the level considered tolerable by conservation officials, and in some cases the loss by erosion was over 300 tons per hectare.[8]

Even seemingly minor changes in weather patterns can have catastrophic consequences for agricultural production. Recent decades —especially the 1960s—have been marked by remarkably benign weather; the odds against having climate as favorable as that of the 1960s have been calculated to be on the order of 10,000 to 1.[9] Several recent reports suggest that with respect to both short-term and longer-run cycles we may be entering a period that is much less favorable for agricultural production. Whether or not the frigid winter of 1977 marks the beginning of a major unfavorable weather cycle, it would seem unrealistic to assume that the exceptionally favorable experience of recent decades will continue indefinitely.

Most importantly, even under the most optimistic demographic assumptions, population growth will continue well into the twenty-first century, if not beyond. Having reached the four billion level in 1976, the world's population can be expected to double again in roughly thirty-five years.

Several premises form the starting point of the analysis. First, one need not necessarily accept the more apocalyptic or deterministic prophecies that have become fashionable in recent years to recognize that global food production is likely to appear on any short list of the more important international problems facing mankind during the coming decades. Those who argue that the problem is merely one of distribution ("The problem is that the food is here and the hungry are there") and not of production are likely to be proved seriously and dangerously in error.

Second, although some areas of the world will always be more productive than others, excessive dependence on surpluses produced by any one nation or region is undesirable. In 1973 American farms accounted for 36 percent of world production of wheat, corn, soybeans, rice, and sorghum. Almost a third of this harvest was sold abroad, accounting for 58 percent of the world export market.[10] Although 1973 was not a typical year, these figures point to a potentially dangerous degree of dependence on a single source. Vagaries of weather can result in significantly reduced harvests in even the most efficient and productive areas of the world. Two or three consecutive years of substandard American harvests would almost certainly have adverse international consequences, especially if combined with a major crop failure in another region. A recurrence of the devastating weather conditions that helped create the dust bowl of the 1930s would be a crippling blow to any efforts to create adequate food reserves. We cannot dismiss with complete confidence predictions that the next phase in the long-term weather cycle will be far less favorable for agriculture than the immediate past. Even after the record American harvests of 1975, world grain reserves for emergencies were reduced to a thirty-day supply, largely because of Soviet purchases.

Third, American grain yields have increased dramatically during the past three decades, but there can be no assurance that this trend will continue. Indeed, barring some major breakthrough in the science and technology of agriculture, the far safer assumption is that future increases in yield will be marginal, and perhaps insufficient to keep up with growing demands. Moreover, although food is a renewable resource, many fertilizers, pesticides, and the fuels necessary to operate modern farm equipment are not. Because all of these depend to some extent on petroleum, there is reason to fear that the period of low-cost increases in food production is probably behind us. According to one estimate, tripling of fuel costs will ultimately result in doubling of food prices.[11]

Fourth, a long-run solution to the world food problem will require not only that the Soviet Union become self-sufficient in the production of cereals but also that the USSR join the United States, Canada, Australia, and Argentina as consistent net exporters of grains on a massive scale.

The Evidence

In order to make a plausible case in support of the proposition cited earlier, it is necessary to demonstrate that:

1. There is a significant gap between the actual and the potential production of Soviet agricultural goods. Comparative time-series data on agricultural production in Russia and elsewhere will be presented.

2. The causes of the shortfall of Soviet agricultural production can be identified. In order to assess the line of reasoning to be developed here, the most desirable evidence is data that would reveal directly the impact of Soviet agricultural institutions and policies on the motivations and performance of farm workers, managers, and bureaucrats. An alternative strategy is to assess competing explanations for the poor performance of Soviet agriculture. If they are found wanting, then at least a tentative network of indirect, circumstantial evidence in support of the hypothesis will have been erected.

3. The resources that would enable the Soviet Union to cope with its agricultural problem are in fact available. It must be shown that any shortfall in agricultural production cannot be traced to factors that are beyond human control (geography or climate, for example) or that may depend upon unavailable critical resources such as farm machinery, fertilizers, pesticides, or scientific and technical knowledge.

4. The consequences of Russia's inability to cope with its agricultural problems are international in character and not merely confined to Soviet society.

Soviet geography and climate do not compare favorably with those of the most productive areas of American agriculture. It is therefore neither fair nor instructive to make *direct comparisons* between yields achieved today by American farmers and their Soviet counterparts. However, there are other types of analyses that may be undertaken.

First, we can compare the *rate of increase* in Soviet production with that of the United States. This procedure permits each nation to compete against its own past record, factoring out any advantages of climate or soil that may favor the American farmer. We can further protect ourselves against unwarranted acceptance of the hypothesis by selecting a base-line period in which Russian performance was, by every account, very mediocre. With respect to agricultural production, 1913—the last peacetime year prior to the Bolshevik revolution—has been described as "a mediocre czarist year that Soviet statisticians cite as a prerevolutionary base to demonstrate that nation's progress under communism."[12] In 1913 American agriculture was already relatively advanced in the use of farm machinery, fertilizers, and other components of modern farming, whereas Russian agriculture was exceptionally backward and inefficient, even by the standards of the time. The most fertile chernozem soils were

Table 1. Agricultural Production and Yield: Russia and USSR

	1913	1921	1925	1930	1935	1940	1950
Total sown area	118.2		105.4			151.8	146.3
Total area in grain	104.6	59.9				110.5	103.2
Wheat							
production	26.3	6.5	19.9	26.9	30.8	31.7	31.1
area	33.0		20.8	33.8		40.3	
yield	0.80		0.96	0.80		0.79	
Rye							
production	22.7	9.9	23.1	23.6	21.4	21.0	18.0
area	28.2		27.3	28.8		23.1	
yield	0.80		0.85	0.82		0.91	
Corn							
production	2.1		4.5	2.7	2.8	5.1	6.6
area	2.2		3.1	3.9		3.6	
yield	0.95		1.45	0.69		1.42	
Barley							
production	12.1	2.5	6.1	6.8	8.1	12.0	
area	12.7		5.9	7.4		10.7	
yield	0.95		1.03	0.92		1.12	
Oats							
production	17.0	5.8	11.6	16.6	18.3	16.8	13.0
area	19.1		11.6	17.9		20.2	
yield	0.89		1.00	0.93		0.83	
All grains							
production	86.0						
Potatoes							
production	31.9		34.9	49.5	69.7	75.9	
area	4.2			5.8		7.7	
yield	7.60			8.53		9.86	

Sources: United Nations Statistical Year Book (various years); *Statesman's Year Book* (various years); Kenneth R. Whiting, *The Soviet Union Today* (New York: Praeger, 1962), p. 174; Inna Kniazeff, "L'Agriculture sovietique eu 1963–1964: Premier bilan de la politique agricole de N. S. Khrouchtchev," *Annuaire de l'U.R.S.S., 1965* (Paris: Edition du Centre National de la Recherche Scientifique, 1965); Howard P. Kennard, comp. and ed., *The Russian Year Book, 1914* (London: Eyre and Spottiswood, 1914); Roy D. Laird, "Prospects for Soviet Agriculture," *Problems of Communism*, 20, no. 5 (1971): 31–40; *New York Times*, 3 Nov., 1977, 12 Dec., 1977.

Note: Production = million metric tons
　　　Area = hectares (2.471 acres)
　　　Yield = tons per hectare

1955	1960	1965	1970	1971	1972	1973	1974	1975	1976	1977
146.5	203.0		223.5	224.9						
127.5	121.7									
47.3	64.3	59.7	99.7	98.8	86.0	109.7	83.9	66.3	96.9	105.0
61.1	60.4									
0.77	1.06									
16.5	16.4	16.2	13.0	12.8	9.6	10.7	NA	NA		
19.0	16.2									
0.87	1.01									
14.6	9.8	8.0	9.4	8.6	9.8	13.4	12.1	7.3		
8.9	11.2									
1.64	0.88									
10.4	16.0	20.3	38.2	34.6	36.8	55.0	54.2	35.8		
9.3	11.0									
1.12	1.45									
11.8	12.0	6.2	14.2	14.7	14.1	17.4	15.3	12.5		
15.0	12.8									
0.79	0.94									
			186.8	181.0	165.0	222.5	195.5	104.0	223.8	194.0
71.8	84.3	88.7	96.8	92.7	78.3	107.7	81.0	88.7		
9.1	9.1									
7.89	9.26									

being depleted by erosion and exhausted by annual planting of
wheat. Machinery[13] and chemical fertilizers were virtually unknown
on Russian farms, and even the use of manures[14] was severely
restricted by the shortage of livestock. As one contemporary source
described the situation in 1913, "the yield per acre of the Russian
cereals remains low to a degree which is profoundly uneconomical."[15]
Hence, during the past six decades, the Soviet Union has had "an
easy act to follow" with respect to improving the level of agricultural
production. Moreover, during much of the period in question,
American farmers have sought to limit production of many key crops
in order to prevent prices from falling below production costs. These
factors should bias comparisons against rather than in support of the
hypothesis.

Comparing Soviet and Canadian agriculture may provide some
additional insight. Much of the land in both nations lies too far north
for optimal farming. Indeed, whereas most of the USSR lies north of
the forty-second parallel, virtually all of Canada lies north of the
forty-ninth parallel.

Table 1 provides some figures on Soviet production of basic grains
and potatoes. The data are not wholly free of difficulties. They have
had to be drawn from several sources, no one of which is complete.
For example, United Nations figures for the USSR are unavailable
prior to 1952. Moreover, the reliability of Soviet agricultural statistics
is not beyond dispute.[16] One source suggests that harvests are
typically overstated by about 15 percent.[17] Finally, figures for
the interwar period are not strictly comparable with those for the
post-1945 period. In 1940 the USSR annexed Estonia, Latvia, and
Lithuania, and 16,173 square miles of Finnish territory were taken as
a result of the treaty ending the "Winter War." The Baltic region
included some of the more productive agricultural areas in Eastern
Europe. In 1939 a large portion of eastern Poland was also added to
Soviet territory when that nation was partitioned by Hitler and
Stalin. These problems may render the absolute figures in table 1 less
than completely reliable, but any resulting biases tend to work
against rather than in support of the hypothesis.

Production figures for the Soviet Union, Canada, and the United
States indicate that, although Soviet harvests and yields per hectare
have increased since the czarist era, the rate of increase lags far
behind that of the two North American nations (tables 1–3). Even if
we discount the disastrous Soviet harvest in 1975, the results are far

Table 2. Agricultural Yield and Production for Selected Crops: Canada

	1910	1920	1930	1940	1950	1960	1970	1975
Wheat								
yield	14.1	14.5	16.0	18.8	17.1	21.1	26.6	NA
production	132	263	398	540	462	490	332	665
Barley								
yield	22.4	24.8	24.3	24.0	25.9	28.1	41.4	NA
production	29	63	135	104	171	207	415	442
Oats								
yield	28.1	33.5	31.9	30.9	36.3	40.9	51.5	NA
production	244	530	423	380	420	456	367	308
Rye								
yield	13.4	17.5	15.2	13.5	11.4	18.6	22.1	NA
production	2	11	22	14	13	10	22	NA
Potatoes								
yield	64	72	84	78	192	144	171	NA
production	30	NA	48	42	97	45	55	60

Sources: *Canada Year Book* (various years); *Agricultural Statistics*, 1974; *United Nations Statistical Year Book* (various years).

Note: Yield = bushels per acre, except cwt per acre for potatoes.
Production = millions of bushels, except millions of cwt for potatoes.
NA = not available.

from impressive.[18] Admittedly, the Soviet regime has often given higher priority to heavy industry and the military than to the agricultural sector. It is also true that increasing land under cultivation may add rather marginal soil on which yields could be expected to be below average. Nevertheless, using only the 1913 acreage as a base line, we could have expected far higher yields than have been achieved in the subsequent decades because there is no objective reason why Soviet production should not have improved at a rate comparable to the increases recorded in the United States or Canada. Indeed, to repeat a point made earlier, there are at least two reasons the rate of increase in the Soviet Union should in fact have exceeded that of the latter two nations. First, the 1913 base line for Russia was far lower than the comparable figures for the United States or Canada as agricultural methods in the latter two countries were far more efficient. Second, for much of the subsequent period a primary goal of American and Canadian agriculture was to *limit* production in

Table 3. Agricultural Yield and Production for Selected Crops: United States

	1913	1920	1930	1940	1950	1960
Wheat						
production	751	843	887	815	1,019	1,355
acreage	52.0	62.4	62.6	53.3	61.6	51.9
yield	14.4	13.3	14.2	15.3	16.5	26.1
Rye						
production	40	62	45	40	21	33
acreage	3.1	4.8	3.6	3.2	1.7	1.7
yield	12.9	12.9	12.5	12.5	12.4	19.6
Corn						
production	2,273	3,071	3,080	2,457	3,075	3,907
acreage	100.2	101.4	101.5	86.4	81.8	71.4
yield	22.7	30.3	20.5	29.9	37.6	54.7
Barley						
production	158	171	301	311	304	429
acreage	7.7	7.4	12.6	13.5	11.2	13.9
yield	20.5	23.1	23.9	23.0	27.1	31.0
Oats						
production	1,039	1,444	1,275	1,246	1,369	1,153
acreage	37.2	42.7	39.8	35.4	39.8	26.6
yield	27.9	33.8	32.0	31.2	34.8	43.4
Rice						
production	11	23	20	24	39	55
acreage	0.7	1.3	1.0	1.1	1.6	1.6
yield	0.65	0.79	0.89	0.91	1.09	1.53
Soybeans						
production			14	78	299	555
acreage			1.1	4.8	13.8	23.7
yield			12.7	16.3	21.7	23.5
Potatoes						
production	199.5	221.3	206.3	226.2	259.1	257.1
acreage	3.5	3.3	3.1	2.8	1.7	1.4
yield	57.0	67.1	66.5	80.8	152.4	185

Sources: The Statistical History of the United States from Colonial Times to the Present (Stamford, Conn.: Fairfield Publishers, 1965), Series K265–94; *Agricultural Statistics*, 1976.

Note: Yield = tons/acre (rice); hundredweight/acre (potatoes); bushels/acre (all other).

Production = metric tons (rice); hundredweights (potatoes); bushels (all other).

1970	1971	1972	1973	1974	1975
1,352	1,618	1,544	1,705	1,796	2,133
43.6	47.7	47.3	53.9	65.6	69.7
31.0	33.9	32.7	31.8	27.4	30.6
37	49	29	26	19	18
1.4	1.8	1.1	1.0	0.9	0.8
25.8	28.1	26.9	25.4	21.5	22.0
4,152	5,641	5,573	5,647	4,663	5,766
57.4	64.0	57.4	61.9	65.4	66.9
72.4	88.1	97.1	91.2	71.4	86.2
416	464	423	422	304	383
9.7	10.2	9.7	10.5	8.2	8.7
42.8	45.7	43.6	40.3	37.2	44.0
917	881	692	669	614	657
18.6	15.8	13.5	14.1	13.2	13.7
49.2	55.9	51.2	47.4	46.5	48.1
84	86	85	93	112	128
1.8	1.8	1.8	2.2	2.5	2.8
2.06	2.11	2.10	1.91	2.01	2.07
1,127	1,176	1,271	1,547	1,214	1,521
42.2	42.7	45.7	55.8	52.4	53.6
26.7	27.5	27.8	27.7	23.2	28.4
325.8	319.4	296.0	299.4	342.1	315.6
1.4	1.4	1.3	1.3	1.4	1.3
229	230	236	230	246	251

order to prevent prices from falling below production costs, thereby driving farmers off the land. These figures are all the more striking when one recalls that the sown area in Russia has doubled since 1913, whereas that in the United States has declined sharply for many of the commodities listed in table 3. Yet between 1913 and 1970–77 total Soviet grain production has slightly more than doubled (an annual increase of well under 2 percent) whereas that in Canada has risen by about double the Soviet rate, and the comparable American figure is a sixteenfold increase.

What are the causes of this very unimpressive record? The hypothesis proposed earlier suggests that the answer is to be found in structural features of the Soviet system of agriculture. But before accepting this interpretation we need to consider whether a more parsimonious explanation may be found in a lack of resources or in some other factors that may be beyond the control of the Soviet leadership. More specifically, competing hypotheses might explain the data by reference to (1) shortages of investment and manpower, (2) insufficient farm machinery, (3) shortages of chemical fertilizers, or (4) inadequate scientific and technical information about modern agriculture.

Soviet agricultural difficulties cannot be attributed to shortages of capital investment or manpower. Cultivated area in the Soviet Union almost doubled between 1913 and 1972, and irrigated land has increased from 4 million hectares to over 12 million hectares since 1913. During the current five-year plan, capital outlays for agriculture have totaled more than 131 billion rubles ($175 billion).[19] Fully 31 percent of fixed capital and 25 percent of the Soviet labor force is employed in agriculture; in each case the comparable figure for the United States is 4 percent.[20] Depending upon the commodity, the labor input per unit of output on Soviet state and collective farms exceeds that of American farms by from 60 percent to 1,530 percent. For the commodities of primary concern in this discussion—grain and potatoes—the labor-production ratios on state farms exceed those of the United States by 80 percent and 320 percent, and the ratios for collective farms are 630 percent and 410 percent higher.[21]

An alternative explanation for the poor performance of Soviet agriculture is insufficient access to modern farm equipment. The data do not, however, provide much support for this interpretation. Recall that prior to World War I tractors and combines were virtually unknown in Russia. Although complete data for the interwar period are unavailable, there has been a rather dramatic growth during the last quarter of a century in the amount of modern farm equipment in use on Soviet farms (table 4).

In comparison, the period of most rapid mechanization of American agriculture appears to have taken place much earlier, and during the past two decades there has been relatively little growth in the number of farm machines in use. For example, during the mid-1950s tractors in use on American farms outnumbered those in the USSR by a ratio of more that 5.5:1. By 1975 that ratio had been reduced to 1.7:1. Although these figures tell us nothing about the quality of the equipment, they do suggest that difficulties in Soviet agriculture are not primarily attributable to lack of modern farm machinery. Indeed, there is at least anecdotal evidence that the problem arises not from insufficient equipment but, rather, from a lack of incentives to keep the equipment in good repair and bureaucratic inefficiencies that prevent its optimal use.

Another potential explanation is that insufficient use of chemical fertilizers is the primary cause of poor harvests. There is no dearth of evidence that this was in fact one of the main reasons for agricultural backwardness during the czarist period. Even during the years immediately following World War II, application of such key fertilizers as phosphates, nitrogen, and potash was at a relatively low level compared to the United States or Canada. Yet since that time, and especially during the post-Khrushchev era, the use of all fertilizers has grown at an impressive rate, far outstripping the growth rate in the United States (table 5). In 1950 American farmers used 17.5 million metric tons of fertilizers, more than three times the amount used on Soviet farms. By 1973 the absolute level of fertilizer consumption in the Soviet Union (59.9 million metric tons) had far surpassed the United States (37.9 million metric tons), and the trend is continuing. Although lower fertilizer usage per hectare by the Soviet farmer may account for some of the production gap between him and his American counterpart, it does not by itself explain the unimpressive record of the past six decades.

Finally, it does not appear that we can attribute the poor performance of Soviet agriculture to inadequate scientific and technical knowledge. The USSR has access to the same knowledge that is available in the United States, Canada, and elsewhere. The genetic theories of the Lysenko school may have set back Soviet agriculture, but Lysenko's influence appears to have declined after

Table 4. Agricultural Machinery in Use: USSR and United States (thousands)

	1913	1940	1955	1960	1965	1970	1971	1972	1973	1975
Soviet Union										
Tractors				1,112	1,613	1,977	2,045	2,112	2,180	2,400
Harvesters				497	520	623	639	656	670	690
Production of tractors	0	48	170	292						

	1913	1920	1930	1940	1950	1955	1960	1965	1970	1975
United States										
Tractors	14	246	920	1,545	3,394	4,345	4,688	4,787	4,619	4,109
Trucks	10	139	900	1,047	2,207	2,675	2,834	3,030	2,984	2,870
Grain combines	1	4	61	190	714	980	1,042	910	790	655
Corn pickers		10	50	110	456	688	792	690	635	585

Sources: For Soviet Union data: *United Nations Statistical Year Book* (various years); Whiting, *The Soviet Union Today*, p. 202. For United States data: *The Statistical History of the United States from Colonial Times to the Present*, Series K150–51, K152; *Statistical Abstract of the United States, 1974* (Washington, D.C.: Government Printing Office, 1974), p. 610; *United Nations Statistical Year Book* (various years); *Agricultural Statistics*, 1976.

Table 5. Fertilizer Consumption: USSR and United States (million metric tons)

	1913	1920	1930	1940	1950	1955	1960	1965	1970	1973	1975
Soviet Union											
All fertilizers	0.19			3.2	5.3			27.0	45.6	59.9	NA
Phosphates						0.68	0.82	1.50	2.21	2.73	3.83
Nitrogen						0.48	0.77	2.28	4.61	6.22	7.36
Potash						0.73	0.77	1.89	2.57	3.61	5.00

	1913	1920	1930	1940	1950	1955	1960	1965	1970	1973	1975
United States											
All fertilizers	5.8	6.5	7.4	.7.6	17.5	19.4	21.3	27.4	34.7	37.9	36.8
Phosphates						2.13	2.33	3.18	4.15	4.61	4.08
Nitrogen						1.75	2.48	4.19	6.76	7.51	7.79
Potash						1.70	1.95	2.56	3.66	4.21	4.04

Sources: For Soviet Union data: *United Nations Statistical Year Book* (various years). For United States data: *United Nations Statistical Year Book* (various years); *Agricultural Statistics*, 1976.

the death of Stalin in 1953, and by 1965 he had lost his position. In any case, any harmful impact of Lysenko and his theories would actually support rather than detract from the proposition under consideration. That is, the forced collectivization of Soviet farms and the prominence of Lysenko are both examples of efforts to make agriculture serve political or ideological ends.

Other Evidence

To this point the analysis has assessed and rejected the thesis that lack of resources is sufficient to explain the poor performance of Soviet agriculture. There are a few additional bits and pieces of indirect evidence that may have some bearing on this issue.

1. Soviet farmers are permitted to cultivate small "private plots" on their own time and to consume or sell the yield. The private plots, limited in 1939 to one and a half hectares or one-quarter hectare on irrigated land, constitute only 1.4 percent of the agricultural area and 3.2 percent of the sown land. Despite periodic official efforts to restrict them, the private plots account for approximately 32 percent of gross agricultural output.[22] They are typically used to produce fruit and vegetables rather than grain (table 6), but even for a single commodity the disparities in yields are striking. In 1959 the potato yield on private plots was 4.28 tons per acre, whereas on state and collective farms it was 2.67 tons.[23] Such data suggest that when given even a modicum of decision-making freedom and incentives, Soviet farmers are capable of producing harvests that far outstrip those of the collective and state farms. These figures provide support for the observation that "the quickest way of ensuring an increase in production of many much-needed items is to permit some enlargement of private farming activities."[24] If all agricultural lands were returned to farmers, what would be the consequences? One can only speculate, but it seems a reasonable guess that production would improve spectacularly.

2. The Bolshevik revoluton and the subsequent civil war seriously damaged agricultural production. The cultivated area fell, and the grain harvests of 1919 and 1920 were but a small fraction of that achieved in 1913, or even in the midst of war in 1916 (74 million metric tons). Efforts by the Lenin government to establish collective

farms were an almost total failure. As a result, the New Economic Policy, put into force in 1921, permitted peasants to keep their land and to sell their produce. With these incentives, production improved dramatically; by 1925 and 1926 harvests were almost back to the prewar and prerevolution levels. In 1930, however, full collectivization of agriculture was ordered to be completed by 1932. During that period, not only did grain harvests fall off, but many peasants killed off their livestock rather than contribute them to the collectives.

3. The private sector in Polish agriculture plays a far more significant role than it does in the USSR. Polish farmers usually come closer to meeting production quotas than do their counterparts in the Soviet Union. Although cross-national comparisons of this type should be made with great caution (for example, it may be that Polish quotas are typically set at a more modest level than those in the USSR), the point may at least be suggestive. Soviet agricultural production also suffers in comparison with that of other Communist

Table 6. Sources of Soviet Agricultural Production for Various Commodities (percentages)

	Grain	Cotton	Sugar Beets	Potatoes	Vege-tables	Meat	Milk	Eggs	Wool
1962									
State farms	40	18	7	10	30	26	21	13	32
Collective farms	58	82	93	20	28	30	34	11	46
Private plots	2	0	0	70	42	44	45	70	22
1967									
State farms	43	20	10	14	34	31	27	24	40
Collective farms	55	80	90	23	26	29	34	13	40
Private plots	2	0	0	63	40	40	39	63	20
1971									
State farms	46	24	8	14	37	32	29	36	42
Collective farms	53	76	92	23	26	33	36	14	38
Private plots	1	0	0	63	37	35	35	50	20
1973									
State farms	46	26	9	16	39	33	29	43	43
Collective farms	53	74	91	23	37	34	38	14	36
Private plots	1	0	0	61	34	33	33	43	21

Source: Statesman's Year Book (various years).

nations that have taken a less rigid form of collectivization or
that have maintained significant elements of free enterprise in
agriculture.[25]

4. American corporations that have entered the food business have
found that it is wise to stay out of the farming end of the enterprise,
in part because persons at corporate headquarters are less able to
make sound decisions than the farmer himself.[26] Agriculture is an
enterprise that is poorly suited to the bureaucratic routines and centralized management that typically characterize large organizations,
be they corporations or governments.

5. Further insight can be derived from an examination in more
detail of data for Estonia, Latvia, and Lithuania. These nations were
a part of the Russian Empire until the end of World War I, at which
time they achieved independence. The 1939 Nazi-Soviet Pact placed
Estonia and Latvia within the Soviet sphere of influence, and five
weeks later a secret protocol to that treaty transferred Lithuania from
the Nazi to the Soviet sphere. In October 1939 the three Baltic nations
were forced to sign mutual assistance treaties with the Soviet Union
that permitted the latter to station troops within their frontiers. In
June 1940 the Soviet army occupied Estonia, Latvia, and Lithuania.
Rigged elections a month later resulted in governments that
"petitioned" to be incorporated into the USSR, requests that were
"granted" in August 1940. Forcible collectivization of agriculture in
these three nations was completed in 1949. Estonia, Latvia, and
Lithuania thus provide an interesting test case of the effects of Soviet-
style collectivization, as we can compare results for (a) 1913, the
favorite base line of Soviet statisticians; (b) the interwar years during
which Estonia, Latvia, and Lithuania were independent; and (c) the
three and a half decades since the Baltic nations were annexed by the
Soviet Union.

The results are summarized in table 7. Harvests in 1913 produced
mediocre results. After achieving independence, and during the two
decades prior to annexation by the USSR, results in each of the three
nations improved, both in total production and in yields per hectare.
In some cases the improvement was rather dramatic. Since Soviet
annexation, the area under cultivation has grown in each case, but
the rate of production increase has lagged behind what might have
been expected.

Students of Soviet agriculture have advanced various explanations

Table 7. Agricultural Production: Estonia, Latvia and Lithuania (thousand metric tons)

	1913	1920–1924	1934–1939	1960	1965
Estonia					
Rye		146	168		
Wheat		17	72		
Barley		106	94		
Potatoes	689	666	827	1,303	1,481
Oats		134	146		
All Grain	428			363	711

	1913	1920–1924	1934–1938	1960	1965
Latvia					
Rye		198	372		
Wheat		16	171		
Barley		166	205		
Potatoes	645	676	1,610	1,688	2,007
Oats		260	381		
All Grain	880			570	946

	1913	1920–1924	1934–1938	1960	1965
Lithuania					
Rye		523	616		
Wheat		82	250		
Barley		175	257		
Potatoes	1,375	1,297	2,195	2,259	2,601
Oats		235	384		
All Grain	1,449			856	1,691

Source: Statesman's Yearbook (various years); data for 1939 unavailable for Latvia and Lithuania.

for this poor record: inadequate material incentives, insufficient psychic rewards, excessive size of production units, too much centralization of decision making, and supervisory requirements that can poorly be met in large-scale agricultural enterprises.[27] The common denominator in this list is the suggestion that Soviet agricultural difficulties appear to arise not from a lack of adequate resources or technology but from several defects inherent in the system of agrarian collectives.

First, administration is sufficiently centralized to keep many key decisions far removed from the peasant and the land, but not enough to prevent almost comical foul-ups between bureaucratic organizations—for example, between those responsible for the farms and those concerned with production of tractors. No doubt compounding the difficulties are problems arising from organizational inertia and some dysfunctional aspects of bureaucratic politics that are certainly neither an invention nor a monopoly of the USSR.

Second, adequate incentives are lacking. Tangible incentives are important, but perhaps equally so are the intangible rewards or, in this case, the lack of them: "The Soviet kolkhoznik [collective farm worker] is completely denied the stimulus and satisfaction that an individual receives from personally deciding when, how and what work should be done."[28]

Third, there is an apparently unshakable faith in large production units, even though there is ample evidence that they are highly inefficient. Between 1953 and 1974 the average size of both collective and state farms doubled to 3,130 and 6,012 hectares respectively. Unlike industrial production, agriculture may not benefit very much from specialization of tasks, a division of labor, and the like. As one economist has put it: "When it comes to eliciting maximum output from a piece of land, the family farm is hard to beat whether it produces for self-sufficiency or for others."[29]

Large production units also suffer from another disadvantage. The larger the unit, the harder it is for any member to see the direct effect of his own labor and the more difficult it is to justify going to extraordinary lengths when necessary, as the typical farmer may often have to do. The "free rider" problem can exist in any organization, but it may be especially significant in large-scale agricultural enterprises such as state and collective farms. The industrial worker or unit may have production quotas, and it is possible to obtain information about failure to meet them on a daily basis. In agriculture, production results are available less frequently, typically once a year in the case of grain harvests.

Fourth, even if we assumed a willingness on the part of some elements within the Soviet leadership to move toward agricultural policies that emphasize production rather than ideological purity and political control, agriculture may become (or remain) the sector least

likely to attract the ablest and most creative individuals. It is a
plausible though unproven hypothesis that the disastrous 1963
harvest contributed to the ouster of Nikita Khrushchev a year later.
After 1972 grain production fell far short of established quotas,
Agriculture Minister Vladimir Maskevitch was dismissed. And at the
conclusion of the Twenty-fifth Party Congress in March 1976,
Agriculture Minister Dmitri Polyanski lost his position in the
Politburo, and two weeks later he also lost his portfolio. As long as
poor harvests are blamed on individuals rather than on fundamental
defects in the system itself, it would seem likely that the ablest
officials would attempt to avoid any association with agriculture,
leaving that sector to those less able or willing to provide badly
needed reforms.

In summary, the nature of the agricultural enterprise, the size of
Soviet production units, the absence of strong psychological and
material incentives, and the lack of freedom to make decisions locally
appear to interact in such a way as to create a system that seems
better suited to maximizing central control rather than production.

International Effects

Our attention is focused not on the consequences of Soviet grain
purchases for the American consumer or on the rate of inflation in the
United States but, rather, on the broader international effects. Table 8
provides some data on Soviet imports and exports, prices on international grain markets, and grain reserves. Soviet imports during the
mid-1960s had little effect on world prices because grain reserves held
by the major producers were then still relatively large. The next
Soviet grain purchases, in 1972 and 1973, were of gigantic proportions. Although bargain prices were paid for the initial purchases of
American grain under terms of the ill-advised agreement signed by
the Nixon administration just prior to the 1972 presidential election,
dramatic price increases were recorded in 1973. By 1974, when the
USSR once again made large purchases, the price of wheat reached
$193.40 per ton, an increase of 200 percent over the wholesale price
three years earlier and 157 percent higher than the average price of all
imports in 1971. An excellent American harvest, coinciding with a
temporary embargo on exports to the Soviet Union, combined to
prevent the full potential effects of the bad 1975 harvest from raising

prices to the levels reached a year earlier.[30] Ample American reserves may prevent the mediocre 1977 harvest in the USSR from driving world prices back toward 1974 levels.

No doubt part of these increases can be attributed to higher production costs arising, for example, from sharply higher prices for oil and fertilizers. But by virtue of their great size, Soviet purchases had a dramatic effect. During 1973, Soviet imports of cereals accounted for 15.1 percent of the world total and for 20.1 percent of all wheat imports. During the period 1972–76, Moscow imported some 90 million metric tons of grains, a trend that seems certain to continue in the light of the 1977 harvest.

We can gain some perspective on the potential significance of the reduced levels of grain reserves by comparing their 1973 levels— 104 million metric tons of food and feed grains combined—with projected need should the world's climate revert to conditions that prevailed between 1600 and 1850, as predicted in a recent report.[31] As a result of a mere one-degree-centigrade drop in the mean temperature in the Northern Hemisphere, projected requirements to prevent famine in India and China alone would be 80–100 million metric tons each year. Canada would lose 75 percent of its export capacity, and that of the Common Market nations would be reduced to zero. Under such circumstances, both American and Russian yields would also decline. Should such projections turn out to be valid, it seems self-evident that artificial barriers to maximum food production, however useful they may be in meeting the political and ideological needs of the Soviet ruling class, are a luxury that mankind will be unable to afford.

Adequate grain reserves are not only needed to cope with periodic catastrophes brought on by regional crop failures. They are also an essential part of any program to rebuild and return to productivity the environment that has been destroyed by those whose poverty left them no other choice. Programs of reforestation, letting land lie fallow, or reducing herds that contribute to "desertification" of marginal areas can be accomplished only in conjunction with international food programs that support those presently scratching out an existence on such lands.

Table 8. Soviet Imports, Grain Prices, and Grain Reserves, 1963–1973

Net Soviet Exports (Imports)	1963	1964	1965	1966	1967	1968	1969
All cereals (thousand metric tons)	3,025	(5,032)	(2,311)	(4,485)	3,899	3,432	6,805
Wheat & wheat flour (thousand metric tons)	1,052	(6,155)	(4,744)	(4,801)	3,685	3,432	6,383
Average price* Wheat ($ metric ton)	73	75	71	71	74	74	73
Corn ($ metric ton)	61	64	67	67	67	59	62
Wheat reserves** (million metric tons)	53.5	47.0	48.7	34.3	36.7	42.3	60.3

Sources: Agricultural Statistics, 1974, tables 1 and 69.

*All international purchases.
**U.S., Canada, Australia, and Argentina (total).

Policy Implications

With growing awareness that the world could face a major food crisis before the end of the century, American food policies have come under increased international scrutiny and a good deal of criticism. It is ironic that the Soviet Union, whose agricultural failures have contributed significantly to the problem and whose policies have been almost wholly indifferent to the needs of the poorest countries, has almost completely escaped demands upon or criticism of its food policies.[32] Indeed, Soviet spokesmen have consistently denied that there is a potential world food problem. For example, at the Rome Food Conference in 1974, Soviet Vice-Minister for Foreign Affairs Nikolai N. Rodinov stated that the globe could support ten times its present population because less than half of the world's arable land was under cultivation. The incredible hypocrisy of the Soviet position

1970	1971	1972	1973
4,086	5,602	(11,069)	(18,568)
5,716	5,825	(4,048)	(10,574)
72	75	76	102
69	74	69	98
68.7	53.3	49.3	28.9

is evident when we recall that at the same time the USSR was importing vast amounts of grain, with the consequences described in table 8!

For Third and Fourth World nations, the Soviet experience with collectivized agriculture suggests that those trying to achieve self-sufficiency in food production might profitably examine the record to determine whether it may not pose negative lessons for their own efforts. It also suggests that international aid programs directed toward assisting the developing nations to achieve higher production should perhaps devote as much attention to the political and psychological issues of organization and incentives as to the more technical problems of mechanization, use of fertilizers and pesticides, and the like. This is not necessarily to argue that the Canadian or American model of the single-family farm is optimal for all places or crops; it is only to suggest that a high degree of skepticism toward the Soviet model seems warranted.[33]

For the food-exporting nations, one of the more difficult problems is establishing an appropriate grain export policy that balances competing domestic and international demands. In the absence of controls, the Soviet Union clearly possesses the buying power to dominate the international grain markets, especially as the rapid escalation of world oil prices has provided the USSR with greatly increased export income. The 1974 Soviet-American agreement on grain purchase will stabilize international markets to some extent by requiring the USSR to spread out its purchases more evenly over years of good harvests and bad. But the agreement does little for the poor nations of the world that depend upon grain imports to meet basic nutritional needs and that are already faced with vastly higher costs for imported oil. Based on the past record, there is scant reason to expect that the Soviet Union will take much interest in providing food aid to those in direst need. As one observer has put it, the Soviet-American grain agreement will "ensure the survival of Soviet cattle rather than human lives. One wonders if this concern ever occurred to our [American] negotiators in Moscow. One can be fairly certain the thought never dawned on the Soviets, whose dismal humanitarian record is open for all to see."[34]

This is a valid criticism, but it does not really suggest a policy option. As long as the Soviet Union has the resources and the desire to make large-scale grain purchases, only an embargo by the major producers (the United States, Canada, Australia, and Argentina) will prevent it from doing so. Aside from the obvious domestic political problems that any such agreement would entail—farmers within the grain-exporting nations can hardly be expected to welcome artificial reductions of demand for their products—there are other difficulties.[35] Systematic exclusion from grain markets might cause Soviet leaders to lose interest in even the appearances of a policy of détente. In any case, for both domestic and international reasons, there seems to be little inclination in Washington to use the threat of withdrawing access to American grain as a lever in bargaining with Moscow.[36] Questions might also be raised about the legality of excluding the USSR from grain markets of the world by concerted action of the major producers, even though such actions would seem to be consistent with agreements among producers of several other commodities to establish embargoes or to take other actions that interfere with free markets. Finally, nothing would prevent other nations from purchasing the grain and reselling it to the Soviet Union.

What, then, can be done to ensure that the Soviet Union begins to play a more constructive role on the food issue? Perhaps the only realistic answer is, "very little." The political objections to any policy that might be effective are probably too powerful. Yet, to confess the lack of policy prescription does not detract from the urgency of the problem. In the light of the bountiful American harvests of 1975, 1976, and 1977, it might be engaging in hyperbole to suggest that the state of Soviet agriculture constitutes a "clear and present danger" to the global community. There is, however, reason to fear that it does constitute at least a "probable and future danger." Global population will almost double by the end of the century, and most dramatically in the poor nations that, for a variety of reasons ranging from weather to a lack of even the most basic components of modern agricultural technology, are at present unable to feed themselves adequately. It seems unlikely that production of basic foods in the United States, Canada, Australia, and other exporting nations can maintain the growth rate of recent years. It is therefore an almost inescapable conclusion that unless the Soviet Union can consistently export large quantities of food in the coming decades—that is, on a scale comparable to recent American exports—vast numbers of people are doomed to live on the margins of starvation. Failure of the Soviet Union to restructure its agricultural system in a way that will permit it to do so constitutes a clear threat against the poor of the world.

The Politics of Resource Scarcity

The Arab oil embargo of 1973–74 and subsequent price increase rank among the most significant international developments of the past decade. These events reflected fundamental changes taking place in the international order. First, the period signaled the end of an era of cheap, plentiful energy and increased our awareness of the finiteness of the natural endowment of the planet. Second, resource issues have become increasingly politicized as was evident in the proceedings of the Sixth and Seventh General Assembly Sessions on Raw Materials and Development of 1974 and 1975. Third, the demands of less developed nations for a "new international economic order" became a serious item on the international agenda. Finally, the unanticipated success of OPEC in exposing and exploiting the energy vulnerabilities of the industrial world presaged some basic changes in the international distribution of wealth and power toward the resource-rich nations of the Third World.

The experiences of OPEC encouraged other states to try similar tactics in an effort to stabilize and increase the prices of the primary commodities they export. The essay by Alan Winberg emphasizes that OPEC's achievements were made possible by a number of special conditions that may not apply to the circumstances within which other cartels operate. Even the cartel groups that enjoy immediate success can be expected to eventually weaken and break down as conflicts among producers become more salient. Charles Doran's essay assesses the impact of OPEC on the structure of the international political systems. The unprecedented relationship between exporters and importers is described as being one of codependence rather than interdependence, which presumes a cooperative relationship and the relative absence of coercive interactions.

4

In the final essay in this section, Jack Salmon examines the proposals by Gerard O'Neill and the L-5 Society to beam energy from space colonies to earth and to tap the mineral wealth of the moon. In contrast to the earth-centric focus of the other essays in this volume, the L-5 proposal would create an "open system" for minerals and energy. Even though this type of solution to problems of resource scarcity may be technologically feasible and have many other attractive features, it poses many unknowns that ought to be carefully examined. Not the least of these is the prospect of novel political relationships between earth and satellite colonies as well as between the colonies themselves.

Resource Politics: The Future of International Markets for Raw Materials

Alan R. Winberg

I

We have reached a major turning point in international relations. In the natural resource field there is a continuing shift of control over investment and production from generally economic forces to a mixture of both economic and generally political forces. Recent international meetings indicate that eventually trade in all materials will come under some form of intergovernmental regulation.*

At the Fourth United Nations Conference on Trade and Development, UNCTAD IV, held in Nairobi, Kenya, in 1976 and at the Conference on International Economic Cooperation, held in Paris in 1976 and 1977, states discussed several proposals and approaches for improving trade in primary commodities.[1] Among the issues discussed were instability of prices; instability of earnings for exporters; inadequacy of returns; inadequacy of investment; lack of processing of primary resources in exporting countries; availability of energy; security of supply; the need for more transparency on intercorporate and intracorporate sales. At these meetings, much was said but few issues were resolved. A deadlock was quickly reached between exporters and importers of raw materials. Predictably, those states favored by the existing system are very hesitant to see things change. It is equally clear that those states that desire change will eventually use every tool they have to make the system work more in their favor.

*The material presented in this chapter is the sole responsibility of the author and cannot be taken as representing the views or positions of the government of Canada.

As seen in Nairobi, a new source of conflict is developing between primary commodity exporters and primary commodity importers. As this conflict becomes more defined, present relationships and patterns of state behavior will change drastically. The less developed nations of the world are starting to band together to form much more cohesive political blocs than the Group of 77. Evidence of this development may be found in the recent efforts to organize producer associations or common fronts of exporting countries. The purpose of these associations is to set prices and production levels for mineral and agricultural products and to give producers a stronger position from which to deal with consumers. The major consumers of raw materials are industrialized nations, and the markets for raw materials are often dominated by large transnational corporations whose operations tend to confer the most benefit on these same industrialized, raw material–importing nations. Initially, these blocs of developing nations may be regional in nature, but as producers of raw materials realize the vast political and economic advantages of uniting their forces and cooperating to control price and production levels, the blocs will likely become interregional.

The health of the world economy plays a key role in the success of producer associations, of course. In periods of recession, world markets for raw materials tend to become very weak, and concerted action to raise prices does not meet with much success. However, if these associations exert pressure when the world economy is on an upswing, it is likely that they can make important gains.

The dramatic success of the Organization of Petroleum-Exporting Countries (OPEC) has certainly demonstrated the advantages of such producer cooperation and has made the world realize the power that may be derived from the possession of resources and resource reserves. Significantly, OPEC has shown the developing world just how vulnerable the rich, industrialized nations may be. In consequence, accelerated efforts have recently been made for the formation of new associations or the expansion of existing associations by producers of iron ore, copper, bauxite, coffee, bananas, mercury, phosphates, tea, jute, hard fibers, pepper, coconuts, and rubber. Is action based on OPEC's example possible for some or all of these groups?

For a producer association effectively to stabilize or raise prices of a given commodity for a period of, say, eighteen months, the association must meet certain conditions. In the first place, the members of the association must supply a large share of the world market. The smaller their share of that market, the less their ability to control prices is likely to be. The amount of leverage they can wield will depend upon the shape of the supply and demand curves[2] of the commodity in question. Some leverage may be exercised by associations supplying even as little as 20 percent of the world market.

Second, the world demand for the product must be relatively inelastic; that is, the quantities in demand would not be much diminished by a small rise in price. This would be so if the commodity were an essential good, especially if it were one that accounted for only a small part of the expenditure of a single consumer or that represented only a small fraction of the cost of the final product, as is true of certain raw materials.

A third requirement is that it be difficult for producers of the commodity who are not members of the association quickly to increase their existing production of the commodity or to bring new sources into production. As well, it should be equally difficult to substitute some other commodity for the one produced by the association.

Fourth, it is necessary that the structure of the world market for the commodity allow an OPEC-like producer action. It will be shown below that markets that are vertically integrated facilitate such action in the short run. In vertically integrated markets, the same firms undertake every stage of the production and marketing process. For example, the world oil industry is vertically integrated to a very high degree. Major transnational firms, and sometimes consortia of transnationals, undertake exploration, drilling, extraction, storing, transport to refineries, refining into various gas and oil products, transport of refined fuels to retail outlets, and quite often outright or partial ownership of these outlets. In the processing and transforming of most raw materials, technical advantages may be gained from vertical integration. Vertical integration and centralized control of all stages of production provide increased security of supply, improved coordination between successive stages, greater overall efficiency, and elimination of middlemen who may interfere with certain stages of production or marketing. Firms running vertically integrated operations may enjoy the advantages of near-monopolistic conditions with resulting increases in profits.

Fifth, the members of a producer association, or at least some of them, have to be in a healthy financial position (or, failing this, in a relatively strong, stable political position). An association needs some initial financing to take measures that could stabilize prices. Any stabilizing action carried out by producers, such as creation of buffer stocks or imposition of quotas, requires that supplies be either bought up or cut back. This means that producers will have to accept lower revenues for a certain time. Initially, this burden could be borne by those producers with the most favorable economic situation. The least costly method of cutting back supplies is domestic production quotas, but this requires a strong, stable political position in the country concerned, because it means persuading or forcing domestic producers to accept an initial reduction in revenue in hopes that restrictive action will lead in time to a higher export price and increased revenues. The financial capacities and political strengths of producers will determine the credibility of their actions and the likelihood of consumers taking retaliatory actions. If consumers believe producers are capable of taking and sustaining strong action, perhaps they will make concessions without such action being taken.

And finally, the members of the association must act in a cohesive and united manner so that the association can adopt and carry out an integrated policy, backed by all its members. Recent attempts at coordinating supply and price have demonstrated that the association is most likely to be successful when only a few countries control a large portion of the supply. When this is the case, there is less danger of one producer, tempted by a strong market, abandoning the association and increasing supply, thus taking advantage of the higher price.

Clearly, the majority of producer associations now being formed cannot meet these criteria for success to the same extent that OPEC has, and so one would not expect them to achieve a success of OPEC's proportions through similar means. However, it may be possible for producers to raise revenues on a more moderate scale by concerted action in several cases, notably copper, bauxite, and possibly iron ore, and in the agricultural sector, pepper, broad-leaved timber, coffee, cocoa, and perhaps tea. Even where OPEC-type action seems less possible, cooperation among producing countries could still be expected to bring significant benefits, such as stabilization of prices, improved marketing efficiency, a stronger posture with regard to synthetic substitutes, more leverage when dealing with trans-national firms, and better utilization of resources. This is especially applicable in the cases of zinc, lead, manganese, tin, jute, sisal, rubber, oil seeds, and oils.

One method by which potential associations could make up for weaknesses they might possess when operating alone would be to form a common front with one or more other cartels. For example, the present members of the copper producer association, CIPEC (Conseil Intergouvernemental des Pays Exportateurs de Cuivre [Intergovernmental Council of Copper Exporting Countries]), are not in a financial position to cut back production substantially or to accumulate stockpiles. This financial weakness prevents CIPEC from becoming a strong producer association in the near term. If CIPEC were to be supported by the bauxite producer association, however, both would be much strengthened. Indeed, cooperation between the International Bauxite Association and CIPEC would be virtually essential for both associations because of the high cross-elasticity of substitution between copper and aluminum. Because one may be substituted for the other with relative ease, the price of copper affects the amount of aluminum used in production and vice versa. However, an alliance between copper and aluminum producers is highly unlikely at this time.

One interesting example of intercartel cooperation was the formation, in December 1974, of a state-owned multinational corporation for the marketing of coffee, set up on the initiative of the Venezuelan president, Carlos Andres Perez. Agreement was reached between five Latin American countries. Venezuela, a member of OPEC and possessor of large amounts of unabsorbable revenues, offered to use these OPEC revenues to buy surplus coffee production and thereby guarantee a minimum price to the other members. Although most OPEC member-states are not heavily involved in mineral trade, Iran has indicated that it may be interested in funding a copper buffer stock. This trend toward cooperation between cartels, especially where there is an overlap between memberships, illustrates how dynamic and far-reaching the changes created by the establishment of producer associations may eventually become.

But why this new interest in producer agreements? Highly cohesive producer associations controlling a very large part of total production have existed before. Without exception, these cartels eventually collapsed. There is no reason to expect new formations to become permanent institutions, even though, among international raw material exporters, it is true that certain leaders are now adopting longer-term plans and have realized the advantages of cooperating.

Nevertheless, all of these associations or cartels possess certain inherent instabilities. None is permanent. For one or more of the reasons outlined below, eventually the association will lose its leverage in the marketplace, and cohesion among its members will disintegrate.

For example, once the price of a commodity rises above its fair economic price,[3] new sources will be brought into production. Because price can be held at a certain level only by controlling supply, the life of a cartel may depend to a great extent on the length of the period required for bringing in new sources of the commodity in question or for developing a substitute. Moreover, as the price rises consumers can be expected to reduce their demand for the commodity as much as possible, and tastes will tend to change. The association, therefore, must plan well to minimize the danger of such a result. If the producer association or cartel does not manage the supply and price of the commodity efficiently, it is even possible that its actions could do more damage than good in the long run. An excessive price held for a long period may encourage the establishment of new sources, the development and use of substitutes, and a change in tastes to the extent the price of the commodity might fall to a point much below the original level. Even while the price is high, this does not guarantee that total revenues to exporters will be higher. Total revenues are determined by both price and quantity sold. If demand is very elastic (greater than unity), total revenues will drop because of the decrease in quantities demanded.

The cohesion of the cartel will also be subject to increasing strains as time passes because of different characteristics and needs of its members. There always exists the danger that a state will base its strategy on a cartel or producer association only to find the cartel subverted by one or two other members. In the present international system, based on the sovereignty of nation-states, it is very difficult to ensure that members will act in good faith with regard to production quotas, for example. Some members may need to earn foreign exchange more than others, making the temptation to disregard production quotas strong. The problem becomes even more complex when some members are more economic producers than others. For example, in an iron ore association with Brazil as a member, Brazil could sell its ore at a much lower price than the other members and still make a profit because of the high quality of the ore. Although

Brazil's long-term interests would best be served through cooperation with the cartel, under certain conditions the possibility of conflict with the other members would be great.

Further, if the commodity is nonrenewable, the difference in the amount of reserves held by different members can reduce the cohesion of the association. For example, studies have shown that Algeria's oil will last only fifteen years at present exploitation rates, but Saudi Arabia's will last for centuries. Thus, a conflict of aims exists between these two OPEC members. Algeria would like to take advantage of the present inelasticity of the demand for oil[4] by setting a much higher price than is now being charged. In this way, it would obtain maximum revenues for its oil over the next ten or fifteen years to use in developing other industries and energy substitutes. Saudi Arabia, on the other hand, does not want to speed up the development of substitutes and in any case could experience difficulties in absorbing greater revenues in the near term.

Yet another problem endangering the producer group's cohesion is the social pressure to increase or decrease supply that may exist within the societies of different association members. State enterprises may not be preoccupied solely with maximizing profits. They may be concerned with providing employment or protecting the environment. Goals will be different among association members. In general, the only way that prices can be raised or stabilized by a producer association is by controlling supply. This fact has important short-run implications for employment in producer countries.[5] In the case of OPEC, this aspect of controlling production was relatively unimportant for most members because relatively few persons are employed in oil extraction. It becomes more difficult, however, in mineral extraction where more people are employed. And the group of agricultural commodities present a very difficult employment problem for a government wishing to cut back production. This is the situation facing the group of Latin American coffee-producing states where production comes from thousands of small peasant producers.

Political problems within producing countries can also reduce the association's cohesiveness. In the long run, the positive effects of the association's actions within its member countries will depend on government policy. The vast majority of Third World producers, especially those whose exports are based on mineral extraction, have a most unequal income distribution. Past experience has shown that benefits from united producer action in mineral extraction have been distributed largely between mine workers and the government. How much accrues to peasants or to nonunionized labor depends solely on the political will of the government concerned. The same could be said for some agricultural commodities.

The case of coffee again provides a good example. In many producing countries, it appears that the gains from higher world prices have gone to the larger-scale farmers and plantation owners. Before frosts in Brazil sent coffee prices soaring in 1976, governments of many exporting countries had been trying to cut back coffee production by imposing quotas on all existing producers. They paid the (higher) world price to these producers for their (reduced) production. This system of control prevented small-scale peasants from increasing existing production and also restricted new peasants from moving into coffee production. Thus, the most profitable production and highest profits were left to larger-scale producers. However, this is not the only method that has been used to cut back supply. In Tanzania, the domestic price was lowered, and supply fell accordingly. A large tax was applied to all coffee exported. Although producers get lower prices, the government spends the new export tax receipts on measures directed toward improving the lot of the peasants. If the governments were not sincere, however, this arrangement could be even more detrimental to the peasants than the first one outlined: with the export tax, small producers have to accept reduced production and lower prices; if the revenues from the export tax are not spent for their benefit, they would be much worse off. If major political instability or loss of domestic control results from a government's domestic implementation of a producer association policy, it is possible that this country may not be able to continue to take common action with other producers, reducing the cohesiveness of the association.

The length of a cartel's life depends on its ability to take successful action, and the degree of success possible depends in turn on the commodity in question. But the built-in instabilities of a cartel are such that in the long run even the strongest will weaken.

Clearly, faced with the threat of actions that may be taken by a producer association, consumers can be expected to become increasingly organized as time passes. This has been true of oil consumers reacting to OPEC.

In general, if producers limit their goal to obtaining stable prices, the association will be much more stable than if a higher price were pursued. Clearly, as prices increase above normal levels, the payoff to producers who drop out and operate outside the cartel becomes greater.

II

Several industrial countries, such as Australia, Canada, New Zealand, Sweden, South Africa, and the USSR, are substantial exporters of a wide variety of raw materials. Some of these exporters, Australia and Sweden in particular, have supported the formation of producer associations for the commodities they export. Others have refused to support these associations, hoping to improve trade in raw materials by international commodity agreements negotiated by both producers (net exporters) and consumers (net importers). Certainly, negotiated agreement between consumers and producers seems to be the most peaceful and satisfactory way to solve the problems of international trade in commodities. But producers and consumers may not have common ideas as to the magnitude of specific problems or future predictions of trends in supply and demand.

Consumers often are hesitant to enter into these agreements. History has shown that consumers often profit from fluctuations in raw material markets because these fluctuations tend to keep less industrialized producers in a very weak bargaining position with regard to terms of trade. Although they may have to pay higher prices in boom periods, the most important net importers of raw materials are industrialized nations, and the performance of their economies does not depend exclusively on stable raw material markets as does that of many net exporters. Thus, although it cannot be denied that both producers and consumers have a common long-run interest in stable markets, achieving this goal is not really of immediate concern to consumers.

In commodity agreements, initially, it is usually the consumers who can afford to finance the agreement but the producers who benefit. Critics in importing countries are quick to point out that agreements are usually undermined by producers who dump supplies during periods of low prices and create artificial shortages when the market becomes stronger. This activity provides a strong argument against consumer participation in commodity agreements.

In a world based on equal, sovereign states, every state watches out for its own self-interest. Often, short-term consequences have a much greater effect on government decisions than possible long-term results. From this perspective, producers will be less interested in negotiating with consumers when markets are strong, and consumers will not be interested when markets are weak. In transitional periods between strong and weak markets, consumers have no immediate interest in raw material markets and are not likely to agree to finance stabilization measures. This dichotomy cannot be resolved without fundamental changes in the international system that would change, in turn, the nature of relations between states. For the present, satisfactory commodity agreements can be successfully negotiated only after producers have demonstrated that they are capable of taking common action. Consumers, too, can be expected to show their power. Once both have demonstrated relative strength, then and only then can a satisfactory agreement be negotiated to each side's mutual benefit.

Since 1945, agreements including both producers and consumers have been negotiated on only six commodities: wheat, sugar, tin, cocoa, coffee, and olive oil. None has a very good record for stabilizing prices, except for the tin agreement, and now it too is suffering strains. Within the International Tin Council, fruitful negotiations have taken place because the producers act in a cohesive fashion, as do the consumers. Consumers tend to negotiate in good faith because there is a serious threat that producers could take OPEC-like action. Of course, the price of tin could not be increased as much as that of oil because there would be a very high rate of substitution. Even though the United States is not a member of the Tin Council at this time, over the last fifteen years it has helped increase demand for tin by building up large strategic stockpiles (over 400,000 tons).

The important point about the tin agreement is that it has worked in the past because both the producer group and the consumer group have been relatively strong and cohesive. Only when both groups have gathered their forces can satisfactory negotiations take place and a workable agreement be reached.

It is to be expected that producers of commodities that are not traded under an international agreement will eventually form into associations or cartels. In general, as pointed out above, inherent instability, possibly accelerated by consumer reaction, will eventually weaken these cartels to the point where the producers will want to negotiate with consumers to guarantee a stable market. The difference between a commodity agreement negotiated at that juncture and those that are attempted at present is that producers would likely have developed a common position of strength from which to carry on negotiations with the consumers, who are already organized to a certain extent, in part because of the transnational companies that dominate the production and transformation industries.

Thus, the organization of international commodity markets may be seen as cyclic in nature, starting with a relatively "free" market in which transnational firms dominate the scene. These markets are characterized by very volatile price fluctuations, which are further accelerated by speculators and transnational firms. Their near monopoly of information in relatively opaque markets often allows them to make substantial economic rents. Rents are also generated from the oligopolistic nature of these industries having large barriers to the entry of competition and often a wide spread between market price and marginal cost. These rents may or may not be passed on to producers, and the extent to which they are shared is determined in negotiations between transnationals and individual producers. The next stage of the cycle is the creation of producer associations that control price and production levels in an attempt to stabilize prices around long-term trends, at the same time increasing their share of rents presently flowing to transnationals. In some cases, producers may attempt to raise prices at levels that increase factor rents. In the third phase, consumers will associate to react to the producer association. Depending on the practices of the producer and consumer associations, the market may become quite disrupted during this phase. In any case, inherent weaknesses in both groups will eventually lead to a negotiated commodity agreement between producers and consumers. Also, attempts may be made to regulate long-term demand. Depending on the commodity, such agreements could include the creation of buffer stocks, production, export or import quotas, countercyclic financing, compensatory financing, and other methods of dealing with short-term fluctuations from long-term trends, none of which are without problems. The life of the commodity agreement will depend on how well future trends in demand and supply were predicted and on how long all parties act in good faith. Inevitably, at some point serious problems must be expected. There is no way to always predict accurately in human society. Nor can one hope that no cheating will go on when there is a payoff to cheaters and when the actors are sovereign nation-states and transnational companies.

The cycle is completed when the commodity agreement breaks down and we find ourselves with a situation similar to the one that existed before the formation of the producer association. At present, we are at the initial stage of the cycle for most commodities, though the market for oil is already at the start of the third stage. It is expected that, after going through the entire cycle initially, the duration of subsequent phases will change. The first three stages would occur much more quickly, and hopefully, the last phase, involving cooperation, will last much longer.

A further factor that will enter into the picture over the next few decades is the possibility of developing important new sources in the deep seabed for several raw materials, especially oil, nickel, manganese, and cobalt. If these sources are controlled by present importers, markets could be radically transformed, and of course present exporters would not pull very much weight in such markets. Creation of an effective international seabed authority, or some other means of regulating the exploitation of the seabed, does not seem very possible in present circumstances. This means that once the necessary technology for ocean mining is developed, the market cycle for the sea's raw materials may not conform to the general pattern. On the other hand, although it is unlikely that these producers will associate in the very near future, if they were to join together they could play a major role in the future exploitation of the seabed and thus possibly protect their position as land producers.

III

Transnational companies play a major role in raw material markets during phase 1 of the above cycle. In the following phases, their importance is reduced. As the market moves into phase 2, the actions taken by producers to stabilize the price of their exports will ultimately enable them to deal with the powerful transnationals that often control these resources. As the cohesion and resulting effectiveness of the cartel develop, much of the transnationals' power will be transferred to the host governments.

A goal shared by all exporters of raw materials, both industrialized and less developed, is to increase the amount of local processing and to have greater control of the transnationals' general operations within its borders. During phase 2 of the market cycle, producers will realize that this can best be achieved by forming a common front with all other producers to decide upon and coordinate appropriate measures—export controls, export taxes, and the like—to force the transnationals that control much of the world's production and processing of raw materials into taking the action most beneficial to the source countries.

As much as it may hurt a peoples' national pride, it is clear that, in the short term, transnational enterprises can be a great help in the development of a country's natural resources. Transnationals bring capital, technology, and marketing skills to the host country. A symbiotic relationship exists, with both the transnational and the source country profiting from the arrangement. Because of imperfect markets and the price differentiation in raw material markets, there are definite advantages for a source country if a transnational (with its technological expertise) is in charge of production and marketing of a given commodity. Indeed, for those products in which markets are vertically integrated, nationalization of an industry has several short-term disadvantages, especially with regard to marketing. Such nationalized enterprises have to compete with the transnationals and with other nationalized enterprises, and such competition would be based solely on price. This inevitably favors the transnational because it can offer more than just a competitive price. Consumers may be more interested in being sure that contracts will be filled on time and with the proper grade or quality. Here, the transnational, because of the contacts it has already built up, can offer established relations with foreign buyers, several sources of supply that would guarantee greater certainty that contracts would be met on time, and a product and quality control well known and understood by the consumer. This explains the transnationals' dominance during phase 1 of the market cycle.

In the following phases, the presence of the transnationals may well be instrumental in transforming the market. The presence of such firms in the petroleum industry was a most important factor (along with past policies of the major oil consumers) in allowing the members of OPEC to increase the price of oil quickly and dramatically. Because the oil industry is vertically integrated, the transnationals simply passed on all price increases (increase in taxes imposed by producers) to the consumers. OPEC's actions received little negative reaction from the transnationals; the annual reports of these companies illustrate how their profits rose just as fast as the price of oil and in equally impressive dimensions.

Thus, in the short term, there are good arguments for individual states to allow the transnationals to retain charge of production and marketing. In the long term, however, the opposite is true, for these advantages can and do become disadvantages. The transnational's ability to transfer technology and capital to the host country does not always compensate for the loss of control of the industry. The transnational's easier access to credit often leads to the take-over of national companies. The transnational uses its established contacts, expertise, and ability to transfer technology and attract capital to extract favors, such as special tax concessions, subsidies, and grants from the source country. All the trump cards are brought into the bargaining process. In the long run, the resource producer wants to escape the industry's vertical integration. The resource producer would prefer to export a finished good rather than a raw material.

The presence of the transnational causes certain other problems. First, these companies have the ability to transfer price, to use the channels of international trade to rake off surpluses, often through sales to affiliates. Copper and bauxite are examples of commodities where this has taken place.[6] In the second place, transnationals also operate with security perspectives; they tend to diversify their sources. The more diversified the sources, the more difficult it will be for an individual producer to resist granting concessions demanded by a transnational, because the transnational can play off one producer against another. Once again, the producers' strength lies in maintaining a common front in negotiations. Even where a strong producer association exists, the transnational can be expected to make attractive offers to single members in an attempt to persuade them to break the common front. Third, because most transnational corporations are vertically integrated, there will be constraints on these companies developing local processing, local uses of the commodity, or local production in the host countries. This tendency is well illustrated by the relations between aluminum companies and bauxite producers. A strong producer association has much more leverage than individual producers when negotiating, first, with transnationals to gain local transformation and, ultimately, with industrialized nations to gain greater access to their markets.

Thus, the problems of producer countries when they confront the transnational companies may also be alleviated if not solved by organizing a common front to coordinate dealings with transnationals. Any action, from imposing stricter controls to nationalization, that is carried out by only one producer is practically doomed to failure. Actions carried out in common are different. If every producer imposed the same tax or restriction, the transnationals would be obliged to acquiesce. United action would allow the producing countries to retain their access both to export markets and to international capital markets (consumers would still require an adequate supply of the commodity in question). An action such as partial or outright nationalization would also solve the transfer-pricing problem, because national agencies or an agency within the association could set up auctioning systems to ensure that consumers paid the full market price. Once formed, strong producer associations are likely to take actions similar to those just described, thus transforming the role of these companies in the second, third, and fourth stages of the market cycle.

IV

The Sixth Special Session of the United Nations General Assembly in April 1974, the Seventh Special Session in September 1975, and a number of specialized conferences in 1976, 1977, and 1978 were devoted to discussions between the industrialized countries and the developing nations to explore the possibilities of starting a transformation process that would lead to the establishment of a new international economic order. The industrialized world is turning its attention to consideration of demands from the developing countries for a new global order that would provide a more equitable sharing of the world's wealth and power, a new system of international relations "based on equity, sovereign equality, interdependence, common interest and co-operation among all States."[7]

Although the industrialized states have endorsed the concept of eventually creating this new order, it is obvious that no major changes can be expected overnight. However, whether or not the industrialized nations wish to redistribute a part of their wealth, the above analysis indicates that, in the field of primary commodities, a gradual redistribution is to be expected in favor of raw material exporters. As we move into phase 2 of the market cycle, producer associations can be expected to become more and more important as tools to advance the diffusion of economic and political power in the world. Over the next decade, one can expect to witness a continuing transfer of power away from the industrially advanced centers toward previously peripheral regions. Those developing nations that are major exporters of vital raw materials will become more and more important in world affairs.

It would be improper to assume that improvements accruing to net exporters of raw materials automatically would make the present international division of wealth and power more equitable. Certainly, real resources would flow from net importers to net exporters. But the workings of a market have nothing to do with justice or equity. The advanced, industrial nations are the greatest net importers, but many developing countries would also be affected, as they were by the quadrupling of oil prices. Developing countries that are net importers of commodities in which markets can be transformed would find themselves in an even less favorable position. Also, some industrial countries, such as Australia, Canada, South Africa, Sweden, and the USSR, are net exporters. Thus, without touching on the question of equity, one could generalize that there would be a diffusion of power away from advanced, industrialized net importers toward raw material exporters.

Some of these exporters may indeed share some portion of their wealth with developing states, and in this regard the establishment of common fronts of producers may be seen as a step toward establishing a new economic order in which there would be a greater probability that the world's wealth and power would be divided more equitably between all nation-states. This probability would be further increased if mechanisms were established to assure the resource-poor complete compensation for the losses they face stemming from higher import prices.

Purely economic market forces do not determine world investment, production, and consumption of raw materials. It has now become crystal clear that eventually trade in all commodities will come under some form of intergovernmental regulation. Economic forces remain important, but they are overshadowed by political forces. In the system, these political forces are centered around individual nation-states, each *competing* to pursue its own particular interests. This leads to a relatively shortsighted perspective, with each state more interested in its immediate needs and goals than in the problems of the global community.

I would argue that the establishment of a new international order will not occur as long as states remain the basic actors in the international system. But, unfortunately, the creation of a world federalist system does not seem very likely in the foreseeable future. Until such a system is established, there will continue to be overproduction; noneconomic transformation of commodities that should be processed in the source countries before exportation; inefficient, wasteful consumption; and violent price fluctuations, creating hardship for individual producers and making planning impossible in many developing areas. In the meantime, the market cycle outlined above will be operative for primary commodities. Notice that as the market progresses through stages 1 to 4, the amount of waste of resources may diminish. Eventually consumers' and producers' shortsightedness will have to give way to eventual commodity agreements that will take into account the nonrenewability of some natural resources and the inputs required to obtain these resources. But even then, the agreements obtained will be related more to the relative political strengths of producers and consumers than to concerns for our ecology or a more equitable distribution of the world's wealth.

Oil Politics and the Rise of Codependence

Charles F. Doran

A transformation in world politics, scarcely anticipated by Western policy makers but nonetheless long building, shook the international system in the fall of 1973. Questions of oil politics and resource scarcity, often given a minor foreign affairs role in the past, now occupied the front stage of the international political arena. At the center of these developments was the emergence of small, weak, largely agricultural polities such as Saudi Arabia and Iran, who suddenly revealed a capacity for global impact on the major powers and on the direction of world economic and financial events.

An important question arises in the light of these developments. How far-reaching is the transformation wrought by the Organization of Petroleum-Exporting Countries (OPEC) in terms of the relations between the advanced industrial nations and the less developed countries of the Third World? Is the upheaval in oil politics akin to a thoroughgoing twentieth-century revolution of class relations among governments, or is it instead more likely to approximate one of the conservative peasant jacqueries of the nineteenth century in which "the more things changed, the more they seemed to remain the same"? In other words, is the OPEC experience a forerunner and catalyst of major structural and economic change throughout the international system or merely a transient perturbation of regional politics?[1]

In order to address these questions effectively, we must place the analysis in the context of the larger debate regarding *dependence* and *interdependence* within the global international system. It is to these concepts that we first turn for definition and assessment of the mechanisms underlying contemporary world politics. We then evaluate the substance of oil politics over the last several years so as to obtain causal insight into the oil price changes themselves and to obtain a yardstick for measuring the impact of energy on future governmental relations. Finally we formulate a new concept, a *codependence*, which we use to characterize the norms and structures that have evolved between oil producers and consumers since 1973 and that appear likely to shape future governmental policies.

Probing the Dependency Thesis

Providing a context in which to examine the birth and maturation of OPEC, the dependency thesis contains a number of distinguishable elements.[2] First, according to the thesis, "dependency" results from highly unequal power and trade relationships between commodity producing countries and the "capitalist metropolist" or core state, especially the United States. While the trade of the commodity producer may be relatively unimportant (in terms of volume or value) to the core state, the significance of the core state to the commodity producer, both as a market for its exports and a source of industrial imports, is thought to be overwhelming. That many of the dependent countries are single-commodity producers having agriculturally based economies means that they are often subject both to wide fluctuations in commodity prices and to imported inflation from the industrial countries. Loss of commercial autonomy is moreover reinforced, according to the dependency thesis, by the military dominance of the superpowers, particularly within their "spheres of influence" where exclusivity of control reinforces the degree of dominance.

Second, the dependency thesis argues, control by the core state is maintained through the channels provided by the multinational corporations having home offices in the core state. Not only do these corporations rebate profits to the core state, thus transferring wealth from the developing to the developed nations, but the corporations also prevent the host governments from gaining control over and knowledge of their own resources. Lacking such control, the developing countries are in a poor position to attempt appropriate planning, to assess taxes adequately, or to obtain a proper ultimate return on their resource endowments. It is also argued that the foreign corporation tends to develop only the extractive or primary goods industries that supply raw materials to the rich countries while neglecting agriculture in general and the larger indigenous economy of the host country. The dependency thesis argues further that foreign corporations have a distortive effect on employment and upon the political life of the host country because the ablest young men and women are absorbed into the foreign corporation and away from possible entrepreneurship elsewhere in the country. Moreover, sometimes the corporate hierarchy is accused of establishing an alliance with the political elite governing the developing country in defiance of what might be argued is in the larger interest of the community as a whole.

Third, the dependency thesis asserts, the terms of exchange between raw materials and industrial goods—namely, the ratio of the prices the developing countries received for their exports and the prices they are charged for their industrial imports—have been shifting steadily against the developing countries. This last assertion is perhaps the keystone of the dependency thesis. It is also super-ficially a simple, empirical matter for testing. But in practice the test is clouded by a number of issues, including which bundle of goods to measure, what temporal end points to select, and how to deal with technological innovation, that is, how to place an appropriate value on the discovery of new products and industrial techniques. In consequence, the issue of faltering terms of trade has become a major debating point for economists and policy makers on both sides of the North/South axis.

Briefly outlined, these are the elements of the dependency thesis. Third World poverty is thought to be not the sole responsibility of the Third World country itself but in large part the result of policies in the advanced industrial world that are "exploitative." Dependence is viewed not only as a legacy of the colonial era but as the result of "neoimperialism," in which more subtle avenues of political and commercial control emanate from the core state through the insti-tutions of capitalism. Very little is said regarding dependence fostered by Communist governments, for example, the present political, military, and trade dependence of Cuba or Eastern Europe upon the Soviet Union. Only the most encompassing explications of the doctrine include such examples of socialist dependence. Yet dependence is often related to the policies of the United States government and by implication to the structure of the current international system, which itself is sometimes labeled as "inherently unjust" because of the processes of exchange and transaction that operate within it.

Before examining the dependency thesis in relation to oil politics, let us turn to a converse concept, *interdependence*, which is often held to be the goal or condition toward which governmental policies are (or ought to be) tending.[3]

Exploring Interdependence

Interdependence implies mutual reliance of two or more partners in a transaction.[4] It also implies the comparative *absence* of power politics in the transaction. In other words, interdependence incorporates and necessitates a high degree of cooperation in the behavior of the actors. Because cooperation and consensus are emphasized and power politics is missing or constrained, interdependence is likely to occur more frequently among relative political and economic equals than among highly unequal states. Interdependence thrives in a setting of relative equality because in that setting exchange can occur on the basis of voluntarism and freedom of choice among possible options.

Interdependence is also said to flourish in an environment composed of increasingly similar governmental policies and behaviors. For example, the increasing importance of world trade as a percentage of GNP, the increasing vulnerability of economies to imported inflation, the increasing importance of centralized monetary machinery such as that housed under the International Monetary Fund (IMF), and the increased use of regional or supranational peace-keeping forces in troubled areas all tend to contribute to a propitious climate for interdependence. Thus, both a convergence of needs and a convergence of capabilities at the international level reinforce interdependence. Interdependence may become a precursor of true political and economic integration, although it may as well ironically emerge as a substitute for that final stage of institutional unification. In any case, if integration among nations is to proceed, some convergence of policies—of the type we have described as interdependent—is essential.

Given these brief discussions of the dependency thesis and of interdependence, to what extent can we say that the recent transformation in oil politics and pricing has moved the international system away from dependency relationships toward a new politics of interdependence? In order to answer that first question, we must examine whether the dependency thesis accurately depicts the relationship among the consumer nations, the oil industry, and the producer nations prior to 1973 and whether and in what way the nature of dependence has been transformed. Second, we must ask how appropriately interdependence describes the new set of political and commercial relationships emerging after the OPEC take-over of the oil market.

Origins of Consumer Oil Dependence and the OPEC Price Surge

Secretary of State Acheson allegedly once identified the American oil industry as an extension of U.S. foreign policy reminiscent of the Clausewitz assertion that war approximated diplomacy by other means. In a number of ways, Acheson's characterization was accurate and perhaps more revealing than he was aware, confirming that at least some elements of the dependency thesis were valid for oil.

In the 1950s, when the profits from foreign oil production were high, the largest oil companies maintained large "concessions" within the oil-producing countries, fully owning all production rights and making all production decisions.[5] Individual host governments rarely knew the size of their petroleum reserves, optional production levels, available marketing choices, or terms of trade considerations. The large, foreign-owned corporations told the governments, for the most part, how much crude oil would be "lifted," at what price, and for what market. The corporations also decided for themselves how much exploration they planned to do. About the only decision role the governments retained involved bargaining over "concession permits" or designation of the right to drill for oil in certain locations. But even here the degree of governmental leverage, as witnessed by the prolonged negotiations in Iraq during the early 1960s, was limited by the amount of knowledge the government possessed concerning the probability of discoveries and by the ability of the large companies tacitly to agree among themselves, however briefly, on priorities.

In fairness to the companies, it must be pointed out that they faced problems of geological uncertainty that were probably greater then than today. Outlines of major formations and reservoirs were still relatively unknown, although as it turned out in the Middle East, at least, the financial cost of producing the resulting wells was not especially high. Initially, the companies assumed all costs of exploration and production, a situation that was used to justify the very rapid "payback" once a producing well was discovered.

Of two minds regarding a later objective favored by many host countries—the training of nationals for posts of high administrative or technical competence—the companies on the one hand sought to provide such training in order to legitimatize their operations within a country but on the other were aware that they were preparing their own obsolescence in so doing. With fully trained nationals, the countries would have little need for foreign companies. The companies also recognized the contradictions inherent in the issue of whether they were distorting the domestic labor market in the host country. If they *failed* to hire nationals and to promote them rapidly to high-salaried posts of considerable responsibility, they were accused of imperialism and exploitation. But they were also held to be guilty of imperialism and exploitation if they *actively sought* and trained managers from within the country, because they were allegedly skimming off the most talented members of the society and diverting them from indigenous entrepreneurship.

The measure of whether the oil corporations did or did not foster dependence among the oil-producing countries is perhaps most aptly revealed in the context of revenue and rebated profits. One caveat, however, is in order. If one subscribes to the view that the private foreign investment capital that migrates from lender to borrower initially should subsequently return in the form of interest and payments on principal or in terms of rebated profits (in the case of direct foreign investment), then, despite any possible subservience involved, the eventual movement of capital from developing to advanced industrial country is thought to be normal and acceptable. On the other hand, if the critical concern with the foreign investment relationship is loss of political or economic autonomy or if one subscribes to the view that capital should move only from advanced industrial to developing country and never in the opposite direction, then *any* rebate of profits or payment on interest and principal will be thought exploitative and therefore unacceptable. Alternatively, if we accept the former view but qualify the justifiability of the relation according to the relative *magnitude* of rebated profits, then we have a much more flexible instrument with which to examine dependency.

Using this last measure of dependency regarding oil matters, we must recognize that several times the cost of investment in oil production abroad by the United States was returned to stockholders in the form of profits. Thus, despite the loss of foreign petroleum assets, most American-based oil companies have at least partially been compensated. In general, they have returned to stockholders more money than the companies originally had invested abroad and at a rate of return at least equal to comparable domestic investments. It is true, however, that the rate of return on foreign oil investments has fallen off sharply during the latter years of the post–World War II period, coinciding with a decline in the impact of this form of dependency.[6]

But the other financial measure of dependency is perhaps more interesting, namely, the question of *control over the level of prices*. Again we must establish the limits or criteria of plausible interpretation. We are faced with an unusual and incontrovertible fact. In the brief period of a few months during the winter of 1973, the price of petroleum rose four times. This abrupt increase in price is set against a background of only very gradual price escalation since 1945. The *suddenness* of the price increase and the *magnitude* of that increase eliminate as a sufficient causal explanation a simple shift in the market forces of supply and demand. The price rose because, it is often said, the Organization of Petroleum-Exporting Countries "gained control of the market." According to this interpretation, the cartel was able to raise the price by constraining petroleum supply, accomplished initially during the oil embargo of 1973, and by eliciting at the same time higher prices from the consumers (a considerable oversimplification of events but a useful summary). This interpretation emphasizes that the oil producers through collusion were able to obtain monopoly prices for their oil and thus in effect were able to "exploit" the consumers or make them dependent.

Alternatively, one could argue the interpretation one sometimes hears in the OPEC countries, namely, that the price of oil had long been depressed or held hostage by the oil companies and that the price rise in part reflected a release of the price from the "stabilizing" efforts of the companies (achieved through regulatory policies of the Texas Railroad Commission). There is much to be said for this interpretation as long as it is not used to explain the *whole* of the subsequent price increase. During the intense history of price negotiations between 1968 and 1973, the companies resisted the efforts of the producer countries to readjust prices upward, a fact poorly comprehended in the industrial countries themselves. Indeed, the consequence of this continuing effort to keep prices down and to maintain control of their assets abroad was that the oil companies in effect were transferring revenue from the developing countries to the advanced industrial countries. In this sense, the companies were acting in their own interests and by extension as an instrument of U.S. foreign policy. By keeping the price of oil arbitrarily low (whatever the actual fraction of the difference between the 1972 and the 1974 price levels), the strategy ensured that the oil-producing countries were losing some of the benefits from their oil production, a consequence that translated dependency for them into direct financial cost.[7]

Conversely, however, to the extent that the post-1973 price levels have been kept arbitrarily *high* by OPEC actions, dependency is inverted, and the advanced industrial countries, and increasingly the United States, are the victims of these actions. Thus, besides demonstrating the very probable existence of producer-country dependency upon the oil companies and the United States prior to 1973, we have also underscored the reversibility of that dependence.

Interdependence: A New Political Reality?

Having argued that dependency was present prior to 1973 in oil matters, can we validly assert that relations between the oil-producing and consuming nations are approaching that of inter-dependence today? Returning to our earlier discussion of inter-dependence, we recall that the definition emphasized the mutual reliance of the partners in a transaction, the comparative absence of power politics, the high degree of political cooperation, and the probable relative industrial and commercial equality of the members. Relations between OPEC and the oil-importing nations of the world scarcely conform to these provisions.

OPEC policy on matters of price and supply has been unilaterally determined. OPEC dictates the posted price of petroleum, and the consumers accept it. Confrontation between OPEC and the International Energy Agency has been more than implicit. Indeed, the IEA program is essentially designed to deter a possible future instance of supply interruptions or selective petroleum embargo. Significant issues of foreign policy disagreement separate prominent members of the cartel and other members of the international community. Despite large volumes of trade flowing between the producer and the consumer nations, denials by the oil producers of the importance of any particular nation as a market, and denials by the oil consumers of the importance of certain OPEC members as essential trading partners, suggest a rather turbulent and precarious set of commercial relations. Military and industrial inequality, moreover, distinguishes rather than consolidates the respective policy groups.

Given these state characteristics and these distinctive styles of commercial exchange, one cannot fairly describe oil relations in terms of interdependence. Oil relations involve both more and less than interdependence. They involve less because they have not yet achieved the level of mutual reliance and cooperation, free from unilateral compulsion, that is a necessary condition of true commercial and political interdependence. On the other hand, oil relations involve more than is implied in the concept *interdependence* because the respective actors are locked into a complex set of exchanges mediated by powerful transnational institutions and shaped by governments with quite exclusive bases of power. Latent ability to employ this power and apparent willingness to do so distinguish oil politics from situations in which the interdependence notion can be more conventionally applied. In fact, oil politics in the late twentieth century displays some traits that are rather unique historically and are thus more appropriately described by a new concept, *codependence*.

Emergence of Codependence

What is codependence, and why is the concept relevant analytically to oil matters? Codependence means that both parties to a transaction are *compelled* to participate. Cooperation exists, but so does the capacity for coercive response. There are two sides to codependence, much as there is a demand and a supply side in economic relations. In the larger political-economic sense, however, the two sides correspond to that which the partners would like to obtain from each other and that which they are unable to avoid—in other words, to *opportunities* and to *punitive consequences*.[8]

Codependence creates a peculiar set of opportunities because each partner offers the other something that is exclusive and unavailable elsewhere. It is perhaps obvious that OPEC in general and Saudi Arabia in particular offer the United States large amounts of petroleum that increasingly are unavailable internally and cannot be obtained elsewhere outside the United States except at higher prices.

Conversely, the United States offers the principal oil-exporting nations, namely, Saudi Arabia, Kuwait, the United Arab Emirates, and Iran—all conservative political monarchies—a number of things they cannot easily obtain elsewhere. First, the United States offers positive support for the capitalist orientation of their economies while at the same time it does not interfere with the right of these societies to determine for themselves how they wish to be governed. Thus, in ideological terms, the United States presents no threat to these governments and indeed reinforces their internal political and economic stability.

Because the principal oil-exporting nations occupy one extreme position ideologically within the Middle East, with such governments as Algeria, Iraq, and Libya at the other extreme, it is important for the conservative states to trade with external governments that do not threaten the structure of their regimes or the commercial base of their economies. Historically conservative in economic terms and rather tolerant of right-of-center regimes politically (despite internal liberal criticism of some of these policies), the United States becomes a very suitable trading partner.

Second, Saudi Arabia and its neighbors recognize that the United States has no territorial ambitions. Of the two superpowers capable of providing military security in a crisis, the United States is thus a much more attractive ally than the Soviet Union, which historically has taken a too-active interest in access to warm-water ports in the region. It is true that American commitments to Israel and its geographic distance from the Gulf area hinder its alliance potential for the major Arab countries. But United States constraints in these regards may actually constitute its strengths. Because of its special relationship with Israel, the United States enjoys uncommon influence in Israeli foreign policy calculations, as other Middle East governments recognize; and because the United States is an "island" state in a geopolitical sense, it possesses the largest "blue-water" navy in the world with unparalleled capacity to maintain open sea-lanes from the Persian Gulf, an objective as important to the oil consumers as it is to the oil exporters. Thus, the United States can offer unequaled security guarantees to selected OPEC governments without exacting additional costs or imperiling these governments in return.

Third, although this consideration should not be exaggerated, the United States possesses modern technology and educational capability not found elsewhere in some instances either in quality or quantity. Although the most visible examples of the importation of high technology from the United States into the oil-producing countries may be in the military area, nonmilitary equivalents can be found in all sections of the economy. Over 6,000 Saudi Arabian students are currently studying in the United States, more than in any other single foreign country. Proportionately large numbers of students from each of the major oil-exporting countries are seeking educations abroad. Educational and technological opportunities are a key to the economic development of these nations, and they value these inputs correspondingly.

Codependence also involves an alternate side not present with true interdependence, namely, the capacity and apparent willingness to use punitive sanctions. But the power of the trading partners in this regard is curiously asymmetric. Saudi Arabia, for example, can undermine the United States commercially or financially by cutting off the supply of oil or manipulating financial reserves. The United States, on the other hand, could disrupt the flow of arms or spare parts or trained technicians to Saudi Arabia, thus subverting Saudi security, especially in a crisis period. In contrast, the United States has very little leverage over Saudi Arabia in other commercial matters, and Saudi Arabia has almost no leverage over the United States in purely military terms. Thus, the coercive potential of each partner over the other is very real but also quite balanced and asymmetric.

Perhaps the ability to raise petroleum prices is the most effective leverage OPEC currently has upon the United States and the other consumer nations. The ultimate sanction the United States possesses in the event of a serious energy disruption is military intervention. Most OPEC members probably correctly discount the probability that this extreme measure ever will be used, in part because the United States would have to reckon with a local balance of power in favor of the Soviet Union. But under present circumstances, whether the Soviet Union would risk war with the United States in defense of one of the conservative oil monarchies is likewise debatable. Hence, the ultimate sanction of military intervention cannot be disregarded by the producers, just as the ultimate OPEC sanction of another oil embargo cannot be ignored by the consumers.

Together, the incidence of both the positive goods and the punitive bads probably makes codependence over the near term stable. Both the United States and principal oil exporters must learn to live together in this uneasy partnership because they cannot live apart. Insofar as a continuous flow of petroleum and industrial goods traverses the Atlantic at prices that do not escalate too rapidly, codependence is likely to prevail. Indeed, the existence of codependence ensures that each trading partner will obtain substantial benefits in the current arrangement and will not want to experience the risks associated with overtly challenging that relationship.

Whether codependence itself is durable in the long term is a function of a number of factors. Three alternative outcomes are possible: (1) intensified dependence of the oil-consuming nations upon OPEC; (2) a return to the historical situation of approximate producer-country dependence upon the United States; (3) progress toward a genuine condition of interdependence. A brief evaluation of the determinants of each of these scenarios follows.

If the principal consumer countries fail to inaugurate significant programs of energy conservation and fail to develop alternative energy sources, the increase in their petroleum demand combined with lagging domestic petroleum supply will force them into a position of increased dependence. Although this condition of dependence will vary greatly across the industrialized nations (with Britain and Norway, for example, benefiting from their North Sea oil reserves), the United States in the absence of a comprehensive energy program could find itself more dependent upon foreign petroleum in 1985 than it was in 1975.

On the other hand, a vigorous U.S. energy program, spearheaded by a significant increase in the tax on gasoline (a conservation measure designed to cut down consumption), and additional, presently unforeseen major petroleum discoveries, could put substantial external pressure on the OPEC cartel. Unless the cartel is able to solve its internal problem of determining an efficient and equitable market-share distribution, perhaps by accepting the price leadership of Saudi Arabia on this question, pressure upon the unity of the cartel will be compounded in the face of the increasing revenue needs of the members. Under the combined circumstances of increased internal OPEC tension and increased external pressure, OPEC may lose its control over prices. Having lost this control over the market, the OPEC membership once again could be subject to comparative dependency upon the industrialized nations for reasons of trade and security.

Alternatively, OPEC consumer relations abetted by the efforts of the energy industry could enter a new era of genuine inter-dependence. This era would be marked by freedom from threatened acts of coercion by either side. For this condition to prevail, the United States would have to recognize the futility of armed interven-tion in the Gulf area. Similarly, the oil-exporting nations would have to recognize the disutility of further oil embargoes. On both sides, coercive responses would disappear as realistic political options.

Perhaps even more significantly, interdependence would neces-sitate a compromise on price. In return for a realistic effort to curb inflation in the industrialized countries, Saudi Arabia would have to prevail on its associated members to accept moderate price increases on petroleum. For the two sides to succeed in establishing a firm basis of interdependent trade, the increase in petroleum prices must not exceed the annual increase in the world rate of inflation. In the absence of threatened coercive responses and in the presence of oil price moderation, such a foundation for interdependence could emerge.

Currently, however, the more complex, perhaps transitional set of relations is best characterized by the concept of codependence. Meanwhile, the impact of codependence on the structure of the international system is worth exploring in terms of both content and scope.

Codependence and Future Middle East Politics

Codependence has changed international relations in two nontrivial ways.[9] First, under the cover of codependence large magnitudes of material resources have been transferred from the advanced industrial countries to the oil-exporting nations. A consequence of this transfer of wealth has been accelerated economic development throughout OPEC's thirteen member countries. How far this growth and development will go in each country is a function of the size of the population base and collateral resources and of the size of the nation's petroleum endowments. But regardless of these important constraints, economic development is proceeding rapidly throughout OPEC, especially in the Middle East.

In political terms, the most striking effect of codependence is the shift in ideological cross-currents. In the Nasser era, for example, pro-Arab sentiment increasingly seemed to be moving to the left. Government by government, traditional political monarchies were being replaced by socialist regimes, often through the coup d'état and with subsequent military participation. Among the last regimes to fall were those in Libya and Ethiopia. Increasingly, the conservative governments in Iran, Saudi Arabia, Jordan, and the sheikhdoms now composing the United Arab Emirates appeared to be vulnerable to the same ideological winds of change. But the acquisition of petro-dollars altered the political geography of the Middle East. Not only have the conservative monarchies survived essentially intact, but they in turn, because of their enormous surplus revenues, have begun to transform the orientation of other previously moderate-to-radical regimes.

During the Lebanese civil war, the impact of Saudi Arabian foreign assistance was critical to the survival of the conservative Christian minority. Likewise, the behavior of President Assad of Syria when he intervened against the Palestinians and the leftist Moslems was influenced by the new Saudi assertiveness in foreign affairs. Similarly, the new inward orientation of Sadat, his concern to attract private foreign investment, and the warmth of relations with the United States all must partially be explained by the change in ideological atmosphere wrought by the politics of codependence.

Finally, codependence is affecting international relations between the United States and the principal OPEC membership by creating in each actor a feeling of special responsibility toward the other. For example, Saudi Arabia cannot afford to let economic or financial conditions deteriorate in the West because the fate of Saudi prosperity rests on the continued growth and expansion of the Japanese and Western economies. Likewise, the United States is obliged to defend the security of Iran and Saudi Arabia against potential external threats because such an increasing portion of U.S. energy and GNP is bound up in commerce with these nations. Thus, codependence has made the United States and the OPEC leadership each respectively the ward of the other. Each must protect the other in order to survive politically itself and to prosper commercially. This nascent awareness on both ends of the OPEC oil pipeline perhaps best describes the new politics of codependence.

Resupplying Spaceship Earth: Prospects for Space Industrialization

Jack D. Salmon

"Energy is the basic natural resource."[1] A number of metals and other resources are in increasingly short supply,[2] but given adequate energy supplies at acceptable costs it is possible to recycle, substitute, dig deeper, or otherwise at least partially evade most other shortages. However, the laws of thermodynamics tell us that energy itself cannot be recycled, which can be understood to mean that an energy system dependent on fossil fuels must eventually come to an end; if the system tries to save itself by accelerated use of fossil fuels, the end comes all the sooner. Further, the heat produced as the end product of all energy production and use is becoming recognized as an ultimate, and adamant, limitation on mankind's economies regardless of their basic energy source. According to R. U. Ayres and A. V. Kneese, continuation of present rates of growth in energy consumption for another 250 years would find man's production of heat on earth equal to the earth's absorbed solar flux—a condition they rather mildly describe as "totally unsuitable for human habitation."[3] Local "heat islands" already affect our social and ecological existence; within much less than 250 years, thermal burden would become a severe limitation.

None of the conventional technological solutions proposed for energy seems able to rescue us from our problems of energy shortage or thermal excess. Despite efforts now being expended on petroleum resources, almost no one argues that petroleum fuels can meet global demands for very far past the year 2000. Improved efficiency and resort to some exploitation of oil shales and tar sands can extend that time frame several decades but only at considerably increased economic and environmental cost. Coal use is already controversial across a wide spectrum of issues: environmental, health, safety, social, and political.[4] As S. David Freeman's famous observation put it, the two things wrong with coal are that we can't mine it and we can't burn it. President Carter's energy plan places increased emphasis on coal, but even administration officials have indicated doubts about the ability of coal technology to overcome its limitations.[5]

Nuclear technologies face similar restrictions of increasing price, limited quantities of fuel, and environmental controls. Breeder technology evades the problem of fuel limitations, but all fission reactors face controversy over increasing costs, declining plant efficiencies, safety, social acceptability, vulnerability of the system to terrorism, thermal pollution, and other related problems.[6] All fission technologies, but particularly the breeder, face the combined technical and ethical-political questions of intergenerational cost transfer associated with the production of large quantities of extremely dangerous materials that must be safely stored for periods of thousands of years into the future. The prospect of nuclear fission as a major component of future global energy systems is perhaps best described as cloudy and uncertain.[7] Nuclear fusion is a technology with an attractive potential, but it is not clear whether or when economically acceptable fusion power will be available. Nor is it clear that fusion will be socially or environmentally acceptable. Doubts have already been expressed about possible radioactivity and thermal pollution problems,[8] and we would do well to remember that at a similar stage in the commercialization of fission power there were few economic, social, or political problems foreseen for that energy system.[9]

A growing realization of the limitations of conventional "technological fixes" and of the increasing pressure upon the self-restorative capacity of the ecosphere has produced a new literature of "scarcity politics." Its contributors range from the relatively sanguine E. F. Schumacher and Amory B. Lovins to the pessimistic Robert Heilbroner, William Ophuls, William and Paul Paddock, and Garrett Hardin.[10] The now famous series of Club of Rome studies has aroused considerable public and elite interest in such questions as whether it is necessary, or possible, to reshape social and political values away from existing growth economics toward alternative technologies, "soft energy paths," stationary-state economies, and significant variations on existing patterns of social values. It is probably true, as Lovins claims, that the value changes necessary to

accomplish alternative technology solutions and a simplified life style
are no more drastic than those changes that will be necessitated by
increasingly stressful attempts to continue growth as usual. But
Dennis Pirages and Paul Ehrlich have pointed out that the "dominant
social paradigm" is hospitable to large-scale, centralized, elite-
dominated, growth-oriented energy and economic systems.[11] The
recommendation of alternative technology and changed life styles
amounts to a frontal assault upon a very powerful ideological
position. Even should the assault succeed, it is unlikely to do so
rapidly. Solutions of the type preferred under the dominant social
paradigm will be seized upon if they show some possibility of
allowing its continuation.

But there is a further reason for resistance to the "scarcity politics"
proposals, one shared by a sizable proportion of humanity. The
wealthier nations of the world see continued high-energy industrial
economies as necessary for preservation of their rather plush life
style, but it is quite clear that much could be cut from that life style
before significant deterioration in quality of life occurred. However,
this is not true for most of the world's population: the people of the
Third, Fourth, and Fifth Worlds require access to vast supplies of
relatively inexpensive energy and industrial products if they are to
have a real possibility of escaping from the developmental dungeon
in which they now languish. They have little fat to shed, and growing
appetites.

Social and political pressures thus push us powerfully toward
solutions within the dominant social paradigm; ecological and
resource limitations push increasingly in the opposite direction.
There is little doubt that, as the problem is currently formulated, the
basic logic of the scarcity school is correct: our planet is finite, with a
finite capacity to produce energy and raw materials and with a finite
capacity to absorb the environmental insults of heat and other forms
of pollution. At some point in the future, the planet's ability to support life would be overloaded by growth of man and his machines;
the only real questions are when and under what conditions this
would occur. But it is not clear that the "alternative technology"
solutions of the scarcity school are sufficient. Conservation clearly has
its limits. Unconventional technologies based on renewable resources
(geothermal heat flows, ocean temperature gradients, rooftop solar
collectors, windmills, and so on) also have their limitations and are
quite unlikely to adequately satisfy the demands generated by the

growing populations and increasing industrialization of the developing world. The ecology may be preserved by these techniques, but at social and political costs that many nations will prefer to reject.

We thus arrive at a dilemma. Our conventional fossil-fuel economies and the newer nuclear-energy systems pose questions of both supply adequacy and ecological acceptability; the unconventional technology advocated by the scarcity school may resolve ecological problems but may be unable to meet continued and probably rising demands on a global scale. Any concept that purports to meet ecological requirements, to avoid exceeding the planetary limits of resources and environmental regenerative capacity, and to do so within the general framework of the dominant social paradigm should be immensely attractive to harried policy makers and worried citizens.

One such concept, space industrialization, has recently been proposed and is rapidly gaining support. In addition to purporting to meet all the above-listed demands, it has the additional strong appeals of adventure and glamorous endeavor in a worthy cause. On 15 December 1977, resolutions were introduced in the U.S. Congress (House Concurrent Resolutions 447 and 451, 95th Congress, 1st session) calling for a study of this proposal as a possible national goal for the United States. This essay will attempt a preliminary examination of some of the political requirements the concept must somehow meet and propose possible solutions.

The High Frontier: Industrialization of Space

The possibile solution is an outgrowth of the technology and science of the last decade; prior to about 1970, it would have been science fiction or, at best, speculative science. Technology developed for the Apollo moon voyages, coupled with geological findings on the moon, provided the needed technological advances and data base. Prof. G. K. O'Neill of Princeton in 1969–70 assigned his undergraduate physics seminar a problem: "Is a planetary surface the right place for an expanding technological civilization?" From the initial surprising findings flowed other questions, resulting in what is now a well-developed conceptual design for development of human civilizations in space.

Only a brief description of the major components of the design can be given here. More detailed technical, economic, and conceptual information is available in a rapidly growing literature, including Professor O'Neill's recent book, *The High Frontier*.[12]

The basic constraints on space development are the technical and economic limitations placed on any concept requiring that massive quantities of material be repeatedly lifted from the earth's surface to any point in space. NASA's new space shuttle and later follow-on vehicles will carry large tonnages at reduced costs but would still be inadequate to economically transport into space and maintain there any significant number of people or industrial facilities. But the Apollo geological studies show that the moon's crust contains high proportions of various metals, silica, and oxygen. O'Neill's conceptual breakthrough was in designing a system whereby nearly all (over 90 percent) of the construction materials needed in space would be obtained from the moon. This sharply reduces the economic cost, resource drain, and environmental burden on earth of constructing numerous large space facilities. Only the original, basic facilities would originate on earth.[13]

Lunar mines—essentially surface strip mines—would produce unselected soil that would be literally thrown away from the moon by another key part of the design, an ingenious electromagnetic mass launcher capable of slinging large quantities of materials toward a "catcher" in space. The catcher would then transfer the material to a space industrial city—a "Pittsburgh in space"—for processing. These space cities would be located in appropriate orbits or at Lagrange point 5, a large volume of space equidistant from the earth and the moon in which a body placed in stable orbit would remain indefinitely. Solar power in any desired quantity would be used for a variety of high-value industrial activities and for agriculture to feed the work force. Industry would have the necessary facilities (including conditions of vacuum and zero gravity, if desired), and housing would be in very large "space stations" with earthlike environments. The largest would be capable of housing as many as ten million people in a suburban to semirural population density, with large areas for trees, parks, even rivers and lakes. Because the reserve supplies of raw materials and energy in space are far larger than those available on earth, many such space colonies could be built and mass migration to space might be possible, with consequent energy and materials savings to the earth.

One of the major activities of these industrial societies would be construction of very large (10,000 MW) solar power stations (SPS) to orbit the earth and supply electricity to the planet by means of a microwave or laser relay. This energy would be provided by our neighborhood fusion reactor, the sun, in inexhaustible quantities for millions of years into the future at minimal environmental and thermal cost to the planet. This additional energy at low ecological cost would permit the developing nations to improve their status and the developed nations to maintain theirs. If the observed pattern of declining population growth in industrial societies holds, the population growth problem should eventually and "naturally" be reduced somewhat.

In addition to the very considerable romance of the "high frontier," which has already attracted some fervent supporters, studies indicate that the industrial cities could produce both more habitats and large solar power satellites at a rapidly accelerating rate. Within time periods ranging from ten years up, depending upon the urgency with which the work is pursued, the first space industrial cities could have replicated both themselves and enough power satellites that satellite solar power (SSP) would constitute a large proportion of the U.S. electrical supply. Within twenty years, SSPs could be ready to meet all new U.S. electrical needs and begin to replace other energy systems. Depending on various economic assumptions, the sale of power alone would have paid off the entire project cost within twenty-five to thirty-five years, after which profits could be shown while rates dropped. Some space industries would be able to produce very valuable products for export to earth, further improving the economic picture. If several countries are active participants and larger programs are mounted, the systems could begin to have worldwide impact by early in the twenty-first century.

This concept is a technological optimist's solution to *all* the conventional scarcity problems. By importing energy to the earth at very low resource, environmental, and thermal cost, the "limits to growth" barriers are pushed back considerably. This buys time to attack other components of the economic, environmental, and social dilemma that so depress Heilbroner and others. The possibility of less stressful and more rapid industrialization of the developing countries, coupled with the possible longer-term migration of significant numbers of people to off-planet locations, may greatly aid in solving the problems of population growth and world social inequality. It is even arguably possible that peace would break out on earth, for incentives to covet one's neighbor's resources would seem to be less and the adventures of the high frontier would absorb national energies. Should apocalyptic war happen, parts of the race might survive in space and begin again.

Problems on the High Frontier

After hearing Professor O'Neill's presentation before his U.S. Senate subcommittee, Sen. Wendall Ford (D-Kentucky) asked, "Professor, is paradise all bad?"[14] There is now a growing literature of technical and economic analysis of the concept, most supporting its feasibility. Limited research and development programs are underway in both government and private agencies, a citizen's lobby (the L-5 Society) exists, international agencies (including the UN) are taking interest —for a concept that first came to public notice only four years ago, this is a very respectable record. But there has been little attention paid to problems of international politics, political or organizational dynamics, or sociopolitical consequences in general. Senator Ford's question may be the intuitive reaction of a practical politician, aware that there must be some unrecognized snake somewhere in this garden. Such potentially revolutionary programs require very careful advance assessment and evaluation.

Among the necessary elements of space industrialization are several factors directly related to international politics. Three such factors will be subjected to a preliminary examination: international law, international organization, and national security policies.

National Security Implications of Space Industrialization

One reason the United States is currently short of oil is that for many years a system of tariffs and import quotas kept importation of foreign oil to a minimum, encouraging consumption of oil produced from domestic wells. This policy, which someone has called "Drain America first," was justified on the grounds that development of domestic energy sources would make the United States independent of foreign sources in time of war. "Project Independence" has been explicitly justified on the same grounds. Additional examples of national concern over the security of energy sources could easily be cited from Japan, France, the United Kingdom, and others. But as the American example shows, we need not assume that policies urged on the grounds of national security necessarily help that cause. Project Independence and President Carter's energy program would again emphasize development—and thus faster depletion—of U.S. fossil fuels. Thus, a rather temporary independence has a long-run potential of creating greater dependence.

Space industrialization will probably be adopted, if at all, primarily because of the long-run energy potential of the system. For economic and social reasons, provision of abundant and low-cost base-load energy is of very high priority, but it is equally important that vital sources of energy be protected against destruction or capture. Project Independence is justified by the assumption that domestic resources can be protected, whereas foreign supplies may be interrupted. Analyses of the probability that American troops could capture, hold, and produce Arab oil fields under hostile action suggested that the bet was rather poor; little more has been heard of the idea. Would SPS be secure or vulnerable?

There are a number of components in the complete SPS system, all essential to successful operation and growth: earth-based launch and microwave reception installations; mining and mass-launcher facilities on the moon; the industrial city in space; the SPS itself. All are vulnerable to sabotage, but this is true of any major installation and would presumably be dealt with by normal antisabotage methods. There is no obvious reason why sabotage would be more successful here than in any other power system.

Direct attack on the lunar facilities or the space industries, if mounted from earth or near-earth space, would have a long lag time due to the distances involved. Antiballistic missile systems are very poor performers in atmosphere but, under the favorable conditions of vacuum and long warning times, might become feasible. The availability of vacuum and massive electrical power suggests the possibility of laser-based defenses, already under study for use in the more troublesome atmospheric environment. Direct attack on the earth launch facilities or microwave reception system does not seem in principle any different from attacks on existing power plants and distribution centers: there is no known guaranteed defense in either case, only the general deterrent posture for the superpowers or the conventional defenses available to all nations.

The weakest point is the SPS itself. The SPS and its ground antenna are the only system elements that, if destroyed, would cause immediate loss of energy. Destruction of the other components—industrial colony, earth and lunar launch facilities—would have only delayed effects. All SPS designs are large and relatively fragile targets, close to earth (approximately 22,000 miles or less), and in fixed orbits. They appear to be relatively easy targets, and their destruction would have large and immediate effects on national defense and economic systems. This makes them high-value targets of the type to which an enemy would devote enough of his striking force that defense would be very difficult and successful defense unlikely.

One very recently developed technology may drastically alter this evaluation. The very high energy lasers under development, particularly the free electron laser, would be major competitors with microwave techniques as a means of power transmission to the ground. In several ways (smaller antenna size on earth, probably lower environmental impact, greater size flexibility), lasers may well be preferable. But such lasers are also, unavoidably, weapons of exceptional power and speed. As offensive weapons, they would be the primary targets of an enemy; as defensive weapon (ABM mode, or "preemptive strikes"), they might be able to defend themselves fairly well. This dual role of potential weapon and economic tool seems certain to lead any enemy to still more strenuous efforts to destroy it and renders defense, again, doubtful. The laser-relay SPS, if feasible, requires very careful analysis: the social impacts may be so severe as to outweigh any technical gains.

But destruction of an SPS would be a major, unambiguous act of war and presumably would not occur unless core national interests have become involved. To the extent that deterrence works, the SPS should be protected; if deterrence fails, the SPS is simply another item on a long list of hard-to-defend targets. Major nuclear or fossil-fueled generating plants are also vulnerable, although more numerous and less significant as individual targets.

The best and perhaps the only effective defense for an SPS may be similar to the defense currently used by the United States and the USSR for their cities and industries: a mutual vulnerability so naked that each side holds the other's cities as hostages for good behavior. Alternatively, to build upon the functionalist argument, an SPS system that is internationalized and produces power for several nations may thereby become a common good immune to rational destruction. I will return to this point later.

National security policies must deal with many situations short of war: diplomatic pressure or economic rewards and punishments are normal parts of international relations. Use of "the oil weapon" by some members of OPEC has proven sufficient to alter the foreign policies, or affect particular actions, of a number of nations. It is this peacetime leverage, more than the fear of a cutoff in time of actual war, that gives great impetus to the attempts by a number of nations to reduce their dependence on foreign energy supplies.

An SPS system under national control would serve very well as a peacetime energy supplier, quite beyond the influence of any other nation. The sun cannot be "turned off"; there is no monopoly on space solar power by one or a few nations due to a peculiar concentration of the resource in a few areas; tankers cannot be harassed or shipping lanes closed; the price cannot be affected by foreign action. Because its input is from a self-renewing source of (for practical purposes) infinite capacity, investment in this option is different than strategies based on exploitation of fossil resources, which would become increasingly expensive and increasingly limited over time. Because the system output is electricity, a synthetic energy form that could be used to synthesize other energy forms such as hydrogen, the SPS system could be a fundamental building block in a varied and quite "independent" energy system.

Although there is clearly need for more detailed study, a first-pass national security evaluation suggests that the space industrialization/ SPS system has a mixed potential. Unfortunately, its key role in peace makes it a vital target in war, and its destruction could be a mortal blow. If it is possible to design an internationalized SPS in such a way that it cannot be an effective economic weapon but does become less significant or attractive as a target, we can have the best of both worlds.

An international public policy favoring an internationalized SPS system requires creation of a suitable legal and organizational matrix.

A Legal Regime for Space

Over a period of several centuries, there developed a net of national
and international law to govern the activities of both states and
private individuals on and in the sea. Because of the technological
limitations that existed until quite recent times, the legal regime of the
sea dealt with the margins of the ocean (territorial waters), with a
narrow layer at the top of the ocean within which fisheries were conducted, and with rules for navigation and passage on international
waters. The sea floor and deep ocean activities in general were rarely
important enough to be legally noticed. But recent technological
developments, economic pressures, and national security concerns
have combined to produce not only interest in but considerable
conflict over a restructured and extended law of the sea. In particular,
the political and economic demands of the poorer nations for a share
of the sea's wealth have been resisted by the wealthier nations who
possess the technology necessary to exploit the ocean.

Space law has a similar, if shorter, history.[15] It has grown rapidly
but incrementally, following technological feats that aroused a need
for some legal integument, and has roots in several areas: arms
control and national security, desire to advance international
cooperation,[16] economic needs, political rivalry, and even civil
damage claims (who is responsible if a chunk of French satellite falls
on a Japanese tourist in Chicago?). It seems reasonable to assume that
serious consideration of space industrialization will arouse the same
type of questions as have arisen since technology made it possible to
exploit ocean resources more fully. The course of law-of-the-sea
negotiations may thus be quite significant for space law as well.

Who owns nonnational resources? Who can own them, and under
what conditions? How may they be used? How are economic costs
and benefits to be apportioned? These questions must be dealt with
in international public policy for space, as they are now being
threshed out in maritime law.

However, the differences between sea law and space law may be as
significant as the similarities. In particular, space law is still a rather
new field with few precedents, vested interests, or entangling
rules.[17] Such principles and practices as do exist are quite broad and
generally enabling as much as restricting. This adolescent state may
benefit space industrialization: if there can be described soon an
appropriate, architectonic model to organize and guide development,

decisions may be made and programs established in the near future with some confidence.

The complex and interdependent nature of large-scale space industrialization makes it desirable that our conceptual models deal with whole systems. A legal equivalent of the systems design method much used in NASA's engineering development may be appropriate, in which one attempts to construct an integrated model of all relevant systems and then to optimize performance of the total system rather than maximize the performance of a particular part. This of course requires that social, political, and economic factors be part of the analysis, integrated with technological designs. NASA has stressed the additional values produced by space program "spin-offs" into the civilian economy, such as biomedical devices, ceramics, and systems engineering; a social and technological assessment project of the magnitude required by space industrialization might well prove quite valuable for its secondary social and methodological spin-off, as well as for its primary purpose. The study might show insuperable difficulties and avoid diversion of vast resources into a doomed program; if the results are promising, problem areas and solutions would have been illuminated and the project both improved and speeded.[18] House Concurrent Resolutions 447 and 451 (95th Cong., 1st sess., 15 December 1977) specifically request the Office of Technology Assessment to undertake a "thorough study and analysis" of space industrialization "as a national goal for the year 2000." This may serve as the vehicle for comprehensive studies of the type recommended here.

The legal profession is probably the most advanced nontechnological profession in space matters. Several international treaties, both bi- and multilateral, already cover a number of specific topics. National and international legal conferences meet frequently, the American Bar Association has a Committee on Aerospace Law, there is a legal subcommittee of the UN Committee on the Peaceful Uses of Outer Space, and legal panels have been prominent features in more technically oriented conferences (for example, the International Astronautical Federation).

Our chief current source of space law is the 1967 Treaty on Principles Governing the Activities of States in the Exploration and Use of Outer Space, Including the Moon and Other Celestial Bodies, now in force for over seventy states.[19] But it is now comparatively old, predating the Apollo moon landings and O'Neill's synthesis. It has already become the subject of many suggestions for revision.[20]

This treaty established the broad principle that "use" of celestial bodies is open to all nations; but neither any territory in outer space nor outer space itself is "subject to national appropriation by claims of sovereignty." Exploration and peaceful experimentation are permitted, but implementation of a space industrialization program of the type and scope envisioned by O'Neill will clearly raise allegations of illegality if any single nation attempts such a program. Certainly, the mining of lunar materials and their transport into space for construction purposes is more than a strict reading of the treaty permits; J. H. Glazer has even argued that construction of permanent, fixed-orbit, manned facilities might be construed as "national appropriation" of a portion of outer space.[21] But claims to exclusive rights have already been made. A Canadian study in 1967 recommended that Canada claim an area of space for use by synchronous orbit satellites,[22] and in December of 1976 a claim to control of geosynchronous orbit space over equatorial states was advanced by a group of eight equatorial nations (Bogotá communiqué, 4 December 1976). A new space treaty must deal with such claims.

Further, outer space and celestial bodies are reserved by the treaty for "the benefit and in the interests of all countries, irrespective of their degree of economic or scientific development, and shall be the province of all mankind." This principle seems very close to what the developing nations are demanding in law-of-the-sea conferences; clearly, space law must deal with this demand in some form.

C. Q. Christol has proposed an evolutionary approach, involving creation of an international organization to manage space development. He argues that the present vague space regime permits nations or organizations under their supervision to exploit space resources provided only that no claims to sovereignty are made and that the use is both peaceful and internationally beneficial. Even so, "the problem of exploiting the natural resources of the space environment is very similar to that posed in the exploitation of the resources of the deep seabed and ocean floor. In each instance there is a need to focus on the management of such resources by way of an operating regime or authority, which, in order to be most effective, would undoubtedly take institutional form."[23] In particular, the pressure coming from developing and noncoastal countries for a share in the ocean's benefits will surely be matched in space development as developing and non-space-traveling nations become aware of potential benefit

and seek to channel it in their direction. Institutionalizing the
program in an agency subject to international control, thus giving
all nations a role and a share, seems a likely preferred strategy for
"have-nots."

Because of this potential for loss of their existing monopoly, major
space-going nations may prefer other, less structured alternatives.
The similar situation in law-of-the-sea negotiations has produced a
warning from William Rogers, as U.S. undersecretary of state for
economic affairs, that "Many of the developing countries are trying
to impose a doctrine of total internationalization on the industrial
countries, which alone have the technological and financial capacity
for mining the seabeds in the foreseeable future. The U.S. has offered
to find financing and to transfer the technology to make international
mining a reality. But total internationalization is out of the question.
. . . There are limits beyond which we cannot and should not go."[24]
Outright violation of international space law by some great power
would be costly and potentially destabilizing: a national program to
acquire exclusive control over important extraterrestrial resources
and to construct large platforms in space would arouse national
security fears in other major powers. Presumably, strong counter-
pressures would be aroused. But full internationalization seems too
much to expect at this time.

Reinterpretation of existing law and principles may, however,
permit important space development by some middle road between
national exclusivity and unlikely "space government." Glazer has
sought to apply traditional state-centric law to outer space development and has found several possible avenues.[25] Under his flexible
interpretation of current international law, one possible option would
be resurrection of the concept of a "free city" that was applied to
Danzig and Trieste. A multilateral treaty might create a class of
internationalized, less-than-sovereign legal entities in space, with
sufficient legal capacity to accept limited legal rights and obligations.
These entities would be neither solely national instruments nor
themselves nations and would thus neatly evade the problems of
"national appropriation" while simultaneously allowing their sponsoring nations to exercise control in the most significant matters.
Perhaps the North Atlantic Treaty Organization, the European
Economic Community, the Council of Mutual Economic Assistance,
or other multinational groups could sponsor such a free city, thus
maintaining the existing legal regime while evading broader
international control.

Something similar to the free city may be in the minds of both O'Neill and Peter Glaser.[26] They refer to what are probably international, or at least multinational, space industry operating organizations that seem to resemble the International Telecommunications Satellite Consortium (INTELSAT). Intelsat was created by multilateral treaty as an "international public utility" to operate and regulate international satellite communications. Such a model might meet legal requirements as postulated by Glazer but does present some political and organizational problems.

Christol and others, drawing on analogies from current sea-law controversy, assume that national resource competitions in space will not automatically benefit all nations and therefore contemplate the necessity of some variety of international organization to meet demands for greater equity of benefits. Glazer's models, however, would attempt to avoid a future in which space development is "monolithically centralized," instead preserving an essentially single-country exploitation model or creating a special-purpose "loophole" device such as the free city for use by groups of nations. Christol's model suffers from the usual infirmities of large international organizations, which must be multifunctional, deal with very important matters, and satisfy a broad range of national interests; Glazer's are still likely to spark the rivalry and controversy that would be aroused by unambiguous single-nation actions, without providing any offsetting benefits.

A third alternative might build on Glazer, plus the models provided by the U.S. Constitution and some of the usual features of U.S. antitrust laws. Space colonization and industrial exploitation as described above are clearly complex, interdependent, specialized enterprises. We may analytically subdivide the whole in several ways, only one—location of activity—of which will be used here for illustrative purposes:

1. Earth-based (at least until well along in the program) activities, such as surface-to-orbit shuttles, managerial coordination, financing, marketing, and industrial production
2. Lunar-based mining and associated operations
3. Colony-based industrial fabrication
4. Satellite power station operations

Accepting Glazer's premise that it will be easier and just as suitable to adapt existing law rather than to invent new modes, we may construct an "antitrust" space law regime that permits any one country or international organization to operate in no more than one (or two or three, depending upon the degree of "safety" desired) of the above listed subdivisions. A central coordinating organization would probably be necessary for efficient operation, but it could be international and could be barred from direct involvement in operating areas. Those who propose measures to control the multinational oil corporations frequently construct similar models.[27]

Space exploitation will require extensive interdependence between the several operating divisions listed above, but antitrust provisions would require their legal and political separation. The coordinating agency, under the logic of separated powers as in the U.S. Constitution in which each "branch" has a self-interest in both cooperation with the other branches and in checking their unrestrained growth and power, may be able to avoid both extremes of "monolithic centralization" and nationalistic aggrandizement. Each member nation should be able to assure that its interests would not be endangered, whereas a norm of cooperation would be necessary for successful exploitation. The American federal government has operated for two centuries on a similar model: some degree of inefficiency and risk of deadlock has been accepted as the price for prevention of tyrannous government, while the overarching need for cooperation forces compromise. Perhaps a similar, functional division of powers in space can provide a key to both legal and political institution building. Additionally, such a model automatically spreads financial burdens and benefits across a number of countries, thus easing the problem of raising capital and simplifying the problems of distribution of profits.

Some Organizational and Political Possibilities

The organizational and political devices used for space exploitation will be shaped by, and will continue to shape, the legal model established. Current space law and practice, as well as normal international rivalry, seem to rule out the possibility of some single nation dominating all areas of space industrialization. The 1967 Outer Space Treaty requires that all space activities must be under "authorization and continuing supervision by the appropriate State Party to the Treaty" (Article VI), which equally clearly rules out the possibility of a wide-open private-enterprise approach in which governments stand aside. Finally, unless something highly unexpected happens in the theory and practice of world government, there is unlikely to be anything approximating "space government" on the supranational level.

Assuming a space law regime that is neither a single, all-embracing government nor a real anarchy, organizations involved in space industrialization must utilize models that are flexible. An international legal regime and its organizational components must work both on earth and in space and must work with individuals and groups who will no doubt also remain subject to their own national laws in areas and roles not controlled directly by international space law. A similar condition exists in regard to ocean law, in which individuals may be subject to international law, to the laws of their nation of citizenship, or to the laws of other nations, depending on the particular conditions.

There is a tendency to extrapolate from existing models of space organization into the future, although this probably will produce an inappropriate model for space industrialization. Existing space organizations deal with narrow functional and usually technical problems: communication satellite operation, resource surveys, meteorology. Although complex, these are relatively impersonal and small scale, focused on technology.[28] Models of organization that have appeared in space industry literature, such as the "Ensat"[29] or "Sunsat"[30] models, assume a relatively narrow-focus, technology-dominated, functional organization held together primarily by economic motivations. There is a clear analogy to Intelsat.

E. B. Skolnikoff has modeled the effective international organization, particularly those which are technology related, as being characterized by highly specialized and technical subject matter, having a clearly defined and restricted function, with a membership limited to only those nations directly involved in the technology and operation (thus, a small number in most cases) and with an organizational structure allowing representation and control based on the recognition of unequal power, stakes, and expertise of the members.[31] In brief, the organization is administrative rather than overtly political. Intelsat seems to meet most of these requirements rather well and has been successful. But can this model apply to space industrialization?

According to the O'Neill scenario, within some thirty years there would be a human population in space numbering at least ten thousand and perhaps as much as a million. Because of the rapid growth capabilities of the system and the presumed great attractiveness of life in space, that number could grow geometrically—into the billions. Certainly, even numbers of people approaching a million would be beyond the scope of Skolnikoff's model: in 1970 more than ten national governments had populations of less than one million, and a majority of the world's nations had fewer than ten million persons. This scale of human population suggests that politics will be at least as important as bureaucratic organization.

In addition to sheer numbers of people in space, there is the expectation that very large proportions of national and international energy systems will depend upon satellite solar power. Massive economic stakes will be involved. National, even planetary, economic and social well-being could depend upon the energy, industrial products, and perhaps raw materials produced in space. Simultaneously, according to the plan, the space industries themselves would be in the process of reducing their dependence on earth by developing asteroid resources, space agriculture, and machine facilities. This reversal of roles, from space "colonies" dependent on earth to the opposite condition, will clearly have political consequences.

Something analogous to this process has happened before in human history, in the great colonial migrations of the seventeenth through the nineteenth centuries in the Western world and in other cases throughout recorded history. Colonies begin as administrative, functional organizations but develop internal and external politics. "Mother countries" have always insisted upon a significant voice in the affairs of their daughters, and successful colonies usually have sooner or later drawn free. During this process both the colony and the sponsoring nation had to adjust to the development of new economic relationships, new value constellations, new types of both cooperation and friction—that is, to conflict and its resolution by political means. Whether one sees space communities as historically similar to colonies that will seek liberation or as economic dependents that will grow in power and eventually rival the mercantilist core powers that established them,[32] there is clearly a potential for rivalry between nations on earth over control of space industry, between groups in space, and between earth and the colonies. The Skolnikoff technology-oriented model is clearly not applicable to space industrialization.

At the opposite extreme would be an organizational mode dominated by representational and economic equity concerns rather than functional expertise, with multipurpose functions and something approaching universal membership. The organization would deal with high stakes, intense public interest, and a complex set of demands. Formation of this organization would be of great significance, because the terms of its charter would be an important part of the stakes. It is not unreasonable to expect development of what approximates a universal government for space to be slow in formation, diluted to a least common denominator, and difficult to work. Indeed, it seems unlikely to happen at all.

Between the narrow, "nonpolitical" functionalism of an Ensat and the pitfalls of a space government lies the "separation of powers" model. This model is essentially a variety of functionalism, proposing that the advantages of cooperation will be sufficient to entice nations into accepting a buffered system within which they cannot control but can prevent others from controlling, while still gaining the material advantages sought.

Advocates of space industrialization, particularly for energy production, typically cite economic studies indicating that their preferred alternative is less costly than other alternatives and point to its possibility of very profitable long-term operation. Even though these are good advocacy points, it is still true that any project designed to supply a major portion of the world's energy will be enormously expensive. Current space industrialization studies indicate initial costs will run from as low as $40 billion to perhaps $200 billion over twenty-five years. For comparison, the 1975 Federal Energy Agency estimated cumulative capital requirements in 1975–85 alone for electric generating plants at almost $200 billion, to implement Project Independence. In increasingly burdened capital markets, as nations attempt to deal with not only the capital needs of increasingly expensive energy but a host of other demands, there will probably be great reluctance by any one nation to shoulder an additional capital burden of this size.

There is a history of U.S.-Soviet negotiations on ways to save money by joint space projects and of somewhat more successful arrangements between the United States and several noncommunist countries for cost sharing, such as contract launches of satellites.[33] All these projects together would aggregate far less than the minimal initial costs of space industrialization. It is clear that saving money does not always overcome political objections, but it helps.[34] For the wealthier nations, there should be a willingness to pay some political price in order to obtain important economic help. The poor nations conversely may be able to pay only a small portion of the economic cost but be willing to do so in return for some political voice in a program of very great potential importance to them. By dividing the space industry system into several program elements and organizing economic and political participation around them, it should be possible to accommodate a number of variations in national size, wealth, goals, and so on.

An organization composed of and responsible to several different nations, with nationals of several countries involved, should be sufficiently full of security leaks to make it very difficult for any nation to mount a security threat through the space industry system. The complex ramifications of organizational coordination should create sufficient bureaucratic structure and interties to allow nation-states a number of options for normal interest-group maneuvering as part of the check-and-balance system. In brief, the technological motivations of efficiency, economy, and effectiveness may, in this case, require for their political acceptability the use of a political structure capable of frustrating any level of efficient action that might constitute a threat. If space industrialization is to proceed, the political price must be paid.

Summary

It is a curious fact that human societies frequently exhibit an inertia akin to that of physical bodies under Newton's laws. Although the advice of Schumacher, Lovins, and others urging a simplified life style and ecological adjustments may be the essence of wisdom, it violates the dominant social paradigm of the industrialized societies that would have to accept and live by it and offers little attraction to developing nations. These societies have demonstrated a preference for social problem solution by means of very large-scale, complex technology: nuclear power systems, concentrated industries, massive waterworks to move rivers rather than people, supersonic planes rather than a slower pace of life. The energy crisis has brought forth chiefly programs for increased energy supply; population explosions have produced the advice that we should "increase the banquet of life" rather than limit the diners. In view of this observed regularity of human behavior, coupled with the apparent technical and economic feasibility of space industrialization, it seems quite reasonable to believe that this paper is dealing with a high-probability future.

We have not been particularly good at dealing prospectively with the sociopolitical aspects of technological developments, even when they could reasonably have been foreseen long before their arrival. Many of the social and political ramifications of nuclear energy systems, ocean-mining technology, computerized personal data systems, and other recent technologies could have been—and sometimes were—foreseen, but little or nothing was done about them until quite late. Technology assessment and forecasting and social impact assessment are gaining respectability and attention as means of changing that pattern.

For technological development of the potential importance and comparatively fast time scale of space industrialization, we urgently require simultaneous efforts toward assessment and institution modeling. This essay presents preliminary models for both international law and organization and a preliminary assessment of some basic national security questions aroused by the concept of space industrialization. No fundamental obstacle to realization of the concept is apparent. Design criteria for central elements of the legal, organizational, and security components of the concept are described. In keeping with Ophuls definition of "design" as the approach that seeks to produce an outcome "by establishing criteria to govern the operations of the process so that the desired result will occur more or less automatically, without further human intervention,"[35] basic structural and motivational elements are emphasized. Thus, the legal structure recommended emphasizes incremental change and use of existing national and international legal models; the organizational structure assumes that nations will continue to exhibit nationalist concern for security and participation; the national security model emphasizes the neutralization of the system rather than its active defense.

International
Environment Management

In his essay, "The Tragedy of the Commons," Garrett Hardin maintains that a management regime is necessary to regulate common property resources. Nowhere is the need for management more evident than in the case of the heightened pressure to exploit the wealth of the oceans with the inadequacy of land-based agriculture and resources to meet exponentially growing demands. The intransigence of the delegates to the Third United Nations Law of the Seas Conference, which began in Caracas in 1974, is illustrative of the obstacles encountered in developing a system of resource management.

The three essays in this section address two fundamental issues of resource management: first, the assignment of responsibility for environmental preservation and, second, the forms of regulations that will be the most effective and equitable. In the first article, George Kent suggests reasons to question reliance on individual nation-states, particularly in regard to the management of ocean fisheries. Establishment of 200-mile territorial waters, for example, does not necessarily prevent overfishing, nor does it promote equity. A possible alternative is the "common heritage principle," first placed before the General Assembly by Arvid Pardo in 1967, which presumes an international governing agency that would regulate the exploitation of ocean resources and distribute the benefits equitably. In the second essay, James Larry Taulbee discusses alternative legal strategies for environmental management, drawing a distinction between approaches that assign liability for injury or damage and those that would impose regulations or set environmental standards. Although neither of these approaches has as yet been developed into an effective set of legal instruments for encouraging ecological responsibility, the latter appears to have more potential. To be

5

successful in coping with environmental problems, however, we may have to make radical changes in the existing state system.

Whether individual nation-states should unilaterally take responsibility for resource management and environmental preservation or defer to international institutions is an issue discussed in the third essay. Donald C. Piper asks whether unilateral actions, such as the extension of territorial waters for fishing or regulations designed to limit the risk of oil pollution, are a necessary stopgap procedure for coping with immediate environmental problems. In the long run, these unilateral initiatives may prove to be an important first step in the cumbersome process of formulating international law.

Ocean Fisheries Management*

George Kent

The Context

The international law of fisheries in effect until 1978 was codified in one of the four conventions produced at the First United Nations Conference on the Law of the Sea, held in Geneva in 1958. This Convention on Fishing and Conservation of the Living Resources of the High Seas obtained enough signatures to come into force in March 1966. It affirmed the generally accepted pattern whereby coastal states had full jurisdiction over the fisheries resources of their territorial seas and all states had free access to fishing on the high seas beyond those coastal jurisdictions.[1]

The Second United Nations Conference on the Law of the Sea, held in 1960, again in Geneva, tried but failed to reach agreement on a standard width for the territorial seas of coastal states. As a result, there has been a great deal of variation in claims, with some states, such as the United States, claiming territorial seas of only 3 miles' width and other states, particularly Latin American states, claiming territorial seas of up to 200 miles' width.

Other variations have been introduced by some states, claiming jurisdiction for special purposes beyond their territorial seas. Several states have claimed special conservation or pollution control zones. Several have made claims to exclusive fishery zones beyond their territorial seas. The United States, for example, passed a law in 1966 (P.L. 89–658, 80 Stat. 908) establishing a contiguous fishery zone out to a distance of 12 miles from the United States' coasts. This was superseded by the Fisheries Conservation and Management Act of

*Adapted by permission from *Ocean Management* 4 (1978):1–20.

1978, which established U.S. jurisdiction over fisheries out to 200 miles from shore.

By the end of 1977, virtually all major nations had claimed, or indicated their intention to claim, jurisdiction over fishing out to 200 miles off their coasts. The aggregate effect of these many unilateral actions is the creation of an entirely new order of the oceans, an order that is being established whether or not it is ultimately sanctioned in the form of a new multilateral convention on the law of the sea.

Although there are broad similarities, it should be clear that widespread agreement on the convention developed at the Third United Nations Conference on the Law of the Sea would have effects quite different from those that would emerge from a new customary law based on the accumulation of unilateral actions. An agreement to conventional law would establish that law in fine detail, it would establish uniformity across states, it would create clarity as to the content of the law, and it would provide detailed means for dispute settlement. Moreover, the draft convention provides for innovative new institutional arrangements with respect to the exploitation of minerals of the seabed out beyond national jurisdictions. Thus, despite the wave of unilateral actions, the emerging convention on the law of the sea is of very great importance.

After years of preparatory work, the first session of the Third United Nations Conference on the Law of the Sea was held in New York in December 1973. Additional sessions were held in Caracas, Geneva, and New York through the following years. The conference's mandate was "to adopt a convention dealing with all matters relating to the law of the sea," that is, to formulate a wholly new framework for the management of the world's oceans, replacing that codified in 1958.

The range of the issues was indicated by the way the agenda was divided among the three major working committees. Committee I was charged with working out a new regime for governing the seabed out beyond national jurisdictions. Committee II was to delimit and work out the rights and responsibilities of states and other parties in different zones of the sea. Committee III's main task was to develop the rules governing protection of the ocean environment, scientific research, and transfer of technology. The primary responsibility for dealing with fishing was thus lodged with Committee II.

There are three broad areas of consensus emerging from this Third Conference: (1) there will be a territorial sea of up to 12 miles' width for all coastal states; (2) there will be a 200-mile exclusive economic zone in which coastal states will have jurisdiction over the economic resources; and (3) a new International Seabed Authority will be created to manage the exploitation of the resources of the sea floor out beyond national jurisdictions. At the close of 1978, there was still a great deal of disagreement within this framework, however, such as the disputes over the exact structure and powers of the new authority and the question of what should be the rights of states other than the coastal states within the 200-mile exclusive economic zones.

The broad outlines of the likely agreement have been clear from the outset of the conference, but the specifics have undergone continuing negotiation and refinement. This has been apparent in the draft texts that have been produced. The session of the conference that met in Geneva in 1975 produced an *Informal Single Negotiating Text*. After the second of the two sessions held at the United Nations in New York in 1976, a *Revised Single Negotiating Text* was released, superseding the earlier text. This in turn was replaced by the *Informal Composite Negotiating Text*, which came out of another session held in New York in 1977. In each case it was understood that the text was not a negotiated draft but only a basis for negotiations prepared by the chairmen of the three committees. The following survey of the proposals for the management of fishing is based on the *Informal Composite Negotiating Text*.[2]

The Text

According to this draft text, the exclusive rights of coastal states to fish in their adjacent territorial seas would remain total and unqualified by virtue of their sovereignty over those waters (art. 2). Under the new treaty, all states would have territorial seas with a standard limit of 12 miles' width (art. 3).

The rights of all states to fish on the high seas would remain essentially as they are now (art. 116). States are asked to adopt measures to assure that their nationals work toward the conservation of the living resources of the high seas (art. 117), and a gesture toward international management is made in the assertion that "States shall cooperate with each other in the management and

conservation of living resources in the areas of the high seas"
(arts. 118, 119).

The most highly disputed fishing rights are those proposed for the
area between the territorial seas and the high seas, the exclusive
economic zone, extending out to 200 miles from shore. In this area
the coastal state would have "sovereign rights" over the living
resources, but that sovereignty would be tempered by the requirement that "the coastal State shall have due regard to the rights and
duties of other States" (art. 56).

The rights of states other than the coastal state to fish in the
economic zone are indicated in articles 62, 69, and 70, but the
predominance of the rights of the coastal state is clearly established in
the "conservation" provisions of article 61: "The coastal State shall
determine the allowable catch of the living resources in its exclusive
economic zone."

According to article 62, "where the coastal State does not have the
capacity to harvest the entire allowable catch, it shall . . . give other
States access to the surplus of the allowable catch." In determining
what is allowable, the coastal state is asked to take into account such
things as the significance of the fishery to its own economy and its
other national interests, the requirements of developing countries in
the region, and the need to "minimize economic dislocation in States
whose nationals have habitually fished in the zone."

Article 69 gives special attention to landlocked states, saying they
"shall have the right to participate in the exploitation of the living
resources of the exclusive economic zone of adjoining coastal States
on an equitable basis, taking into account the relevant economic and
geographical circumstances of all the States concerned." The meaning
of this and the specific terms of participation are to be determined by
agreement among the concerned parties. The application of this
article to developed landlocked states is limited in that they may
exercise their rights only within the economic zones of adjoining
developed coastal states.

Article 70 is concerned with developing coastal states that either
(1) depend on fishing in the exclusive economic zones of neighboring
states for the fulfillment of their nutritional needs or (2) can claim no
exclusive economic zones of their own. Such states "shall have the
right to participate, on an equitable basis, in the exploitation of living
resources in the exclusive economic zone of other States in a
subregion or region." Unlike the provision for the landlocked states,

this right is not limited to the economic zones of adjoining states. The terms and conditions for the participation of these special groups of developing coastal states in the economic zones of other coastal states are to be determined by agreement among the concerned parties.

In addition to the general rules governing who may fish where, there are also special provisions proposed for the management of different species. For tunas and other highly migratory species, the concerned states "shall cooperate directly or through appropriate international organizations with a view to ensuring conservation and promoting the objectives of optimum utilization of such species throughout the region, both within and beyond the exclusive economic zone." Moreover, "In regions where no appropriate international organization exists, the coastal State and other States whose nationals harvest these species in the region shall cooperate to establish such an organization and participate in its work" (art. 64).

Article 65, on marine mammals, says only that "Nothing in the present Convention restricts the right of a coastal State or international organization, as appropriate, to prohibit, regulate and limit the exploitation of marine mammals."

Anadromous fish are those that swim up rivers and streams to spawn but live out the major portion of their lives in the open ocean. Salmon is the most common example. The basic regulatory principle proposed in article 66 is that "States in whose rivers anadromous stocks originate shall have the primary interest in and responsibility for such stocks." Fishing for anadromous stocks would not be conducted in the high seas but only in the economic zones and territorial seas of coastal states. An exception would be made for cases in which this would result in "economic dislocation" for a state other than the state of origin.

Catadromous species spawn on the high seas but spend much of their lives inland in fresh-water streams and rivers. Some eels are catadromous. Article 67 says that "A coastal State in whose waters catadromous species spend the greater part of their life cycle shall have responsibility for the management of these species." They are to be harvested only in the waters of those responsible coastal states. If they migrate through the waters of another state, harvesting is to be regulated by agreement among the states concerned.

Article 77 specifies that sedentary species are included as part of the natural resources of the continental shelf over which the coastal states exercise sovereign rights for the purpose of exploitation.

Sedentary species are defined in the article as "organisms which, at the harvestable stage, either are immobile on or under the sea-bed or are unable to move except in constant physical contact with the sea-bed or subsoil."

Extended Jurisdiction

The major response of the Law of the Sea Conference to the problems of fisheries management has been to propose the extension of coastal state jurisdiction out to 200 miles. Many developing countries have expressed the view that this would help them to develop economically and would help to slow the widening of the gap between rich and poor. The representative from Barbados, for example, said that the existing law of the sea "reflected the interests of the great maritime Powers" and "served merely to widen the gap between the developed and the developing countries." He argued that "economic necessity justified the principle that a coastal State could unilaterally extend its jurisdiction and control" over coastal resources out to 200 miles.[3]

The urge to extend control is largely due to the recognition that some 90 percent of the ocean fish that are caught are caught near coasts. Because of the concentration of fish there and because of their easier accessibility, jurisdiction over areas near coasts is far more valuable than jurisdiction over areas of equal size in midocean. Of course, the extremely valuable offshore oil, found in the continental shelves, is concentrated along the coasts as well.

Although developing countries like Barbados would gain something, it is now clear that the extension of coastal jurisdictions would be of greatest benefit to the physically large countries, most of which are developed. With its many outlying possessions, Alaska, Hawaii, and its long continental coasts, the United States would gain most of all, 2,222,000 square miles. The next largest gains would be by Australia (2,043,300 square miles), Indonesia (1,577,300 square miles), New Zealand (1,409,500 square miles), and Canada (1,370,000 square miles).[4] The area gained by the United States alone would have "an annual potential production of at least 18 billion pounds of fish for food and recreation, or about 10 percent of the total estimated world production," thus constituting "the largest fisheries resources of any nation in the world."[5] Among the developed countries,

Japan would be an exceptionally great loser, because nearly half of its marine fisheries production has been from near the coasts of other nations.

The developed countries would be able to draw far more benefit from each square mile of extended jurisdiction than the developing countries, for a variety of reasons. As things stand now, many poor countries are not able to make full use even of their narrow territorial seas. Often limited to operations with very small boats, the extension of their legal jurisdictions would have no real impact. In contrast, the developed countries, with more capital and advanced technology at their disposal, would be able to take greater advantage of their increased jurisdiction.

Developing countries could invite developed countries to provide capital and technology for exploitation of their resources through joint ventures or other arrangements. Of course, the developing countries would then be obligated to share the benefits. The joint ventures or other contractual agreements are likely to be of greater benefit to the developed nations because of their greater bargaining power.

Where coastal developing countries do increase their participation in the production of fish, they are not likely to enjoy a proportionate increase in consumption. The decline in long-distance fishing will be met by an increase in international trade. For example, where Japan used to send out its own nationals to fish off the coasts of other nations, it will, in effect, hire the people of the coastal nations to do its fishing by importing from those nations. The pattern of the poor fishing for the rich will continue.[6]

It should also be noticed that most of the landlocked countries are poor, developing countries. Having no coasts, they obviously have no jurisdictions to extend. The rights granted to the landlocked states in the economic zones of other states are very weak. Since the landlocked states would be losing the legally unencumbered right to fish in the wide, resource-rich, and nearby area, which they had enjoyed when that area was regarded as part of the high seas, the landlocked states would be made substantially worse off by the extensions of coastal state jurisdictions out to 200 miles.

There are also extreme differences in the capabilities of the developed and the developing states to patrol and generally administer the new extended jurisdictions. The United States Coast Guard, Navy, National Marine Fisheries Service, and other agencies

have been planning for years in anticipation of their new responsibilities, and they are spending a great deal of money for new facilities
to patrol the area. Many small nations, in contrast, are barely capable
of patrolling their narrow territorial waters. They often experience
incursions into their waters by foreign fishing vessels, but they have
little capacity to do anything about it. Thus, the developing states are
far more likely to suffer from violations of their extended jurisdictions
than the developed states. If they do undertake the great costs of
preventing and prosecuting violations, that cost might well exceed
their gains from having jurisdiction over a wider area.

The problem of continuing inequities in the world cannot be met by
rearranging the geography of jurisdictions. At best, that could only
be a temporary corrective, in the same way that a one-time gift of
resources from the rich to the poor would only temporarily alter the
balance. It is obvious that the skew in the distribution of the world's
wealth is not due primarily to the fact that some nations are better
endowed with natural resources than others. If it were, Japan and
England would be desperately poor, and Latin Americans would
count themselves among the most comfortable.

Although direct control over natural resources is certainly *a* cause
of inequities, it is greatly overshadowed by the role of social
structures, and particularly the structure of trade relationships.
Thus, changing starting points with a one-time grant of enlarged
jurisdictions would not help in the long run because it would not alter
the major structural source of the problem.

Extending jurisdictions also fails to meet the problem of threats to
the integrity of the environment, whether through pollution or
through depletion of resources. Reading Garrett Hardin's metaphor
of the "tragedy of the commons," many observers have come to
believe that the major source of economic inefficiency and of environmental problems is the fact that many people have uncontrolled
access to a common resource.[7] One remedy, supposedly, is to fence
off or somehow partition that common resource into separate, closed
jurisdictions.

The analysis is misleading on several counts. One major difficulty
is that partitioning is different from containment; with partitioning,
the negative effects of one's actions can still spill over to hurt one's
neighbors. One nation's coastal pollution is likely to hurt its
neighboring nation, just as a nation's overfishing is likely to hurt
its neighbor.

If the economic conditions are right for it, overexploitation even of privately controlled pastures may be economically rational. That is, even under single management, there may be strong motivations to exploit renewable resources at rates that exceed the maximum sustainable yield. The fisherman might be better off economically if he were to fish out the entire stock for immediate profit and place his proceeds in a bank to earn interest. Economic rationality can be reconciled with environmental rationality but only with more deliberate institutional interventions than fence building.

Perhaps most seriously, Hardin's metaphor ignores the problem of inequalities in the powers of the parties. In the real world, some people are more capable of shunting the costs of pollution and of overexploitation onto others. The excessive whaling by Japan and the Soviet Union, for example, represents the exercise of oligopolistic power more than it represents a tragedy of unlimited access by large numbers of more or less equal competitors. Partitioning is of little help in dealing with the problem of inequities in the distribution of benefits from the use of the sea.

The lesson that ought to be drawn from the tragedy of the commons is the necessity for positive management at the global level. Hardin himself recognizes the need: "It is doubtful if we can create territories in the ocean by fencing. If not, we must—if we have the will to do it—adopt the other alternative and socialize the oceans: create an international agency *with teeth*."[8] A central authority is needed to systematically alter the structure of incentives in order to reduce the motivation to overexploit both nature and humankind.

Assessment

Beyond the misplaced faith in extending jurisdictions, the major failing of the fisheries articles of the *Informal Composite Negotiating Text* is that, rather than coming to grips with the problems that need to be resolved, they put them off, offering only the bland hope that they will be addressed in negotiations among the concerned parties at some unspecified time in the future. For example, rather than saying what constitutes "equitable" participation for landlocked states, article 61 says only that "The terms and conditions of participation shall be determined by the States concerned through bilateral, subregional, or regional agreements."

One of the major arguments advanced for giving other states the right to fish in the exclusive economic zone of coastal states has been that, where the coastal state has limited fishing capacity, the "surplus" beyond that taken by the coastal state should not be allowed to go to waste. It should be recognized, however, that if a state has full and exclusive rights over fishing in a given area, fishermen of other nations may be admitted, not as a matter of right but through negotiated agreement with the coastal state.

To the extent that other states can demand entry as a matter of right, however, the coastal state cannot demand payment for entry. Thus, to the extent that the doctrine of full utilization requires admission of noncoastal states, it works to the disadvantage of underdeveloped coastal states and to the advantage of nations able to send out fishing fleets.

This would be a matter of concern, except for the fact that in the text there are no clear rights granted to the landlocked states or to "certain developing coastal states" for access to the exclusive economic zones of other states. That could be accomplished only through a specification of what those states could claim as rightfully theirs in the absence of agreement between them. That specification is needed to clarify their positions, for it is what a state can command in the absence of agreement that establishes its bargaining power in negotiations. As the draft stands, noncoastal states have very weak rights and only a weak basis for claiming those rights. As long as future arrangements are left to ordinary political negotiations, with no clear new rights granted to the landlocked or the developing states, those states will remain at a great disadvantage.

Thus, apart from the delaying tactics, there is also an intolerable ambiguity with respect to rights and obligations. With provisions as fuzzy as those in article 61, it is no wonder that the landlocked states, together with the other geographically disadvantaged states, protested that the first *Informal Single Negotiating Text* "did not take account of the legitimate rights and interests of the Group" and that, in the Revised Text, "no noticeable progress has been achieved." What is the purpose of these arduous negotiations if so much is to be left to future negotiations?

The 1958 law-of-the-sea conventions did not stand, largely because they were ambiguous on critical points. Some slack in interpretations in international agreements is generally needed to accommodate different perspectives, but when the lack of clarity goes too far, the life of the agreement is endangered. At some points, phrasing known to be a source of difficulty in the 1958 conventions has been retained in the current draft. Article 77's definition of sedentary species, for example, is the same definition used in the 1958 Geneva Convention on the Continental Shelf. Oysters, clams, and other kinds of mollusks are clearly included, but the new text does nothing to resolve the disagreements over whether crustaceans such as crabs, lobster, and shrimp should be regarded as sedentary species. The Soviets, for example, have argued that crabs walk on their continental shelf and thus are Soviet property, while the Japanese have argued that crabs swim and thus are free to be taken by any nation.

The fisheries articles of the text reflect a mixture of ad hoc accomodations to particular interests, especially to the interests of the major maritime powers. The provisions on anadromous species, for example, reflect an accommodation between the United States and Japan who, in the past, have been in serious conflict over salmon fishing in the Pacific. Article 65 on marine mammals offers only a disclaimer of responsibility, leaving the control of whaling in the ineffectual hands of the International Whaling Commission—as if no improved management structure were needed. The provisions on fishing show no clear bases in principle for allocating rights and responsibilities among the concerned parties. They show no serious appreciation of the gravity of the problems of fisheries management.

Broadly, the text says that coastal state interests are to prevail for all but migratory species. Many issues of detail remain unresolved. More significantly, however, the major response—extending state jurisdictions—is inherently inadequate. Despite the fact that the problems of production, conservation, and allocation of fisheries resources are so much more intense now than they have ever been in the past, the proposals embodied in the text do not begin to meet these urgent problems of fisheries management on a global scale.

The Common Heritage Idea

Traditionally, all oceanic resources have been understood as either *res nullius* or *res communis*. *Res nullius* resources are understood to be *no one's*, and subject to appropriation. *Res communis* or *common property* resources are understood as being *anyone's*, and not subject to appropriation. They are equally accessible to all, available for anyone's use. Under *res communis*, resources belong to those who first use or take them. Fish taken on the high seas, for example, have traditionally been *res communis* resources. They are public goods, like the air, or like highways or parks or open pastures that anyone may use freely. Both *res nullius* and *res communis* are very different from the common heritage idea, by which some resources should be regarded as *everyone's*, and subject to their joint management.

The common heritage principle, providing a wholly new understanding of the nature of property rights, was first placed before the United Nations General Assembly in 1967 by Ambassador Arvid Pardo of Malta. In accordance with his proposal, in 1970 the General Assembly passed a resolution, the Declaration of Principles Governing the Seabed and Ocean Floor and the Subsoil Thereof, beyond the Limits of Nations' Jurisdictions (Res. 2749, XXV), in support of the common heritage principle.

The principle is being interpreted at the Law of the Sea Conference as applying only to the resources of the sea floor beyond national jurisdictions, which in effect means it is to apply only to the exploitation of manganese nodules out beyond 200 miles from the coasts of nations. However, it could conceivably be applied to fisheries or to any other kind of resources. It is useful, therefore, to describe the idea at a sufficiently high level of abstraction so that it could be applied to many different kinds of resources.

The irreducible essence of the common heritage idea appears to be that resources regarded as part of the common heritage of mankind are to be governed in accordance with these major principles:

1. *Peacefulness*. The resource should be used only for peaceful purposes.

2. *Equity*. The benefits derived from the use of the resource should be distributed equitably. This in turn means: (a) as a *common* heritage, everyone is entitled to share in some measure in the benefits from the use of the resource, which necessarily implies nonappropriability, such that no individual, corporation, or government has the right to claim the resource for its own exclusive benefit; (b) a greater share of the benefits should go to the poor.

3. *Environmental Integrity*. As the heritage of the future as well as the present, users of the resources should show respect for the environment, limiting both depletion and pollution.

4. *Common management*. To give effect to these principles, a governing agency responsible for their implementation must be established. That agency, acting in behalf of all humankind, should provide for participation by all affected parties in the making of its decisions.[9]

This common heritage idea should be understood as a wholly new concept of property rights, a modern alternative to the traditional ideas of exclusive ownership or of free and unlimited access. In earlier times, the laissez-faire doctrine helped to meet the problems of speeding the extraction of needed resources and accelerating industrial development. The older, essentially anarchic property concepts served good purposes in an era of relatively small clashes, expanding resource frontiers, and modest environmental impacts. But now that the limits of natural and human exploitation have been approached, the old ideas fail us.

New and different modes of management are needed. The common heritage idea, anticipating a wholly new kind of resource management, can provide the basis for that new order.

Recommendations

The thought that the common heritage principle should be extended to all of ocean space has already been articulated, most prominently in the draft ocean space treaty presented by Malta to the Seabed Committee, and in Elisabeth Mann Borgese's draft "Constitution for the Oceans."[10] Constructive ideas have also been developed in the Resources for the Future's Program of International Studies of Fishery Arrangements and by the American Society of International Law.[11]

The difficulty is that those with political power have not taken these proposals very seriously. Their time has not yet come. But that is only part of the problem. Advocates should not assume that these ideas have been ignored only because of the obstinacy and irrationality of those in power. The evidence is that the arguments have not been persuasive, and that is partly an observation on the arguments themselves.

They can be improved. Earlier proposals for the creation of some sort of global authority for the management of fishing ought to be restudied, and the reactions to them ought to be carefully reviewed. The lessons from these experiences can be used to guide the formulation of new proposals, proposals that are more sensitively attuned to the major actors and their concerns.

Can we discover, for example, why it is that the developing countries have not been more ardent in advocating the common heritage idea? Some observers suggest that the developing countries simply failed to understand their own true interests. Aaron Danzig found their position to be "amazing" and "stupid": "With a choice of placing the resources . . . in a common pot for the benefit of all mankind but primarily for the benefit of the developing countries, or alternatively, each country appropriating for itself as much as possible, one would expect the developing countries to opt for the common pot. Unfortunately, the opposite has turned out to be true. The developing countries have joined a stampede to divide the best part of the ocean treasure *colonial style*."[12]

How can we understand this new "Third World colonialism"? Danzig seems to favor his explanation that it is due to a conflict of interest among the developing states themselves (for example, some have wide and some have narrow continental shelves) and to dismiss the problems of "the developing countries distrust of anything proposed by an imperial power."

I think Danzig underestimates their distrust. The Third World fears that any new international organization will very likely be captured by the powerful nations of the world and turned to serve their interests. There is strong evidence for this in the history of the United Nations and its more specialized arms such as the Food and Agriculture Organization, the International Whaling Commission, and countless fisheries commissions. The distrust is greatly reinforced by their observation of the behavior of the more powerful nations in the negotiations over the constitution of the International Seabed Authority, which is to administer whatever is left of the common heritage when the Law of the Sea Conference concludes.

Apart from the suspicions by the weak that it would be turned to favor the strong, all nations fear that any new authority might gain too much power. Through the usual processes of accretion of power to the center, sooner or later the agency might impose unwarranted constraints on the freedom of action of the separate nations.

To meet those problems of fear and distrust, it is useful to distinguish between *comprehensive* management and *positive* management.

An agency with comprehensive authority would have responsibilities over the full range of activities, with nothing excluded from its purview. This question of its scope, however, is separate from the question of the degree to which the agency exercises power. It may be comprehensive but weak, if the authority is only allowed to offer guidelines and recommendations with respect to a broad range of activities. Having positive management power would mean that the authority would be able to act decisively with respect to some issues, whether those issues are narrowly specified or cover the entire range.

Surely, what is needed is an international organization with teeth. One of the major reasons for the failure of the International Whaling Commission is that it has not had the power to impose effective restrictions on each of its members without each member's consent. The nations of the world must come to see that accepting restrictions on their freedoms can be in their own best interests.

At the same time, however, it should be acknowledged that only certain teeth are necessary. Past proposals may have suggested vesting too much power, over too broad a range, in the central authority. To allay the legitimate fears, the positive functions of the central authority ought to be limited to a very narrow range. It should have clear and strong powers, but only in precisely specified areas, with all residual powers clearly retained by the separate nations. The constitution of the new authority should also include safeguards to prevent unwarranted and uncontrolled expansions of its jurisdiction. Remedies of this sort can help to meet the well-justified distrust ordinarily aroused by proposals for creating new central agencies.

One example of a narrowly specified function for a central authority is dispute settlement. Careful statements of how the agency is to undertake this work could be outlined in its constitution, with clear indications of the limits beyond which it may not go. A relevant model is provided in the dispute-settlement provisions of the text.

Another example would be the surveillance of fishing fleets to help prevent violations of coastal state jurisdictions. The global authority could be given powers to prevent or to punish such violations, or more narrowly, it could be limited to the task of monitoring ship traffic and informing nations when their waters appear to be violated. This would permit a broad sharing in the benefits of advanced technology such as satellite surveillance systems. Through services of this kind, the apparent centralization of power could actually enhance the control of individual nations within their jurisdictions, much as the institution of police within residential communities enhances each citizen's freedom to act without interference from others. Central authority can protect interests.

Conservation would be another arena in which the central authority could be given precisely limited functions. Coastal states might be granted the primary authority to manage the fish stocks off their shores, but the central agency might be authorized to intervene *if* the coastal state permitted serious and sustained overexploitation of the fish stocks or otherwise abused the resource.

This policing function need not be tyrannical. As Hardin argues, what is needed is *mutual coercion, mutually agreed upon.* If the coastal states participated in deciding the bases on which the central agency was to act, the constraints on their freedom to overexploit would be collectively self-imposed. Through this kind of action, nations acting jointly, in their own interests, can take the radical step of abolishing the unconstrained freedom to fish, whether within or beyond national jurisdictions.

For those with faith in the common heritage idea, there is much more work to be done. The major failings of the existing and anticipated nonmanagement of fisheries need to be documented more convincingly. There must be a better and clearer design of the institutional arrangements that can give effect to common heritage principles. More attention needs to be given to the design of transition strategies to achieve the implementation of those new arrangements.

It must be kept in mind that the proposals are to be addressed to skeptics, not just to the faithful. It should be possible to show that the proposed new methods of management would actually meet the major problems of concern and would accomplish that without incurring excessive costs. The most demanding challenge, perhaps, is the need to show, through analysis of the data, that most nations would in fact be better off, in material or other terms, with the proposed system of positive global management. Despite our wishes, lofty and abstract humanitarian and environmental goals are not enough to sway political decisions. Whether the major benefits are supposed to be material or of other kinds, the bases for the promises need to be persuasively demonstrated.

In some important ways, the agenda for the Law of the Sea Conference has been too narrow, making it impossible to deal with the essential structural sources of major problems. For example, the question of equity in fishing has been viewed entirely in terms of production: who catches what amounts of fish. Because of the patterns of trade, however, the inequalities in consumption are even more striking than they are in production. To broaden perspectives, Pardo and Borgese, and others, are trying to show how the law-of-the-sea issues should be understood as essential elements in the pursuit of a new international economic order. These connections between problems of ocean management and the more general organization of world order need to be explored more thoroughly.[13]

If the Third Law of the Sea Conference concludes with nothing more to propose for fisheries management than those elements embodied in the text, we must conclude that the problems remain on the world's unfinished agenda. The issues must be taken up again.

If a global authority for the positive management of fisheries is too much to hope for in the short run, it may be possible to move toward that objective in particular sectors. A model management structure might be created, for example, for tuna in the South Pacific, which has only recently been recognized as a problem in need of attention.

Merely redrawing lines on maps to say who may fish where would redistribute the initial stakes, but the game would remain the same. The remedy would still be essentially anarchic and thus would still tend to serve the interests of the powerful. If the social forces at work remain the same, the same old rules of power politics will prevail, and the long-run trends will remain the same. The major problems of fisheries management, such as overfishing and the skewed distribution of benefits, have not yet been attacked at their source. They can be solved only with new global structures for the positive management of the world's fisheries for the benefit of all mankind.

Law, Organization, and Environmental Concerns

James Larry Taulbee

I

A review of the literature on environmental and resource problems demonstrates a trite but nonetheless true proposition: strategies for dealing with international environmental problems depend upon one's basic conception of the present situation. Although the proposition may be trite because the same principle applies to every issue area in international politics, this does not diminish the importance of the observation. In environmental and resource questions, as in other issue areas, controversies can be directly related not only to differing assessments of the factual base but also to differing opinions as to what data constitute the factual base. Presently, as with any new or highly politicized issue area, it is the second of these questions—the description or definition of the situation—that has produced the greatest amount of controversy.

This is readily apparent in the steady-state or limits-to-growth debate. On the one hand, the logic and evidence of the work of the limits-to-growth advocates support the idea that the situation generated by human industrial activity will, in a relatively short time, alter the terms of human existence and perhaps make human survival questionable.[1] On the other hand, in opposition to this apocalyptic view, many scientists question the methods and conclusions of the limits-to-growth advocates and argue that the evidence available does not support the contention that the world is facing an immediate global environmental and resource crisis.[2] For example, another MIT-based study completed at approximately the same time as *The Limits to Growth* focused on "environmental problems whose cumulative effects on ecological systems are so large and prevalent that they have world wide significance."[3] This study identified less than ten processes and substances that required immediate remedial action. Similarly, Herman Kahn and his associates have consistently challenged the assumptions and conclusions of the steady-state economists.[4]

The general courses of action that derive from these two contrasting factual assessments might be characterized as world order radicalism versus world order gradualism. From the perspective of world order radicalism, the severe and imminent threat of disaster means that strict limitations and guides *must* be adopted and an enforcement authority with power to make conclusive determinations as to compliance must be fabricated. The capacity of states to pursue unilateral policies detrimental to the world community as a whole *must* be controlled. In sum, the logic of the advocates of world order radicalism differs little from that used by those who have found the necessity for transformation in the impact of technology on warfare or the demands of modern socioeconomic trends.[5]

Needless to say, the prescriptions of world order gradualists differ markedly. World order gradualists tend to assume either that there is no imminent problem or that there is no problem that is not amenable to a technical "fix." As a group, they assume that both resources and technology will be available to meet any future problem. In one sense, the difference between the two groups might just as well be termed world order pessimism versus world order optimism.

If we assess the merits of these various arguments, one factor is apparent—we have very little scientific knowledge about the biosphere and the interdependence of its subsystems. The problem of assessment is complicated by the fact that many of the problems are the result of exponential processes. No crisis is perceived, because the logic of exponential progressions runs counter to common sense and concern with the environment is a relatively new phenomenon. It may well be that at present we do not know enough to appreciate the scope of the problem or to define exactly where it is we stand.

In the past, the controlling assumption was of "earth as an open space." Little attention was given to the ecological impacts or risks of technological innovation. Writers have viewed industrialization as a constant advance toward control or mastery of the environment. Few writers recognized that technological innovations involve social

choices and that these choices could have widely varying consequences for society.[6] That the process of converting "nature" to
goods might have spillover costs potentially dangerous to humanity
still has not been fully accepted by the majority.

The problem of food production provides an excellent example.
Lack of knowledge is most evident in the debate over ocean
resources. At present there is considerable disagreement over how
much food the ocean might yield. There is no consensus on how
much of a fishing effort the ocean can support and still maintain a
natural reproductive equilibrium. Nor have such fundamental
questions as migration patterns of certain species been determined
with precision. After rising 6–7 percent per year for twenty years, the
world fish catch has declined, on average, 6 percent a year since 1971.
The causes for the decline have not yet been isolated with certainty.

The dislocations caused by introduction of "green revolution"
technology provide an interesting demonstration of innovation as
choice. Green revolution wheat strains have produced impressive
yields on the most fertile lands in such countries as India. However,
the focus on high technology and the amount of capital required to
utilize green revolution methods have diverted money and research
efforts from attempts to improve traditional methods of agriculture.
This is of great importance because there is accumulating evidence
that green revolution technology does not result in sufficient
increases in yields on less fertile acreage to recover the costs of
necessary inputs.[7] Moreover, the social side effects on land tenure
and agricultural employment practices have been enormous.[8] Finally,
the dependence on technical inputs necessary for green revolution
methods caused further problems when the prices of these inputs
soared in the wake of the 1973–74 rise in oil prices and the Indian
government, lacking viable alternatives, was forced to cut back
production.

The point is that while it may not be possible to demonstrate to
everyone's satisfaction that the world faces impending disaster, there
are numerous disturbing trends in population, energy production,
and industrial waste activity. Given the finitude of the earth's
resources, it does seem evident that the pace of present trends cannot
be sustained indefinitely into the future. A crisis may not be
imminent, but neither is it temporally or physically remote. It must be
kept in mind as well that the lead times for international action are

extremely long. Put somewhat differently, the key is to make carefully deliberated decisions while there are real alternatives, rather than by default when there are no options.

It does not require a sophisticated observer of the international system as presently organized to see that resources for both legislation and enforcement at the international level are painfully lacking; nor is there a great probability that these resources will be substantially increased in the immediate future. International institutions suffer from both limited authority and a lack of financial support. If the problems are such that there is a threat of imminent and irreversible catastrophe, there is little hope of survival. If any lessons may be drawn from history, the one that stands out with respect to international politics is that demonstrating a necessity for change does not guarantee that states will adopt appropriate strategies. In fact, nothing in recent state behavior suggests that the tempo of bargaining processes will suddenly increase to approximate the tempo of scientific and technological change.[9]

As an example, we may use past experience in lawmaking for the oceans. The most critical problem *is* the time span involved in negotiating international instruments. For the four major conventions produced by the 1958 Geneva Conference, the elapsed time for the policy-making process averaged twenty years or more depending on where one designates the beginning.[10] Even so, the scope of these conventions was limited. None could be considered to have "global" effect.

The Convention on Fishing and Conservation of the Living Resources of the High Seas took seventeen years to become a legal document. At the end of this period, it was binding only on twenty-two countries whose portion of the total world catch of pelagic fish made up slightly less than 14 percent.[11] More discouraging is the fact that by the time the Convention on Fishing and the Convention on the Continental Shelf entered into force, both were made obsolete by technological developments. In particular, the technology-based definition of the outer limits of the continental shelf was obviously dysfunctional before the convention entered into force.[12] A reading of the *Proceedings* of the continuing UN Conference on the Law of the Sea demonstrates that there is still little consensus on the control and management of marine resources.

The roots of the problem are relatively easy to trace. Successful cooperation in scientific activities up to the present has been based upon the implicit assumption that all mankind will benefit from the results. However, science is Janus-faced in that it is both an agent for improvement of mankind's lot and the author of most of the more urgent problems that threaten mankind's survival. In terms of gathering scientific data, it is often difficult to sort innocent information gathered purely for the sake of knowledge from information gathered for military or economic purposes. The techniques for sea-bottom exploration are the same for the oil geologist, the military planner, and the physical oceanographer. Additionally, most of the basic research carried on in the world today is nationally oriented and tied closely to military planning. For example, the United States has consistently blocked attempts to give the United Nations a major role in space communications.[13]

The result is that agencies such as the International Telecommunications Union (ITU), the World Meteorological Organization (WMO), and the World Health Organization (WHO) regulate areas of undisputed common interests and of little significance to peace. International organizations tend to spring up on an ad hoc basis as responses to specific problems. Indeed, the continuing organization resulting from the Stockholm Conference is one such example. Thus, for any new problem ,the diffusion of authority and competence resulting from this process requires the participation of a number of organizations whose functional missions overlap. Ernst Haas has observed: "As tasks of the U.N. become legitimate, they also become self-encapsulating and self-sufficient, preventing the more precariously established tasks to profit from the success of the legitimate ones."[14] Each organization tends to restrict its activities to a narrow range of subjects for which it will take responsibility. So, when the Intergovernmental Maritime Consultative Organization (IMCO) was asked to consider the problem of oil pollution of the sea from sources other than ships, it characteristically responded that this was a problem that touched on the areas of responsibility of more than one international agency and consequently joint work was necessary.[15]

There is little question that more scientific knowledge is needed to make intelligent policy decisions on environmental problems. However, again, scientific data often have a negative effect, and better knowledge does not always produce more rational and responsive solutions. New evidence may introduce new concepts and new interests that fragment the existing policy consensus.

Differences in perception of interest may spur some states to action and may cause intransigence on the part of the others. The data used for different political ends become a source of tension. This is evident in the recent sharp politicization of ocean affairs, particularly in the International Oceanographic Commission (IOC) where a broad difference of opinion has arisen between developed and less developed states. Many developing states have put sharp restrictions on or are denying permission altogether to scientific expeditions from developed states in waters or areas the developing view as within their jurisdiction.[16]

In a similar vein, the less developed states have acquired considerable expertise in maneuvering major policy issues of concern to the developed states in order to gain marginal bargaining leverage on other issues, such as colonialism. From this perspective, the need to acquire more technical data for "rational" decisions has been manipulated for leverage by a large number of states recently mobilized into participation through learning about the significance of the issues. An already unwieldy process has become even more so.

II

Insofar as international law as a separable consideration is concerned, its scope and effectiveness are limited by the twin laissez-faire principles of national sovereignty and freedom of the high seas. And it should not be overlooked that law is a technique for formalizing cooperative ventures, not an alternative strategy per se. The international legal order, because of its decentralized structure and the nature of contemporary politics, is particularly reliant upon voluntarism. Taken together, these "international facts of life" put states in a legal position to exploit to the limits of relevant technologies without regard for injury to the environment either within their own national territories or on the planetary commons.

These general characteristics, of course, affect almost all areas of state action. What is important for our purposes is the extent to which these facts of life dominate the international law of environmental protection. For example, broad definitions of national sovereignty mean that many of the more potentially dangerous processes such as population growth are totally excluded from regulation through international action. Where other areas of the law have carved out extensive exceptions to the sovereignty principle, surveys of the current status on international law, both conventional and customary, reveal a rather motley collection of limited and often still emerging limitations on state action with regard to the environment. Principles that might impose responsibility and liability for acts injurious to the environment of other states are still vaguely defined; nor has there been any recent great effort to regulate activities through treaty.

Environmental concerns are somewhat more apparent in the law of the sea.[17] There has been considerable effort given to regulating certain specific polluting activities, particularly within the last five years. Treaties in the field have also conferred on coastal states certain jurisdictional rights in areas beyond territorial waters that permit them to regulate injurious activities in those areas. Moreover, arguments analogous to "environmental injury" from sources beyond territorial jurisdiction, at least when the source is located on the high seas, have been made to allow states to take reasonable action to prevent or abate the threat. Such a right is contained in the 1969 IMCO Convention Relating to Intervention on the High Seas in Cases of Oil Pollution Casualties. The acceptance of this argument as a part of general international law, however, is a matter of great controversy. According to the traditional law of treaties, this principle will only affect the high contracting parties and will not be a matter of general obligation for all states. These observations are made to illustrate the fact that legal change does not flow inevitably from social or technological change.

If activities both within territorial jurisdiction and on the high seas are considered, there is still no general principle of international law that obligates states to refrain from injury to the environment itself, as distinguished from injury to the environment of a particular state. This should be contrasted with developments in some national legal orders where injuries to the environment are subject to regulation not only through civil procedures (law of torts), so that a mode of redress is available to individuals through their own initiative, but often through criminal penalties as well. The condition of the planet as a whole may be part of a general moral awareness, but there is little evidence that this awareness has found its way to international law. The Stockholm Declaration is a beginning, but one should keep in mind the comments of Joseph Stalin, who said of those instruments signed in the course of World War II: "A declaration I regard as Algebra, but an agreement as practical arithmetic. I do not wish to decry Algebra, but I much prefer practical arithmetic."[18] The test of Stockholm will be whether the principles so grandly proclaimed will be reflected in the practical arithmetic of state behavior.

The limitations of the law as a technique for dealing with new phenomena are reflected in the application of the responsibility/liability framework to environmental problems. The idea that legal responsibility for injury should be imposed upon the party who caused the damage has an old and honorable history; but establishing a law of environmental protection in this manner requires that we proceed on a case-by-case basis. Apart from the time involved in international adjudication, the major long-term environmental issues do not present themselves as a discrete set of problems, each with a definite technical/legal solution. Also beyond the episodic character of the liability framework is the consideration that the results of any particular litigation using the framework provide only a standard as to levels of injury *not* permitted. Seldom does litigation in liability cases serve the dual function of imposing responsibility for past acts and allocating the costs of future ones.[19] Furthermore, adducing proof of liability in many cases would be impossible. Lawyers tend to think in terms of paradigm cases, such as the oil spills, where problems of proof are comparatively easy. In contrast, most problems will occur as penumbral, not paradigm, cases. How would proof be adduced in the case of injury to fisheries at some distance from the coast from land-based or ocean-based sources that discharge relatively small quantities of pollutants but do so relatively often? The Rhine fish kill of 1969 provides an example of the difficulties authorities may have in establishing not only the cause of an injury but the origin of the injurious substance as well.

One alternative to the liability framework is the establishment of a legal regime that would set permissible levels for polluting discharges. This would conceive of environmental injury as an "external cost" imposed by those persons engaged in economic activity on those persons who are not so engaged.[20] The assumption in any such regime is that such economic activity has a positive benefit to the community at large, and thus some sacrifice in the form of external costs such as a certain level of pollution must be borne by the community to support the enterprise. The legal regime would accept some pollution to balance the value of the environment as a protected interest against the value of the enterprise to the community. The thrust would be to set a permissible limit of injury.

As an approach, this is attractive as a means of dealing with readily identifiable and immediate concerns. However, as a long-term strategy, it suffers from many of the same defects of the liability framework. First of all, it requires that the concept of the environment as a legally protected interest be developed. As indicated before, there seems to be little movement in this direction. Second, such a legal regime makes the same assumptions as the liability framework as to the possibility of defining discrete problems amenable to legal-technical solutions. Third, such regimes are difficult to establish.[21] The establishment of any legal regime must deal with what Richard A. Falk and others have called the paradox of aggregation (or the tragedy of the commons). Perceptions of states as to the value of particular activities and the level of injury they are willing to accept to support them vary widely. The problem is vividly illustrated by the failure of the International Whaling Commission. Reliable data supplied to the IWC for the purpose of promoting better conservation policies were used initially by some countries to whale more efficiently. Enforcement of current agreements is almost impossible because of the difficulty in detecting violations and the minimal penalties involved if detected. For individual whalers, the immediate payoffs in violating the agreements were worth both the risk of detection and the long-run probability of eliminating the industry through depletion of stock. In short, evasion pays.

States resist changes in established regimes for many reasons, not the least of which is uncertainty with respect to the parameters of such change. This can be seen, for example, in the response to Canada's attempt to control or prevent certain potential sources of marine pollution in coastal waters up to 100 miles from shore. The Canadian legislation is an attempt to balance the right of free navigation against the right of defense against anticipated hazards. Under the Canadian law, the right of free navigation may be exercised only if certain preconditions are met.[22] The United States, in particular, has vigorously protested that such a unilateral extension of authority over areas generally considered to be high seas is clearly impermissible. The argument, as with most cases where change is the issue, can be characterized as a claim for law in development (*lex ferenda*) versus a claim for the law as currently interpreted (*lex lata*). Although a reasonable expectation would be recourse to a third-party review and a decision at equity, Canada has steadfastly refused to submit the issue to adjudication.

The recent decision by the International Court of Justice in the fisheries case (*United Kingdom* v. *Iceland*, 1975)[23] provides some insight into both the reluctance of Canada to submit the question of "environmental self-defense" to third-party review and the difficulties in moving beyond established practices. The ICJ argued that in such cases cooperative action was the controlling norm. Thus, although a coastal state may have "preferential rights" with respect to fisheries, navigation, environmental control, and conservation, such rights require the agreement of states affected by their exercise. Under such reasoning, Canada would be forced to negotiate with each state that found itself adversely affected by legislation.

The point is obvious. States in pursuit of important interests that challenge the status quo are unlikely to permit tribunals to apply a technique that embodies by definition the status quo and not broader considerations of public policy. The clearest evidence of this is the tendency toward unilateral action by states who feel their interests have not been sufficiently protected by multilateral or bilateral efforts.

Two final points are important here. First, the definition of environmental quality adopted will tend to structure priorities. Second, the place any environmental concern has in the international arena may be determined by political factors unrelated to any objective analysis of its importance. For each of the broad categories of concern, there are source constituencies—scientists, conservationists, exploiters, and so on—that have different stakes in the problem and the solution. Thus, it is a mistake to think of definition in terms of fixed and immutable alternatives, or in terms of universal principles. Rather, the definition will probably vary from region to region, turning on local assessments and configurations of source constituencies, hopefully balanced by a consideration of preserving the integrity of natural life-support systems.

Some standards must be set and priorities developed for issues that affect the global commons, such as the high seas. Yet, if the preceding analysis is accurate, there will be an inevitable tension between the local and the global view. Here again, the limits of law as a technique must be stressed.

The status of the Continental Shelf Convention may serve as an example. There is one weak convention and there are numerous agreements, mainly bilateral, tailored to the particular needs of the states involved. In no area where there is potential for successful economic exploitation of the shelf have all coastal states subscribed to the 1958 convention.[24] Moreover, despite the progress of the current Law of the Sea Conference, the present tendency is toward further particular systems.[25] Success or failure in reconciling this particular manifestation of local-global tension may well foretell success or failure in meeting environmental challenges.

Perhaps the dimensions of the problem can be more clearly seen if the question is asked: why should the decentralized international legal order be expected to deal any more efficiently with environmental questions than do the relatively centralized municipal legal orders? The control of powerful, selfish interests is difficult even in municipal legal orders where presumably more resources for control are available. Enforcement of existing standards or the evolution of new standards often results in cumbersome, time-consuming, and expensive legal actions. The results have seldom been a function solely of legal and technical considerations.

Add to this the fact that most of the problems are generated by the needs and by-products of valued human activities such as generating power or making fertilizer. Take the simple environmental problem generated by both of these activities—the regulation of residual discharges. On what basis does one weigh the costs of residual discharges against the external costs or damages avoided by reducing them? Even in domestic legal systems, the regulation of such problems is based upon crude estimates, hard bargaining, and intuition.

In sum, the characteristics of public and private legal institutions severely limit the planning horizon, imparting a view far shorter than that necessary to deal with major pollution problems. Long-term improvements in environmental quality will seldom result from a comparison of short-term costs versus short-term gains. A successful strategy requires that action be based upon anticipated consequences of current action rather than perceived costs of past actions. Needless to say, it is the latter view that is embedded in the law. The transfer from an open-space to a closed-space concept of the world would require a radical restructuring of goals. International law as a technique is not an instrument to generate such new goals but, rather, is an instrument to preserve them once generated.

III

The question raised by the foregoing analysis is whether or not any decentralized system of world order, even if some of the more glaring deficiencies are remedied, is capable of meeting the emerging challenges posed by technology, overpopulation, and resource depletion. From the argument above, it would seem that neither the system as presently organized nor a new structure within the UN system nor a new organization outside of it can effectively perform the requisite planning, coordination, and review functions. International agencies have been largely confined to helping governments help themselves and to encouraging governments to help each other.

The science of "muddling through" and the view of policy as a compromise of interests may be luxuries. Although in the eighteenth and nineteenth centuries mistakes in calculation could be rectified over time and generally concerned only a limited number of states, decisions and policies made today, especially by the powerful and developed, could have deleterious and lasting effects on the future quality of life on a global scale. Are we then left at worse than scratch? A hopeful answer to this question requires an imaginative leap beyond the constraints on thinking imposed by political realism. Is the sovereignty system as durable and resistant to change as a realistic analysis would indicate?

To return, then, to the question raised in the first section of this essay—and considering environmental imperatives in conjunction with questions that relate to the organization of security in the postwar world—the inescapable conclusion would seem to be that long-run survival may require a replacement for the state system. We are, however, faced with the dilemma that the state is still the fundamental actor, spiritually, effectively, and legally, though technology has rendered it functionally unviable. The dilemma is heightened because present structural parameters of the system are profoundly conservative of diversity. As Cyril Black has pointed out, the fundamental effect of diversity in the international order of the near future will be the instability that it engenders.[26]

The view that technology has made the state obsolete has gained increasing credibility in light of twentieth-century developments. Plans for alternatives to the sovereignty system must number in the thousands. Yet, few of these confront directly the problem of transition. As an example, the literature dealing with futurology stresses the technical problems of postindustrial societies, not the political problems of a future international order. There is little or no analysis either of the nature of political change or of the effects of rapid change on the system or of the problems inherent in modernization. The effects of changes in technology are treated as if they will occur in a vacuum. Critical to any prediction about the future status of society is an assessment of the requisites of political stability in terms of capacities of participants, resource distribution, and ideological direction. These are all political questions that futurologists (and economists) tend to disregard. The result is prediction without explanation—that is, a picture of what may happen without a suggestion as to why. This tendency to ignore political questions is symptomatic of the literature as a whole. As Professor Falk has commented: "Most proposals to organize a peaceful world society have badly underestimated the objective grounds of conflict and the dynamic process of a competitive world order."[27] In fact, rarely asked is the question: what does peace in the future imply about the relative distribution of power and resources among the world's nations and peoples? By the same token, what does environmental quality imply about the relative distribution of resources?[28]

For example, how does the desire of less developed states for economic modernization affect this issue? The less developed countries fear that the rich will use environmental problems as a device to deny them an equitable piece of the action. This concern became so great that the opposition of the less developed countries threatened to abort the 1972 Stockholm Conference. In a meeting with the secretary-general of the conference, Maurice Strong, these countries voiced the following concerns:

1. that environmental concerns would be defined as the rich cleaning house and diverting resources from development needs to pollution abatement;
2. that developed nations would create rigorous environmental standards for products traded internationally resulting in a form of neo-protectionist discrimination which would exclude non-conforming goods from poor lands;
3. that emphasis on non-polluting technology and re-cycling might eliminate or reduce demand for some raw materials or agricultural products;

4. that developed states might dictate environmental standards to
the lesser developed lands without considering how to relate
these to the peculiar conditions of these lands.[29]

The attitude of the less developed countries was perhaps best
expressed at Stockholm by Indira Gandhi: "How can we speak to
those who live in villages and slums about keeping the oceans,
the rivers and the air clear when their own lives are contaminated
at the source?"[30]

Objectively, there is much evidence to support the argument that
states are becoming increasingly interdependent. What the attitude
of the less developed states demonstrates, however, is the importance of how elites perceive the character of this interdependence.
Patterns of transactions may indicate a growing togetherness, but
political perceptions include other salient factors as well. If there were
a one-to-one relationship between systems of interdependence as
measured by technological or transactional links and the willingness
of states to participate in international cooperative ventures, we
might have more confidence in future projections of possible
solutions to environmental problems.[31]

The mere existence of problems that are transnational in scope is no
guarantee that states will respond. This is not to deny that in the past
twenty years the number of transnational functional organizations
has increased dramatically. However, it is to question the contentions
of advocates of functionalism as a strategy for order that the system
has markedly changed as a result. The result has been an increase in
confusion as much as a contribution to order. The conclusions of
James Sewell in his studies of WHO and the International Atomic
Energy Agency point to the failure of functionalism to generate new
elements or world community.[32] Even a sympathetic Robert Angell
must admit that an upsurge in transnational contacts has not
perceptibly altered existing patterns.[33]

In the long run, functional pluralism may be an answer, but what
do we do in the meantime? The primary resources for the regulation
of state behavior remain in the category of persuasion and influence
rather than sanction and edict. Can the area of noncoercive regulation
be enlarged? The achievements of international organization do
include some notable gains in noncoercive regulation. International
organizations have created a record of persistence, flexibility, and
ingenuity in the development and exploitation of devices for

inducing cooperative behavior. Inis Claude notes that it is striking how much can and must be done even in domestic political orders without the threat of sanction.[34] Our questions relate to whether the scope of such cooperation is increasing fast enough to meet the environmental challenges and to whether the inducements toward cooperative behavior are sufficient to offset the factors that encourage fragmentation. Carlos Romulo has summarized the problem admirably: "What makes our age unique, I suppose, is that the immediate and the ultimate questions are locked together."[35] Emphasizing this perspective to states and seeking cooperative responses in return may be the only strategy we have in the attempt to reconcile the necessity of survival with the desire to live well.

14

Unilateral Acts of States with Regard to Environmental Protection

Don C. Piper

For any student of international relations and of international law, the propensity of national decision makers on occasion to undertake unilateral acts toward other states that have not been theretofore legally prescribed and to assert that the acts are legally permissible is well recognized. One can identify such unilateral acts as the U.S. quarantine of offensive military weapons against Cuba in 1962,[1] the 1945 proclamation by President Truman asserting U.S. jurisdiction over the adjacent continental shelf for the purpose of exploring and exploiting the petroleum resources there,[2] and the proclamations in recent years by several states (for example, Iceland) of an exclusive fishing zone for the purpose of preserving the coastal fishery for local nationals. In each of these instances, the national decision maker asserted the right of the state to engage in certain prescribed activities that had not theretofore been recognized under the existing rules of international law. In acting unilaterally to assert a legal right, the decision maker declares that the existing rules of international law, either conventional or customary rules, are inadequate, inappropriate, or unsatisfactory in a new situation that has been brought about either by technological advances or important reasons of national security. Because of the asserted inadequacy or inappropriateness of the existing rules of international law and the necessity of national action either to preserve an existing situation or to prevent a possibly undesirable situation, decision makers opt to undertake unilateral action and unilateral lawmaking rather than engage in the long process of negotiation with other interested parties and the ultimate formulation of appropriate conventional law.

With regard to unilateral acts, one can assert that such acts, not being legally recognized by the existing rules of international law, constitute infractions of the law and must be treated as dysfunctional lawmaking activities. I have on occasion tried to argue a contrary view, that in some instances the unilateral action by decision makers may be one of the ways in which the rules of international law may be brought up to date to meet changing requirements and situations and that within limits the process of unilateral action may facilitate the growth and development of the rules of international law.[3]

The unilateral actions mentioned above were concerned with matters of national security or the regulation of access to a particular resource considered to be essential to the coastal state. In this regard, one would expect, because of the increased concern expressed by governments and international organizations about environmental protection, that some national decision makers would conclude that unilateral action was both necessary and appropriate in order to provide the required protection to the national environment.

With this expectation, I undertook the task of seeking to identify the unilateral acts by states undertaken for purposes of environmental protection. I looked for new acts of states—that is, acts that would have an impact on nonnationals and that were not already legally recognized as part of a state's right to regulate activities within its own territory, air space, territorial sea, or contiguous zone, or already recognized by existing conventional law with regard to activities outside of its jurisdiction and with regard to nonnationals.

Based upon previous examination of unilateral acts by states in various matters, I began this investigation of unilateral acts for environmental protection with the following rough model as a statement of the unilateral lawmaking process.

I. A perception by a national decision maker of an environmental danger resulting from the presence or possible introduction of some polluting substance originating from outside of the state's territory.

II. A perception of the national decision maker that the existing rules of international law, either conventional or customary, either are silent on the matter, are inadequate to provide the necessary degree of protection, or interfere with the enactment of the desired measures of protection.

III. The perception by the national decision maker that he will be unable to conclude a satisfactory cooperative arrangement with other national decision makers, either because of a lack of time or because of a fundamental clash of values and legal interests.

IV. The unilateral assertion by a national decision maker of a legal right to undertake certain specified action to prevent or minimize the danger of environmental destruction, which action may result in a limitation or qualification of the existing rights of other states. The asserted action is set forth as consistent with basic principles of the international legal system and as both necessary and reasonable to the danger. Any limitation of existing rights of other states is asserted to be permissible because the right of environmental protection takes legal precedence over other rights.

V. Responses by other national decision makers to the unilateral action may be

A. No response from many national decision makers because they perceive that there is no specific interest or legal right at issue of value to them

B. Implicit or explicit acceptance of the unilateral assertion as consistent with the principles of international law because

1. the action appears to be both necessary and reasonable

2. the action is perceived as contributing to the growth and development of international law

3. the action may be beneficially invoked by the state to protect its own interests

C. Explicit protest by national decision makers either to the particular specific action or to the principle because the widespread application of the principle may be perceived as disadvantageous to a state's existing rights.

VI. Possible discussion of the unilateral action at subsequent multilateral conferences and possible incorporation of the legal principle in treaty law or the rejection of the principle as inappropriate for treaty law.[4]

To determine how widespread the practice of the invocation of unilateral acts for environmental protection has become and what types of unilateral action are being undertaken, I examined the *New York Times* and *International Legal Materials* for the period since 1965. In this examination, I concentrated solely on unilateral acts relating to environmental protection; I did not examine fishing control zones, many of which have been unilaterally proclaimed, because they have already been widely identified and reported and pertain to both economic and resource protection rather than environmental protection per se.[5]

My initial expectation was that I would be able to identify a modest number of nondramatic but nevertheless specific unilateral acts by states to protect their national environment. Much to my surprise, the number of unilateral acts that I have identified is very small, and the acts relate exclusively to dangers to the marine environment that could be caused by navigation accidents and oil spills.

In expecting a modest number of unilateral acts, I recognized that the protection of the marine environment would be of interest primarily to coastal states rather than to all states and, among that subset, more likely to states with a long coastline than to states with a very modest coastline. I also recognized that from a technological point of view there is a limit to the activities that a state can undertake unilaterally that will have any practical consequence on the protection of the marine environment. Although the protection of the atmospheric environment is of interest to all states, there appears to be little that a state can do unilaterally to prevent the spread of atmospheric pollution into its territory. An activity by a state such as the refusal of landing rights to the Concorde because of a danger to the atmospheric environment, although perhaps relevant to the general problem of environmental protection, does not really represent a "new" state activity because it can be subsumed under the existing right of a state to control the passage of commercial aircraft into and over its airspace.

The acts that I have identified are three completed acts and one proposed action. The completed actions are: (1) The Canadian Arctic Waters Pollution Prevention Act, 1970, (2) The USSR Statute on the Administration of the Northern Sea Route Attached to the Ministry of the Maritime Fleet, 1971, and (3) the United Kingdom Prevention of Oil Pollution Act, 1971. The unperfected action is the proposal by Indonesia, Malaya, and Singapore to close the Straits of Malacca to supertankers because of the danger of destructive oil spills in the shallow waters.

The most dramatic of these unilateral acts, and perhaps the most far-reaching in its principle, if not in application, would appear to be the Canadian Arctic Waters Pollution Prevention Act, 1970, which became effective in 1972.[6] The most significant part of the act for our consideration is the establishment by the Canadian government of an Arctic waters zone for 100 miles from Canadian Arctic territory located north of the sixtieth parallel.[7] In this area the government may establish shipping safety control zones in which it will issue regulations for ships in the zones, including "prohibiting any ship of that class or of any of those classes from navigating within any shipping safety control zone." Under the legislation, ships may be prohibited from navigation in the zones unless they comply with several specified standards, such as hull and fuel tank construction, including the use of double hull construction.[8] Owners of ships or cargo that navigate the safety zones must also provide evidence of financial responsibility in amounts to be established by orders-in-council.[9] The legislation also asserts the right of the government to remove or destroy any ship within Arctic waters that is in distress, stranded, wrecked, sunk, or abandoned and that is depositing waste in the Arctic waters or is likely to deposit waste.[10] The act also sets forth penalties and civil liability for violations and provides for inspection of ships to determine if there is compliance with the prescribed standards.

The purpose of the act is apparently to prevent the deliberate or accidental discharge of oil into Arctic waters that would result in substantial damage to the Canadian Arctic ecology. In explaining the need for the legislation, the Canadian government declared: "The proposed anti-pollution legislation is based upon the overriding right of self-defense of coastal states to protect themselves against grave threats to their environment." The government also stressed the security considerations inherent in the idea of self-defense in the statement: "It is the further view of the Canadian government that a danger to the environment of a state constitutes a threat to its security." The government also explained that the unilateral legislation followed an unsuccessful attempt by it to secure at the 1969 conference of the Intergovernmental Maritime Consultative Organization (IMCO) "effective pollution prevention measures . . . for coastal states and the world's marine environment."[11] Because of the urgent importance of the matter and of its own primary responsibilities and because the Canadian government does not regard the Northwest Passage as constituting the high seas, the government was prepared to act unilaterally and thus to take a step toward the creation of new customary rules of international law regarding coastal state rights and not await the creation of treaty rules relating to environmental protection. Moreover, the government rejected the view set forth by the United States that the action had no basis in international law.

It should be noted that the Canadian legislation is not based upon an extension of Canadian sovereignty over the Arctic waters or a claim that the waters in question are internal waters. The basis for the legislation rests upon the asserted right of self-protection—the right of a state to take necessary and reasonable measures to protect against a danger to its security.

The immediate response of the United States government was to challenge the unilateral nature of the action and not its purpose of protecting against environmental pollution.[12] The United States claimed that the unilateral action had no basis in international law and that the "United States can neither accept nor acquiesce in the assertion of such jurisdiction." The United States also proposed that the legality of the Canadian action be adjudicated by the International Court of Justice, but the Canadian government declined the suggestion, taking "into account the limitations within which the court must operate and the deficiencies of the law which it must interpret and apply."[13] (In order to deny the court's jurisdiction, the Canadian government modified its acceptance of the optional clause of the Statute to exclude the antipollution legislation.)

Because of its claim of a right to prevent navigation that is not in accord with the prescribed standards, the Canadian government is in fact asserting a right to limit the application of the existing rules of international law regarding freedom of navigation. The right of navigation is limited by the priority right to prevent environmental destruction. In the interplay of these two asserted legal rights, those who defend the legislation utilize a "self-protection" perspective and declare that the regulations are both necessary to prevent dangerous oil spills and proportionate responses to the danger.[14]

Others argued at the time that the matter required multilateral action and that the legislation was especially inappropriate in the light of the discussions for a future UN conference on the law of the seas. Because of the importance of the matter, it was asserted that states should not act unilaterally but should seek appropriate action at the multilateral conference. Indeed, one scholar has declared: "Canada has struck a blow against pollution and for today's crusade for the environment, but it is a blow also at international law and its law of lawmaking. A blow at international law by Canada is perhaps the most unkindest cut of all."[15]

Notwithstanding the protests by the United States, the Canadian government appears to be determined to maintain its prerogatives as set forth in the legislation, although there is no evidence to indicate that the legislation has been invoked against any specific vessel. The explanation may be that vessels have not sought to proceed through Canadian Arctic waters, or that they have been dissuaded by the legislative requirements from attempting any passage. Consequently, it is not possible to offer a definitive statement regarding the practical consequence of the legislation for other states. The consequence for Canada is that there has not been any reported oil spill in Canadian Arctic waters.

Another decree relating to Arctic pollution, the Statute on the Administration of the Northern Sea Route Attached to the Ministry of the Maritime Fleet, was issued by the Soviet Union in 1971.[16] This decree is less specific than the Canadian legislation in that it does not refer to a specific zone for the territorial scope of the decree, other than an undefined reference to the northern sea route. Moreover, the decree does not contain the specific standards that vessels must meet in order to navigate the northern sea route as are set forth in the Canadian legislation.

As set forth in the decree, one purpose of the administration of the northern sea route is to take "measures to prevent and eliminate the consequences of pollution of the marine environment or the northern coast of the Union of Soviet Socialist Republics and effectuating supervision of vessels for this purpose and of other floating means which may be a source of pollution." In carrying out this purpose, the administration may regulate the movement of vessels along the sea route, establish rules for navigation, determine the condition of vessels before they traverse the sea route in order to establish their conformity to the increased requirements of safe navigation in ice, visit vessels and, if they do not conform to the increased requirements, prohibit their transit through the northern sea route.

One of the defects of the decree is that it does not identify either criteria or standards for determining the "increased requirements for safe navigation in ice." Notwithstanding the brevity of the decree, it is clear that one of its purposes is to enable the Soviet Union to prohibit passage of vessels through the sea route if they do not meet standards that are necessary to prevent accidents that will result in environmental damage. I have been unable to locate any data regarding the number of vessels that use the northern sea route, what percentage of these vessels are non-Soviet flag vessels, and whether vessels have been prohibited from transit because they did not meet the requirements.

Both the Canadian and the Soviet actions are intended to prevent polluting activities, and somewhat similar action is being contemplated by Indonesia, Malaya, and Singapore. According to news reports, these three states propose to act in concert and unilaterally close the Malacca Straits to supertankers because there is substantial risk of environmental pollution in the shallow waters of the straits from accidental oil spills from the supertankers. They propose that supertankers will be required to use the Lombok and Makassar straits. The use of these two straits will add 900 miles to the sea trip for tankers proceeding from the Middle East to Japan.[17] Until a specific decree is published or legislation enacted by the states, it is not possible to know the specific terms of the limitation on supertankers and the legal basis for the limitation.

The unilateral acts discussed above relate to action by states that may deny to vessels the exercise of a previously recognized right, namely, the right to navigation in a specific area of the high seas. A different approach is set forth in the United Kingdom Prevention of Oil Pollution Act, 1971.[18] That act provides that in the event of an "accident" from which the discharge of oil "will or may cause pollution on a large scale in the United Kingdom or in the waters in or adjacent to the United Kingdom up to the seaward limits of territorial waters," the secretary of state may undertake certain action to prevent or reduce the oil pollution. These actions may include direction to persons to undertake or refrain from undertaking certain action (for example, moving the vessel) and ultimately, if all other procedures are inadequate, ordering the sinking or destruction of the vessel.

The act gives substantial discretion to the secretary of state and does not define what constitutes an accident, leaving unanswered the question of whether the deliberate discharge of quantities of oil by a vessel is sufficient to invoke the act or whether the term *accident* is to be taken in its normal meaning. In addition, the secretary must determine without the benefit of legislative criteria or standards what constitutes "pollution on a large scale." The act does prescribe that persons suffering damages as a result of action taken by the secretary that was not "reasonably necessary" or was disproportionate to the possible damage may seek to recover compensation from the secretary of state.

Under the Oil in Navigable Waters (Shipping Casualties) Order, 1971, the provisions of the act may be extended to foreign vessels outside of the territorial waters of the United Kingdom "in any case in which the Secretary of State is satisfied that there is a need to protect the coast of the United Kingdom or the waters in or adjacent to the United Kingdom up to the seaward limits of territorial waters against grave and imminent danger of oil pollution."[19] As is the case in the basic legislation, the secretary of state has substantial discretion to determine when the act should be invoked against a foreign-flag vessel. If the act is invoked, the United Kingdom asserts its primary right of jurisdiction over that of the flag state.

Although there are some differences, the act is generally compatible with the 1969 International Convention Relating to Intervention on the High Seas in Cases of Oil Pollution Casualties.[20] The act is apparently in force and may be invoked against any foreign vessel whether or not it is covered by the convention. In addition, the act differs dramatically from the convention, which calls upon the endangered state to engage in consultations with the flag state and other interested states except in situations of extreme urgency before initiating action.

In each of the cases that we have examined, the basic concern of the coastal states has been the prevention of the introduction of oil from outside a state's territorial limits into its territory to the damage of the local environment. In at least three of the four cases, one can identify a specific event that appeared to stimulate national action. In the case of the United Kingdom, it was the damage caused by the oil spill from the *Torrey Canyon* in 1967. In the case of Canada, it was the successful transit of the Northwest Passage by the *S.S. Manhattan* with the expectation that the *Manhattan* would soon be followed by tankers loaded with oil from the Arctic oil fields. In the case of the three Pacific states, it was the ten-mile-long oil slick near Singapore in January 1975, caused when the Japanese tanker *Shawa Maru* went aground in the Malacca Straits.

In each of these cases and in the case of the Soviet Union as well, the national policy has been the unilateral assertion of a restriction on the recognized right of navigation. The justification for the restriction is that the right of navigation must be qualified in response to the unquestioned right of a state to protect its local environment. The right of navigation of the high seas, it is asserted, although long established, is not an absolute right and is subject to reasonable qualification.

Although all of the actions aim for environmental protection, they differ in their legal approach. The Canadian government's approach declares to all parties, prior to any untoward act, that the enjoyment of the right of navigation will be permitted only if certain conditions are met in advance. That is, to enjoy a right, one must meet certain specified preconditions. The Soviet Union also takes this approach, although the decree does not specify the precise conditions that are necessary for navigation through the northern sea route. The approach followed by Indonesia, Malaya, and Singapore is to prohibit one right of navigation and to offer an alternative right.

The approach taken by the United Kingdom, however, is quite different. The legislation does not upset the enjoyment of an existing right of navigation but does provide that if that right is abused by an oil spill penalties, including the possible destruction of the tanker, will be imposed. One therefore may enjoy an existing right, but with the knowledge that an abuse of that right may result in substantial penalties. It would appear that the approach taken by the United Kingdom, because it does not interfere under normal circumstances with the exercise of an existing right, would be less unsettling to the existing rules of international law and the international lawmaking process.

There is no doubt that unilateral assertions of international legal rights by states with regard to environmental protection or with regard to any other matter may be unsettling to the law and the lawmaking process and may place a strain upon the law. The strain on the law may subside over time as other states articulate agreement with the shared value and accept the utility of the unilateral action as a means of promoting their own interests and facilitating the growth and development of the international legal system. It is just as possible, however, that unilateral action will result in a fundamental disagreement over shared values and respective legal rights, perpetuating a strain on the legal rules that can only be resolved, if at all, by third-party dispute settlement.

In addition, as I have suggested, one must also consider that the unilateral actions we have identified may not have been undertaken solely for the purpose of achieving environmental protection. One may accept at face value the statements of concern about environmental protection and still understand that a decision maker's motives may not match completely the public explanation for unilateral action. To assert an extreme position, one must acknowledge that legal rhetoric may be employed to cover less obvious or perhaps less noble purposes than those articulated by the decision maker. It is not out of the question that the acting states had mixed motives in undertaking the unilateral action, although there is no evidence to suggest that this was the case. Nevertheless, we must be alert to the possibility of multiple motives by the acting states and differing and perhaps erroneous perceptions of these purposes by other states.

In the cases that we have examined, comments or protests from other states regarding the specific unilateral actions, their apparent and related or hidden purposes, or the values of environmental protection appear to have been minimal. In part, this may be the case because only a very limited number of states believe that either their interests or their rights are affected by the actions. In this regard, the Japanese government indicated a desire to discuss the question of the Malacca Straits with the interested governments. Although the United States government protested the Canadian action, it did so by indicating that its concern was more with the mode of the Canadian action than with the specific application of the legislation to Arctic waters. The United States asserted:

We are concerned that this action by Canada if not opposed by us, would be taken as precedent in other parts of the world for other unilateral infringements of the freedom of the seas. If Canada had the right to claim and exercise exclusive pollution and resource jurisdiction on the high seas, other countries would assert the right to exercise jurisdiction for other purposes, some reasonable and some not, but all equally invalid according to international law. Merchant shipping would be severely restricted, and naval mobility would be seriously jeopardized. The potential for serious international dispute and conflict is obvious.[21]

The United States protest implicitly identifies the dilemma for other states in responding to unilateral acts for environmental protection. Unilateral action for environmental protection, which may be desirable and reasonable from a technical point of view, must be challenged because the customary rules of international law cannot be sufficiently refined to permit such actions without opening up the law to other, less reasonable assertions. The U.S. response suggests that, given the nature of customary international law, the principle of the law must be defended in each and every instance without the opportunity for reasonable variations or exceptions. Yet, it is certainly debatable that customary international law does not permit variations between states (for example, the variation in the recognition of the width of the territorial sea up to a maximum of

12 miles), which suggests that some legal fine tuning may be possible with regard to environmental regulations.

Although there are important substantive and legal differences in the matter, an examination of the International Court of Justice's decision in the fisheries jurisdiction case (*United Kingdom* v. *Iceland*) provides a useful perspective for examining the unilateral acts relating to environmental protection.[22] In the fisheries case, the court emphasized the preferential rights of the coastal state with regard to the protection of the coastal fishery but declared that the Icelandic 50-mile fishing zone could not be opposable to the United Kingdom because of the latter's recognized existing fishing rights and because the fishing zone did not take into account the United Kingdom's rights as set forth in the 1961 exchange of notes between the two governments.

In its opinion, the court upheld the concept of "preferential rights" for the coastal state with regard to fishing rights but indicated an important distinction between "preferential rights" and "exclusive rights." With regard to preferential rights, the court declared: "The contemporary practice of States leads to the conclusion that the preferential rights of the coastal State in a special situation are to be implemented by agreement between the States concerned, either bilateral or multilateral, and, in case of disagreement, through the means for the peaceful settlement of disputes provided for in Article 33 of the Charter of the United Nations."[23] However, the court distinguished preferential rights from exclusive rights in the following manner: "The concept of preferential rights is not compatible with the exclusion of all fishing activities of other States. A coastal State entitled to preferential rights is not free, unilaterally and according to its own uncontrolled discretion, to determine the extent of those rights. The characterization of the coastal State's rights as preferential implies a certain priority, but cannot imply the extinction of the concurrent rights of other States and particularly of a State which, like the Applicant, has for many years been engaged in fishing in the waters in question, such fishing activity being important to the economy of the country concerned."[24]

In the cases we have been considering here, it is difficult to argue that the coastal states were seeking to establish exclusive rights. There is no evidence that they wish to prohibit all navigation or that they wish to act in a discriminatory fashion and prohibit foreign navigation in order to protect or develop national navigation activities. It is possible to argue, however, that the states are asserting preferential rights in the sense that in order to achieve environmental protection they are asserting that the particular protection of the national marine and coastal environment takes precedence over the general right of navigation on the high seas. It should be remembered, however that the court emphasized that preferential rights must be implemented by agreement of the parties concerned. If one can paraphrase the court, one might declare that a coastal state has preferential rights on the high seas over other states in order to prevent environmental destruction but that the implementation of the protective activities must be accomplished by agreement among the parties concerned.

Recent policy statements by international organizations or conferences also clearly affirm a state's responsibilities with regard to environmental protection, and most of them stress the importance and necessity of cooperative action on a regional or local basis. The cumulative effect of these policy statements emphasizing cooperative action is certainly to establish an expectation that cooperative action is the norm and that any noncooperative action will be questioned.

This cooperative approach, which calls upon states to take into account the interests of other states, is set forth inter alia in principles 21, 22, and 24 of the Declaration of the United Nations Conference on the Human Environment, 1972; in article 30 of the UN Charter of Economic Rights and Duties of States; in the Organization for Economic Cooperation and Development (OECD) Council Recommendation on Principles Concerning Transfrontier Pollution; in the OECD Guiding Principles Concerning International Economic Aspects of Environmental Policies; and in the Final Act of the Conference on Security and Cooperation in Europe, 1975.

Notwithstanding this predominate emphasis upon cooperative action, recommendation 92 of the United Nations Conference on the Human Environment acknowledges that the possibility of unilateral legal action by states warrants consideration by international bodies. That recommendation states:

that in respect of the particular interests of coastal States in the marine environment and recognizing that the resolution of this question is a matter for consideration at the Conference on the Law of the Sea, they [governments] *take note* of the principles on the rights of coastal state discussed but neither endorsed nor rejected at the second session of the Intergovernmental Working Group on Marine Pollution and refer those principles to the 1973

IGMCO Conference for information and the 1973 Conference on the Law of the Sea for such action as may be appropriate.[25]

The principles referred to above are:

1. A state may exercise special authority in areas of the sea adjacent to its territorial waters where functional controls of a continuing nature are necessary for the effective prevention of pollution that could cause damage or injury to the land or marine environment under its exclusive or sovereign authority.

2. A coastal state may prohibit any vessel that does not comply with internationally agreed rules and standards or, in their absence, with reasonable national rules and standards of the coastal state in question, from entering waters under its environmental protection authority.

3. The basis on which a state should exercise rights or powers, in addition to its sovereign rights or powers, pursuant to its special authority in areas adjacent to its territorial waters, is that such rights or powers should be deemed to be delegated to that state by the world community on behalf of humanity as a whole. The rights and powers exercised must be consistent with the state's primary responsibility for marine environmental protection in the areas concerned; they should be subject to international rules and standards and to review before an appropriate international tribunal.

In assessing the significance of the unilateral actions and their possible contribution to the growth and development of international law, it is useful to view the acts as part of the process of emerging treaty law. Indeed, one can speculate that some of the unilateral acts might have been initiated in order to focus other states' attention upon an issue, or perhaps even to obtain a bargaining advantage for subsequent multilateral lawmaking activities. As a consequence, the unilateral acts should be seen as problem-focusing rather than as problem-solving actions.

If problem focusing or bargaining were part of the strategy of the Canadian and Soviet governments, evidence suggests that they were successful in their efforts. Article 235 of the *Informal Composite Negotiating Text*, released following the 1977 session of the Law of the Sea Conference (LOS III), supports their argument that Arctic waters require special attention and provides for the right of the coastal state to "establish and enforce non-discriminatory laws and regulations for the prevention, reduction and control of marine pollution from vessels in ice-covered areas . . . where particular severe climatic conditions and the presence of ice covering such areas for most of the year create obstructions or exceptional hazards to navigation, and pollution of the marine environment could cause major harm to or irreversible disturbance of the ecological balance. Such laws and regulations shall have due regard to navigation and the protection of the marine environment based upon the best available scientific evidence."[26]

In the same manner, the proposal of Indonesia, Malaya, and Singapore to close the Malacca Straits relates to the question of a coastal state's right to establish regulations to prevent vessel-source pollution within the 200-mile economic zone and to the question of the right of archipelagic states to designate "archipelagic sealanes" for the passage of foreign vessels, which is also being discussed at LOS III. The right to make such a designation and thereby restrict passage in other sea lanes is affirmed in article 53 of the 1977 *Informal Composite Negotiating Text*.

The United Kingdom legislation relates to the International Convention Relating to Intervention on the High Seas in Cases of Oil Pollution Casualties, 1969. The legislation does not completely match the convention, because some of the legislative provisions are less restrictive upon the government than the comparable provisions in the basic treaty. Nevertheless, the legislation supports the purpose of the treaty. The legislation is also supported by the LOS III discussions and the 1977 *Informal Composite Negotiating Text*. Article 222 sets forth that

1. Nothing in this Chapter shall affect the right of States to take measures, in accordance with international law, beyond the limits of the territorial sea for the protection of coastlines or related interests, including fishing, from grave and imminent danger from pollution or threat of pollution following upon a maritime casualty or acts related to such a casualty.

2. Measures taken in accordance with the Article shall be proportionate to the actual or threatened damage.

Because these unilateral acts are part of the continuing discussion of emerging treaty law, one cannot offer a definitive conclusion as to their contribution to the international legal order regarding environmental protection. Although their present legality may be debatable, the acts do not represent such a radical departure from the existing norms that their basic principles and values are deemed to be unworthy of discussion. Nevertheless, it is not clear at the present time whether the unilateral acts will be incorporated into conventional or customary law, as the principle of the U.S. continental shelf proclamation was quickly incorporated into both customary and conventional law.

Although the weight of the court's decision and international organization resolutions argue against uncontrolled unilateral action, unilateral rights may still be asserted by national decision makers in specific situations, especially those relating to accidental pollution. If these unilateral acts for environmental protection are to be accepted by states of the international community as consistent with the general principles of international law and community values and thereby deserving of respect and adherence, one can suggest that the following concepts of international law are appropriate as standards for such acts.

Necessity. Although one need not demand compliance with Daniel Webster's famous dictum regarding necessity and self-defense, it would appear to be appropriate for states to insist that any state acting unilaterally to protect its environment provide persuasive evidence of the need for unilateral action to prevent environmental destruction. To be most persuasive, the evidence would support the need for immediate and unilateral action rather than subsequent and possibly delayed cooperative action. The element of necessity would be most persuasive if it were attested to by outside experts. (The Convention Relating to Intervention on the High Seas in Cases of Oil Pollution Casualties requires that a list of experts be maintained to be available to assist the coastal state contemplating interventionary acts to prevent oil pollution.) The use of a second party to affirm the necessity and reasonableness of the action would be similar to third-party dispute settlement without the legal structure and the binding quality of the decision.

Proportionality. It is reasonable to expect that any action unilaterally undertaken by a state to protect its environment must be proportionate and reasonable to the environmental danger. Indeed, the International Convention Relating to Intervention on the High Seas in Cases of Oil Pollution Casualties requires that "Measures taken by the coastal state in accordance with Article I shall be proportionate to the damage actual or threatened to it." The concept of proportionality of response appears to be sufficiently well established in international law as a limitation on the scope of unilateral acts (for example, self-defense and reprisals) to suggest its appropriate application in limiting unilateral actions regarding environmental protection. As a practical matter, it must also be apparent to any decision maker who contemplates unilateral action that the action is much more likely to be accepted and regarded as legally appropriate if the action is clearly proportionate to the actual or threatened environmental danger.

Third-party review of acts in dispute. Although the Canadian government has taken the position that "a danger to the environment of a State constitutes a threat to its security" and has amended its acceptance of the optional clause to the Statute of the ICJ to exclude disputes regarding environmental activities, the argument that environmental matters are of such importance that they cannot be reviewed by a third party even to the extent that they affect the existing rights of other states is not persuasive.

Nor is the argument that the law regarding the high seas is in a period of transition persuasive as a reason to reject third-party review of acts in dispute. It may be the case that the law regarding high-seas rights is in transition, but the principles of recognition of rights of other states and of third-party dispute settlement would appear to be well established and not in transition or doubt. Indeed, as the court declared in the fisheries jurisdiction case, a state entitled to preferential rights "is not free, unilaterally and according to its own uncontrolled discretion, to determine the extent of those rights." This being the case, if one is to promote the rule of law, one must promote third-party review of unilateral acts if they result in a dispute between states regarding their respective rights.

The reluctance of the Canadian government to accept the court's jurisdiction may be explained in part by a concern that the court would apply "old" or existing law that would not permit the desired action. Although the customary rules of international law may not easily be fine tuned to accommodate special situations, the court's willingness to accommodate "preferential rights" in the fisheries jurisdiction case suggests that it may be receptive to appropriate unilateral action as long as that action takes into account the rights of other states.

Although one can speculate that agreement among states on the appropriate law may be difficult to secure because the coastal state may argue *de lege ferenda* and the aggrieved party will argue the *lex lata,* it is possible that because of the recognized need for environmental protection the parties could resolve their disputes as to the applicable law by requesting a decision *ex aequo et bono.*

Nondiscrimination. Any action undertaken by a state for environmental protection must be implemented in a nondiscriminatory manner as between nationals and aliens and as between various aliens. Action undertaken for environmental protection that gives to the coastal state territorial or economic advantage at the expense of the rights of other states would deserve quick rejection by the members of the international community.

Social Dangers and Challenges

The effects of ecological deterioration will take many forms: some will be readily obvious, others less so. In such circumstances, attributions of cause and effect in the complex interface between natural and social systems will be difficult, especially where cause and effect are separated in space and time. This suggests the need to develop a more sophisticated understanding of the interaction of social and natural systems. The three essays presented in this final section draw attention to several problems of this type that might otherwise remain undiagnosed.

Rapid growth in international activities such as trade, travel, communications, private investment, and interstate agreements is often regarded as the basis of a new era of peace and prosperity. In a more critical perspective on these trends, Andrew Scott expresses a concern that the international system is approaching a condition of "hyperactivity" in which the volume of interactions, including those related to a growing degree of ecological interdependence, will outstrip the ordering capacity of the system. The following article by David Orr and Stuart Hill analyzes two contrary political and social responses to ecological problems implicit in the work of Robert Heilbroner and E. F. Schumacher. At both the national and international levels the tendency toward centralization ought to be balanced by selective decentralization, particularly in the energy and agricultural sectors.

The social costs of environmental deterioration will fall heavily on future generations. In the final essay in this volume, Marvin Soroos calls upon the present generations to be more conscious of how their ecologically related actions will affect the life opportunities of the

6

future of the planet. For this reason, it is important to recognize that conflict, cooperation, violence, and peace often cut across generational lines. Thus the immediate social challenge is to incorporate the interests of posterity into present decisions.

15

The Logic of International Interaction*

Andrew M. Scott

"It has become a platitude to say that the whole world is now
interdependent. . . . Yet what a tremendous platitude it is! . . . If
this platitude is unalterably true, its implications must profoundly
affect the conditions of human life for the future; it must transform
all our thinking about social organization; it must modify all our
programmes and policies. Clearly we ought to be thinking seriously
about it, and asking ourselves what it involves."[1] The condition
Ramsay Muir referred to as a "tremendous platitude" in 1933 has
become far more pronounced in the intervening forty-odd years, yet
theory has still not caught up with the evolving reality, and so
statesmen and analysts must make do, for the most part, with
concepts designed for a preinterdependent world. Because these
ideas are not adapted to the present, paradoxes and difficult
questions abound: Why is it that the great increases in human
knowledge have not yet led to a corresponding increase in the
capacity to control international events or even to anticipate them? If
man's physical capabilities are increasing at an unprecedented rate,
why is it that his international problems are also increasing? Why is
it that nations, even the most powerful of them, have difficulty
accomplishing the ends they desire and avoiding the ills they want
to avoid?

In this article I want to go beyond the facts of interaction and
explore dynamics for, until they are understood, there is little chance
of successful system management. In brief, the argument will be that
in a large and complex system, such as the international system,

*Reprinted by permission from *International Studies Quarterly* 21, no. 3 (September
1977): 429–60.

interaction is a key variable and is a potent source of consequences. As the level of interaction in the international system increases, the number of difficult system problems increases, inadvertent consequences become more important, system management becomes more and more difficult, and the international system as a whole becomes increasingly fragile. In exploring the logic of interaction, this article will emphasize some neglected aspects: first, the costs of interaction, for more is not always better; and, second, the part that powerful apurposive forces play in the working of the international system.

The growth of interaction represents a long-term trend. In the distant past, civilizations existed without being aware of each other. One of the historical by-products of the travels of a Marco Polo, a Columbus, or a Cortez, was to introduce one civilization to another.[2] As the tempo of interaction picked up, formal introductions became unnecessary. We may conceive of the assemblage of actors as having moved along a continuum, over a period of time, from a condition characterized by a very low level of interaction to one characterized by a relatively high level. During the fifteenth century, most societies touched each other only occasionally, and what happened in one society was apt to be little influenced by what happened in other parts of the globe. In the sixteenth century the tempo of interaction around the Mediterranean basin picked up, and, as a consequence of the great explorations, developments in the New World and Asia began to influence European nations.[3] In the eighteenth century a global economy took shape, and the Seven Years' War (1756–63) afflicted almost all of Europe and North America and reached to India. The nineteenth century opened with the far-reaching Napoleonic Wars, and the twentieth century brought the first conflict to be called a world war. The depression beginning in 1929 became worldwide, and when war was renewed in 1939 it was, of course, another world war.

Interaction, as the term is used here, includes: (1) the actions of nation-states, intergovernmental organizations, nongovernmental international organizations, and subnational groups; (2) transactions and flows that reach across national boundaries, such as trade, investment, tourism, international broadcasting, and the diffusion of technology. Reasons for the increase in interaction are not hard to find. First, the number of actors has climbed steadily over a long period, accelerating sharply after World War II. Second, the political and economic resources that actors have been able to devote to interaction activities have risen sharply. Third, the repertoire of actions available to different kinds of actors has broadened. Technological innovations such as trains, planes, radio, film, television, missiles, nuclear weapons, and communications satellites create new opportunities for interaction. Social innovations have also played a role. One thinks of information and cultural exchange programs, economic aid, technical assistance, military advisory teams, covert support of "liberation" activities, arrangements for insuring foreign investment, and so on. Finally, structures on the international scene have played an important role in increasing interaction—the North Atlantic Treaty Organization, the World Bank, the United Nations and its many agencies. These factors, taken together, may allow an actor to launch a multitude of actions into the international arena in a short space of time.

The growth of interaction has persisted over several centuries. Some forms of interaction have declined, of course, such as the slave trade or passenger travel by ship, but many others have been increasing, sometimes exponentially. Because of the persistence of this growth and because the factors that account for it show no signs of diminishing in number, the presumption must be that the increase in interaction will continue into the future unless important changes take place. The international system has been and is at present moving rapidly along the interaction continuum toward a condition of hyperinteractivity.

Interaction and International Structures

C. F. Bergsten, Robert Keohane, and Joseph Nye distinguish between the structural level and the process level in analyzing international interaction.[4] Structures have to do with organizations, arrangements, and rules and set the parameters for day-to-day interaction processes. Their character at a given time will reflect the interests and the relative power of key actors, will contribute importantly to increases (or decreases) in the amount of interaction at the process level, and will also affect the characteristic forms that interaction takes. The free trade system of the nineteenth century was a structure created and maintained primarily by the British, and it resulted in substantial increases in capital flow and world trade. The economic structures created after World War II were largely the work of the United States. The Bretton Woods system and the major economic institutions associated with it—the International Monetary Fund (IMF), the General Agreement on Tariffs and Trade (GATT), the International Bank for Reconstruction and Development—were designed to facilitate trade and investment, and without them world trade would not have increased fivefold, as it did, between 1950 and 1970.[5] The North Atlantic Treaty Organization raised the level of political and military interaction among signatory nations and also helped give that interaction its special character. The same was true of structures much narrower in scope. The International Air Transport Association (IATA) fostered an increase in air travel and influenced its character.

In each of the functional areas sometimes used to classify behavior in the world arena, the same pattern can be seen: structural arrangements influencing processes of interaction. Rules and regulations flow down from the structural level, as indicated by the downward-pointing arrows in figure 1 and help shape the relevant behavior at the interaction process level.

At the process level, there may be a great deal of interactive behavior as thousands of business concerns engage in millions of transactions and extensive communications. This behavior operates within the constraints imposed by structural arrangements, but it is not *wholly* controlled by them. Feedback mechanisms allow for a reciprocal influence of interaction behavior on structural arrangements, as indicated by the upward-pointing arrows. Typically this reciprocal influence is continuous, with structural provisions shaping an interactive process and that process, in turn, leading to a modification of rules and institutions, which changes then have a new impact on the process in question.[6]

Figure 1.

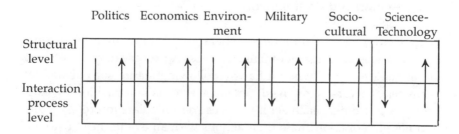

There is also lateral interaction and influence at both levels, as indicated in figure 2. This schema provides a way of classifying types of interaction and interdependence that is useful for some purposes: (1) the influence of structural arrangements on an interaction process; (2) the reciprocal impact of a process on structural arrangements; (3) the impact of sets of structural arrangements on one another; (4) the direct impact of interaction processes on one another. Each of these types has contributed something to the overall growth of interaction.

Figure 2.

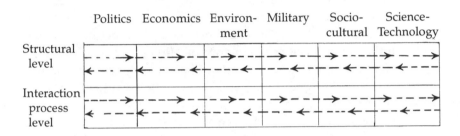

	Politics	Economics	Environ-ment	Military	Socio-cultural	Science-Technology
Structural level						
Interaction process level						

Lateral interaction at the structural level will vary depending on circumstances. Because the United States was the linchpin of a number of structures after World War II, interaction across functional areas was extensive. There was political and military coordination through NATO as well as the coordination of national economic policies via informal collaboration and through the IMF, GATT, and the Organization for Economic Cooperation and Development (OECD). The network of structures associated with the Warsaw Pact provided for a similar, though even higher, level of coordination.

Aggregation and Combination

Aggregation, a little understood characteristic of many international processes, is of fundamental importance. A process may be referred to as "aggregative" when it has the following features: a substantial number of actors is involved; no single actor is in a position to shape process outcomes; each actor pursues its immediate interests; actors do not plan or coordinate their actions with an eye to the consequences those actions may bring about when they are all taken together, that is, when they are aggregated.

Because the international system is highly interactive, actions must, and do, impinge on one another even though taken without regard to the possibility of such impact. Ecologists are fond of pointing out that it is not possible to throw anything away. No matter where we put old bottles and beer cans, or nuclear wastes, they are still somewhere. The same thing holds for the international arena, but we have yet to fully appreciate that fact and grasp its implications. Actors continue to think of the international arena as a vast sink into which they can toss all kinds of behaviors and artifacts and then forget about them. Yet, the bits and pieces go somewhere, and many of them aggregate with one another. Actions leave residues in the form of consequences.

Only elements that are similar to one another can aggregate, of course. Pollutants discharged into the atmosphere from countless points around the world aggregate and constitute what we term the problem of global air pollution. Wastes discharged into rivers and those pumped into the oceans by ships, industrial concerns, and cities aggregate to constitute the problem of pollution of the seas. Thousands of boats and ships from scores of countries fish the oceans and create the problem of overfishing. Births and deaths around the world aggregate into a global population problem, and empty stomachs aggregate to create a world food problem. Aggregation takes place at the process level, and, in many cases, structural constraints either do not exist or are too weak to guide the process in question.

Aggregation is not the only process going on in the "sink" of the ecosphere and the international arena. Because behaviors and their consequences cannot be thrown away, it is apparent that scores, or perhaps hundreds, of aggregative processes are going on at a given time and that these processes must necessarily interact with one another. In the preceding section, it was noted that interaction processes can have a direct impact on one another, an impact that is only marginally affected by structural arrangements. This lateral influence may be referred to by the term *combination*.

Combination involves the linking of processes *within* functional categories as well as *across* functional boundaries. The resulting combinations, which may be quite elaborate, often offer impressive examples of interdependence. For example, industrial and municipal waste disposal practices may lead to increases in air pollution, which may change environmental conditions, which may in turn lead to changes in temperature and rainfall, which could precipitate a sharp drop in food production, which might lead to hunger and then to political instability and, perhaps, to war. As functional boundaries in the international system become more permeable, because of the increased prominence of diffusion processes, opportunities for combination increase sharply. Developments in the political realm may affect those in the communications field, which may affect economic processes, which may in turn have an impact on environmental processes, and so on.

Aggregation is not very well understood, save in connection with certain market processes, but combination is far less understood, in part because the number of pathways by means of which processes can link with one another multiplies so rapidly with increases in the permeability of functional boundaries. The essential point is, however, that through combination entire trains of consequences can link up with one another, *and all without deliberate collective calculation or management, because the combining takes place at the process level rather than the structural level*.

Some interactive processes are directed effectively by means of structural arrangements, and others are not. One can envision a scale of "directedness" extending from the completely directed at one extreme to the completely undirected at the other. Any international process could be located somewhere along that scale, although a given process might migrate over a period of time. For example, if structural controls were to weaken for some reason or if a process became harder to control, it would move from the more directed toward the less directed end of the scale.

Aggregative and combinatory processes are constantly at work in the international arena and the ecosphere, and, at best, they are only semidirected. This lack of direction is the key to the paradox of how it is that activities that could not exist but for the actions of men and their institutions are nevertheless not under effective control by men. Together, aggregation and combination remove whole clusters of processes from the realm of effective direction. To the extent that they are not subject to deliberate, collective direction, their outcomes must be shaped by something else, that is, by impersonal forces and the little understood dynamics of combination. Combinatory sequences, although often exceptionally important, are self-manufacturing.

Inadvertent Change

It has long been recognized that men may intend to achieve one consequence and end up achieving a quite different one. Actor X may threaten Y in order to induce compliance, but Y may be angered rather than intimidated and may therefore become less rather than more compliant. The common components in such cases are: a purposive act, which produces consequences, which are either different from those intended or go beyond them. As the international system becomes more interactive, this kind of miscalculation continues to be important, but more powerful dynamics also come into play. A central characteristic of the international system at present is its impressive capacity to produce inadvertent consequences, and the way it does this deserves close study.

If half a dozen chefs were using the same mixing bowl at the same time to prepare their favorite dishes, the expectations of each would be frustrated by the actions of the others. If we were trying to anticipate the nature of the final outcome, traditional culinary knowledge would not be of much help and we would have to develop a new style of analysis. So it is with the international system. Hundreds of actors are pouring actions into the international arena at the same time, and those actions are being variously deflected and aggregated and combined with one another.

In an undirected aggregative process, the behavior of individual actors is purposive, but the process as a whole knows no purpose and is under no overall direction. Each actor may contribute something to the result, but no one controls that result, no deliberate social choice is involved, and therefore the outcomes are unplanned. It cannot be otherwise. If a process is neither understood nor directed by the actors involved, unplanned consequences are inevitable. If an aggregative process is semidirected, the same forces will be at work but will be less pronounced. A process that is only partly under control does not become quiescent because the control element has ceased to be adequate but, rather, continues to function and *produces results only some of which are intended.*

The growth of multinational corporations exemplifies a semi-directed aggregative process at work. The structural arrangements fashioned after World War II incorporated a strong element of purpose. GATT, IMF, and the World Bank were designed to facilitate the growth of trade and were remarkably successful. The aggregative economic activities that these arrangements engendered began to have consequences of their own, however, one of which was the rapid growth of the multinationals, an outcome the economic planners did not really envision but that the rules of the game they instituted did allow for. The production of inadvertent consequences by semidirected processes is normal and should be anticipated whenever such processes are at work. They are evident if one looks at matters having to do with resources, food production, population, the environment, inflation, trade and payments, the rich nation/poor nation split, and economic development.

The production of inadvertent consequences has become a serious problem and for reasons that are quite understandable. As the number of actors and forms of action climbs, the number and variety of inputs into the international arena skyrocket. There are more things and larger quantities to be aggregated—commercial trans-actions, industrial wastes, aggressive behaviors, cooperative actions, technological innovations, social innovations, communications be-havior—and therefore more aggregative and combinatory processes must come into play. This is not because anyone creates them deliberately; it is because the logic of interaction requires it. Whenever there is interaction there is aggregation; aggregative processes, by themselves and in combination with one another, produce inadvertent consequences. Therefore, as the amount of interaction in the international system increases so, too, will the production of inadvertent consequences, other things being equal.

As noted already, miscalculation continues to play an important role in producing inadvertent consequences, for actors are increas-ingly in the position of trying to act on the system, or to achieve results through its workings, while having only vague and inadequate ideas about those workings. As the international system becomes more interactive, it necessarily becomes more complex. Each year more ships, planes, trains, and trucks set forth to carry larger quantities of a greater variety of materials and persons to an increasing number of destinations. Countless linked decisions and actions and reactions are required to maintain distribution networks and keep things moving through them. Patterns of dependence and influence become increasingly complicated.[7] The emergence of each new actor or new type of interaction creates the possibility of hundreds of new actions and new dyadic relationships.

The international system is a man-made creation, and new com-

ponents are being added to it each month. It has, in fact, achieved a
degree of complexity that can no longer be fully comprehended. It
may seem strange that men can construct something more complex
than they can understand, but that is not uncommon in an interactive
world. Americans, for example, have fashioned both a national
economy and an urban society so intricate that they can neither
comprehend the two fully nor manage them effectively. This is the
Labyrinth Effect. Daedalus, so mythology tells us, designed the
Labyrinth in Crete for the Minotaur at the order of King Minos. Later,
the angry king imprisoned Daedalus and his son Icarus in the
Labyrinth, but so well had the designer done his job that even he
could not find his way out of it.

The secret of man's capacity to create extreme complexity lies in the
incremental character of many of his social constructions. Parts can be
fitted together piece by piece by actors who do not understand the
whole and do not need to. They need to understand only those components of the broader system that are immediately adjacent. The
growth of multinational corporations exemplifies this incremental
feature of aggregative processes. A corporate manager needs to know
how to expand his company's operations abroad, but he need not
understand the general impact of multinational corporations on the
international economic system. It is by incremental means that men
have created the international system. Man's knowledge of that
system is growing, of course, but it is not clear that it is growing as
rapidly as is the complexity of the system itself. It may be, indeed,
that understanding of the international system, relative to what there
is to be understood, has actually declined since, say, World War II.
Part of the difficulty lies in the fact that the system is in continuous
and rapid change and therefore some of that which is true today will
not be true five years from now, and unlearning is about as painful as
learning.

As the web of interaction has become more dense the international
system has also become more effective as a transmission medium.
Ideas, technologies, fads, and modes of behavior now move easily
across national boundaries and diffuse with epidemiclike characteristics. Perturbations in the international system that might once have
spent their force locally are now transmitted through an entire region
or across the globe—unemployment, payments problems, resource
scarcities, environmental hazards, or inflation.[8] The consequences of
any significant action are likely to be more extensive and more

pervasive than would have been the case ten, fifteen, or fifty years ago, and therefore those initiating actions are much less able to anticipate consequences.

Predictability also tends to decline the more distant in time an initial act is from its remote consequences. A major action does not produce all of its consequences at one time but may go on generating them almost indefinitely. For example, all the returns are by no means in on the 1973 oil price increase. Five years from now it will still be producing consequences, but they will have become increasingly dilute, of course, in the sense that outcomes produced will be increasingly shaped by second-order and third-order consequences of the change and by trains of action set in motion by factors independent of the price change.

Typically, actors plan first-order consequences. These are likely to flow quite directly from their actions and can be calculated with a degree of confidence, and it is in order to achieve them that an action is taken in the first instance. Rarely, however, are the actors able, even if they were to try, to anticipate the higher-order consequences of their actions. The Organization of Petroleum-Exporting Countries (OPEC) raised the price of oil in order to increase their income from its sale. They succeeded in doing so and therefore correctly anticipated that first-order consequence. In addition, however, the change had a variety of other consequences: worsening the economic position of Fourth World nations and increasing the amount of malnutrition and starvation in them; increasing the size of arms shipments to the Middle East; exacerbating the Arab-Israeli conflict; changing the relations of OPEC members to one another; further undermining the economic situation in countries such as England, France, and Italy; speeding the process of nuclear proliferation, with whatever additional consequences that may have; contributing to a variety of important international power shifts; encouraging demands for the development of a new international economic order and encouraging the United States to reassess a variety of economic policies; and, by altering the cost of energy, influencing the worldwide direction of technological and economic development. To what extent did OPEC anticipate these consequences; and were the consequences of these consequences correctly anticipated?

Men knew enough to develop DDT to kill mosquitoes, but they did not know enough to anticipate the ecological consequences that would flow from the widespread use of that chemical. Physicists and engineers knew enough to develop the atom bomb during World War II, but statesmen and policy analysts were not able to anticipate the profound effect that the development of nuclear energy would have on military strategy, the conduct of diplomacy, power relations among nations, medicine, energy production, and the environment.

Distant and higher-order consequences are called into existence over a period of time by processes of aggregation and combination and by complex mechanisms involving multiplier, dampening, triggering, and threshold effects. Some actions may be dampened out and generate little in the way of discernible consequences, save as they contribute to a process of aggregation. Others, however, may generate whole trains of consequences, and the initiating actor often cannot tell which is which ahead of time. The point is important, for it explains how it is that, in an interactive system, an initial action or set of actions may lead to consequences that will seem shockingly disproportionate.

Garrett Hardin's villagers, with their few sheep, did not intend to precipitate the tragedy of the commons.[9] The householder, with spray can in hand, is trying to set hair or kill household odors, but that action, when aggregated, may have higher-order consequences that will endanger the ozone layer. Because of the complexity of the system in which they are involved, actors are often unable to trace the connection between actions they may be contemplating and the consequences that will, in fact, result.

A mist lies between an actor and the distant consequences of its actions. If it cannot know those consequences, then it is not in a position to weigh gain to itself against costs to the community, even if it were inclined to do so. It could endanger the commons in good faith—and in total ignorance. Or it might sense that a self-serving action was not wholly in accord with community good without being fully aware of just how disproportionate its advantage and community costs might be. Lyndon Johnson was probably aware that waging the Vietnam War without dampening domestic economic activity would cause inflation, but did he realize how great, how persistent, and how costly that impact would be? He may have been aware that some of this inflation would leak into the world economy, but did he have any conception at all of the impetus that leakage might give to worldwide inflation?

Observers are accustomed to analyzing problems in terms of the *purposes* of actors, and so it is their tendency to assume that an actor who sets a train of events in motion must have planned the entire sequence and can therefore be held responsible for it. In fact, however, actors of any significance, however carefully they plan their actions, will generate inadvertent consequences. They need only go about their normal day-to-day affairs and the processes of aggregation and combination will guarantee a rich harvest of surprises. To a considerable extent, then, men are not deliberately fashioning the world in which they live but are creating it, from day to day, without really knowing what they are doing. *In the international system, the significance of purposive action is declining relative to the part played by the apurposive and the inadvertent.* The machinations of major actors are no longer the nearly exclusive source of "history," and evil often appears without evildoers and trouble without troublemakers.[10]

Problems, Requisites, and System Fragility

The character of the problems in a system is related to the character of the system. As diffusion mechanisms have become more common and more important, they allow combinatory processes to work more easily. In many cases the key boundaries are not those of nation-state borders but the limits of a given diffusion process. In an international system characterized by ease of diffusion, it is not surprising that system problems are also easily diffused. The geographic scope of problems increases, and linkages between them become closer. Simple and local problems are progressively replaced by those that are complex and are either regional or global. It becomes increasingly difficult to decompose a complex problem into its component parts so that they can be dealt with singly, and yet it also becomes increasingly difficult to deal with the entire complex of problems at one time.[11]

The number of problems confronting major actors at a given time is also related to the characteristics of the international system. Because that system is technologically innovative, problems are likely to be plentiful. Before the technology was developed to mine the sea depths, nations did not have to worry about regulating that activity. Before the advent of nuclear energy, nations did not have to concern themselves with nuclear proliferation and the control of nuclear testing. Before the advent of intercontinental ballistic missiles, major nations did not have to try to limit the number of delivery vehicles that potential enemies might have or worry about the prospects of being overwhelmed by a first strike. Before men could achieve orbital flight, there was no need to outlaw the military use of space stations on the moon or the manufacture of suborbital bombs. As technology continues to accelerate, so too will the production of problems from this source.

Another source of problems, also related to the changing character of the international system, is the increase in the number of system and structural requisites. The term *system requisites* refers to those needs that must be satisfied if the system is to function normally. These requisites can be placed in the following general categories: environmental requisites; physical resource requisites; system flow requisites (materials, people, energy, technology, information); requisites associated with trained personnel and their services; control and guidance requisites.

The needs of the international system evolve as the system evolves. A high level of international trade has not always been a system requisite, but it is now. That trade, in turn, could not be maintained without high levels of productivity in trading countries, rapid means of moving freight, sophisticated communications and computer systems, and institutions to regulate and facilitate trade and payments. The production and distribution of large quantities of petroleum have not always been vital. The number of life-support systems that must be kept operational climbs as the international system becomes more interactive. Tomorrow's system requisites will be somewhat different from today's and will be more numerous.

The term *structural requisites* refers to needs associated with the maintenance and functioning of important managerial and control structures. These structures will normally be brought into existence in order to satisfy a system need, a system requisite. A system need can often, of course, be satisfied by any of a number of structural arrangements. As noted, it has been a system requisite for some time that large quantities of petroleum be produced, transported, and made available for consumption. Until 1973 this requisite was satisfied through structural arrangements dominated by the large oil companies, the United States, and the United Kingdom. In time, the requisites of that structure failed to be satisfied, and a new set of structural arrangements emerged, dominated this time by OPEC. This new structure also has its requisites, however, including such things as the continuation of a high level of cooperation among major OPEC participants as the price-setting negotiations of December

1976. Actors are often unclear about the distinction between system requisites and structural requisites and tend to assume that the collapse of a set of structural arrangements to which they are attached would be equivalent to the denial of a *system* requisite and would therefore endanger the viability of the international system itself. For example, threats to the Bretton Woods institutions might be perceived as threats to international exchange itself.

The increase of interaction in the international system, involving as it does an increase in complexity and differentiation, will require the development of larger numbers of controlling and regulating structures or, at least, an expansion in the functions of existing structures. In either case, this will mean that the number of structural requisites will increase and that, by definition, the number of points of structural vulnerability will become more numerous.

Not only does the number of system and structural requisites increase as the system becomes more interactive, the number of things that can interfere with their satisfaction also increases—accidents, sabotage, official miscalculation, congestion, panics or massive losses of confidence, and inadvertent synergistic consequences resulting from aggregation and combination. "So far as we can determine, proliferating vulnerabilities are a universal concomitant of progression from relatively simple to increasingly complex technological-economic systems."[12] Important flows may be slowed or stopped. Environmental or structural requisites may cease to be satisfied. The services of key personnel may be lost through disaster or strike. Vital resources may become depleted. Control arrangements may prove inadequate to the job to be done, resulting in, say, runaway inflation, the collapse of international trade, epidemic terrorism, or nuclear war. Interaction points toward a rise in the frequency of major system crises but also toward a rise in the frequency of mishaps such as oil spills and nuclear accidents. Relatively minor mishaps may, of course, combine with one another and become significant in the process of so doing.

As long as everything goes smoothly, the operation of the international system is impressive. The complexity and division of labor that allows it to perform so well are also a source of vulnerability, however.[13] A system cannot but become more vulnerable when it must maintain an increasing number of major population centers and an increasingly involved network of interlocking processes and when it must rely upon an increasing number of elaborate and interrelated technologies. In the same way, the larger the number of flows it must depend upon, the greater is the potential danger from congestion. "It is almost a truism that the higher the level of technological-economic development, and the more urbanized the society, the more dependent its members become upon the uninterrupted delivery of essential supplies and the performance of other equally essential services."[14]

The flows in a system move through channels, but channel and flow do not always constitute a perfect fit. Congestion comes whenever a flow is greater than a channel can handle efficiently, and this could result from an increase in the flow, as with international air travel, or because of a constriction in the channel, as with the closing of the Suez Canal in 1967. In the international system, opportunities for congestion are many and increasing. Even the elimination of congestion can sometimes set up disruptive wave actions that will propagate widely.

Congestion in the international system may be thought of as roughly analogous to "friction" in a mechanical system. As the international system becomes more complex, the number of points of friction must increase, and the total amount of friction in the system will increase rapidly unless, of course, some new way is discovered to reduce it. Unfortunately, the flow of decisions needed to deal with congestion—decisions that must come from governmental and nongovernmental sources—is itself subject to congestion.[15]

Major actors today are presented with a flow of problems as if they were being ground out of a sausage machine. The factors touched on above help explain why this is the case. System requisites and structural requisites, although analytically distinct, both contribute to the sum of problems with which leading actors must deal. As long as the number of requisites increases, the future will offer a progressively richer array of potential dangers and an increasing likelihood of simultaneous crises. The increasingly close linkage of subsystems in an interactive world also increases the likelihood of crises, linked crises at that. A crisis in one sector, that is, might precipitate a crisis in another and another, and, in that way, a rolling crisis might advance like a wave through the entire international system. Other things being equal, then, system fragility must rise with an increase in system interaction. This is simply one more inadvertent consequence of systemic development. There was no plan to create a global system so interactive and fragile that its own survival would be at risk; it just happened.

Order and Disorder

Order is not a natural, spontaneous product in complex social systems but must be imposed by deliberate effort. When individuals interact with one another in a large organization, a city, a nation, or the international system, their affairs will go smoothly only if there is a framework of rules to channel and direct their activities. These rules are provided by the control structures referred to earlier, and the structures themselves may be a product of law, formal agreements, informal agreements, or custom. Rules there must be, however, for uncoordinated action will produce only disorder. Even market activities, which may seem spontaneous, have to be organized in the first instance, must operate in accordance with the rules of the game, and must be policed.

As the level of interaction in the international system rises, the amount of effort devoted to system control must increase if the preexisting level of control is to be maintained. The more actors and actions and flows there are, the more time and energy must be devoted to overcoming congestion and other forms of friction. More individuals and more organizations must devote a greater proportion of their time and energies to satisfying the increasing number of system and structural requisites and seeing to it that needs are met, at least minimally. Harold and Margaret Sprout have noted that "the more complex a system becomes, the greater also becomes the cost of providing against breakdown from whatever cause."[16]

If the effort devoted to management and control does not increase as the system becomes more elaborate and interactive, then existing control capabilities must become increasingly attenuated. In the last twenty-five years, the level of interaction and complexity in the international system has increased greatly, but without being countered by a corresponding increase in effort devoted to control and management. In such circumstances, to stand still, or to move forward only slowly, is to move backward. That is why the evidence of drift and of weakening control is so abundant.

The imposition of order in the international arena is peculiarly difficult. Order is created by means of structures and associated rules of the game, but these can only be created on the basis of agreement among sovereign nation-states. Typically, it is hard to get agreement on the nature of a problem and harder still to get agreement on a solution. Getting agreement on almost anything is time consuming, and the more complex the matter, the greater is the time required.[17]

Order can be achieved and maintained only by dint of effort, but disorder can arise without anyone working at it. Quite different processes are involved in the two cases. Actors often get into trouble via processes of aggregation and combination that have an element of the automatic about them—inflation, recession, pollution, and so on—and this means that they cannot control the *amount* of trouble they find themselves in. In a practical sense, it may be beyond their control. Yet they must get out of trouble through reliance on analysis and purposeful collective action. Problems may be generated effortlessly at the process level, whereas solutions can be achieved only through hard-won agreement at the structural level.

The practical implication of this is that, in a highly interactive and rapidly changing international system, problems will often be generated faster than solutions. It took only a few years to move from high explosives to fission weapons and then to fusion weapons, but adequate control of nuclear weaponry has still not been achieved. The technology for exploiting the sea depths has been developing rapidly, but getting agreement on the way that technology can be used has been moving slowly. A number of the problems created by the multinational corporations took shape quickly, but getting agreement on what to do about the multinationals is still years in the future. In the meantime, of course, they will continue to evolve and, because of processes of aggregation and combination, will produce more inadvertent consequences and more problems for nation-states.

Because problems may be produced by one set of mechanisms but must be dealt with by a quite different set of purposeful procedures, if they are to be dealt with at all, it is easy for problem creation and problem solution to get out of phase. That is to say, it is quite possible for actors to get into more trouble than they can get out of, and that is what is happening. The conclusion that problems are being generated faster than solutions is not a comforting one. It suggests that problems not dealt with, aggregating and combining in accordance with their own peculiar dynamics, might produce an unexpected, and perhaps catastrophic, higher-order consequence. Apart from that, they must, in time, constitute an unmanageable system overload.

It may be a characteristic of all highly complex systems that interaction tends to outrun control capabilities.[18] Be that as it may, it is clear that the international system has been going through a protracted entropic or disorder crisis. The amount of inadvertent change being generated through processes of aggregation and combination, combined with normal problems involving hostility and competition, has been overtaxing the collective capacity of actors to deal with the situation through purposeful efforts. The international system is markedly undergoverned in comparison with other complex social systems, and yet deliberate control over its evolution continues to decline. As the international system moves farther out the interaction continuum toward the extreme of hyperinteractivity, the issue of control must become increasingly critical. The sooner significant remedial action is undertaken the better, for as the ratio of directed elements to undirected declines there will be progressively more disorder to cope with.

Remedial Action and Interaction Costs

The problem of maintaining system control is created by the tendency of interaction, and its associated features, to outrun deliberate collective guidance. Remedial action therefore can be directed toward (1) the improving of management capabilities; (2) slowing, stopping, or redirecting the growth of interaction; (3) both of the above.

A technological breakthrough might ease the managerial task for a time, but it could be only a short-term remedy.

There is no way that technology can solve the information problem once and for all, for the increase in interaction continues without let-up and constitutes a ceaseless demand for ever better communication. The best that can be done is to buy time, and not much at that. The level of information flow that is adequate one moment will seem cramped and inadequate six months later. The arrival of the electronic computer significantly improved man's capacity to handle vast amounts of data, but the demand for more and better computers has not slackened and the pressure on man's information-handling capabilities is as great now as when the computer age dawned.[19]

Men can improve their managerial capabilities, but only slowly. Have we advanced so far beyond those who saw to the building of the pyramids or who administered the Roman Empire? Man's capacity to

give deliberate guidance to complex social systems still leaves much
to be desired.

For example, we do not yet have a tool of analysis that allows
estimated benefits from a prospective increase in interaction to be
offset against its costs and that facilitates a recognition of the full
range of costs involved. Serious cost-benefit analysis is rarely
undertaken in connection with system interaction because the presumption is that most forms of interaction (including the economic
but excluding war) are unquestioned goods. Costs, if they are
considered at all, are presumed to be negligible.[20] This presumption
has received support from the literature dealing with free trade,
comparative advantage, and economic growth and development.
Few things are cost-free, however, and international trade is not one
of them.

An important cost of interaction has to do with obsolescence. A
highly interactive system, characterized by a high rate of change and
innovation, must necessarily be characterized also by a high rate of
obsolescence. Taking the system as a whole, the new cannot be
brought in without displacing the old. As we put new cars on the
road, we propel old cars to the junkyard, so to speak. In the same
way, the more rapidly the international system changes because of
increased interaction, the more rapidly knowledge becomes obsolete.
Actors will find themselves continually moving out of situations they
have begun to understand into those that are unfamiliar.

Obsolescence is a handmaiden of change, a cost associated with
social, political, economic, and technological innovation, and it may
take many forms: new power relations replace the old; familiar
stereotypes become dated, and established expectations prove to
have been mistaken; treaties are abrogated or ignored, and informal
rules cease to be observed; institutions lose their vitality; alliances and
blocs dissolve; ideologies lose their followings, and values that were
once functional become counterproductive; yesterday's technologies
are replaced by today's. The rate of obsolescence will increase as the
rate of interaction increases, and the burden of coping with it will
become heavier as the international system continues toward a
condition of hyperinteractivity.

One way to reduce the costs of interaction would be to reduce the
amount of interaction itself. Because our experience has lain largely in
increasing interaction, we don't have much to go on, and so at this
juncture little more can be done than to touch on a few of the obvious

points. There would be costs involved in any deliberate effort to slow the growth of interaction, but they would vary depending on the way in which the slowing were done. For example, speeding the diffusion of technology might allow for greater dispersal of production facilities and thus might offer a low-cost means for reducing trade in finished goods.

Because increases in interaction are fostered by social and technological innovation, among other things, slowing the rate of innovation would, over time, serve as a brake on interaction. In effect, if this option were utilized, actors would be deliberately allowing congestion to develop. Instead of trying to improve rates of flow and reduce system friction, they would be utilizing friction as a means, imperfect but nevertheless effective, of slowing the growth of system interaction. Shifts in the *direction* of technological and social innovation might also serve to slow down interaction.

The growth of interaction is also fostered by structural arrangements. If the Bretton Woods institutions were successful in facilitating the expansion of international trade and investment, might not a modified set of arrangements, including higher prices, serve to slow that expansion? Disincentives could, of course, be applied gradually and selectively.[21]

Another line of attack might be for individual actors to seek to lower the level of their involvement in the international system. A net reduction in system interaction would then take place, and individual actors, because they had moved in the direction of autonomy, would be less vulnerable to crises running through the international system. An extreme example of autarky would be Japan prior to the visit of Admiral Perry. China, from 1949 until the death of Mao, has pursued a policy of limited involvement with the Western world. Autarky does have its costs, however, including lower living standards and a slowed rate of economic development. As the Sprouts have observed, "national communities, especially those dependent on a technologically advanced industrialized economy, face increasingly the unwelcome *choice between high-cost autarky and high-risk inter-dependence.*"[22]

Since the growth of interaction cannot long be sustained without periodic changes in structural arrangements, the deliberate failure to update the rules of the game would serve to brake the growth of interaction, but this high-cost remedy might be almost as bad as the disease itself.

The idea of slowing the rate of interaction could not fail to be controversial, for powerful interests as well as familiar principles and assumptions would be challenged. Yet, policy makers in developed countries must sometimes try to cool off a national economy that is overheating, and the same logic might be applied to the international system. One could confidently anticipate that it would generate no less resistance at that level, however. On 15 November 1976, the *New York Times* News Service reported, for example, that OECD economists were predicting that economic recovery would slow markedly unless the United States and major industrial nations adopted more expansionary economic policies. At about the same time, an international group of private economists warned of a slowdown unless "slow growth" antiinflationary policies were quickly reversed. Nations have trouble living with sustained international economic growth but are alarmed by anything that threatens to slow it.

Beyond doubt, high costs would be associated with a deliberate slowing of the rate of growth of interaction, and in all likelihood those costs would not be distributed evenly. For example, by promoting change, interaction often undermines existing structures and creates opportunities for their replacement. At present, therefore, a slowing in the rate of change might tend to work to the disadvantage of developing countries seeking to improve their bargaining positions vis-à-vis the developed nations. A slowing of the rate of interaction would also tend to slow their rate of economic development and might be perceived as an effort to lock the less developed nations into their present condition. The preponderance of the interaction in the international system is accounted for by the developed nations, however, not the less developed, and it might therefore be possible to devise policies that would rest more heavily on the former than on the latter. At best, slowing interaction would involve costs, and they would be substantial, but the costs involved in *not* slowing the growth of interaction may be prohibitive. In its evolution, the international system has become so interactive that no attractive alternatives remain, only alternatives that differ in their unattractiveness. The present situation is highly unstable, and if successful collective efforts to control the growth of interaction are not forthcoming and the aggregate of autarkic efforts by individual actors proves insignificant, then automatic limiting processes must come into play.

The world depression of 1929–39 showed such a limiting process at work. A level of economic and commercial activity had been achieved incrementally that could not be sustained. Nations lacked the collective ability to manage the world economy they had created, and a drastic, unplanned reduction in economic interaction took place. The flight from multilateralism to bilateralism led to a spasmodic contraction in world trade. The costs associated with this contraction were immense, but in the end, the international economic system had retreated to a level of interaction that was manageable. The elements of the international economic system are more tightly linked now than they were in 1929 and the level of economic activity is much higher, so that automatic corrections, if they were to come, might be much more painful.

Summary

The early identification of emergent international problems is largely a conceptual matter, and the analyst will be aided if he has an understanding of underlying system processes. This paper has argued that interaction is a key variable in the development of the international system, that the system is evolving from a relatively low level of interaction to a very high one, and that this shift brings with it a number of profoundly important consequences. Because these consequences are related to interaction and to one another, one can speak of the "logic" of interaction:

   1. Inputs are flowing into the international arena and the environment in increasing numbers and with greater variety.
   2. These inputs are aggregated and combined in intricate ways.
   3. When behaviors flowing from a multitude of microdecisions are aggregated and combined, the results constitute not macrodecisions but, rather, processes partially or wholly lacking in direction.
   4. Undirected or partially directed processes produce surprises and inadvertent consequences as a normal part of their functioning.
   5. Because the variety of inputs into the international system is increasing, the number of undirected processes also increases, and therefore the production of inadvertent consequences becomes both more common and more important.
   6. The international system is becoming more elaborate and differentiated, and as a consequence the number of system and structural requisites climbs.

7. Due to the increase in the number of requisites and the number of undirected or semidirected processes (and the inadvertent consequences associated with the latter), the international system is generating an increasing number of problems.

8. The improved processes of diffusion associated with an increasingly interactive international system guarantee that these problems will tend to broaden in scope and to become more tightly linked with one another.

9. It follows that as the number of requisites and problems increases the international system as a whole will become increasingly fragile and the costs involved in keeping the system operating will escalate sharply.

10. As the international system becomes more differentiated and complex, actors find its workings harder to comprehend.

11. This means that they will find it difficult to determine where long-term interests lie and what the higher-order consequences of their own actions and the actions of others will be.

12. Furthermore, because of the complexity of the system and the inertia represented by its many interlocking processes, actors find it increasingly hard to shape events and pursue their interests effectively. For major actors, this difficulty will be aggravated by the necessity of trying to deal with a more or less continuing flow of system-generated crises. Actors will have a declining sense of efficacy and a growing feeling that they are not so much directing events as being swept along by them.

13. Management capabilities will increase, but only slowly, and these advances will be more than offset by the growth of interaction.

14. System management and control will therefore become more attenuated, the drift toward undirectedness will accelerate, and the disorder crisis will become progressively more acute.

This logic can be altered and can be brought under control, but it will require strenuous collective effort on the part of leading actors. At present, because the role of apurposive forces in the functioning of the international system is systematically underestimated, those actors are not yet in a position to manage the system of which they are a part. If significant collective changes are not made, the international system will continue to be propelled at an increasing rate of speed toward a condition of hyperinteractivity. However, because the multiple demands of hyperinteractivity can never be satisfied, arrival at that destination can never occur. Somewhere along the way an accident must take place.

Leviathan, the Open Society, and the Crisis of Ecology*

David W. Orr and Stuart Hill

In light of the intensity of the ecology debate, it is curious that so little attention has been given to the political implications involved in the creation of an environmentally sustainable society. With some exceptions,[1] the few scholars who have addressed these issues have assumed that the resolution of ecological problems will require the centralization of political power and the imposition of authoritarian controls on liberal societies. These measures, they argue, are necessary to mobilize the resources and capabilities of society, to tighten social discipline, and to provide efficient planning and administration. The lack of subsequent debate about the implications of such a course for democratic societies might be explained by the "obvious" congruence between the magnitude of the crisis and the need for social discipline. But whether authoritarianism is an obvious and necessary response depends a great deal upon tacit assumptions about the causes and dimensions of the crisis and upon one's estimate of the capacity of large-scale centralized government to resolve complex environmental issues.[2]

In the paper that follows, we propose to examine the case for centralization and explore possible alternatives. Although the focus of the paper is on national political systems, the problems of political organization are in many respects similar to those at the international level. That we have chosen to deal with the domestic level, however, reflects our belief that ecological reform of modern societies is a necessary precursor to and component of international solutions.

In the first section, we will review and critique the work of three of

*Adapted by permission of the University of Utah from the *Western Political Quarterly* 31, no. 4 (December 1978).

the most influential proponents of centralization: Robert Heilbroner, Garrett Hardin, and William Ophuls.[3] The second section will examine the opposite case for a decentralized society implicit in the work of E. F. Schumacher and others.[4] In the third and final section, we will consider the possibility of selective decentralization, which maximizes the possibility of resolving ecological problems while preserving social "resilience."

Ecology and Leviathan

There is an old assumption that political democracy depends in large part upon the existence of natural abundance. Alexis de Tocqueville, for example, once suggested that the stability of American democracy depended on "a love of equality and liberty" *and* "a limitless continent."[5] Although Tocqueville did not develop the theme, the Hobbesian implications of scarcity are nevertheless clear.

Among contemporary thinkers, Tocqueville's assumption is implicit in the writings of Hardin, Heilbroner, Ophuls, and others. But in contrast to Tocqueville, who could not have foreseen the possibilities of future scarcity, these scholars assume that we are now approaching the condition the authors of *The Limits to Growth* called "overshoot." Robert Heilbroner, for example, states that "We are entering a period in which rapid population growth, the presence of obliterative weapons, and dwindling resources will bring international tensions to dangerous levels for an extended period."[6] William Ophuls similarly states that "We have come to the final act of the tragedy of the Commons."[7] These scholars agree that the combination of resource scarcity, overpopulation, and the lack of a long lead time for measured changes threatens to overwhelm the capacities of both physical and social systems.

For Hardin the structure of our plight is analogous to the tendency of eighteenth-century English villagers to abuse common grazing land.[8] The conflict he describes between individual and collective interest is similar to that described in Rousseau's stag hunt and to the game theoretician's model of the prisoner's dilemma. In each of these matrices, the system rewards self-interest while penalizing altruism, so that the collective "tragedy" occurs because everyone behaves according to his rational self-interest.

Heilbroner offers a slightly different perspective in which the interaction of population growth, the spread of nuclear weapons, and the resources and pollution limits to industrial growth will create intolerable stresses on social systems in advance of physical carrying capacity. He foresees a world of decreasing stability characterized by conflicts over redistribution between and within nations. In contrast to Hardin, he depicts the tragedy as neither inevitable nor "structural" but, rather, as a product of recent trends and the lack of sufficient adjustment time.

The problem of adjustment is compounded for all three because we cannot rely on individual altruism or enlightenment. Heilbroner asserts that there is little evidence to "encourage expectations of an easy subordination of the private interest to the public weal."[9] Hardin also suggests that those motivated by altruism simply eliminate themselves because the integrity of the commons is always at the mercy of the few not subject to conscience. Ophuls similarly maintains that "individual conscience and the right kind of cultural attitudes are not by themselves sufficient to overcome the short term calculations of utility that lead men to degrade their environment."[10] Accordingly, "passionate" men need external checks to their wills and appetites, as once suggested by Edmund Burke.

If individuals are unreliable, the possibility still exists that social institutions can provide the necessary strength and flexibility for adaptation to new conditions. Heilbroner, however, assures us that "one can[not] avoid the conclusion that the required transformation will be likely to exceed the capabilities of representative democracy." This conclusion applies with equal force to socialist societies: "For what portends in that longer run, is a challenge of drastically curtailing, perhaps dismantling, the mode of production that has been the most cherished achievement of both systems."[11] Ophuls, looking specifically at the United States, is equally apocalyptic, stating that our "current institutions are incapable of meeting the challenge of scarcity."[12]

Despite some difference in emphasis, all three agree that (1) we are at the threshold of an unprecedented planetary ecological crisis; (2) reliance on individual good will, conscience, and/or education is not sufficient; and (3) democratic institutions are inadequate to meet the challenge. Because "Freedom in a commons brings ruin to all," the responses they recommend are variants of Hardin's system of "mutual coercion mutually agreed upon,"[13] in which the individual's "right" to encroach on the commons is replaced by a system of centralized controls.

In a later essay Hardin extended this line of thought by suggesting that the division of nations into those with rapid, uncontrolled population growth and those with slower sustainable rates had created a situation analogous to a partially filled lifeboat surrounded by drowning swimmers.[14] The question he poses is whether those on the lifeboat should admit some of the swimmers; if so, how many, and which ones? The decision, he contends, should be based solely on the grounds of the "safety factor" of the boat and not on altruism.

Aside from the usefulness of the analogy, which has been critiqued elsewhere in this volume, a lifeboat strategy would require even greater political centralization than Hardin admitted in his 1968 essay. The policy of refusing aid to other societies in desperate need would probably entail the closure of international borders to relatively free immigration, travel, commerce, and cultural exchange in order to prevent terrorist reprisals. It might also encourage other states to apply the same logic in reverse to our overconsumption of their resources and energy, leading possibly to our military retaliation.[15]

Heilbroner is even more dismal. "There is, " he states, "no escape from the necessity of a centralized administration for our industrial world."[16] He envisions realistic alternatives to our present system as blending "religious orientation and a military discipline." The road to survival can be found only by monastic societies that are tightly disciplined. What hope exists for the survival of democratic institutions ironically can be found only in the vigorous exercise of executive leadership. The magnitude of the crisis is so great, according to Heilbroner, that the "centralization of power [is] the only means by which our threatened and dangerous civilization can make way for its successor."[17] Ophuls similarly states that scarcity will create "overwhelming pressures toward political systems that are frankly authoritarian."[18] At one point, he feels this new authority might be made "constitutional and limited." This seems to be a rather empty qualification, however, because he stresses the need for an oligarchy or "aristocracy" to determine and justify "certain restrictions on human activities" because the populace "would do something quite different . . . left to its own."[19]

In short, the crisis described by Ophuls, Hardin, and Heilbroner is without historical precedent. Although scarcity is not new, the sudden transition from unparalleled abundance into want is new. Nothing in our present circumstances or in our philosophy of technological progress can prepare us for the descent they envision: a collapse not only of the material foundations of Western life but of much of its intellectual basis supporting science, technological growth, and material progress as well. If we accept this Hobbesian scenario, we might logically accept the leviathan they propose— except that we now know more about the capabilities and limits of leviathan than Hobbes did.

There is little doubt that most persons identifying themselves as environmentalists concur in the belief that centralized authority will be necessary to resolve the ecological crisis. Necessity aside, growing demands have led to greater centralization and expansion of government throughout the twentieth century. Is there then reason to take issue with what some consider to be an absolute necessity, and with observable trends? Although it is clear that modern societies have long since passed the point (if it ever existed) when dispensing with centralized leadership could be seriously considered, there is some reason to suggest moderation in our expectations about the capacity and potential of large-scale government.

Although Heilbroner and Ophuls are not particularly clear about what they mean by centralization, we might infer that it minimally implies government responsibility for a growing number of functions that are now handled privately or are left to nature. Moreover, since the ecological crisis they describe is one of bewildering complexity, including everything from climate change down to the "cogs and wheels" of nature, we might reasonably expect greater specialization and a consequent increase in the internal complexity of government as suggested by Ross Ashby's "law of requisite variety."[20] We might also expect a drastic increase in the coercive capacity of the state necessary to maintain public order and to prevent revolution during the retreat from general affluence to controlled scarcity described by Heilbroner and Ophuls. Military power would also be necessary to reduce the vulnerability to international terrorists, to protect supplies of raw materials, and to protect the state from attack by others in even more dire straits. Whatever the merits of Hardin's lifeboat analogy, in real life the drowning swimmers are not helpless and nations do not simply disappear. They sometimes make reprisals.

Assuming that their diagnosis of the ecological crisis is correct, can the state cope with the added burdens prescribed by Heilbroner, Ophuls, and Hardin? There are those who have wondered only some-what facetiously whether the state now is itself governable. To add to its present functions those of managing the commons and super-vising nature while maintaining public order may overstrain our organizational capacity, not to mention our credulity. Without explicitly stating the case, they assume (1) that an authoritarian state can cope with its own increased size and complexity; (2) that it can muster sufficient skill to exert control over the external environment; and (3) that these conditions can be maintained in perpetuity. A fourth and crucial assumption, that we have no practical choice, will be considered later.

1. Taking these in order, the first assumption is made without acknowledgment of the effects of increased size and complexity upon the internal functioning of the state. Beyond some threshold, however, there may be limits to our capacity to manage the apparatus of government. Langdon Winner, for example, states: "The complexity of what it must know about its own internal composition and its external environment appears to place a severe limitation on the ability of a large organization to understand its situation. To be more precise, this means that those who direct the activities of the organization will often make crucial choices in relative ignorance of the universe in which they are to act."[21] According to Daniel Metlay, these limits are the result of "informational overload" and "limited channel capacity."[22] More directly, the limits result from the inherent problem of accurately monitoring and controlling large, complex systems. How close we may be to these limits is debatable, but some have conjectured that we are not far off.

The increased size and complexity of government suggest a second limit inherent in the unavoidable competition between bureaucratic agencies. From the work of Graham Allison and others, we know that governments seldom, if ever, act as "rational actors" but are, rather, interlocking, competing bureaucracies.[23] Government policy is not the product of rational consideration of options but more often reflects the relative bargaining strength of bureaucratic rivals. The belief that government could be united around the common goal of protecting the environment or any other single focus belies the evidence at hand. But even if we could dismiss this evidence, a bureaucratic perspective cautions us from assuming that policy implementation could avoid the debilitating effects of bureaucratic competition.

The management of a large, complex state is also subject to limitations characteristic of pyramidal structures generally. As the size of an organization increases, the need for hierarchically arranged control likewise grows. The effects of growth, however, are not necessarily benign. Chris Argyris, for example, argues that pyramidally arranged organizations promote incompetence, lower morale, and result in impaired effectiveness.[24] Organizations so constituted tend to become "self-sealing" from their environment and subsequently unable to "learn." Employees are governed by methods of unilateral direction, coercion, and hierarchical control, which leave little room for individual initiative. According to Argyris, emphasis upon rationality and suppression of emotion and intuition create persons unable to experience either self-satisfaction or human growth. The effects of self-sealing would impair the objective performance of an organization and particularly its capacity to innovate. Similarly, Kenneth Boulding has stated that "the larger and more authoritarian the organization, the better the chance that its top decision-makers will be operating in purely imaginary worlds. This is the most fundamental reason for supposing that there are ultimately diminishing returns to scale."[25] There is accordingly considerable potential for internal decay and consequent collapse of Heilbroner's large authoritarian state.

2. The second assumption made by Heilbroner, Ophuls, and Hardin is that a large centralized state could in fact reverse or slow ecological deterioration to some acceptable level. They assume, in short, that government effectiveness in dealing with the physical world will rise commensurate with the increase in the size and power of government itself. There are reasons to commend this view, not the least of which is the historical tendency for societies to respond to external military threats by increasing social discipline and simultaneously the power of central governments. Similarly, some might argue that centralized governments have proven more effective than their less centralized counterparts in promoting industrialization and economic growth. But whether the capacities of centralized government are suited to what Heilbroner and Ophuls seem to suggest are qualitatively different circumstances of the ecological threat is questionable.

The crisis they describe is subtle, complex, and long-term, but the solution they provide is the rather blunt instrument of the myopic, centralized, administrative state. It is interesting to note that Hobbes himself, who is credited as the intellectual godfather of this view, assumed that both society and "leviathan" would be relatively simple.[26] Part of the difficulty lies in the customary tools of administration, which include government regulation and bureaucratic fiat. Neither of these has proven to be particularly effective in dealing with ecological or other problems in the past, because administrative agencies are frequently overly influenced by the very groups they supposedly regulate.[27] Hardin and Ophuls are aware of this but offer no solution to the problem. The second shortcoming, once described by Murray Edelman, is that a large portion of bureaucratic activity is purely symbolic and is intended not to solve problems but only to appear as if doing so.[28]

If the tools of administration are suspiciously weak, we might similarly wonder about the suitability of the typical bureaucratic methods described as "disjointed incrementalism."[29] Government normally divides and subdivides responsibilities and attempts only small changes at the margin of the status quo. The result is that administrators seldom if ever adopt systemic approaches, which we are assured will be necessary to resolve the ecological crisis. Incrementalism implies not only small adjustments but also preoccupation with the present. Governments do not anticipate problems; more characteristically, they react long after the problems have become acute. There is little reason to think that an even more centralized administrative state will do much better, and at least some reason to think that it may do worse.[30]

Finally, Heilbroner, Hardin, and Ophuls argue that authoritarian government can provide the necessary initiative and leadership for the vast social changes they describe as necessary. Aside from the question of how we construct such an entity, we can question whether government is a suitable agent for the paradigm shift they propose. Governments, for reasons mentioned above, are more often conservative forces, even when speaking in revolutionary idiom. Our pessimism is compounded when we consider that the behavioral and structural changes they consider to be essential will require great creativity and social innovation. But research at the small group level shows that authoritarian groups are not as creative as their democratic counterparts, especially when confronted by complex problems.[31] There are obvious difficulties in extrapolating findings at this level to that of the state, but at a minimum such evidence should caution us against expecting the authoritarian state to be a source of much innovation, especially after bureaucratic routines become established.

3. Third, the solution proposed by Heilbroner, Hardin, and Ophuls

would be unforgiving of failure by centralized government. Social and ecological stability would both depend upon the good judgment and continuity of leviathan. Such a system lacks redundancy and diversity, which in other disciplines, notably ecology, are known to be synonomous with long-term stability. Highly centralized systems have little margin for error or tolerance of failure. If the body of scientific knowledge about ecological systems should prove to be inadequate, or if the commitment to ecological stability should erode for any reason, we could reasonably expect the collapse of the system. There is no obvious difference between this and the collapse of previous authoritarian societies, except that modern societies have grown more interdependent and dependent upon technology and, accordingly, have farther to fall. Their recovery in any meaningful sense of the word would be problematic at best.

There is, moreover, reason to expect the eventual erosion of the state's commitment to ecological concerns. For one thing, at least since Roberto Michels, we are aware of the possibility that elites will act to enhance their own tenure regardless of the consequences to the larger organization.[32] Second, the state has customarily derived a substantial portion of whatever legitimacy it had from the performance of large-scale projects, including the building of pyramids and military conquest.[33] More recent "megaprojects" included putting men on the moon and managing the ongoing miracle of compound economic growth. The state also derived legitimacy from its monopoly of the means of organized violence. George Modelski goes so far as to suggest a direct causal connection between the rise of the modern state and war, which culminates in "excessive centralization of government and the emasculation of local and functional activity."[34] But, presumably, megaprojects and war (including the environmental costs of preparation for war) would no longer be suitable for the straitened circumstances that Heilbroner and others predict. Ironically, the likelihood of maintaining domestic or international order in conditions they describe will require even greater levels of military strength. Moreover, without megaprojects and war, there is something of a void. How does the state justify its existence? Implicit in Heilbroner, Ophuls, and Hardin is the questionable belief that an ecologically based authoritarian state could derive its legitimacy from its alleged capacity to preserve the environmental balance. But the maintenance of a complex and subtle ecological balance affords little opportunity for visible achievement and thus a minimal base for government legitimacy.

In short, the case for a highly centralized, authoritarian solution is not sufficiently grounded in what we know (or may conjecture) to be the limits of large-scale organization. We are warned of an impending crisis without precedent but in the end are given the timeworn tool of authoritarian government. Even if we could achieve consensus on their diagnosis, we still have substantial room to question their prescription. But if not an authoritarian government, what?

A Decentralized Alternative

One answer proposed by other environmentalists, including Edward Goldsmith, E. F. Schumacher, John Todd, and Amory Lovins, is social and political decentralization.[35] This view does not represent any significant difference of opinion about the urgency of the crisis; rather, it represents different estimates of the dynamics of the crisis, the potential for citizen participation, and the efficacy of large-scale organization.

The case for decentralization, drawing from Kropotkin and later anarchists, rests on three propositions. First, those favoring decentralization argue not only that centralized institutions are inappropriate but that centralization itself is one of the principal causes of the problem. Implicit in this view is the idea that the ecological crisis, in its present acute form, originated partly in the transfer of power and wealth from smaller units in society to larger ones, particularly the modern corporation. They argue thus that a necessary, if insufficient, condition for a solution to the crisis will be a redistribution of power and wealth so that all share equally in the costs and benefits of society. Large organizations, whether the state or the corporation, will further increase the reliance on "high" technology, itself a major source of ecological hazard, while they simultaneously lower social adaptability. Denis de Rougemont argues further that the highly centralized state represents the triumph of power over freedom: "Whether we like it or not 'huge' means highly centralized; 'expensive' means state intervention in large-scale investment and a great leap forward in GNP, that yardstick of national spending; while 'dangerous' implies greatly increased police control and the supremacy of a supposedly infallible technocracy."[36]

Second, those favoring decentralization maintain that the crisis is due in part to the loss of a sense of appropriate scale and meaningful purpose. This is most evident, according to E. F. Schumacher, in the design of the modern economy, which is based on high rates of energy and resource use, mass consumption—in a word, greed. In its place he proposes an economy of "permanence," which "implies a profound reorientation of science and technology."[37] This requires that methods and machines be inexpensive enough to be generally accessible so that the cost of the average workplace does not exceed the annual earnings of an able worker. Moreover, Schumacher argues that the scale of technology ought not to exceed our knowledge of its effects and that both technology and the methods of production ought to be designed to stimulate human creativity. The modern paradigm of economics that emphasizes mass consumption should be replaced with what he calls "Buddhist economics" that give priority to human creativity, community, and the production of necessary goods.

Although Schumacher does not deal directly with the role of government, it is clear nevertheless that Buddhist economics would entail an increase in the number of decisions made at the community and household level; the creation of local markets; a sharp reduction of large economic concentration; and less need for government supervision. To the extent that economic and political structures are linked, this course also implies a substantial devolution of political power to the local level.

The authors of *Blueprint for Survival* propose the decentralization of urban concentrations and the creation of a society made up of decentralized, self-sufficient communities in which people work near their homes, have the responsibility of governing themselves, of running their schools, hospitals, and welfare services, in fact of constituting real communities.[38] To promote the conditions of "full public participation in decision-making," the authors recommended the redesign of society to favor smaller communities. A similar emphasis is found in David Morris and Karl Hess's *Neighborhood Power*, which calls for "a return to a human scale of organization, a return of power to the people . . . and a return to a sense of community."[39] They argue that small-scale technology is capable of supporting a viable productive base at the neighborhood level. There is also a burgeoning knowledge of the technical components of rural self-sufficiency pioneered by the Rodales in Emmaus, Pennsylvania, the New Alchemists in Massachusetts, and a rapidly growing number of others.

A third divergence between the centralizers and decentralizers concerns the different assessments of the ability of the individuals to participate effectively in public affairs. Implicit in the views of Heilbroner and other centralizers is a model of self-centered, "rational" man, who is unwilling to act in the larger community interest and unable to decipher the complexities of ecological problems. Those favoring decentralization argue on the contrary that centralization is itself a cause of ecological disruption and that a return to a smaller-scale, decentralized social order where participation is encouraged is essential to any permanent solution. Under these conditions, they assume that men will act in the community interest. The fact that they do not in present circumstances, accordingly, says more about the effects of hierarchically organized society based on specialized expertise than about the potential for citizen participation.

Despite the popular response to the writings of Schumacher, decentralization does not as yet constitute a clear policy option for the United States or for industrialized countries. Proponents of small-is-beautiful are often vulnerable to criticisms of utopian thought generally.[40] It is an inescapable fact that we live in a highly interdependent, urbanized, mass society presided over by centralized institutions that are unlikely to disappear anytime soon. Nor is it immediately evident what ought to be decentralized and why. Clearly, some functions and services are appropriately handled at the societal or the international level. How these might be distinguished from those that might be descaled is not as apparent as some enthusiasts have suggested. Neither is it clear what relationship might exist between centralized and decentralized institutions. Schumacher confines his argument to the need for descaling both the tools and the size of productive units to "human scale." Whether this can be carried out within large structures such as corporations is not clear. Goldsmith and others propose the general decentralization of population but offer no clear idea of the role and functions of any centralized government. Small scale, alone, is not necessarily a source of stability or human fulfillment.

Moreover, decentralization, whether applied to population, the economy, technology, or political power, ironically, will depend upon the assistance and active involvement of government. Although grass-roots efforts are important, they are unlikely to generate societal-wide changes without deliberate assistance from the federal government in the form of changes in the tax laws, rebates, direct grants, research and development on alternative technologies, and extension services to aid their diffusion. Given the scale of effort required and the constraints that may be imposed by growing resource and energy shortages, only government has the necessary leverage to reverse the drift toward centralization. To do so, however, would require the creation of long-range plans for decentralization and the adoption of "nonincremental" strategies (for example, the NASA program) requiring large start-up funding, substantial ongoing budgets, and a sustainable political consensus.[41]

Another problem that has received less attention concerns the difficulty of designing and implementing institutions for a decentralized social order. The transfer of many functions to the state and local level will require active citizen participation, the success of which will depend upon whether citizens will in fact participate in such circumstances and upon the creation of suitable channels to do so. In addition, the quality of participation will hinge upon a stable consensus on decision-making procedures and upon the creation of means to integrate citizens and experts in the policy-making process.

Toward a Resilient Society

We seem to be caught in a dilemma. Drift or deliberate change toward further centralization of government and society as advocated by Heilbroner and Ophuls creates vulnerability to large-scale breakdown and may unwittingly exacerbate environmental stresses. Decentralization, if feasible, would reduce some environmental problems, but it might also lead to parochial society or, even worse, unmanageable chaos. Whereas proponents of both alternatives tend to offer either-or choices, it would appear to be preferable to selectively decentralize society in ways that balance the requirements of system coordination with the advantages of a more flexible social order.

But decentralization of what? By what criteria do we decide to encourage decentralization or centralization? The movement toward greater centralization of services, industry, population, agriculture, and technology evident throughout the twentieth century has commonly been justified on grounds of economic or technical efficiency. These criteria, however, seldom reflect the true costs of change due to hidden subsidies, tax provisions, and the failure to include both social and environmental "externalities." The growth of central government in the same period was propelled in large part by the need to control what Andrew Scott described in the previous chapter as "inadvertent consequences" arising from an increasing number of complex interactions. Centralization in both society and government owes more to happenstance and the accumulated effects of small decisions than to any conscious design.

One criterion for decentralization would be to compare the effects of alternative policies on social resilience, which we might define as the capacity of the society to withstand the collapse of any one of its subsystems. We might accordingly give greater priority to the preservation of diversity, redundancy, and self-sufficiency, which may not be narrowly "efficient" but which might nonetheless promote resilience. A second and related criterion is to compare the net energy efficiencies of alternative policies. H. T. Odum has argued that energy is the common denominator of all systems and that we can use it as a more accurate measure of costs than that provided by conventional economics.[42] Accordingly, we can compare the "net energy" efficiencies of alternative policies, including social costs and also the energy value of nature's services that would be displaced. Whether energy can be used as a more general accounting unit remains to be seen, but in an age of energy scarcity it makes obvious good sense to compare policies against the yardstick of energy efficiency. We might also assume that high energy efficiency would tend to imply lower environmental impacts.

To turn to the practical implications, one possibility for decentralization is the option of utilizing small and intermediate technologies to create what Amory Lovins has described as a "soft energy path." Lovins and others have marshaled an imposing body of evidence to demonstrate both the feasibility and the desirability of soft alternatives to a "hard," centralized, high-technology, capital-intensive approach to energy production.[43] The soft path implies a gradual, planned transition to small-scale technologies that rely on renewable or income energy sources of sun and wind; the matching of energy sources with the appropriate quantity and quality of end-use needs; and the decentralization of energy production. Much of the technology necessary for the soft path already exists and needs only engineering and design work to make it suitable for widespread adoption.

A soft path promotes resilience in a variety of ways. First, the risks of large-scale accidents such as those incurred by nuclear power are eliminated. Second, large-scale ecological disruptions from mining and drilling and pollution from the combustion of fossil fuels are sharply reduced. Third, the soft path is invulnerable to centralized failures or to sabotage. Fourth, the soft path does not require the irreversible commitment of capital for research and development, for deployment of costly generating stations, and for fuel-recycling facilities. Fifth, the soft path, in relying on the energies of the public, and decentralized application, creates one of the prerequisites for social resilience and for a renaissance of local autonomy. Much of the burden of designing and implementing soft energy systems could be placed on state and local governments and individual citizens. In short, a decentralized energy system requires no "Faustian bargains," vast centralization, expanded police powers, or irrevocable commitments.

The agricultural sector offers a second possibility for decentralization. U.S. agricultural production is increasingly dominated by large, energy-intensive agribusinesses. But high agricultural centralization is accomplished at a substantial price. According to Carol and John Steinhart, it takes nearly ten calories of energy input to produce one calorie of food value.[44] Agriculture requires large energy subsidies in the form of operating costs, chemical fertilizers, pesticides, transportation, food processing, and distribution. Large-scale agriculture imposes other costs. Runoff from animal feedlots and fields is a major source of nonpoint water pollution. Moreover, the lack of care implicit in an industrial approach to the land has led to soil erosion rates estimated nationally to be between 9 and 12 tons an acre per year.[45] By comparison, topsoil is formed under ideal conditions at 1.5 tons an acre/year. The social costs of agribusiness are no less devastating. Self-congratulation about the fifty-six persons one farmer feeds conceals one of the largest forced migrations in modern history. Dislodged from the land by market factors, high taxes, and rising costs, rural populations migrate to the cities where they impose other inefficiencies in the form of higher costs for urban services, roads, schools, hospitals, police, housing, and welfare. The belief that this exodus to the city represents a victory for efficiency is one of the sadder delusions of our time.

The irony is that small family farms are often not only more productive per acre but more energy efficient as well. One recent study found that Amish farms using a fraction of the energy of typical U.S. farms nevertheless produce about 4 percent more per hectare.[46] The Center for the Study of the Biology of Natural Systems at Washington University compared "organic" farms with other farms using chemical fertilizers and pesticides and found that organic farms were as productive per acre but used only one-third as much energy.[47] A return to smaller farms, however, would require changes in tax laws, the encouragement of alternative marketing systems suited for the smaller producer, the development of smaller farm equipment, and changes in the dominant "paradigm" of agriculture.

Third, the revitalization of rural life suggests the possibility of decentralizing population. To some extent, this is already occurring. Since 1970, nonurban areas have been growing at a faster rate (3.1 percent) than urban areas (2.2 percent). These trends, however, have not been planned or encouraged by the federal government. James Sundquist's study of population distribution in Europe showed that since 1945 European governments, to encourage greater population distribution, have utilized a variety of techniques, including aid to investors, tax concessions, cash grants, disincentives to growth, decentralization of government agencies, dispersal of universities, and comprehensive regional planning.[48] In contrast, population patterns in the United States, according to Sundquist, largely reflect economic decisions made by large corporations. European experience, however, suggests the possibility of using government powers to encourage trends toward a more decentralized population and greater regional self-sufficiency.

A fourth possibility for decentralization lies in the broad area of public policy making. Increasing centralization of government has led to a shrinkage of meaningful citizen participation. Some have argued that the public would not participate and even should not participate in complex policy issues. As to whether the public should participate, my own preferences are more Jeffersonian for reasons that lie partly in the events of the recent past, including the Vietnam War, Watergate, and the FBI/CIA abuses of power. Evidence from a variety of sources suggests that people *do* participate, given meaningful opportunities, and that participation in one area of life encourages involvement in other areas.[49] The design of participatory institutions has been addressed in recent work by Donald Schon and John Friedman, who have proposed alternative ways to create "learning" of "transactive" societies in which the public is much more extensively involved in the design and implementation of policy.[50] Their work also stresses the need to minimize hierarchy and centralization, involving what Schon describes as a "shift away from center-periphery to network modes of growth and diffusion."[51] A similar approach is evident in the work of the psychologist Carl Rogers, who has proposed what he calls a person-centered approach to participation, in which roles are less structured and hierarchy minimized or abolished altogether.[52]

It is interesting to note that technology, which has been a prime cause of centralization throughout much of the century, now offers a number of opportunities to reverse the trend, allowing for greater public involvement. Computers, fiber optics, and two-way video networks might be combined to facilitate the novel possibility of a mass, geographically dispersed, participatory system. Space, time, information costs, and a large population have in the past constrained direct participation, but information processing and communications technologies have rendered these less important, so that the fundamental limits to public participation are now those of choice, social inertia, institutional inflexibility, and lack of imagination. Whether desirable or not, we can now realistically speak of the possibility of decentralization and participation within a common framework of macrocontrol.

For at least two reasons, decentralization in each of the four areas noted above would require the redistribution of income. First, should economic growth slow or stop altogether it is highly unlikely that the poor would quietly resign themselves to perpetual poverty. The prospect of growth has always been used by the rich to avoid facing issues of equity on the premise that everyone in the growth state was becoming better off. But in conditions of ecological scarcity, inequity could strain social order to the breaking point. Lee Rainwater similarly states that "societies with much more equality than our own are the only kinds of societies that are likely to be able to live with slow growth without a totalitarian government."[53] Accordingly, he recommends an equity ratio of not more than four to one. A second reason for equity is alluded to by Michael Best and William Connolly, who suggest that solutions to ecological problems will require closing off the private escape routes of the rich so that all share in collective achievements and collective failures.[54] The equalization of life's chances accordingly would create common incentives to find collective solutions.

Finally, it is necessary to mention briefly the effects that selective decentralization might have on government. It certainly does not imply the demise of central government. On the contrary, it suggests the expansion of government powers for planning and social guidance, as well as greatly enhanced powers in new areas, including the control of science and technology. It further implies that government would engage much more intensively in issues of macro-societal design in order to avoid the proliferation of environmental and other problems. Selective decentralization does imply, however, the use of government power to encourage the devolution of capability in the specific areas noted above through the use of existing policy incentives and sanctions. In these areas the role of government must shift from monopolizing power and initiative to facilitating regional and sectoral resilience. Problems that are unsolvable from the centralized perspective may frequently be disaggregated and solved at a lower level. There is often an implicit assumption that big problems require big solutions, but it is at least as plausible to argue that big problems may on occasion yield more readily to a series of smaller solutions. There is, moreover, evidence from diverse sources, including behavior during the recent energy shortfall, and from studies of the management of common pool resources that local management is often more effective than centralized control.[55] Nor is it always necessary to create vast bureaucracies such as the new Department of Energy to promote ecological goals. The use of such techniques as depletion quotas, severance taxes, effluent taxes, and public trusts, which diffuse the burden of administration and allow for wider participation, are realistic and perhaps better means to achieve environmental reforms.[56]

As noted at the outset, the assumption by many that massive ecological problems can be solved only by the creation of equally gargantuan authoritarian institutions is symptomatic of a general distrust of broad participation as well as an unjustifiably optimistic assessment of authoritarian government.

Following a half-century or more of steady growth in the size and complexity of social institutions, including government, it is time to question the appropriate scale of things. In a relatively brief period of time, this view has won a number of converts, including Daniel Bell who has recently argued that "the problem of decentralization becomes ever more urgent. The multiplication of political decisions and their centralization at the national level only highlight more nakedly the inadequacies of the administrative structures of the society. . . . We have little sense of what is the appropriate size and scope of what unit of government to handle what level of problem."[57] Seen in this light, the ecological crisis is as much a challenge to our social and political creativity as anything else. There are two tragedies to be avoided: the very real possibility that we will wantonly destroy our life support system, and the almost equally grim prospect that we will jettison the open society and much of our Western heritage in the name of survival. But neither of these outcomes is necessary.

Ecology and the Time Dimension in Human Relationships

Marvin S. Soroos

Introduction

For centuries there has been a prevailing assumption in the advanced industrial societies of the West that human progress was inevitable and that each generation could be counted on to leave an enriched legacy for those that will follow.[1] In the past fifty years, this faith in human progress has been reinforced by remarkable technological advances in communication and transportation, a greatly increased availability of consumer goods, and advances in medicine that have allowed for better health care and extended life spans, to mention a few of the factors that have been regarded as enhancements to the general quality of life. What serious setbacks have taken place during the twentieth century—two world wars and the great economic depression of the 1930s—have been viewed as temporary perturbations in the human condition from which even more advanced societies have arisen within little more than a decade.

In recent years ecologists have come to the ominous realization that the industrial approach to improving living standards is seriously undermining the environmental systems that are so critical to a quality form of human existence. Reserves of certain nonrenewable resources are being depleted within a matter of a few generations. Renewable resources, such as forests, fertile agricultural land, and fisheries, are being irreversibly damaged or destroyed through excessive or improper use. Pollutants in water systems and the atmosphere have been building to levels that pose health hazards and could even significantly alter the earth's climate. The detonation of thermonuclear weapons or major failings of atomic power plants could render large areas of the planet uninhabitable within a matter of hours. No longer can it be assumed that future generations will be better off than their ancestors. On the contrary, it appears that the contemporary generation occupies a pivotal role in human history. Decisions made in the not too distant future may sharply reduce the life opportunities of many future generations or, alternatively, lay the groundwork for an enriched quality of human life for our descendants.

As long as the welfare of future generations is not being compromised by the practices of earlier generations, it is appropriate for us to be concerned almost exclusively with the immediate problems that affect the lives of those of us living now. It follows that inquiry into social matters would focus upon conflicts that arise between us and our contemporaries, in particular competing interests that are currently being acted upon. This intragenerational perspective had been the predominant orientation of past social inquiry.

Alternatively, when there is a realistic possibility that future generations will be adversely affected by the practices of their ancestors, it is important to acknowledge a realm of social relationships that transcends time, to realize that concepts such as conflict, peace, violence, and cooperation can be applied to social relationships between members of two or more generations. The purpose of this essay is to explore the implications of this expanded conception of social interrelationships in the context of the planetary ecological problems that have been discussed in this volume.

Time and Social Relationships

At the most basic level, a social relationship exists whenever one human being has an impact on another. The parties to the social relationship may, of course, be collectivities—families, organizations, corporations, nation-states, alliances, and the like. A variety of types of social relationships can be identified on the basis of two conceptions of time. First, on the basis of chronological time, a distinction can be drawn between latitudinal and longitudinal relationships. Second, time defined in terms of generations distinguishes intragenerational from intergenerational relationships.

The elements of a *latitudinal* social relationship are present at approximately the same chronological time—during a specified day, month, year, or perhaps even decade. This implies that the interests of the two parties are operative during the same period of time and, moreover, that what impact the actions of one party has on others will be experienced within the same time frame. In contrast, the components of a *longitudinal* relationship do not occur simultaneously. The related interests of different groups may be operative at widely different times, and considerable time may elapse before the actions of one party impact on the other one. To avoid confusion, it should be emphasized that an extended series of latitudinal interactions, as in the continuing series of confrontations between Israel and the Arab states, does not constitute a longitudinal relationship.

An *intra*generational social relationship takes place when the interests or actions of contemporaries are salient to one another. In *inter*generational relationships, the social links are between members of different generations, as between parents and children or between grandparents and grandchildren. Because the actions of one generation can have consequences long after its death, it is very possible for two generations to have a social relationship even if their life spans do not overlap.

The distinctions that have been drawn on the basis of chronological and generational time allow us to identify four types of social relationships as portrayed in table 1.

No significant time gaps are present in type I relationships, examples of which are most day-to-day business transactions or armies engaged in combat. In type II relationships, only the chronological time dimension is extended. An example is the conflict between the immediate economic interests of a lumber company and the future long-term recreational interests of environmental groups. In type III relationships, only the generational dimension is drawn out. The proportion of national annual income in any given year that is allocated to social security benefits for the retired generation illustrates this third type of social relationship.

Table 1.

Generational Time	Chronological Time	
	Latitudinal	Longitudinal
Intragenerational	I	II
Intergenerational	III	IV

Both time dimensions are extended in type IV relationships. Relationships between people whose life spans do not overlap fall within this category because by definition they will be both inter-generational and longitudinal. Practices that bring about irreversible environmental damage, such as the depletion of a nonrenewable resource or the extinction of species of wildlife, eventually take on the attributes of this fourth type of relationship.

Most social inquiry, with the exception of studies of family life, has focused upon the first of the four types of social relationships, in which time is a relatively unimportant factor. In the remainder of this paper, let us examine the other three realms of social interaction, especially the intergenerational varieties, which take on added importance in view of the ecological predicament that man faces. The next sections explore the nature of conflict, cooperation, violence, and peace in the relationships that transcend chronological and generational time.

Time in Conflict and Cooperation

In the context of this essay, let us simply assume that conflict is present whenever two parties have interests that are mutually incompatible. In other words, the full realization of one party's interests precludes fulfillment of those of a second party.[2] If the parties to the conflict are of different generations, the conflict is intragenerational in nature. Likewise, a conflict is longitudinal to the extent that there is a gap between the times the competing interests emerge.

Time can affect awareness of interest incompatibility. If there is a considerable gap between the chronological times at which com- peting interests are operative, intervening events can be expected to obscure the relationship that exists between the two parties. Thus, earlier generations acting on their immediate interests are unlikely to be sensitive to their impact on the well-being of later generations at some distant point in the future. Moreover, when succeeding generations are in a position to act on their interests, there may be little evidence of how their opportunities have been compromised by their ancestors.

Time can also affect the resources that parties can bring to bear on behalf of their interests in a conflict situation. The relative capabilities of the parties have been referred to as the degree of symmetry in the conflict relationship. In symmetrical conflict situations, the parties are relatively balanced in their capacity to push for their interests. In asymmetric conflicts one of the parties is in a distinctly advantageous position.[3]

Conflicts characterized by an extended time dimension will have a greater tendency to be asymmetric. Resources are more readily marshaled in pursuit of short-term interests that can be readily identified than in support of some tentatively defined concern in an uncertain future. Moreover, the generation that is currently in its most active and productive age ranges has far more capacity for advancing its interests than do those that are not yet participants in political arenas. This type of imbalance is particularly problematic for those generations as yet unborn and therefore precluded from articulating and working for their own welfare at the time their life opportunities are adversely affected by the action of preceding generations.

Let us now explore the potential for cooperation in social relationships that transcend time. Cooperation takes place when two parties assist each other in fulfilling their objectives. In cooperative interchanges, the providing of assistance usually requires sacrifices in the expectation that they will be more than offset by benefits resulting from the reciprocating sacrifices of the other party.

Cooperation that is both intergenerational and longitudinal (type IV) is fundamental to family relationships in most cultures. Parents provide for the young until they reach maturity and become self-reliant. When the parents need assistance in old age, the younger generation then provides for its parents. This willingness within the family to make sacrifices for young and old is fostered by bonds of affection and a sense of duty. Outside of family bonds, legal contracts may be drawn up to insure that those making the sacrifices will be reciprocated at an appropriate time in the future.

When there is no overlap in the life spans of generations, mutual assistance becomes impossible. Later generations can offer nothing in return for the sacrifices of their deceased predecessors, except perhaps to honor them in history texts. Thus, the fate of future generations depends upon the willingness of their ancestors to make sacrifices that will not be reciprocated. How likely are these unreciprocated sacrifices? Will the earlier generations, as Kenneth Boulding suggests, ask the question, "What has posterity done for me?"[4]

Time in Violence and Peace

Violence is present when the death or injury of one person can be attributed to specific actions of another, as in the case of an aggressive personal attack, act of war, torture, terror, or imprisonment. These direct forms of violence are usually attempts to resolve an interest incompatibility that is well known to the affected parties. As suggested above, longitudinal conflicts of interest tend to be obscured by intervening events and are therefore less likely to be perceived and to provoke violent actions.

Direct forms of violence are an impossibility between two generations whose life spans do not overlap. Even if life spans do overlap, direct intergenerational violence, except in the instance of isolated family quarrels, is unlikely in view of strong loyalties and affections and of other more important lines of conflict that cut across generations. Thus, while it is not unusual for fathers and sons to fight in the same army, it is inconceivable that they would fight against one another as members of armed groups identified with competing generations.

Shall we conclude that violence is a moot issue in an analysis of intergenerational relationships? If the term is limited to the direct, physical types of attack that have just been described, the answer would be affirmative in most contexts. A quite different conclusion may be reached, however, if the meaning of the concept is extended to include what Johan Galtung has referred to as "structural violence."[5] This concept was coined to refer to those situations in which human suffering and a failure of people to achieve their full potential are attributable not to a personal act of an individual but to the complex pattern of interactions of a social system. In this way, the concept *violence* is extended to neglect, slavery, repression, discrimination, exploitation, and other forms of social injustice. In his contribution to this volume, Ole Holsti applies the concept to Soviet agricultural policies that necessitate imports of food that could otherwise go to hungry people elsewhere.

Structural forms of violence can be present in any type of social relationship, including those that are intergenerational in nature. The routine functioning of political and economic systems may be geared to the short-range interests of contemporary, politically active groups, whereas the future interests of others are gradually, quietly, and unwittingly compromised, regardless of how just and vital they may be. A general "let them take care of themselves" attitude toward future generations—or to use the French phrase, "Après nous, le déluge"—is a form of structural violence parallel to neglecting or discriminating against contemporaries.

What does the preceding analysis imply for the meaning of peace? Peace has been defined in negative terms as the absence of physical and structural violence. In positive terms, it is defined as the presence of harmony, cooperation, or integration that contributes to human well-being. As with conflict, cooperation, and violence, the concept *peace* can be applied to intergenerational and longitudinal relationships. Thus, the meaning of peace is extended beyond the universal welfare of the members of one generation at one period in history to include the welfare of human beings regardless of generation. The time at which one's interests become operative or the generation in which one is born has no more validity as justification for discrimination or neglect than do other arbitrary ways of classifying human beings, such as by race, sex, religion, or nationality.

To illustrate the importance of an awareness of social relationships that cut across chronological and generational time, let us turn our attention, first, to several problems of global ecology and, second, to potential incompatibilities between long-range environmental priorities and more immediate aspirations for economic development.

Ecological Imperatives and the Interests of Future Generations

Warnings of rapidly worsening ecological problems suggest the emergence of some very fundamental lines of intergenerational and longitudinal conflict. Increasingly high levels of resource consumption and discharges of pollutants have been sustaining the comfortable, middle-class life styles of the contemporary residents of the industrial world. Large families contributing to a population explosion have likewise served certain short-term interests in less developed countries. A continuation of these rapid, exponential growth trends may lead to serious problems for future generations, potentially in the form of widespread starvation, resource shortages, high rates of inflation, industrial collapse, political instability, and warfare and other forms of physical violence. Although some of these conditions have been prevalent in the poorer regions, what is new is the increasing possibility that living standards in the developed world may decline sharply within the next century if not much sooner.

In referring to natural resources, it is customary to distinguish between renewable and nonrenewable types. The nonrenewable riches of the planet are a single-shot natural endowment that all generations must rely upon to satisfy their material needs. In recent decades, low prices for raw materials encouraged high, wasteful rates of consumption of many types of nonrenewable resources. As a result, a lion's share of the accessible reserves of a number of critical resources, most notably petroleum, is being consumed by only a handful of the thousands of human generations that have populated the planet. Future generations will have to make do with a badly depleted stock of less accessible resources.

It can be argued that longitudinal and intergenerational conflicts over renewable resources may not be as irreconcilable as would be inferred from the warnings of ecological "alarmists." A number of developments or practices could ameliorate the resource problems of future generations, such as the discovery of substantial additional reserves, mining and smelting of lower-grade ores, shifts to plentiful substitutes through the use of new technological processes, recycling previously used materials, changing tastes and life styles, and even space colonization, a possibility that is discussed in the chapter by Jack Salmon in this volume. Unfortunately, implementing some of these possibilities may require huge capital outlays and high levels of energy consumption, emit large quantities of harmful pollutants, require technologies that cannot be developed sufficiently soon, or necessitate social changes that are politically unfeasible. Moreover, these alternatives fail to circumvent the "entropy law" described by Nicholas Georgescu-Roegen: man's creation of usable low-entropy resources is achieved only by drawing heavily on finite reserves of other scarce forms of low-entropy resources, such as fossil fuels.[6]

Because renewable resources such as fertile land, fisheries, and forests are normally replenished in relatively short periods of time, we would not anticipate that intergenerational conflict over their use would be as sharp. If care is taken in harvesting these resources, their consumption by one generation should not jeopardize their availability to future generations. Problems arise for future generations when steps are not taken to preserve them, because of either ignorance, neglect, mismanagement, or economic considerations. In regard to the latter factor, Garrett Hardin has illustrated how investing immediate profits from clear-cutting forests may have a greater financial payoff in the long run than sustained yield harvesting, even if the forest is not replanted and is of no further economic value.[7]

There are numerous examples of the destruction of renewable resources to the disadvantage of future generations. Improper agricultural practices can render once fertile land useless for agricultural purposes. Vast areas farmed by the ancients in Mesopotamia and India have in effect become barren deserts.[8] Deforestation of large areas in the interests of current consumption has contributed to erosion and flooding and to the extinction of many species of plants and wildlife as well as significantly reduced the forest reserves available for harvest in the future.[9] Intensive harvesting of a number of species of fish and whales has left the remaining stock below levels necessary for successful regeneration. It is particularly noteworthy that worldwide harvests of fish began falling in 1970 following twenty years of unprecedented growth in catches, despite greater investments in fishing technology and vessels.

Pollution poses similar patterns of longitudinal and intergenerational conflicts of interest. Some pollutants build up very gradually, without undesirable effects being detected for years. Only when accumulations of these substances reach a threshold do serious, harmful consequences become apparent. A case in point is DDT, which over time, through a process of biological magnification, is becoming concentrated at dangerous levels in the tissues of higher-order organisms, including human beings. Another example is the eutrofication of many fresh-water lakes and rivers in Europe and North America, attributable in part to chemical fertilizers, livestock manure, human sewage, and industrial wastes.

Prudence and a sense of responsibility to future generations would seem to dictate caution until possible harmful effects of pollutants have been thoroughly studied. In many cases, however, the future costs are discounted in favor of the immediate economic efficiencies of discharging the pollutants. Some forms of environmental pollution may be irreversible; in the case of others, restoration of the damaged ecosystem may be possible, but at a great expense that must be borne fully by future generations.

Mention should also be made of the increasing worldwide commitment to the nuclear generation of power. Future generations are being left with the permanent, unsolicited task of safeguarding nuclear dumps that will be highly radioactive for thousands of years. Likewise, the dangerous and very costly task of decommissioning spent nuclear power plants is being deferred to future generations. In effect, future generations are being permanently enslaved to the debris from the nuclear power industry of their ancestors without having shared in the electricity that was produced.

Population Policies in Intergenerational Perspective

Along with high-technology industrialization, rapid rates of population growth have been among the root causes of the ecological predicament we now face. The ethical questions pertaining to population and intergenerational conflict are perhaps more perplexing than is the case with the resource and pollution problems that were just discussed.

With regard to population size, the principal interests of the potential members of future generations would appear to be twofold: (a) to be born and (b) to live in a world in which opportunities for fulfillment are not severely limited by overpopulation. When human beings are considered individually, these two interests are not incompatible. A dilemma arises, however, when the human population is analyzed as a collective. If birth rates continue at high levels, it is inevitable that a large proportion, if not all, of the earth's inhabitants will experience a very marginal standard of living characterized by acute scarcities of food and natural resources. Alternatively, reducing birth rates to allow for a more attractive material standard of existence for the smaller number fortunate enough to be born denies an opportunity for human life and fulfillment for "potential" people.

The currently fertile generation has the responsibility for determining which of these two directions will be taken, either of which could be interpreted as a form of intergenerational violence. The position of the Catholic Church would suggest that denying the opportunity for life is the more serious form of intergenerational transgression. In contrast, Nobel laureate George Wald has called for a "better world for fewer children."[10] The latter position is also supported by Garrett Hardin, who asks whether "it is not desirable that at least some of the grandchildren of people now living should have a decent place in which to live?"[11]

Brief mention should be made of several other potential lines of intragenerational conflict in the realm of population policy. The contemporary generation may desire many children for reasons of personal enjoyment and emotional fulfillment, security in old age, social approval, or religious conviction. Moreover, short-run political considerations may dictate deferring indefinitely the social resistance that would inevitably develop along intragenerational lines if strong measures necessary to limit population growth are implemented. In contrast, those born into the future generation would benefit from a commitment by earlier generations to limit birth rates to the degree necessary to avert future overpopulation.

The question of death rates raises another potential type of intergenerational conflict, in this instance of a latitudinal nature. The possibility of extending the human life span indefinitely by medical technologies, such as by transplanted or artificial organs or by drugs that reduce the rate of aging, would appear to be a very attractive possibility to many currently living. A consequence of a substantial increase in life span for many would be an even more rapidly growing population that would become very top-heavy in the less productive older age groupings. Such an eventuality would place heavy burdens of support on younger generations in addition to cutting into their share of resource consumption. The interest of future generations would be better served if preceding generations live only a natural life span, averaging about seventy to seventy-five years.

What intergenerational conflict is present between the interests of the current generation in having many children and the future generation's interest in a limited number of contemporaries is asymmetric to the extreme. Those who are born will have little or no voice in how many others will share in the resource-limited planet with them.

Immediate Problems versus Future Priorities

Concern has been expressed that awareness of the problems of future generations will draw attention away from the immediate, day-to-day struggle for survival of the poorer half of the world's population. For those whose survival prospects are in the present marginal, what motivation can there be to make sacrifices for the future? It may be argued that concern for the future is a luxury that can be enjoyed only by those who are secure in the present.

The question of whether priority should be given to present or to future problems comes to a head when we consider the economic aspirations of the less developed countries (LDCs) of what are known as the Third and Fourth Worlds. As suggested by David Orr (chapter 4 of this volume), the dwindling reserves of nonrenewable natural resources and the limited capacity of the ecosystem to absorb pollutants will probably not allow these countries to follow the path to industrialization that was forged by the Western developed countries (DCs) over the past century. Nor can the bulk of the people in the LDCs expect to enjoy the material standard of living now being enjoyed in the developed world.

Four groups could potentially share in the remaining finite reserves of natural resources of the planet: (*a*) the present generation in the DCs, (*b*) the present generation in the LDCs, (*c*) future generations in the DCs, and (*d*) future generations in the LDCs. A potential conflict relationship exists between any pair of these four groups. The present generation in the DCs occupies the pivotal position in that the other three groups are dependent on its resource policies.

There are four general policy options available to the dominant group in the DCs. First, it may choose to look after only its own interests and to leave others to fend for themselves, which appears to be the drift of the present policies. Second, it could make the sacrifices necessary to commence a frontal attack on the immediate problems of poverty and inequality in the LDCs, possibly along the lines of proposals for a "new international economic order." A third option would write off present and future generations in the poorest countries in the interests of conserving resources for future generations in the DCs. Among those advocating this position are William and Paul Paddock in their adaptation of "triage"[12] and Hardin in his advocacy of "lifeboat ethics," which was discussed in chapter 7 herein.[13] The moral dilemma posed by the second and third alternatives can possibly be avoided by a fourth course of action, the development of less resource-intensive technologies that can reduce levels of consumption in the industrial regions while allowing for an enhanced standard of living in the less developed regions and the conservation of resources for future generations in all regions. The proposals of E. F. Schumacher for "intermediate technologies" fit with the fourth option.[14]

The Challenge for Social Inquiry

The intergenerational perspective on social relationships raises a number of challenges for social inquiry. Let us consider several of the more important issues, then briefly explore some possible responses to them.

1. How prevalent and serious are intergenerational and longitudinal forms of conflict and violence? I have offered only a few illustrations of the applicability of these perspectives to ecologically related problems. In what other realms of human relationships are these forms of conflict and violence a matter for serious concern?

2. An answer to the first question assumes answers to the question of how intergenerational conflicts of interest and violence can be identified. This is an important but difficult task, given uncertainties about the future, such as technological innovations that, if they occur, may either reduce or increase the degree of conflict between the interests of present and future generations.

3. It is important to learn more about how current actions and policies affect the life opportunities of future generations. As time passes, the range of alternative strategies with a potential for coping with emerging problems tends to dwindle to the options that are the most costly and disruptive.

4. To what extent should earlier generations assume responsibility for the well-being of future generations? What rights do the members of future generations have to use natural resources for the realization of their potential as human beings? Given that many of our potential descendants have not as yet been born, can it be argued that "potential" people have interests that should be respected prior to their birth?

5. On the basis of what criteria can the interests of one generation be equitably compromised with the competing interests of future generations? What rights can the current generation justly claim in pursuit of its own imminent interests as opposed to responsibilities for serving those of future generations?

6. What procedures of conflict resolution can be employed to achieve equitable settlements of nonconcurrent and intergenerational types of conflict? This is a particularly challenging task, given the asymmetry in the support for the competing positions.

An in-depth analysis of answers to the questions just raised is beyond the scope of this paper. The following suggestions illustrate a few of the types of responses that could be considered in social research as well as in public and private circles beyond the academic community.

A general broadening of perspective is needed in which concern with the day-by-day turn of events is complemented by a consciousness of the changes taking place in a very dynamic and perhaps pivotal era. Attention must be given to the implications current policies may have for the well-being of succeeding generations and, most importantly, to the relationship the generations of the 1970s have to fellow human beings of the future. Toward this end it would be appropriate to call attention to the historically unique circumstances that will impact upon future generations, using the medium of an international conference along the lines of the recent United Nations–sponsored gathering on the condition and problems of women.

Forecasting probable future developments takes on added importance as a means for learning more about the potential lines of conflict of interest between present and future generations. Projections of trends in population, resource consumption and depletion, and pollution are particularly critical. Forecasts are also needed on the probability that a variety of technologies in fields such as energy will become operational within a given time frame. It is important to be conscious of the implications that technologies could have for the welfare of future generations in order to understand how they may alter lines of conflict between immediate and future interests.

A continuation of current trends and policies could have disastrous, irreversible consequences for future generations. The tendency for many governments to plan only two or four years in advance needs to be counteracted. General long-term goals for mankind must be discussed and competing values reconciled. Designs of alternative future worlds should be formulated, analyzed, and reviewed in many circles, including, whenever possible, those who would be affected. Finally, steps toward the realization of a more desirable future should be undertaken sufficiently early to increase the probability of successful implementation.

It is unlikely that future interests will be well served by a course of events that evolves from a relatively uncoordinated and unregulated interaction of the competing, partial designs of a multiplicity of groups. The planning and sacrifices for the sake of future generations of some groups in a highly interrelated world society may be negated by others that do not share such a sense of responsibility for future generations. This in essence is a variation on the "tragedy of the commons" type of problem.[15] Thus, the designing of alternative futures must assume a universal perspective, incorporating proposals for strong institutions that can coordinate efforts to further the interests of future generations.

In the case of intergenerational conflicts involving succeeding generations, the younger generation may have some opportunities to work for their interests. This possibility assumes greater conscious- ness among young people of the opportunities that remain open to their generation. The young should recognize the ways in which their interests may be in conflict with those of their parents' generation and how immediate decisions will affect them well into the future. To achieve these objectives, education programs for the young should place greater emphasis on preparing students to anticipate the unique problems, opportunities, and decisions they are likely to encounter during their lifetimes.[16] The interests of the young could also be better served if efforts are made to implement Margaret Mead's proposal for prefigurative patterns of learning in which the old learn from the young, complementing the predominant post- figurative directions of education in which the young are taught by the old.[17]

Within governments and legal systems, it is imperative that the principle be established and reinforced that the rights of future generations be protected if threatened by immediate actions. Insti- tutional mechanisms should be established that would insure more input from younger generations in goal setting and policy making in governments that are now almost exclusively directed by members of older generations. Special allowance must be made for the advocacy of the interests of as yet politically unaware generations. This could perhaps be accomplished by providing future generations with legal standing and appointing special legal representatives with responsi- bility for defending their legal rights, along the lines of what have become known as class action suits or the proposal that Christopher Stone has advanced for giving trees, rivers, and mountains legal standing.[18]

Conclusions

The intergenerational perspective places new responsibilities on humanistically oriented scholars. In recent decades, there has been a growing tendency for them to view their role in terms of developing knowledge that will further the cause of justice by contributing to the advancement of the "underdogs" of the global society, in particular those who are on the short end of national or world distributions of resource consumption in any given era.[19] An additional concern must be support for the interests of future generations who are underdogs in a different way. There is a major task ahead in calling attention to the nature of intergenerational conflicts of interest and to the ways in which current actions and policies have significant implications for the lives of those who will inhabit the planet in the future.

In taking an intergenerational perspective, there is danger that concern will be diverted from the compelling problems of poverty, misery, and death that a substantial proportion of the world's population already faces. Philosophies such as Hardin's lifeboat ethics would rationalize structural violence toward the underdogs of the current generation under the guise of responsibility to posterity. There are also dangers inherent in a preoccupation with a short-range, intragenerational view of social relationships. What may be ignored is a drift by mankind into an even more problematic future and a failure to recognize how some strategies devised to cope with problems in the immediate future tend to compound the difficulties that posterity will face. In such an event, whatever positive contributions result from our efforts will be short-lived and dysfunctional over the long run.

The challenge is to learn how present and future interests may be reconciled so that the current, pivotal generations can live in harmony with future generations. The preceding analysis emphasized intergenerational conflict and violence. Some of these lines of conflict are indeed very serious. In other instances, current generations may be misperceiving their real interests and needs. For example, adjustments in life styles and consumption habits for the sake of future generations, such as altering beef-oriented diets, may be more rewarding to present generations than had been anticipated. In many contexts, the interests of a series of generations may be found to be complementary, as in the avoidance of wars and the realization of arms control and reduction. Finally, there is an underlying intergenerational harmony of interest that is perhaps more fundamental than any others. Concern and compassion for future generations can offer present generations a greater sense of purpose and personal identity and fulfillment. This harmony of interest is expressed well by Boulding.

the welfare of the individual depends on the extent to which he can identify himself with others, and . . . the most satisfactory individual identity is that which identifies not only with a community in space but also with a community extending over time from the past into the future. If this kind of identity is recognized as desirable, then posterity has a voice, even if it does not have a vote.[20]

Notes
Bibliography
Contributors
Index

Notes

Foreword

1. Kurt Vonnegut, Jr., "Only Kidding, Folks?" *Nation*, 13 May 1978, p. 575.
2. See Amilcar Herrera et al., *Catastrophe or New Society? A Latin American World Model* (Ottawa: International Development Research Centre, 1976).
3. Fernando Henrique Cardoso, "Toward Another Development," in Marc Nerfin, ed., *Another Development* (Uppsala: Hammarskjöld Foundation, 1977), pp. 21–39; quotations from pp. 27, 23.
4. Quotations taken from "Optimism, Abundance, Universalism, and Immortality: The Philosophy of F. M. Esfandiary," an interview conducted by Mico Delianova, *Futurist* 12, 3 (June 1978): 185–89.
5. Pierre Teilhard de Chardin, *The Future of Man* (New York: Harper Colophon, 1969), p. 23.

Introduction

1. Eugene Odum, *Fundamentals of Ecology*, p. 3.
2. Herman Kahn, William Brown, and Leon Martel, *The Next 200 Years*, p. 1.
3. The subject of environmental issues at the international level has been explored by Harold and Margaret Sprout in *The Ecological Perspective on Human Affairs* and in *Toward a Politics of the Planet Earth*.
4. See, for example, Edward Hyams, *Soil and Civilization*; Vernon Gill Carter and Tom Dale, *Topsoil and Civilization*; and J. Donald Hughes, *Ecology in Ancient Civilizations*.

Chapter 1: Watch for the Foothills

1. Donella Meadows et al., *The Limits to Growth*.
2. For full details on World3, see Dennis L. Meadows, *The Dynamics of Growth in a Finite World*.

Chapter 2: Exploring Global Ecological Futures

1. Kenneth Boulding, "The Economics of the Coming Spaceship Earth," pp. 11–12.
2. Bertrand de Jouvenel, "Political Science and Prevision," p. 32.
3. Johan Galtung, "Peace Research," p. 62.
4. Barry Commoner, *The Closing Circle*, pp. 216–17.
5. Bertrand de Jouvenel, *The Art of Conjecture*, pp. 183–84.
6. Donnella Meadows et al., *The Limits to Growth*, p. 23; Mihajlo Mesarovic and Eduard Pestel, *Mankind at the Turning Point*, p. 17.
7. Herman Kahn, William Brown, and Leon Martel, *The Next 200 Years*, p. 7.
8. Wassily Leontief, *The Future of the World Economy*.
9. See Harold Guetzkow et al., *Simulation in International Relations*; Paul Smoker, "Social Research for Social Anticipation."

10. See Olaf Helmer, *Social Technology*.

11. See Roy C. Amara and Gerald Salancik, "Forecasting"; and Nazli Choucri, "Forecasting in International Relations."

12. Often cited is Abraham H. Maslow's value framework presented in *Toward a Psychology of Being*, p. 3. See also William Eckhardt, *Compassion*.

13. See Gerald Mische and Patricia Mische, *Toward a Human World Order*.

14. Editors of the *Humanist*, "The Humanist Manifesto II."

15. Lynn White, "The Historical Roots of Our Ecological Crisis."

16. Mankind 2000 and the Union of International Associations, *Yearbook of World Problems and Human Potential*.

17. For example, Grenville Clark and Lewis B. Sohn, *World Peace through World Law*; and David Mitrany, *A Working Peace System*.

18. Saul H. Mendlovitz, ed., *On the Creation of a Just World Order*.

19. Meadows, *Limits*, pp. 156–84.

20. See Herman Daly, ed., *Toward a Steady-State Economy*; Dennis C. Pirages, ed., *The Sustainable Society*; and Amory B. Lovins, *Soft Energy Paths*.

21. Richard A. Falk, *A Study of Future Worlds*, pp. 286–96.

22. Arthur I. Waskow, "Towards a Democratic Futurism," pp. 90–91.

23. Gerald Feinberg, *The Prometheus Project*.

Chapter 3: Population Dynamics and Future Prospects for Development

1. I would like to express my appreciation to my colleague R. Kenneth Godwin for his criticisms of an earlier draft of this essay.

2. Steven Polgar, "Population History and Population Policies from an Anthropological Perspective."

3. Joseph B. Birdsell, "Some Predictions Based on Equilibrium Systems among Recent Hunter-Gatherers," pp. 230–31.

4. Ansley J. Coale, "The History of the Human Population."

5. Donella H. Meadows et al., *The Limits to Growth*, pp. 25–28.

6. Richard E. Leakey, "New Fossil Evidence for the Evolution of Man."

7. W. F. Bodmer and L. L. Cavalli-Sforza, *Genetics, Evolution, and Man*, p. 539.

8. Marshall D. Sahlins, "Notes on the Original Affluent Society," p. 85.

9. Frederick L. Dunn, "Epidemiological Factors," p. 224.

10. Edward Deevey, Jr., "Pleistocene Family Planning," p. 248.

11. Birdsell, "Some Predictions," pp. 236–37, 239; Dunn, "Epidemiological Factors," pp. 222, 225.

12. James Woodburn, "Population Control Factors," p. 244; Richard B. Lee, "What Hunters Do for a Living," pp. 37–39; Dunn, "Epidemiological Factors," p. 223.

13. Dunn, "Epidemiological Factors," p. 223; Colin Turnbull, "Population Control Factors," p. 245.

14. Dunn, "Epidemiological Factors," pp. 222, 228.

15. Lee, "What Hunters Do," p. 33; Turnbull, "Population Control Factors," p. 245; Sherwood L. Washburn, "Population Control Factors," p. 245; Woodburn, "Population Control Factors," p. 244.

16. Lee, "What Hunters Do," pp. 37–38; James Woodburn, "An Introduction to Hadza Ecology," p. 54.

17. Lee, "What Hunters Do," p. 36.

18. Sahlins, "Notes," p. 86.

19. John C. Caldwell, "Toward a Restatement of Demographic Transition Theory"; Ansley J. Coale, "The Demographic Transition"; Michael S. Teitlebaum, "Relevance of Demographic Transition Theory for Developing Countries."

20. Paul Ehrlich, *The Population Bomb*.

21. James E. Kocher, *Rural Development, Income Distribution, and Fertility Decline*; William Rich, *Smaller Families through Social and Economic Progress*.

22. Joseph W. Eaton and Albert J. Mayer, *Man's Capacity to Reproduce*; John Andrew Hostetler, *Hutterite Society*.

23. Gunnar Myrdal, *The Challenge of World Poverty*.

24. Moye W. Freymann, "Foreword," in Richard L. Clinton, ed., *Population and Politics*.

25. Philip Slater, *The Pursuit of Loneliness*; Denis Goulet, *The Cruel Choice*.

26. Maurice F. Strong, "One Year after Stockholm"; Ignacy Sachs, "Ambiente y estilos de desarrollo"; Richard L. Clinton, "Hacia una teoría del ecodesarrollo"; Richard L. Clinton, "Ecodevelopment."

27. E. F. Schumacher, *Small Is Beautiful*.

28. Teitlebaum, "Demographic Transition Theory."

29. Pi-chao Chen, "China"; Loren Fessler, "China"; Leo A. Orleans, *Every Fifth Child*; H. Yuan Tien, *China's Population Struggle*; Geoffrey McNicoll, "Community-Level Population Policy."

30. Lauchlin Currie, *Accelerating Development*.

31. Wayne A. Cornelius, "Urbanization and Political Demand Making"; Lars Schoultz, "Urbanization and Political Change in Latin America."

32. Frederick C. Thayer, *An End to Hierarchy! An End to Competition!*

33. Amory B. Lovins, "Energy Strategy."

34. G. Tyler Miller, Jr., *Living in the Environment*.

35. Richard L. Clinton, "Politics and Survival."

Chapter 4: Modernization and the Ecological Perspective

1. Thomas S. Kuhn, *The Structure of Scientific Revolution*, p. 24.

2. Cyril Black, *The Dynamics of Modernization*, p. 7; S. N. Eisenstadt, *Tradition, Change, and Modernity*, p. 231; Kenneth Boulding, *The Meaning of the Twentieth Century*, pp. 27–53.

3. Talcott Parsons and Edward Shils, *Toward a General Theory of Action*, pp. 76–86.

4. Karl Deutsch, "Social Mobilization and Political Development."

5. Gabriel Almond and G. Bingham Powell, *Comparative Politics*, p. 94, n. 18.

6. Marion Levy, *Modernization and the Structure of Societies*, 1: 31.

7. Samuel P. Huntington, "Political Development and Political Decay."

8. Levy, *Modernization*, 1: 11–15.

9. Black, *Dynamics*, p. 7.

10. Herman Kahn, William Brown, and Leon Martel, *The Next 200 Years*, pp. 1–25.

11. Daniel Bell, *The Coming of Post-Industrial Society*, p. 263.

12. Nicholas Georgescu-Roegen, *The Entropy Law and the Economic Process*, pp. 276–314.

13. Donella H. Meadows et al., *The Limits to Growth*.

14. For examples, see H. S. D. Cole et al., *Models of Doom*; Mancur Olson and Hans H. Landsberg, eds., *The No-Growth Society*; Wilfred Beckerman, *In Defense of Economic Growth*.

15. Mihajlo Mesarovic and Eduard Pestel, *Mankind at the Turning Point*, pp. 143–57.

16. Jan Tinbergen, Antony J. Dolman, and Jan van Ettinger, eds., *Reshaping the International Order*, pp. 37–38; Wassily Leontief, *The Future of the World Economy*, pp. 1–11.

17. Barry Commoner, *The Closing Circle*, pp. 138–75.

18. Lewis Mumford, *The Myth of the Machine*; pp. 51–104; William Leiss, *The Domination of Nature*, pp. 45–72.

19. Mumford, *Myth*, p. 284.

20. Ibid., p. 328.

21. E. F. Schumacher, *Small Is Beautiful*; pp. 20, 30.

22. Theodore Roszak, *Where the Wasteland Ends*, p. xxi.

23. C. S. Lewis, *The Abolition of Man*, pp. 79–80.

24. Aldo Leopold, *A Sand County Almanac*, p. 251.

25. Harold Sprout and Margaret Sprout, *Multiple Vulnerabilities*, pp. 18–20.

26. Fred Hirsch, *The Social Limits to Growth*, p. 185.

27. Mumford, *Myth*, pp. 186, 283.

28. Edward Goldsmith, "Is Science a Religion?"

29. Jacques Ellul, *The Technological Society*, p. 143.

30. Theodore Roszak, "The Monster and the Titan," p. 28.

31. John Quarles, *Cleaning Up America*, p. xv.

32. Robert Heilbroner, "Second Thoughts on the Human Prospect," pp. 27–28.

33. Robert C. North and Nazli Choucri, *Nations in Conflict*.

34. Barbara Ward and René Dubos, *Only One Earth*, p. 214; also Harold Sprout and Margaret Sprout, *Toward a Politics of the Planet Earth*, p. 27.

35. Herman Daly, ed., *Toward a Steady-State Economy*, p. 14.

36. Willis Harmon, *An Incomplete Guide to the Future*, p. 119; also L. S. Stavrianos, *The Promise of the Coming Dark Age*, pp. 137–63.

37. Georgescu-Roegen, *The Entropy Law*, p. 281.

38. Sterling Brubaker, *To Live on Earth*, p. 201.

39. Christopher D. Stone, *Should Trees Have Standing?*

40. William R. Catton, "Human Ecology and Social Policy," pp. 15–23.

41. Murray Bookchin, *Our Synthetic Environment*, p. 238.

42. Edward Goldsmith et al., *Blueprint for Survival*, p. 52.

43. Lynton K. Caldwell, *Man and His Environment*, p. 15; Walter A. Rosenbaum, *The Politics of Environmental Concern*, pp. 17–24, 281–95.

44. William Ophuls, *Ecology and the Politics of Scarcity*, p. 163; Robert Heilbroner, *An Inquiry into the Human Prospect*, p. 90.

45. Mumford, *Myth*, p. 408.

46. Davis B. Bobrow, "The Politics of Coordinated Redistribution," p. 199.

47. Michael H. Best and William E. Connolly, "Market Images and Corporate Power," p. 59.

48. Alvin Weinberg, "Social Institutions and Nuclear Energy," pp. 33–34.

49. Sterling Brubaker, *In Command of Tomorrow*, p. 5.

Chapter 5: International Environmental Concern

1. Maurice F. Strong, "One Year after Stockholm."

2. United Nations, General Assembly, *Development and Environment*.

3. General Agreement on Tariffs and Trade, *Industrial Pollution Control and International Trade*, p. 16.

4. United Nations, Conference on Trade and Development, *Impact of Environmental Policies on Trade and Development*, p. 13.

5. On the subject of additionality and compensation, see Shadia Schneider-Sawris, *The Concept of Compensation in the Field of Trade and Development*; and Yvonne I. Nicholls, *Source Book*.

6. United Nations, Economic and Social Council, *Official Records* (1730th meeting), p. 46. On the operation of the bank in this area, see World Bank, *Environment and Development*.

7. UN Conference on Trade and Development, *Impact of Policies*, p. 17.

8. United Nations, Economic and Social Council, *Summary Records*.

9. United Nations, General Assembly, *Official Records* (1423d meeting), pp. 427–28.

10. Miguel A. Ozorio de Almeida, "The Confrontation between Problems of Development and Environment," p. 54.

11. United Nations Office at Geneva, 9th Geneva Graduate Study Programme, p. 9.

12. UN Conference on Trade and Development, *Impact of Policies*, p. 16.

13. Ibid., p. 19.

14. United Nations, General Assembly, *Report of the United Nations Conference on the Human Environment*, pp. 3–33.

15. United States, Information Service, Press Release, 16 June 1972.

16. United Nations, Conference on Trade and Development, *Implications for the Trade and Investment of Developing Countries of United States Environmental Controls*, p. 5; and Walter Ingo, *International Economics of Pollution*.

17. Richard Blackhurst, "International Trade and the Environment," pp. 91–111. See also Lester R. Brown, *In the Human Interest*, pp. 80–81.

18. United Nations, Conference on Trade and Development, *The Impact of Environmental Issues on Development and International Economic Relations*, pp. 15–16. On

the problems of the copper-smelting industry caused by pollution control costs, see United States, Department of Commerce, *The Effects of Pollution Abatement on International Trade—III*, pp. 1–6, 3-2, 3-3, B-48, and B-50. See also Robert Lindsey, "Hard Times in Copper Country."

19. "Japan's Economy in Transition," pp. 44–50. On the general problems of pollution in Japan, see Cynthia Enloe, *The Politics of Pollution in Comparative Perspective*, pp. 221–63, and Marshall I. Goldman, *Ecology and Economics*, pp. 167–71.

20. M. Y. Yoshino, "The Multinational Spread of Japanese Manufacturing Investments since World War II," pp. 357–81.

21. Clyde Farnsworth, "Multinational Corporations Turning Away from Third World Lands," pp. 27, 29.

22. United Nations, Conference on Trade and Development, *Social Evaluations and Pricing of Natural Resources*, pp. 2–3, 14. This paper is strongly critical of the free market mechanism because it "allows the bulk of natural resource production to be channelled for use in developed countries. There is therefore a need for global management of natural resources to ensure a more equitable distribution" (p. 7).

23. UN Conference on Trade and Development, *Impact of Issues*, p. 15.

24. United Nations, Industrial Development Organization, *Report of the Expert Group Meeting on the Study of Synthetic versus Natural Products*.

25. UN Conference on Trade and Development, *Impact of Issues*, p. 16.

26. This information is contained in a letter to the author from Dr. Lee. For a recent analysis of the practices of the World Bank and eight other international development agencies, see International Institute for Environment and Development, *Multilateral Aid and the Environment*.

27. See United States Agency for International Development. *Environmental Impact Statement on the AID Pest Management Program*, 2:304–307.

28. United States, Council on Environmental Quality, *The President's Environmental Program—1977*, pp. M11–12.

29. United Nations, Environmental Program, *Environment and Development*, pp. 5–8, 17, 19.

30. United Nations, Environmental Program, *Ecodevelopment*.

31. United Nations, Conference on Trade and Development, *Environmental Policies and Their Implications for Trade and Development*.

Chapter 6: A Look at America's Potential Roles in a Global Food Crisis

1. United States, Department of Agriculture, *The World Food Situation and Prospects to 1985*, p. 1.

2. Ibid., p. 3.

3. Ibid., p. 50.

4. Ibid., p. 50.

5. Ibid., p. 55.

6. Frances M. Lappé and Joseph Collins, *Food First*; Susan George, *How the Other Half Dies*.

7. Lappé and Collins, *Food First*, p. 265.

8. USDA, *The World Food Situation*, p. 12.

Chapter 7: Lifeboat Ethics versus One-Worldism in International Food and Resource Policy

1. See Kenneth Boulding, "The Economics of the Coming Spaceship Earth"; Lynton K. Caldwell, *In Defense of Earth*; Maurice F. Strong, "One Year after Stockholm"; Mihajlo Mesarovic and Eduard Pestel, *Mankind at the Turning Point*; Richard A. Falk, *A Study of Future Worlds*; and Ervin Laszlo et al, *Goals for Mankind*.

2. Garrett Hardin, "Living on a Lifeboat." See also Garrett Hardin, "Carrying Capacity as an Ethical Concept."

3. Garrett Hardin, "The Tragedy of the Commons." See also Garrett Hardin, *Exploring New Ethics for Survival*; and Garrett Hardin and John Baden, eds., *Managing the Commons*.

4. Hardin, "Lifeboat."

5. Ibid., p. 562.

6. See also James W. Howe and John W. Sewell, "Triage and Other Challenges to Helping the Poor Countries Develop"; George R. Lucas, *Triage in Medicine and Society*; and S. W. Hinds, "Relation of Medical Triage to World Famine."

7. Hardin, "Lifeboat," p. 564.

8. Hardin, *New Ethics*, p. 134.

9. Ruth L. Sivard, *World Military and Social Expenditures—1977*, p. 61.

10. Howe and Sewell, "Triage," p. 61.

11. Quoted in Philip Handler, "On the State of Man," p. 427.

12. Frances M. Lappé and Joseph Collins, *Food First*. See also Susan George, *How the Other Half Dies*.

13. Lappé and Collins, *Food First*, pp. 13–21.

14. George, *Other Half*, p. 14.

15. Lappé and Collins, *Food First*, pp. 156–68.

16. Ibid., pp. 15, 252–69.

17. Hardin, "Lifeboat," p. 563.

18. Ibid., p. 567.

19. Ibid., p. 564.

20. Lappé and Collins, *Food First*, p. 324.

21. Charles F. Gallagher, "Japan and the World Food Problem," p. 6.

22. George Borgstrom, *The Hungry Planet*, pp. 344–54.

23. Lester R. Brown, *In the Human Interest*, p. 33.

24. Nathan Keyfitz, "World Resources and the World Middle Class," p. 32; Donald R. Kelley, Kenneth R. Stunkel, and Richard R. Wescott, *The Economic Superpowers and the Environment*, p. 51.

25. Raymond F. Mikesell, *Nonfuel Minerals*, p. 91.

26. Bension Varnon and Kenji Takeuchi, "Developing Countries and Nonfuel Minerals," p. 508.

27. Mikesell, *Minerals*, p. 25.

28. Harold Sprout and Margaret Sprout, *Multiple Vulnerabilities*, p. 18.

29. J. Calvin Giddings, "World Population, Human Disaster, and Nuclear Holocaust"; D. V. Segre and J. H. Adler, "The Ecology of Terrorism," pp. 180–81.

30. See E. F. Schumacher, *Small Is Beautiful*.

31. Hardin, "Lifeboat," p. 561.

32. Caldwell, *Defense*, p. 48.

Chapter 8: Global Food Problems and Soviet Agriculture

1. There are, of course, other barriers as well—for example, the fear among producers that major reserves will be used to depress prices, the dramatic increase in the price of petroleum products that are essential in the production of fertilizers, and the fact that although the Soviet Union may be the worst offender it is not alone in pursuing counterproductive agricultural policies.

2. Large U.S. surpluses exist at the time of this writing (early 1978).

3. Herman Kahn, William Brown, and Leon Martel, *The Next 200 Years*; David Harmon, "An Optimistic View of Agriculture's Future."

4. Harry Walters, "Difficult Issues Underlying Food Problems," p. 524. See also the report of the Food and Agricultural Organization, released in January 1978, which concluded: "The world food situation remains fragile. There are no grounds for complacency."

5. Michael B. McElroy, Harvard University, quoted in Jerry E. Bishop, "Earth's Ozone Shield May Be Imperiled by More Fertilizer Use, Scientist Says."

6. A report prepared for the National Academy of Science, summarized in the *New York Times*, 6 February 1976, 1:1, 12:1.

7. Considerable uncertainty exists about what constitutes a nutritionally adequate diet for various populations under various environmental conditions. Thomas T.

Poleman, "World Food: A Perspective," p. 511. This is not to say, however, that there is no need for concern about global food production.

8. Erik P. Eckholm, *Losing Ground: Environmental Stress and World Food Prospects.*

9. Joseph M. Winski, "By 2000, Prevention of Starvation May be Chief Global Concern," p. 1.

10. *Statistical Abstract of the United States, 1974*, p. 616. The year 1973 included extraordinarily high American grain sales to the Soviet Union. But even if we apply a liberal discount to these figures, the degree of dependence on American agriculture is very high.

11. John Steinhart, food and energy analyst at the University of Wisconsin, points out that we now use 10 calories of fuel for every calorie of food produced. Quoted in Winski, "By 2000, Prevention of Starvation."

12. *New York Times*, 10 December 1975, 1:1. For this reason, 1913 is the year of the czarist era for which more complete data on Russian agricultural production are available, a fact reflected in the tables that appear in this paper.

13. "The Russian farmer probably suffers from the want of real up-to-date machinery more than from any other one cause." Howard P. Kennard, comp. and ed., *The Russian Yearbook* (1914), p. 163.

14. "It is reckoned that for food and fodder about 600,000 tons of phosphoric acid are taken every year from the soil, but that not more than 165,000 tons are returned to it. On a yearly average each acre of cultivated land in Russia gets in manure 1/6 lbs. of phosphoric acid. In Belgium the amount supplied is about 21 lbs. per acre." Ibid., p. 163.

15. Ibid., p. 167. Despite the backward state of its agriculture during the czarist era, Russia was a significant grain exporter. At that time the Ukraine was called the "granary of Europe."

16. Karl-Eugen Wadekin, "Soviet Agricultural Statistics," p. 279. For further discussions of Soviet farm statistics, see Eberhard Schinke, "Soviet Agricultural Statistics"; Philip M. Raup, "Some Consequences of Data Deficiencies in Soviet Agriculture"; and Roy D. Laird, "Prospects for Soviet Agriculture."

17. Laird, "Prospects for Soviet Agriculture," p. 38.

18. Drought conditions in the USSR no doubt accounted in part for the poor 1975 harvest, but it seems highly unlikely that most of the shortfall from production quotas can be attributed to weather. As early as 1971 an American analyst predicted that basic shortcomings in the Soviet system of agriculture would prevent quotas of the current five-year plan from being met (Laird, "Prospects for Soviet Agriculture"). Moreover, the problems of Soviet agriculture do not appear to be limited to an occasional drought year. Indeed, there is some evidence that much of the period since the Russian Revolution has coincided with the most favorable agricultural weather of the past 1,000 years (Environmental Fund, *The Other Side*, no. 8, March 1976).

19. *New York Times*, 10 Decmeber 1975, 20:4.

20. Keith Bush, "The U.S.S.R.'s Third Major Grain Purchase," p. 6.

21. Roy Laird, "Soviet Goals for 1965 and the Problems of Agriculture," p. 149.

22. Alex Nove, "Soviet Agriculture Marks Time," pp. 164–65; and Raup, "Some Consequences of Data Deficiencies," p. 265.

23. Nove, "Soviet Agriculture," p. 164.

24. Ibid., p. 165.

25. Alex Nove, "Will Russia Ever Feed Itself?" p. 48. There is also some evidence from less developed nations that seems relevant to the issue. One observer writes: "There is impressive evidence of strong latent potential in the private sector of the LDC's for mobilizing the resources and effort needed for agricultural progress when the private economic rewards for doing so are high. Under these circumstances, needed changes in the institutions required to mobilize the resources and direct the effort seem relatively easy to achieve. Institutional resistance is stronger in situations where there is not direct personal economic reward to change, as in the typical public institution" (Pierre R. Crosson, "Institutional Obstacles to Expansion of World Food Production," p. 523).

26. John Walsh, "U.S. Agribusiness and Agricultural Trends," p. 531.

27. In addition to previously cited works on Soviet agriculture, see: Michael E. Bradley and M. Gardner Clark, "Supervision and Efficiency in Socialized Agriculture"; Lazar Volin, "Agricultural Organization"; and Stephen Osofsky, "The Soviet Grain Problem in Perspective."

28. Laird, "Soviet Goals for 1965," p. 154. Even wage incentives may not work effectively in agriculture. For example, the tractor driver who is paid for the area he plows is unlikely to overlook the fact that it pays him to plow shallowly.

29. Pan A. Yotopoulos, in a paper prepared for the Carnegie-Rochester Conference on Public Policy, cited in Lindley H. Clark, Jr., "Future Food," *Wall Street Journal*, 11 November 1975.

30. One line of reasoning is that high world grain prices will actually benefit less developed countries because low prices reduce incentives for them to seek self-sufficiency in food. This argument overlooks the possibility that not all nations are capable of doing so, even given favorable climate. Whereas in the Soviet Union agricultural difficulties are largely the result of deliberate policy choices, there are areas of the world in which there is insufficient fertile land to sustain large and growing populations at even a rather minimal definition of a nutritionally adequate diet.

31. A study by Dr. Reid A. Bryson of the University of Wisconsin, summarized in the *New York Times*, 1 May 1976.

32. For example, at the Rome Food Conference of 1974, the United States came in for harsh criticism—not all of it unwarranted—whereas the USSR escaped almost entirely. One possible explanation is that external critics may perceive the United States as a potentially responsive target of criticism, whereas there is little evidence that Soviet policies are very sensitive to external criticism. Even American writers on global food problems have scarcely been overly harsh in their analyses of Soviet agriculture, which is often treated as a costly idiosyncrasy rather than as a potential source of international problems.

33. Nor should this paper be construed as an argument that American, Canadian, or Australian public policies toward agriculture are free from various irrational elements. Consider, for example, the use of tax funds by the American Department of Agriculture to support the price of tobacco at the same time that the Department of Health, Education, and Welfare is spending large sums on cancer research and the Federal Trade Commission seeks to require stronger warning on the dangers of smoking in cigarette advertising. But absurd as such policies may be, their consequences for coping with the world food problem are relatively limited, especially when compared to the difficulties created by the structural irrationalities in Soviet agriculture.

34. Gerald E. Connolly, Letter to the Editor, *New York Times*, 3 November 1975. Mr. Connolly is executive director of the American Freedom from Hunger Foundation.

35. Temporary embargoes put into effect by the Canadian and American governments in 1975, pending further information on the size of harvests, were greeted with less than unanimous enthusiasm by the farm community, and the "farmer strikers" of 1977–78 in the United States have made frequent unflattering comments about any government policies to regulate grain exports.

36. See, for example, President Ford's speech of 5 January 1976, in which he stated that grain sales and deliveries to the USSR would not be made contingent upon the end of Soviet military intervention in Angola. The Carter administration also appears committed to policies that maximize stable market conditions and export sales.

Chapter 9: Resource Politics

1. This paper is not concerned with temperate zone fibers and foodstuffs, or raw materials in which high-income countries are dominant from the standpoint of reserves, production, and exports. The relevant commodities are thus tropical zone foodstuffs, petroleum, and some minerals such as bauxite, tin, nickel, copper.

2. A supply curve is a curve relating the quantity of a commodity that will be supplied to the price. Generally, the curve is depicted as rising from left to right, indicating that producers will supply more at a higher price. A demand curve relates the quantity

demanded to price. Generally, the curve falls from left to right, indicating that consumers will purchase less at a higher price. Steep curves are "inelastic," and flat curves are "elastic." In a market where supply and demand curves are very inelastic near their intersection, a group of relatively small producers could exercise a great deal of leverage.

3. "Fair economic price" is defined as the absence of factor rents where price equals marginal cost or, more simply, as the price at which existing producers will continue to produce but no new producers will be attracted into the market.

4. All commodities face very elastic demand and/or supply curves in the long run. If the price were high enough, eventually substitutes would be developed or new sources brought into production.

5. In the long run, however, I would contend that the increased revenues gained by the producer association can be managed to improve employment levels and development.

6. See John Tilton, "The Choice of Trading Partners," pp. 419–74. Tilton demonstrates that international exchange depends to a great extent upon where transnational firms have affiliates.

7. United Nations, Office of Public Information, *Charter of Economic Rights and Duties of States*, p. 2.

Chapter 10: Oil Politics and the Rise of Codependence

1. In contemplating the sweep of this question, the following studies place the issue of the role of the Middle East and the larger world system into perspective: Richard N. Rosecrance, *Action and Reaction in World Politics*; Leonard Binder, "The Middle East as a Subordinate International System," pp. 408–29; Manfred Halpern, *The Politics of Social Change in the Middle East and North Africa*; Yahya Armajani, *The Middle East*; George Lenczowski, *The Middle East in World Affairs*; Malcom H. Kerr, "The Arabs and Israelis," pp. 3–31; William Zartman, "Negotiations," pp. 69–77.

2. Andre Gunder Frank, *Capitalism and Underdevelopment in Latin America*; Celso Furtado, "The Concept of External Dependence in the Study of Underdevelopment"; Fernando H. Cardoso, "Dependency and Development in Latin America"; Theodore H. Moran, *Multinational Corporations and the Politics of Dependence*.

3. For a sample of the literature on interdependence, see, for instance: Richard N. Cooper, *The Economics of Interdependence*; George Liska, *Nations in Alliance*; Nazli Choucri, *Global Energy Interdependence*; Douglas R. Bohi and Milton Russell, *U.S. Energy Policy*.

4. Whether all changes in the response of one actor to another stem from *transactions between* actors is sometimes debated. Where the actors involve both governments and corporations, the transactional motif seems, however, especially appropriate because commodity exchanges tend to give political relationships a raison d'être. Bruce Russett, "Transactions, Community, and International Political Integration"; C. F. Bergsten, Robert O. Keohane, and Joseph S. Nye, "International Economics and International Politics," pp. 3–36.

5. Cooper, *Economics*, uses *interdependence* to connote "loss of national autonomy." Our definition of interdependence goes one step further in claiming that a modicum of *cooperation* between actors is essential for a meaningful or effective concept of interdependence.

6. Among the sources to be consulted on this topic are: Mordechai Abir, *Oil, Power, and Politics*; Nasrollah S. Fatemi, *Oil Diplomacy*; Stephen H. Longrigg, *Oil in the Middle East*; J. E. Hartshorn, *Oil Companies and Governments*; David Hirst, *Oil and Public Opinion in the Middle East*; Charles Issawi and Mohammed Yeganeh, *The Economics of Middle Eastern Oil*; Kamal S. Sayegh, *Oil and Arab Regional Development*; Raymond Vernon, ed., *The Oil Crisis*.

7. Regarding oil industry profits, see Neil H. Jacoby, *Multinational Oil*; United States Senate, Committee on Finance, *Oil Company Profitability*.

8. The nature of codependence and U.S./OPEC relations is more broadly discussed in Charles Doran, *Myth, Oil, and Politics*.

9. Relevance of these ideas to the evolution of world order is seen in the discussion of "lifeboat" ethics by Marvin Soroos, chapter 7 herein. Consider also Richard A. Falk, *A Study of Future Worlds*; Edward Azar, *Probe for Peace*, pp. 12–31; and the highly useful recent special issue on the *International Studies Quarterly* on the *International Politics of Scarcity*, edited by Dennis Pirages.

Chapter 11: Resupplying Spaceship Earth

1. A. L. Hammond, W. D. Metz, and T. H. Maugh, II, *Energy and the Future*, p. v.
2. L. D. Roper, *Where Have All the Metals Gone?*
3. R. U. Ayres and A. V. Kneese, *Economic and Ecological Effects of a Stationary State*, p. 16.
4. Leonardo Scholars, *Resources and Decisions*; Hammond, Metz, and Maugh, *Energy*, chap. 1; United States, Council on Environmental Quality, *Energy and the Environment —Electric Power*.
5. *New York Times*, 3 June 1977, p. D13.
6. W. Patterson, *Nuclear Power*; R. E. Webb, *The Accident Hazards of Nuclear Power Plants*.
7. T. E. Jones, "Current Prospects of Sustainable Economic Growth," pp. 159–170.
8. Amory B. Lovins, "Energy Strategy," p. 81.
9. J. F. Hogerton, "The Arrival of Nuclear Power."
10. E. F. Schumacher, *Small Is Beautiful*; Lovins, "Energy"; Robert Heilbroner, *An Inquiry into the Human Prospect*; William Ophuls, *Ecology and the Politics of Scarcity*; William Paddock and Paul Paddock, *Famine—1975!*; Garrett Hardin, "The Tragedy of the Commons."
11. Dennis C. Pirages and Paul Ehrlich, *Ark II*.
12. G. K. O'Neill, "The Colonization of Space," "Space Colonies and Energy Supply to the Earth," *The High Frontier*; P. E. Glaser, "Space Shuttle Payloads," "Solar Power from Satellites"; T. Heppenheimer and M. Hopkins, "Initial Space Colonization"; J. P. Vajk, "The Impact of Space Colonization on World Dynamics," "An Open Door for A Closed World"; United States, National Aeronautics and Space Administration, *Space Manufacturing from Nonterrestrial Materials*, and *Space Settlements*. For a useful social critique of the concept, see P. L. Csonka, "Space Colonization."
13. Proposals to build all space structures on earth have been made, and experimental installations would no doubt be constructed on earth. The cost of solar power stations built on and launched from earth is economically "competitive" after A.D. 2000, according to ERDA (Energy Research and Development Administration, Office of the Administrator, "Final Report of the ERDA Task Group on Satellite Power Stations" [ERDA-76/148], November 1976). The O'Neill space manufacturing system should greatly reduce the cost.
14. O'Neill, *The High Frontier*, p. 270.
15. S. H. Lay and H. J. Taubenfeld, *The Law Relating to Activities of Man in Space*, chap. 3.
16. D. E. Kash, *The Politics of Space Cooperation*.
17. E. R. Finch, "Energy-Ecospace"; G. S. Robinson, "Space Law," pp. 59–64; Seyom Brown et al., *Regimes for the Ocean, Outer Space, and Weather*.
18. Davis B. Bobrow, *Technology-Related International Outcomes*.
19. U.S. Treaties and Other International Acts, Series 6347.
20. Kash, *Politics*; C. Q. Christol, statement before the Subcommittee on Space Science and Applications, Senate Committee on Science and Technology.
21. J. H. Glazer, "Law-Making and Human Settlement at the Lagrangian Points of Trans-National Space."
22. K. Johnson, "Canadian Report Urges Domestic Comsat."
23. Christol, statement.
24. W. Rogers, statement in U.S. Department of State *Current Policy* Series.
25. Glazer, "Law-Making."
26. G. K. O'Neill, *New York Times Magazine*; Glaser, "Solar Power."
27. J. M. Blair, *The Control of Oil*.

28. E. A. Steinhoff, ed., *Organizing Space Activities for World Needs*.

29. O'Neill, "Space Colonies."

30. Glaser, "Space Shuttle."

31. E. B. Skolnikoff, *The International Imperatives of Technology*, pp. 159–60.

32. Robert Gilpin, *US Power and the Multinational Corporation*.

33. Kash, *Politics*.

34. I. L. White, *Decision-Making for Space*.

35. Ophuls, *Ecology*, pp. 228–29.

Chapter 12: Ocean Fisheries Management

1. For a comprehensive analysis, see Douglas M. Johnston, *The International Law of Fisheries*.

2. The work of the conference as a whole is documented in the Supplements to the General Assembly *Official Records* entitled *Third United Nations Conference on the Law of the Sea*. The *Informal Composite Negotiating Text* may be found within these volumes as United Nations Document A/Conf.62/WP.10, dated 15 July 1977. For analyses based on earlier stages of the Third Conference, see Barbara Johnson, "A Review of Fisheries Proposals Made at the Caracas Session of LOS III"; Channing Kury, "The Fisheries Proposals: An Assessment"; Manjula Shyam, "Rights of the Coastal States to Fisheries Resources in the Economic Zone"; and George Kent, "Fisheries and the Law of the Sea." The present paper is an undated version of "Fisheries and the Law of the Sea," which had been based on the *Revised Single Negotiating Text*.

3. Plenary Meetings, Summary Records, 28 June 1974, in UN, *Third United Nations Conference on the Law of the Sea*, 1:63.

4. Robert E. Osgood et al., *Toward a National Ocean Policy*, p. 177.

5. United States, National Marine Fisheries Service, *Fisheries Management under Extended Jurisdiction*, pp. vi, ii.

6. George Kent, "Dominance in Fishing."

7. Garrett Hardin, "The Tragedy of the Commons." For applications of the idea to fisheries management, see, for example, Anthony D'Amato and John L. Hargrove, *Environment and the Law of the Sea*, and Courtland L. Smith, "Fishing Success in a Regulated Commons." The ways in which free access can lead to economic inefficiency are described in Richard J. Sweeney et al., "Market Failure, the Common-Pool Problem, and Ocean Resource Exploitation."

8. Garrett Hardin, *Exploring New Ethics for Survival*, p. 121.

9. In Pardo and Borgese's very similar formulation, the basic principles are that the common heritage cannot be appropriated, it requires a system of management, it implies an active sharing of benefits, it implies reservation for peaceful uses, and it implies reservation for future generations. See Arvid Pardo and Elisabeth Mann Borgese, *The New International Economic Order and the Law of the Sea*. A fuller treatment of the concept is provided in Arvid Pardo, *The Common Heritage*.

10. Elisabeth Mann Borgese, "The Ocean Regime Draft Statute."

11. The Resources for the Future studies are summarized in Francis T. Christy, Jr., "Disparate Fisheries." Also see *Principles for a Global Fisheries Management Regime*. For a derisive view of the idea that fisheries might be treated as part of the common heritage, see William T. Burke, "Some Thoughts on Fisheries and a New Conference on the Law of the Sea."

12. Aaron Danzig, "A Funny Thing Happened to the Common Heritage on the Way to the Sea."

13. See Pardo and Borgese, *New International Economic Order*. An abridged statement of their views may be found in Jan Tinbergen, Antony J. Dolman, and Jan van Ettinger, eds., *Reshaping the International Order*, pp. 305–17. Other perspectives are provided in Robert L. Friedheim and William J. Durch, "The International Seabed Resources Agency Negotiations and the New International Economic Order," and in United Nations, Food and Agricultural Organization, *A Contribution to Discussion of a New Economic Order with Reference to the Living Resources of the Ocean*.

Chapter 13: Law, Organization, and Environmental Concerns

1. Donnella H. Meadows et al., *The Limits to Growth*.
2. H. S. D. Cole et al., *Models of Doom*.
3. Study of Critical Environmental Problems (SCEP), *Man's Impact on the Global Environment*.
4. Herman Kahn, William Brown, and Leon Martel, *The Next 200 Years*.
5. See, for example: Norman Angell, *The Great Illusion*; Ivan S. Bloch, *The Future of War*; John Herz, *International Politics in the Atomic Age*.
6. For an early exception, see Karl William Kapp, *The Social Costs of Private Enterprise*.
7. Nicholas Wade, "Green Revolution (II)," p. 1186.
8. Wolf Ledjinsky, "Ironies of India's Green Revolution," pp. 758–68; Nicholas Wade, "Green Revolution (I)," p. 1093.
9. Dennis L. Meadows and Jørgen Randers, "Adding the Time Dimension to Environmental Policy," p. 232.
10. Zdenek Slouka, *International Custom and the Continental Shelf*.
11. Zdenek Slouka, "International Environmental Controls in the Scientific Age," p. 223.
12. Derek Bowett, *The Law of the Sea*, p. 60.
13. Howard J. Taubenfield, ed., *Space and Society*, p. 14.
14. Ernst Haas, *Tangle of Hopes*, p. 230.
15. Robert L. Friedheim, "International Organizaton and the Uses of the Ocean," p. 235.
16. For an overview of these issues, see Dennis Livingston, "Science, Technology, and International Law," pp. 68–123.
17. For example, see E. D. Brown, *The Legal Regime of Hydrospace*, chaps. 5–7; Edward Wenk, *The Politics of the Ocean*, chaps. 1–2; L. F. E. Goldie, "Development of an International Environmental Law—An Appraisal," pp. 104–65.
18. Quoted in Arthur Schlesinger, Jr., "Origins of the Cold War," p. 30.
19. John L. Hargrove, ed., *Law, Institutions, and the Global Environment*, p. 96.
20. From the viewpoint of the requirements of a market economy, three elements are necessary if science and technology are to be applied in a socially responsive manner: a need expressed in monetary terms, entrepreneurship, and money costs that reflect social costs. All three are fundamentally political problems in that they involve moving resources, burdens, and power from one societal group to another. Economists tend to ignore these difficulties in assessing the costs of cleanup. Keith Pavitt, "Technology, International Competition, and Economic Growth: Some Lessons and Perspectives," pp. 197–98; see also Allen V. Kneese, "The Political Economy of Pollution," pp. 153–66.
21. For a good discussion of these problems, see Charles Cheney Humpstone, "Pollution, Precedent and Prospect," pp. 325–38.
22. Don C. Piper, "Unilateral Acts of States with Regard to Environmental Protection" (chap. 14 herein).
23. See the *American Journal of International Law* 69 (1975): 154–74, for the text of the court's decision.
24. United Nations Secretariat, *Survey of Existing International Agreements Concerning the Sea-Bed and the Ocean Floor*, Doc. A/AC.135/10/Rev. 1 (12 August 1968).
25. Freidheim, "International Organization, " pp. 275–77.
26. Cyril Black, "Challenges to an Evolving Legal Order," p. 22.
27. Richard A. Falk, *The Endangered Planet*, p. 273.
28. Edward J. Woodhouse, "Re-Visioning the Future of the Third World," pp. 1–33.
29. "Development and Environment," Report to the Secretary-General of the United Nations Conference on the Human Environment, 4–12 June 1971, UN Doc. GE 71-12738, pp. 22–30 (1971).
30. Quoted in Edwin P. Morgan, "Stockholm," p. 153.
31. Robert Keohane and Joseph S. Nye, *Power and Interdependence*, pp. 3–19.
32. James P. Sewell, *Functionalism and World Politics*.
33. Robert C. Angell, *Peace on the March*.

34. Inis Claude, *Swords into Plowshares*, p. 398.
35. Ibid., p. 359.

Chapter 14: Unilateral Acts of States with Regard to Environmental Protection

1. Marjorie M. Whiteman, *Digest of International Law*, 5:443–49.
2. Ibid., 4:756–57.
3. Don C. Piper, "Foreign Policy Outputs and International Law," pp. 132–37; and Don C. Piper, "The Cuban Missile Crisis and International Law," pp. 26–31.
4. The reader will readily observe that the rough model I have set forth assumes that unilateral action by states declared to be for environmental protection is in fact primarily motivated by a concern with environmental danger or destruction. It is, of course, quite possible that a state might undertake unilateral action, ostensibly for the purpose of environmental protection, when, in fact, environmental concern is only peripheral to another related issue that the decision maker seeks unobtrusively to promote. If this is the case, the assertion of legal rights regarding environmental protection may be employed to accomplish other and perhaps less noble and/or less legal purposes. The reader will also observe that I assume that the protection of the national environment is a shared value and that the discussion relates to means and not to the appropriateness of the shared value.
5. As a recent example of a fishing control zone, one may cite the U.S. legislation that became effective 1 March 1977. Under the legislation, the United States asserts "exclusive fishery management authority" in a 200-mile zone in order to establish a maximum allowable catch of coastal fish and to allocate that catch among U.S. and foreign fishermen. In accordance with the legislation, the U.S. has concluded a number of agreements with foreign states in which the latter recognize the U.S. authority and are allowed to participate in fishing activities within the U.S. zone. To the extent that states, in creating such zones, assert "management" rights rather than an absolute right to terminate an existing right or demand new behavior, the fishing zones would appear to be different in legal impact from action likely to be taken to protect the environmental quality. For the text of the U.S. legislation, see P.L. 94-265. For an assertion that the U.S. legislation was contrary to existing rules of international law, see John Norton Moore, "Foreign Policy and Fidelity to Law," pp. 802–8.
6. For the text of the act, see, S. Houston Lay, Robin Churchill, and Myron Nordquist, comps. and eds., *New Directions in the Law of the Sea*, 1:199–210.
7. Sec. 3 (1).
8. Secs. 11–12.
9. Sec. 8.
10. Sec. 13 (1).
11. See the Canadian statement of 17 April 1970 in *New Directions*, pp. 213–21. See also the views of the former legal adviser to the Department of External Affairs, J. Alan Beesley, "The Canadian Approach to International Environmental Law," pp. 3–12.
12. See the U.S. statement, 15 April 1970, in *New Directions*, pp. 211–12.
13. Ibid., p. 218.
14. See, for example, Albert E. Utton, "The Arctic Waters Pollution Prevention Act and the Right of Self-Protection," pp. 140–53.
15. Louis Henkin, "Arctic Anti-Pollution," p. 135. See also Richard B. Bilder, "The Canadian Arctic Waters Pollution Prevention Act," pp. 1–51.
16. Lay, Churchill, and Nordquist, *New Directions*, 2:710–11. See also William E. Butler, "Pollution Control and the Soviet Arctic," pp. 557–60.
17. *New York Times*, 28 August 1975, p. 4.
18. For the text of the act, see Lay, Churchill, and Nordquist, *New Directions*, 1:222–28. See also Malcolm J. Forster, "The Prevention of Oil Pollution Act 1971," pp. 771–74.
19. See Lay, Churchill. and Nordquist, *New Directions*, 1:229.
20. For the text of the treaty, see ibid., 2:592–601.
21. See document cited in n. 12 above.

22. See *American Journal of International Law* 69 (1975): 154–74 for the text of the court's decision.

23. Ibid., p. 163.

24. Ibid., p. 165.

25. See Lay, Churchill, and Nordquist, *New Directions*, 2:721–22.

26. For the text of the LOS III discussions, see UN *Informal Composite Negotiating Text* (A/Conf.62/WP.10/Corr. 1 and 2).

Chapter 15: The Logic of International Interaction

1. Ramsay Muir, *The Interdependent World and Its Problems*, p. 1.

2. These early contacts sometimes produced dramatic consequences. Within a century after the arrival of Pizarro, the Inca population had dropped to 25 percent of the earlier figure. This was probably due to the smallpox and measles introduced by the Spaniards and to the disruption of the society's food production, storage, and distribution system. The flow of gold to Western Europe had a pronounced influence on the fortunes of Spain and brought a degree of monetary inflation to Western Europe. See L. Mcintyre, *The Incredible Incas*.

3. Fernand Braudel, *The Mediterranean*.

4. C. F. Bergsten, Robert O. Keohane, and Joseph S. Nye, "International Economics and International Politics."

5. D. H. Blake and R. S. Walters, *The Politics of Global Economic Relations*.

6. I would like to acknowledge a debt to my associate Roger J. Baker, whose comments and suggestions were helpful to me in writing this and several other sections of this paper.

7. Todd R. LaPorte, ed., *Organized Social Complexity*.

8. D. I. Meiselman and A. B. Laffer, eds., *The Phenomenon of Worldwide Inflation*.

9. Garrett Hardin, "The Tragedy of the Commons."

10. Traditional analysis in international politics has focused for the most part on purposive behavior, and the powerful apurposive forces at work have been little probed. Prominent exceptions would include Nazli Choucri and R. C. North (1975), Mihajlo Mesarovic and Eduard Pestel (1974), Donnella Meadows et al. (1972), and, of course, contributions to the literature on geopolitics. Social science literature in general has slighted the apurposive and the inadvertent. Thinkers as diverse as Adam Smith, Karl Marx, and Max Weber have dealt with individual examples of inadvertent outcomes in their analyses, but without examining the dynamics of apurposive change. Surprisingly, contemporary volumes on social change usually overlook the matter also.

11. Mihajlo Mesarovic and Eduard Pestel, *Mankind at the Turning Point*.

12. Harold Sprout and Margaret Sprout, *Multiple Vulnerabilities*, p. 16.

13. There has been a lively debate in the systems literature about whether greater complexity may not increase system stability because of the flexibility provided by backup systems and alternative ways of meeting needs. For some systems, under favorable circumstances, that might be the case. To take full advantage of such flexibility in the event of a breakdown in one sector, however, would require that there be central direction of the system, that system functioning be fully understood by those directing it, that corrective action be swift and well conceived, and that all components respond smoothly, swiftly, and in a coordinated way. These conditions may be satisfied if one is dealing with a regional electric power grid, for then the response could be automatic and preprogrammed. These conditions are *not* met in an international system in which the dominant actors are sovereign nations. In *that* system increased complexity means increased vulnerability and instability.

14. Sprout and Sprout, *Multiple Vulnerabilities*, p. 22.

15. "Congestion" and "friction" have something in common with what others have referred to as "communications costs and loads." See R. W. Cobb and C. Elder, *International Community*, p. 11.

16. Sprout and Sprout, *Multiple Vulnerabilities*, p. 26.

17. If control structures are hard to create, they are also hard to maintain. No control

system exists for all time. The Napoleonic system came and went, and so did the Concert of Europe, the League of Nations, the British Empire, and scores of other arrangements and alliances. A control system may collapse for external reasons or for a variety of internal reasons, including the resistance of subordinate actors. See P. H. Rohn, *World Treaty Index*.

18. Amatai Etzioni, "The Epigenesis of Political Communities at the International Level."

19. Andrew M. Scott, "The Global System and the Implications of Interaction," p. 231.

20. There are exceptions, of course. Labor leaders do not hesitate to charge that multinational corporations export capital and jobs.

21. Robert Gilpin argues that arrangements favoring foreign investment are changing in both host and investing countries and that this will serve as a brake on investment. Robert Gilpin, *US Power and the Multinational Corporation*.

22. Sprout and Sprout, *Multiple Vulnerabilities*, p. 20.

Chapter 16: Leviathan, the Open Society, and the Crisis of Ecology

1. For example, Hugh Stretton, *Capitalism, Socialism, and the Environment*; Davis B. Bobrow, "The Politics of Coordinated Redistribution," pp. 197–219.

2. The argument is similar in most respects to that made by Samuel Huntington that postindustrial society will require authoritarian controls. Samuel P. Huntington, "The Democratic Distemper."

3. Robert Heilbroner, *An Inquiry into The Human Prospect*; Garrett Hardin and John Baden, eds., *Managing the Commons*; William Ophuls, *Ecology and the Politics of Scarcity*.

4. As used here, *participation* will denote involvement in political decision making. *Centralization* is a more complex term used to indicate the extent of governmental authority and/or the degree of social integration. These two uses, however, are not necessarily contradictory. For purpose of discussion, "centralization" will be used to mean the relative extent of government control *and* the related extent of social integration. Presumably, the greater the degree of centralization the greater the power and initiative of government and central structures and less the power and resources of local and state government and structures. To illustrate:

Table 1.

	Participation (examples)	Nonparticipation (examples)
Centralization	Worker democracy Yugoslavia	Dictatorship Stalinist Russia "1984"
Decentralization	Jeffersonian Democracy	Feudal society Tammany Hall Chinese warlord system

5. Alexis de Tocqueville, *Democracy in America*, pp. 279–80.

6. Heilbroner, *An Inquiry*, p. 127.

7. William Ophuls, "The Scarcity Society," p. 52.

8. Garrett Hardin, "The Tragedy of the Commons," in Hardin and Baden, *Managing The Commons*.

9. Robert Heilbroner, "Second Thoughts on the Human Prospect," p. 27.

10. Ophuls, *Ecology*, pp. 154, 235.

11. Heilbroner, *An Inquiry*, pp. 90–93.

12. Ophuls, *Ecology*, p. 167.

13. Hardin and Baden, *Managing the Commons*, pp. 26–28.

14. Garrett Hardin, "Living on a Lifeboat," in Hardin and Baden, *Managing the Commons.*

15. David Orr, "Modernization and Conflict."

16. Heilbroner, "Second Thoughts," p. 26.

17. Ibid., p. 28.

18. Ophuls, *Ecology,* p. 163.

19. Ibid., pp. 226–27.

20. Ross Ashby, "Variety, Constraint, and the Law of Requisite Variety."

21. Langdon Winner, "Complexity and the Limits of Human Understanding," in Todd R. LaPorte, ed., *Organized Social Complexity,* p. 64.

22. Daniel Metlay, "On Studying the Future Behavior of Complex Systems," p. 223.

23. Graham Allison, *Essence of Decision.*

24. Chris Argyris, "Organizations of the Future."

25. As quoted in Amory Lovins, *Soft Energy Paths,* p. 164.

26. Harlan Wilson, "Complexity as a Theoretical Problem," p. 293.

27. Grant McConnell, *Private Power and American Democracy.*

28. Murray Edelman, *The Symbolic Uses of Politics.*

29. David Braybrooke and Charles Lindblom, *A Strategy of Decision.*

30. Beryl L. Crowe, "The Tragedy of the Commons Revisited," in Hardin and Baden, *Managing the Commons.*

31. Dennis J. Palumbo, "Organization Theory and Political Science," p. 357.

32. Roberto Michels, *Political Parties.*

33. Lewis Mumford, *The Myth of the Machine.*

34. George Modelski, *Principles of World Politics,* p. 165.

35. Edward Goldsmith et al., *Blueprint for Survival*; E. F. Schumacher, *Small Is Beautiful*; John Todd, "Pioneering for the 21st Century"; Lovins, *Soft Energy Paths.*

36. Denis de Rougemont, "Choice of Power and Power to Choose."

37. Schumacher, *Small Is Beautiful,* p. 31.

38. Goldsmith, *Blueprint,* p. 157.

39. David Morris and Karl Hess, *Neighborhood Power,* p. 14; see also Scott Burns, *The Household Economy.*

40. George Kateb, *Utopia and Its Enemies.*

41. Paul R. Shulman, "Non-incremental Policy-Making."

42. H. T. Odum, *Power, Environment, and Society.*

43. Lovins, *Soft Energy Paths*; see also Denis Hayes, *Rays of Hope*; Wilson Clark, *Energy for Survival.*

44. J. S. Steinhart and C. E. Steinhart, "Energy Use in the U.S. Food System," p. 311.

45. Luther Carter, "Soil Erosion," p. 409.

46. Warren A. Johnson, Victor Stoltzfus, and Peter Craumer, "Energy Conservation in Amish Agriculture." p. 375.

47. Wlliam Lockeretz et al. *A Comparison of the Production, Economic Returns, and Energy Intensiveness of Corn Belt Farms.*

48. James L. Sundquist, *Dispersing Population,* p. 241.

49. Carol Pateman, *Participation and Democratic Theory.*

50. Donald Schon, *Beyond the Stable State*; John Friedman, *Retracking America.*

51. Schon, *Stable State,* p. 190.

52. Carl Rogers, *On Personal Power.*

53. Lee Rainwater, "Equity, Income, Inequality, and the Steady State," p. 272.

54. Michael H. Best and William E. Connolly, "Market Images and Corporate Power," p. 59.

55. Paul C. Stern and Eileen M. Kirkpatrick, "Energy Behavior," p. 14.

56. Allen Kneese and Charles Schultz, *Pollution, Prices, and Public Policy,* pp. 85–111; Rick Applegate, *Public Trusts*; Talbot Page, *Conservation and Economic Efficiency,* pp. 174–89.

57. Daniel Bell, "The Future World Disorder," pp. 134–35.

Chapter 17: Ecology and the Time Dimension in Human Relationships

1. Bernard James, *The Death of Progress*.
2. Lars Bergstrom, "What Is a Conflict of Interest?" p. 209.
3. Herman Schmid, "Peace Research and Politics," p. 222.
4. Kenneth E. Boulding, "The Economics of the Coming Spaceship Earth," p. 11.
5. Johan Galtung, "Violence, Peace, and Peace Research," pp. 167–69.
6. Nicholas Georgescu-Roegen, "The Entropy Law and the Economic Problem."
7. Garrett Hardin, *Exploring New Ethics for Survival*, p. 216.
8. J. Donald Hughes, *Ecology in Ancient Civilizations*.
9. Eric P. Eckholm, *Losing Ground*.
10. George Wald, "America's My Home," p. 31.
11. Garrett Hardin, "Living on a Lifeboat," p. 567.
12. William Paddock and Paul Paddock, *Famine—1975!* pp. 205–29.
13. Hardin, "Lifeboat."
14. E. F. Schumacher, *Small Is Beautiful*, pp. 171–90.
15. Garrett Hardin, "The Tragedy of the Commons."
16. See Alvin Toffler, ed., *Learning for Tomorrow*.
17. Margaret Mead, "The Future: Prefigurative Cultures and Unknown Children."
18. Christopher D. Stone, *Should Trees Have Standing?*
19. Christian Bay, "Violence as a Negation of Freedom," p. 638.
20. Boulding, "Economics," p. 11.

Bibliography

Books and Articles

Abir, Mordechai. *Oil, Power, and Politics: Conflict in Arabia, the Red Sea, and the Gulf*. London: Frank Cass, 1974.

Allison, Graham. *Essence of Decision*. Boston: Little, Brown, 1971.

Almond, Gabriel, and Powell, G. Bingham. *Comparative Politics*. Boston: Little, Brown, 1966.

Alschuler, Lawrence. "Satellization and Stagnation in Latin America." *International Studies Quarterly* 20 (1976): 39–82.

Amara, Roy C., and Salancik, Gerald. "Forecasting: From Conjectural Art toward Science." *Futurist* 6 (1972): 112–16.

Anderson, Charles H. *The Sociology of Survival: Social Problems of Growth*. Homewood, Ill.: Dorsey Press, 1976.

Anderson, Walt. *A Place of Power: The American Episode in Human Evolution*. Santa Monica, Calif.: Goodyear, 1976.

Angell, Norman. *The Great Illusion*. London: William Heinemann, 1914.

Angell, Robert C. *Peace on the March: Transnational Participation*. New York: Van Nostrand, 1969.

Applegate, Rick. *Public Trusts: A New Approach to Environmental Protection*. Washington, D.C.: Exploratory Project for Economic Alternatives, 1976.

Argyris, Chris. "Organizations of the Future." In Hawley, Willis D., and Rogers, David, eds., *Improving Urban Management*, pp. 175–208. Beverly Hills, Calif.: Sage, 1976.

Armajani, Yahya. *The Middle East: Past and Present*. New York: Prentice-Hall, 1969.

Ashby, Ross. "Variety, Constraint, and the Law of Requisite Variety." In Buckley, Walter, ed., *Modern Systems Research*. Chicago: Aldine, 1968.

Ayres, R. U., and Kneese, A. V. *Economic and Ecological Effects of a Stationary State*. Resources for the Future Reprint no. 99 (1972).

Azar, Edward. *Probe for Peace: Small-State Hostilities*. Minneapolis: Burgess, 1973.

Aziz, Sartaj, ed. *Hunger, Politics and Markets: The Real Issues in the Food Crisis*. New York: New York University Press, 1975.

Barnet, Richard J., and Müller, Ronald E. *Global Reach: The Power of the Multinational Corporations*. New York: Simon and Schuster, 1974.

Barros, James, and Johnston, Douglas M. *The International Law of Pollution*. New York: Free Press, 1974.

Bay, Christian. "Violence as a Negation of Freedom." *American Scholar* 40 (1971): 634–41.

Beckerman, Wilfred. *In Defense of Economic Growth*. London: Jonathan Cape, 1974.

Beesley, J. Alan. "The Canadian Approach to International Environmental Law." *Canadian Yearbook of International Law* 11 (1973): 3–12.

Bell, Daniel. *The Coming of Post-Industrial Society*. New York: Basic Books, 1973.

———. "The Future World Disorder." *Foreign Policy* 27 (1977): 109–35.

Beres, Louis R., and Targ, Harry R., eds. *Planning Alternative World Futures: Values, Methods, and Models*. New York: Praeger, 1975.

Bergsten, C. F.; Keohane, Robert O.; and Nye, Joseph S. "International Economics and International Politics: A Framework for Analysis." *International Organization* 29 (1975): 3–36.

Bergstrom, Lars. "What Is a Conflict of Interest?" *Journal of Peace Research* 7 (1970): 197–218.

Best, Michael H., and Connolly, William E. "Market Images and Corporate Power: Beyond the Economics of Environmental Management." In Dolbeare, Kenneth, ed., *Public Policy Evaluation*, pp. 41–74. Beverly Hills, Calif.: Sage, 1975.

Bilder, Richard B. "The Canadian Arctic Waters Pollution Prevention Act: New Stresses on the Law of the Sea." *Michigan Law Review* 69 (1970): 1–51.

Binder, Leonard. "The Middle East as a Subordinate International System." *World Politics* 10 (1958): 408–29.

Birdsell, Joseph B. "Some Predictions Based on Equilibrium Systems among Recent Hunter-Gatherers." In Lee, Richard B., and Devore, Irven, eds., *Man the Hunter*, pp. 229–40. Chicago: Aldine, 1968.

Bishop, Jerry. "Earth's Ozone Shield May Be Imperiled by More Fertilizer Use, Scientist Says." *Wall Street Journal*, 13 November 1975.

Black, Cyril. *The Dynamics of Modernization*. New York: Harper, 1966.

———. "Challenges to an Evolving Legal Order." In Falk, Richard A., and Black, Cyril E., eds., *The Future of the International Legal Order*. Vol. 1, *Trends and Patterns*, pp. 3–31. Princeton, N.J.: Princeton University Press, 1969.

Blackhurst, Richard. "International Trade and the Environment: A Review of the Literature and a Suggested Approach." *Economic Notes* 3 (1974): 91–111.

Blair, J. M. *The Control of Oil*. New York: Pantheon, 1977.

Blake, D. H., and Walters, R. S. *The Politics of Global Economic Relations*. Englewood Cliffs, N.J.: Prentice-Hall, 1976.

Bloch, Ivan S. *The Future of War*. Translated by R. C. Long. Boston: Ginn, 1902.

Bobrow, Davis B. *Technology-Related International Outcomes: R&D Strategies to Induce Sound Public Policy*. International Studies Association, Occasional Paper no. 3 (1974).

Desmond, Annabelle. "How Many People Have Ever Lived on Earth?" *Population Bulletin* 18 (1962): 1–19.

Deutsch, Karl. "Social Mobilization and Political Development." *American Political Science Review* 55 (1961): 493–514.

Doran, Charles. *Myth, Oil, and Politics: An Introduction to the Political Economy of Petroleum.* New York: Free Press, 1977.

Dunn, Frederick L. "Epidemiological Factors: Health and Disease in Hunter-Gatherers." In Lee, Richard B., and Devore, Irven, eds., *Man the Hunter,* pp. 221–28. Chicago: Aldine, 1968.

Eaton, Joseph W., and Mayer, Albert J. *Man's Capacity to Reproduce: The Demography of a Unique Population.* Glenco, Ill.: Free Press, 1954.

Eckhardt, William. *Compassion: Toward a Science of Value.* Oakville, Ont.: Canadian Peace Research Institute, 1972.

Eckholm, Eric P. *Losing Ground: Environmental Stress and World Food Prospects.* New York: Norton, 1976.

Edelman, Murray. *The Symbolic Uses of Politics.* Urbana, Ill.: University of Illinois Press, 1964.

Editors of the *Humanist,* "The Humanist Manifesto II." *Humanist* 33 (1973): 4–9.

Ehrlich, Paul. *The Population Bomb.* New York: Ballantine, 1968.

———, and Ehrlich, Anne H. *Population, Resources, Environment: Issues in Human Ecology.* 2d ed. San Francisco: Freeman, 1972.

Eisenstadt, S. N. *Tradition, Change, and Modernity.* New York: John Wiley, 1973.

Ellul, Jacques. *The Technological Society.* New York: Vintage, 1967.

Enders, Thomas Ostrom. "North-South Dialogue: Towards One World System or Several?" Ottawa: United States Information Service, Information Release 76–35 (November 1976).

Engler, Robert. *The Brotherhood of Oil: Energy and the Public Interest.* Chicago: University of Chicago Press, 1977.

Enloe, Cynthia. *The Politics of Pollution in Comparative Perspective.* New York: David McKay, 1975.

Etzioni, Amitai. "The Epigenesis of Political Communities at the International Level." *American Journal of Sociology* 63 (1963): 407–21.

Falk, Richard A. *This Endangered Planet: Prospects and Proposals for Human Survival.* New York: Random House, 1972.

———. *A Study of Future Worlds.* New York: Free Press, 1975.

Farnsworth, Clyde. "Multinational Corporations Turning Away from Third World Lands." *New York Times,* 16 October 1976, pp. 27, 29.

Fatemi, Nasrollah S. *Oil Diplomacy: Powderkeg in Iran.* New York: Whittier Books, 1954.

Feinberg, Gerald. *The Prometheus Project: Mankind's Search for Long-Range Goals.* New York: Doubleday-Anchor, 1969.

Fessler, Loren. "China: Development of Population Policy." In Brown, Harrison; Holdren, John P.; Sweezy, Alan; and West, Barbara, eds., *Population: Perspective 1973,* pp. 58–78. San Francisco: Freeman, Cooper, 1973.

———. "The Politics of Coordinated Redistribution." In Pirages, Dennis, ed., *The Sustainable Society,* pp. 197–219. New York: Praeger, 1977.

Bodmer, W. F., and Cavalli-Sforza, L. L. *Genetics, Evolution, and Man.* San Francisco: W. H. Freeman, 1976.

Bohi, Douglas R., and Russell, Milton. *U.S. Energy Policy: Alternatives for Security.* Baltimore: Johns Hopkins University Press, 1975.

Bookchin, Murray. *Our Synthetic Environment.* New York: Harper, 1975.

Borgese, Elisabeth Mann. "The Constitution of the Oceans." In Borgese, Elisabeth Mann, and Krieger, David, eds., *The Tides of Change: Peace, Pollution, and the Potential of the Oceans.* New York: Mason Charter, 1975.

———. "The Ocean Regime Draft Statute." In Borgese, Elisabeth Mann, ed., *Pacem in Maribus,* pp. 331–58. New York: Dodd, Mead, 1972.

Borgstrom, George. *The Hungry Planet: The Modern World at the Edge of Famine.* New York: Macmillan, 1972.

Boughey, Arthur S. *Strategy for Survival: An Exploration of the Limits to Further Population and Industrial Growth.* Menlo Park, Calif.: W. A. Benjamin, 1976.

Boulding, Kenneth E. *The Meaning of the Twentieth Century.* New York: Harper, 1965.

———. "The Economics of the Coming Spaceship Earth." In Jarrett, H., ed., *Environmental Quality in a Growing Economy,* pp. 3–14. Baltimore: Johns Hopkins University Press, 1966.

Bowett, Derek. *The Law of the Sea.* Dobbs Ferry, N.Y.: Oceana, 1967.

Bradley, Michael E., and Clark, M. Gardner. "Supervision and Efficiency in Socialized Agriculture." *Soviet Studies* 23 (1972): 465–73.

Braudel, Fernand. *The Mediterranean.* 2 vols. New York: Harper and Row, 1972.

Braybrooke, David, and Lindblom, Charles. *A Strategy of Decision.* New York: Free Press, 1970.

Brook, E. M., and Grilli, Enzo. "Commodity Price Stabilization and the Developing World." *Finance and Development* 14 (1977), 8–11.

Brown, E. D. *The Legal Regime of Hydrospace.* London: Stevens, 1971.

Brown, Lester R. *World without Borders.* New York: Vintage, 1972.

———. *By Bread Alone.* New York: Praeger, 1974.

———. *In the Human Interest.* New York: Norton, 1974.

———. *World Population Trend: Signs of Hope, Signs of Stress.* Washington, D.C.: Worldwatch Paper No. 8, 1976.

Brown, Peter G., ed. *Food Policy: The Responsibility of the United States in the Life and Death Choices.* New York: Free Press, 1977.

Brown, Seyom; Cornell, Nina W.; Fabian, Larry L.; and Weiss, Edith B. *Regimes for the Ocean, Outer Space, and Weather.* Washington, D.C.: Brookings Institution, 1977.

Brubaker, Sterling. *To Live on Earth.* New York: Mentor, 1972.

———. *In Command of Tomorrow.* Baltimore: Johns Hopkins University Press, 1975.

Burke, William T. "Some Thoughts on Fisheries and a New Conference on the Law of the Sea." In Rothchild, Brian J., ed., *World Fisheries Policy:*

Multidisciplinary Views, pp. 52–73. Seattle: University of Washington Press, 1972.

Burns, Scott. *The Household Economy*. Boston: Beacon Press, 1975.

Bush, Keith. "The U.S.S.R.'s Third Major Grain Purchase." *Radio Liberty Research*, 28 July 1975.

Butler, William E. "Pollution Control and the Soviet Arctic." *International and Comparative Law Quarterly* 21 (1972): 557–60.

Caldwell, John C. "Toward a Restatement of Demographic Transition Theory." *Population and Development Review* 2 (1976): 321–66.

Caldwell, Lynton K. *In Defense of Earth: International Protection of the Biosphere*. Bloomington: University of Indiana Press, 1972.

————. *Man and His Environment: Policy and Administration*. New York: Harper, 1975.

Cardoso, Fernando Henrique. "Dependency and Development in Latin America." *New Left Review* 74 (1972):

Carter, Luther. "Soil Erosion." *Science* 196 (1977): 409–11.

Carter, Vernon Gill, and Dale, Tom. *Topsoil and Civilization*. Rev. ed. Norman: University of Oklahoma Press, 1974.

Catton, William R. "Human Ecology and Social Policy." Unpublished paper, 1977.

Chamberlain, Neil W. *Beyond Malthus: Population and Power*. Englewood Cliffs, N.J.: Prentice-Hall, 1970.

Chen, Pi-chao. "China: Population Program at the Grassroots." In Brown, Harrison; Holdren, John P.; Sweezy, Alan; and West, Barbara, eds., *Population: Perspective 1973*, pp. 79–95. San Francisco: Freeman, Cooper, 1973.

Choucri, Nazli. *Global Energy Interdependence*. Cambridge, Mass.: MIT Center for International Studies, 1974.

————. "Forecasting in International Relations: Problems and Prospects." *International Interactions* 1 (1974): 63–86.

————, and North, R. C. *Nations in Conflict: National Growth and International Violence*. San Francisco: W. H. Freeman, 1975.

Christy, Francis T., Jr. "Disparate Fisheries: Problems for the Law of the Sea Conference and Beyond." *Ocean Development and International Law* 1 (1974): 337–53.

Clark, Grenville, and Sohn, Lewis B. *World Peace through World Law*. Cambridge, Mass.: Harvard University Press, 1966.

Clark, Wilson. *Energy for Survival*. New York: Doubleday, 1974.

Claude, Inis. *Swords into Plowshares*. 3rd ed. rev. New York: Random House, 1964.

Clinton, Richard L., ed. *Population and Politics: New Directions in Political Science Research*. Lexington, Mass.: D. C. Heath, 1973.

————. "Politics and Survival." *World Affairs* 138 (1975): 108–27.

————. "Hacia una teoría del ecodesarrollo: concepto clave para ubicar el papel de las políticas de población en el proceso de desarrollo." *Comercio Exterior* (Mexico) 26 (1976): 64–76.

————. "Ecodevelopment." *World Affairs* 140 (1977): 111–26.

Coale, Ansley J. "The Demographic Transition." In International Union for the Scientific Study of Population, *International Population Conference*, 1 (1974): 53–72.

————. "The History of the Human Population." *Scientific American* 231 (1974): 40–51.

Cobb, R. W., and Elder, C. *International Community: A Regional and Global Study*. New York: Holt, Rinehart, and Winston, 1970.

Cole, H. S. D.; Freeman, Christopher; Jahoda, Marie; and Pavitt, K. L. R. *Models of Doom*. New York: Universe Books, 1973.

Commoner, Barry. *The Closing Circle*. New York: Bantam Books, 1972.

Connelly, Philip, and Perlman, Robert. *The Politics of Scarcity: Resource Conflicts in International Relations*. London: Oxford University Press, 1975.

Cooper, Richard N. *The Economics of Interdependence*. New York: McGraw-Hill, 1968.

Copithorne, L. "International Corporate Transfer Prices and Government Policy." *Canadian Journal of Economics* 4 (August 1971): 324–41.

Cornelius, Wayne A. "Urbanization and Political Demand Making: Political Participation among the Migrant Poor in Latin American Cities." *American Political Science Review* 68 (1974): 1125–46.

Crosson, Pierre R. "Institutional Obstacles to Expansion of World Food Production." *Science* 188 (1975): 523.

Crowe, Beryl L. "The Tragedy of the Commons Revisited." *Science* 166 (1969): 1103–07.

Csonka, P. L. "Space Colonization: An Invitation to Disaster?" *Futurist*, 11 (1977): 285–90.

Currie, Lauchlin. *Accelerating Development: The Necessity and the Means*. New York: McGraw-Hill, 1966.

Daly, Herman E., ed. *Toward a Steady-State Economy*. San Francisco: W. H. Freeman, 1973.

D'Amato, Anthony, and Hargrove, John L. *Environment and the Law of the Sea*. Washington, D.C.: American Society of International Law, 1974.

Danzig, Aaron. "A Funny Thing Happened to the Common Heritage on the Way to the Sea." *San Diego Law Review* 12 (1975): 655–64.

de Almedia, Miguel A. Ozorio. "The Confrontation between Problems of Development and Environment." *International Conciliation* 586 (1972): 37–56.

Debanne, Joseph C. "Evolution of the OPEC Leadership and the New Economic Order." Working Paper 75-18, Department of Management Sciences of the University of Ottawa (May 1975).

Deevey, Edward, Jr. "Pleistocene Family Planning." In Lee, Richard B., and Devore, Irven, eds., *Man the Hunter*, pp. 248–49. Chicago: Aldine, 1968.

De Jouvenel, Bertrand. "Political Science and Prevision." *American Political Science Review* 59 (1965): 29–38.

————. *The Art of Conjecture*. New York: Basic Books, 1967.

Demontribal, T. "For a New World Economic Order." *Foreign Affairs* 54 (1975), 61–78.

De Rougemont, Denis. "Choice of Power and Power to Choose." *Development Forum* 5 (1977): 1–2.

Finch, E. R. "Energy-Ecospace." Paper presented to the International Astronautical Federation, 1976.

Ford Foundation Energy Policy Project. *A Time to Choose*. Cambridge, Mass.: Ballinger, 1974.

Forster, Malcolm J. "The Prevention of Oil Pollution Act 1971." *International and Comparative Law Quarterly* 21 (1972): 771–74.

Frank, Andre Gunder. *Capitalism and Underdevelopment in Latin America*. New York: Monthly Review Press, 1967.

Frejka, Tomas. *The Future of Population Growth: Alternative Paths to Equilibrium*. New York: The Population Council, 1973.

Friedheim, Robert L. "International Organization and the Uses of the Ocean." In Jordan, Robert S., ed., *Multinational Cooperation*, pp. 223–81. New York: Oxford University Press, 1972.

————, and Durch, William J. "The International Seabed Resources Agency Negotiations and the New International Economic Order." Paper presented to the American Political Science Association, 1976.

Friedman, John. *Retracking America: A Theory of Societal Planning*. New York: Doubleday, 1973.

Furtado, Celso. "The Concept of External Dependence in the Study of Underdevelopment." In Wilber, Charles K., ed., *The Political Economy of Development and Underdevelopment*, pp. 118–23. New York: Random House, 1973.

Gallagher, Charles F., "Japan and the World Food Problem." *Fieldstaff Reports* [East Asia Series] 22 (June 1975).

Galtung, Johan. "Violence, Peace, and Peace Research." *Journal of Peace Research* 6 (1969): 167–91.

————. "Peace Research: Past Experiences and Future Perspectives." *Bulletin of Peace Proposals* 4 (1972): 101–2.

————. "Measuring World Development." *Alternatives* 1 (1975): 523–55.

Garvey, Gerald, and Garvey, Lou Ann, eds. *International Resource Flows*. Lexington, Mass.: Lexington Books, 1977.

George, Susan. *How the Other Half Dies: The Real Reasons for World Food Hunger*. Montclair, N.J.: Allanheld, Osum, 1977.

Georgescu-Roegen, Nicholas, "The Entropy Law and the Economic Problem." In Daly, Herman E., ed., *Toward a Steady-State Economy*, pp. 37–49. San Francisco: W. H. Freeman, 1973.

————. *The Entropy Law and the Economic Process*. Cambridge: Harvard University Press, 1974.

Giddings, J. Calvin. "World Population, Human Disaster, and Nuclear Holocaust." *Bulletin of the Atomic Scientists* 29 (1973): 21–25, 45–50.

Gilpin, Robert. *US Power and the Multinational Corporation*. New York: Basic Books, 1975.

Girvan, N. "MNC's and Dependent Underdevelopment in Mineral Export Economics." *Social and Economic Studies* 29 (1970): 490–526.

Glazer, J. H. "Law-Making and Human Settlement at the Lagrangian Points of Trans-National Space." *Columbia Journal of Transnational Law*, forthcoming.

Goldie, L. F. E. "Development of an International Environmental Law—an Appraisal." In Hargrove, John L., ed., *Law, Institutions, and the Global Environment*, pp. 104–65. Dobbs Ferry, N.Y.: Oceana, 1972.

Goldman, Marshall I. *Ecology and Economics: Controlling Pollution in the 1970's*. Englewood Cliffs, N.J.: Prentice-Hall, 1972.

Goldsmith, Edward; Allen, Robert; Allaby, Michael; Davoll, John; Lawrence, Sam. *Blueprint for Survival*. Boston: Houghton Mifflin, 1972.

———. "Is Science a Religion?" *Ecologist* 5 (1975): 50–62.

Goulet, Denis. *The Cruel Choice: A New Concept in the Theory of Development*. New York: Atheneum, 1971.

———. *The Uncertain Promise: Value Conflicts in Technological Transfer*. New York: IDOC, 1977.

Guetzkow, Harold, et al. *Simulation in International Relations: Developments for Research and Teaching*. Englewood Cliffs, N.J.: Prentice-Hall, 1963.

Haas, Ernst. *Tangle of Hopes: American Commitments and World Order*. Englewood Cliffs, N.J.: Prentice-Hall, 1969.

Halpern, Manfred. *The Politics of Social Change in the Middle East and North Africa*. Princeton, N.J.: Princeton University Press, 1963.

Hammond, A. L.; Metz, W. D.; and Maugh, T. H., II. *Energy and the Future*. Washington, D.C.: American Association for the Advancement of Science, 1973.

Handler, Philip. "On the State of Man." *Bioscience* 25 (1975): 425–32.

Hardin, Garrett. "The Tragedy of the Commons." *Science* 162 (1968): 1243–48.

———. *Exploring New Ethics for Survival: The Voyage of the Spaceship "Beagle."* Baltimore: Penguin Books, 1973.

———. "Living on a Lifeboat." *Bioscience* 24 (1974): 561–68.

———. "Carrying Capacity as an Ethical Concept." *Soundings* 59 (1976): 120–37.

———. *The Limits of Altruism: An Ecologist's View of Survival*. Bloomington: Indiana University Press, 1977.

———, and Baden, John, eds. *Managing the Commons*. San Francisco: W. H. Freeman, 1977.

Hargrove, John L., ed. *Law, Institutions, and the Global Environment*. Dobbs, Ferry, N.Y.: Oceana, 1972.

Harmon, David. "An Optimistic View of Agriculture's Future." *New York Times*, 31 January 1976.

Harmon, Willis. *An Incomplete Guide to the Future*. San Francisco: San Francisco Book Co., 1976.

Harrison, Selig S. *China, Oil, and Asia: Conflict Ahead?* New York: Columbia University Press, 1977.

Hartshorn, J. E. *Oil Companies and Governments: An Account of the International Oil Industry in Its Political Environment*. London: Farber and Farber, 1962.

Hayes, Denis. *Rays of Hope*. New York: W. W. Norton, 1977.

Heilbroner, Robert. *An Inquiry into the Human Prospect*. New York: W. W. Norton, 1974.

———. "Second Thoughts on the Human Prospect." *Challenge* 3 (1975): 21–28.

Helleiner, G. K. "Canada and the New International Economic Order."
Canadian Public Policy 2 (1976): 451–65.

Helmer, Olaf. *Social Technology*. New York: Basic Books, 1966.

Henkin, Louis. "Arctic Anti-Pollution: Does Canada Make—or Break—
International Law?" *American Journal of International Law* 65 (1971): 131–36.

Heppenheimer, T., and Hopkins, M. "Initial Space Colonization: Concepts
and R&D Aims," *Aeronautics and Astronautics* 14 (1976): 58–64, 72.

Herz, John. *International Politics in the Atomic Age*. New York: Columbia
University Press, 1959.

Hinds, S. W. "Relation of Medical Triage to World Famine: A History." In
Lucas, George, and Ogletree, T. R., eds., *Lifeboat Ethics: The Moral Dilemmas
of Hunger*, pp. 29–51. New York: Harper & Row, 1976.

Hirsch, Fred. *The Social Limits to Growth*. Cambridge: Harvard University
Press, 1976.

Hirst, David. *Oil and Public Opinion in the Middle East*. London: Farber and
Farber, 1966.

Hogerton, J. F. "The Arrival of Nuclear Power." *Scientific American* 218 (1968):
21–31.

Hostetler, John Andrew. *Hutterite Society*. Baltimore: Johns Hopkins University Press, 1974.

Howe, James W., and Sewell, John W. "Triage and Other Challenges to
Helping the Poor Countries Develop." In Howe, James W., ed., *The U.S.
and World Development: Agenda for Action—1975*, pp.55–71. New York:
Praeger, 1975.

Hughes, J. Donald. *Ecology in Ancient Civilizations*. Albuquerque: University of
New Mexico Press, 1975.

Humpstone, Charles Cheney. "Pollution, Precedent and Prospect." *Foreign
Affairs* 50 (1972): 325–38.

Huntington, Samuel P. "Political Development and Political Decay." *World
Politics* 17 (1965): 386–430.

———. "The Democratic Distemper." *Public Interest* 41 (1975): 9–38.

Hyams, Edward. *Soil and Civilization*. New York: Harper Colophon, 1976.

Issawi, Charles, and Yeganeh, Mohammed. *The Economics of Middle Eastern
Oil*. New York: Praeger, 1962.

Jacoby, Neil H. *Multinational Oil: A Study in Industrial Dynamics*. New York:
Macmillan, 1974.

James, Bernard. *The Death of Progress*. New York: Alfred A. Knopf, 1973.

Jamgotch, Nish, ed. *Thinking the Thinkable: Investment in Human Survival*.
Washington, D.C.: University Press of America, 1978.

"Japan's Economy in Transition." *Business Week*, 7 July 1975, pp. 44–50.

Johnson, Barbara. "A Review of Fisheries Proposals Made at the Caracas
Session of LOS III." *Ocean Management* 2 (1975): 285–314.

Johnson, K. "Canadian Report Urges Domestic Comsat." *Aviation Week and
Space Technology* 86 (27 March 1967): 69–71.

Johnson, Warren A.; Stoltzfus, Victor; Craumer, Peter. "Energy Conservation
in Amish Agriculture." *Science* 198 (1977): 373–78.

Johnston, Douglas M. *The International Law of Fisheries: A Framework for Policy-Oriented Inquiries.* New Haven: Yale University Press, 1965.

Jones, T. E. "Current Prospects of Sustainable Energy Growth." In Laszlo, Ervin, and Bierman, J., eds., *Goals in a Global Community.* New York: Pergamon Press, 1977.

Joskow, Paul L. "The International Nuclear Industry Today." *Foreign Affairs* 54 (1976): 788–803.

Kahn, Herman; Brown, William; and Martel, Leon. *The Next 200 Years.* New York: William Morrow, 1976.

Kapp, Karl William. *The Social Costs of Private Enterprise.* Cambridge: Harvard University Press, 1950.

Kash, D. E. *The Politics of Space Cooperation.* Lafayette, Ind.: Purdue University Press, 1967.

Kateb, George. *Utopia and Its Enemies.* New York: Schocken, 1971.

Kelley, Donald R., ed. *The Energy Crisis and the Environment: An International Perspective.* New York: Praeger, 1977.

————; Stunkel, Kenneth R., and Wescott, Richard R. *The Economic Superpowers and the Environment: The United States, the Soviet Union, and Japan.* San Francisco: Freeman, 1976.

Kennard, H. P., comp. and ed. *The Russian Yearbook.* London: Eyre and Spottiswood, 1914.

Kent, George. "Dominance in Fishing." *Journal of Peace Research* 13 (1976): 35–47.

————. "Fisheries and the Law of the Sea." *Ocean Management*, forthcoming.

Keohane, Robert O., and Nye, Joseph S. *Power and Interdependence.* Boston: Little, Brown, 1977.

Kerr, Malcom H. "The Arabs and Israelis: Perceptual Dimensions to Their Dilemma." In Beling, Willard A., ed., *The Middle East: Quest for an American Policy*, pp. 3–31. Albany: State University of New York Press, 1973.

Keyfitz, Nathan. "World Resources and the World Middle Class." *Scientific American* 235 (1976): 28–35.

Kindelberg, Charles P. "U.S. Foreign Economic Policy, 1776–1976." *Foreign Affairs* 55 (1977): 395–417.

Kneese, Allen V. "The Political Economy of Pollution." *Papers and Proceedings of the Eighty-Third Annual Meeting of the American Economic Association. American Economic Review* 61 (1971): 153–66.

————, and Schultz, Charles. *Pollution, Prices, and Public Policy.* Washington, D.C.: Brookings Institution, 1975.

Kocher, James E. *Rural Development, Income Distribution, and Fertility Decline.* New York: Population Council, 1972.

Kravis, I. B. "International Commodity Agreements to Promote Aid and Efficiency: The Case of Coffee." *Canadian Journal of Economics* 1 (1968): 295–317.

Krueger, Robert B. *The United States and International Oil.* New York: Praeger, 1975.

Kuhn, Thomas S. *The Structure of Scientific Revolutions.* Chicago: University of Chicago Press, 1974.

Kury, Channing. "The Fisheries Proposals: An Assessment." *San Diego Law Review* 12 (1975): 644–54.

Ladejinsky, Wolf. "Ironies of India's Green Revolution." *Foreign Affairs* 48 (1970): 758–68.

Laird, Roy D. "Soviet Goals for 1965 and the Problems of Agriculture." In Shaffer, Harry G., ed., *The Soviet Economy*. New York: Appleton-Century-Crofts, 1963.

——. "Prospects for Soviet Agriculture." *Problems of Communism* 20 (1971): 31–40.

Lall, S. "Transfer-Pricing by Multinational Manufacturing Firms." *Oxford Bulletin of Economics and Statistics*, 1973.

Laporte, Todd R., ed. *Organized Social Complexity*. Princeton, N.J.: Princeton University Press, 1975.

Lappé, Frances M., and Collins, Joseph. *Food First: Beyond the Myth of Food Scarcity*. New York: Houghton Mifflin, 1977.

Laszlo, Ervin, et al. *Goals for Mankind: A Report to the Club of Rome on the New Horizons of Global Community*. New York: E. P. Dutton, 1977.

Lay, S. Houston, and Taubenfeld, H. J. *The Law Relating to Activities of Man in Space*. Chicago: University of Chicago Press, 1970.

——; Churchill, Robin; and Nordquist, Myron, comps. and eds. *New Directions in the Law of the Sea*. 3 vols. Dobbs Ferry, N.Y.: Oceana, 1973.

Leakey, Richard E. "New Fossil Evidence for the Evolution of Man." *Social Biology* 19 (1972): 99–114.

Lee, Richard B. "What Hunters Do for a Living; or, How to Make Out on Scarce Resources." In Lee, Richard B., and De Vore, Irven, eds., *Man the Hunter*, pp. 30–48. Chicago: Aldine, 1968.

Leipziger, Danny M., and Mudge, James. *Seabed Mineral Resources and the Economic Interests of Developing Countries*. Cambridge, Mass.: Ballinger, 1976.

Leiss, William. *The Domination of Nature*. Boston: Beacon Press, 1974.

Lenczowski, George. *The Middle East in World Affairs*. 3d ed. Ithaca, N.Y.: Cornell University Press, 1964.

Leontieff, Wassily. *The Future of the World Economy*. New York: Oxford University Press, 1976.

Leopold, Aldo. *A Sand County Almanac*. New York: Ballantine Books, 1973.

Levine, M. S. "Some Approaches to the Conceptualization and Analysis of Change in the International System." Paper presented to the annual meeting of the International Studies Association, St. Louis, 1974.

Levy, Marion. *Modernization and the Structure of Societies*. Princeton, N.J.: Princeton University Press, 1966.

Lewis, C. S. *The Abolition of Man*. New York: Macmillan, 1970.

Lindsey, Robert. "Hard Times in Copper Country." *New York Times*, 12 December 1976, pp. 1, 9.

Liska, George. *Nations in Alliance: The Limits of Interdependence*. Baltimore: Johns Hopkins University Press, 1952.

Livingston, Dennis. "Science, Technology, and International Law." In Falk, Richard A., and Black, Cyril, eds., *The Future of the International Legal Order*.

Vol. 4, *The Structure of the International Environment*, pp. 68–123. Princeton, N.J.: Princeton University Press, 1972.

Lockeretz, William, et al. *A Comparison of the Production, Economic Returns, and Energy Intensiveness of Corn Belt Farms That Do and Do Not Use Inorganic Fertilizers and Pesticides*. St. Louis: Center for the Study of the Biology of Natural Systems, 1975.

Longrigg, Stephen H. *Oil in the Middle East: Its Discovery and Development*. 3d ed. London: Oxford University Press, 1968.

Lovins, Amory B. "Energy Strategy: The Road Not Taken?" *Foreign Affairs* 55 (1976): 65–96.

———. *Soft Energy Paths*. Cambridge, Mass: Ballinger, 1977.

Lucas, George R. *Triage in Medicine and Society*. Houston: Institute of Religion, 1975.

———, and Ogletree, T. W., eds. *Lifeboat Ethics: The Moral Dilemmas of Hunger*. New York: Harper and Row, 1976.

McConnell, Grant. *Private Power and American Democracy*. New York: Knopf, 1966.

McIntyre, L. *The Incredible Incas*. Washington, D.C.: National Geographic Society, 1975.

McNicoll, Geoffrey. "Community-Level Population Policy: An Exploration." *Population and Development Review* 1 (1975): 1–22.

Makdashi, Zuhayr. *The International Politics of Natural Resources*. Ithaca, N.Y.: Cornell University Press, 1976.

Mankind 2000 and the Union of International Associations, *Yearbook of World Problems and Human Potential*. Brussels, 1976.

Marsden, Ralph W., ed. *Politics, Minerals, and Survival*. Madison: University of Wisconsin Press, 1974.

Maslow, Abraham H. *Toward a Psychology of Being*. Princeton, N.J.: Van Norstrand, 1962.

Mead, Margaret. "The Future: Prefigurative Cultures and Unknown Children." In Toffler, Alvin, ed., *The Futurists*, pp. 27–50. New York: Random House, 1972.

Meadows, Dennis L. *Dynamics of Growth in a Finite World*. New York: John Wiley, 1974.

———; and Randers, Jørgen. "Adding the Time Dimension to Environmental Policy." *International Organization* 26 (1972): 213–33.

Meadows, Donnella H.; Meadows, Dennis L.; Randers, Jørgen; and Behrens, William H. *The Limits to Growth*. New York: Signet, 1972.

Meiselman, D. I., and Laffer, A. B., eds. *The Phenomenon of Worldwide Inflation*. Washington, D.C.: American Institute for Public Policy Research, 1975.

Melville, Herman. "A Canticle." In *The Battle Pieces of Herman Melville*. New York: Thomas Yoseloff, 1963.

Mendlovitz, Saul H., ed. *On the Creation of a Just World Order: Preferred Worlds for the 1990's*. New York: Free Press, 1975.

Mesarovic, Mihajlo, and Pestel, Eduard. *Mankind at the Turning Point*. New York: E. P. Dutton, 1974.

———. "The Politics of Coordinated Redistribution." In Pirages, Dennis, ed., *The Sustainable Society*, pp. 197–219. New York: Praeger, 1977.

Bodmer, W. F., and Cavalli-Sforza, L. L. *Genetics, Evolution, and Man.* San Francisco: W. H. Freeman, 1976.

Bohi, Douglas R., and Russell, Milton. *U.S. Energy Policy: Alternatives for Security.* Baltimore: Johns Hopkins University Press, 1975.

Bookchin, Murray. *Our Synthetic Environment.* New York: Harper, 1975.

Borgese, Elisabeth Mann. "The Constitution of the Oceans." In Borgese, Elisabeth Mann, and Krieger, David, eds., *The Tides of Change: Peace, Pollution, and the Potential of the Oceans.* New York: Mason Charter, 1975.

———. "The Ocean Regime Draft Statute." In Borgese, Elisabeth Mann, ed., *Pacem in Maribus*, pp. 331–58. New York: Dodd, Mead, 1972.

Borgstrom, George. *The Hungry Planet: The Modern World at the Edge of Famine.* New York: Macmillan, 1972.

Boughey, Arthur S. *Strategy for Survival: An Exploration of the Limits to Further Population and Industrial Growth.* Menlo Park, Calif.: W. A. Benjamin, 1976.

Boulding, Kenneth E. *The Meaning of the Twentieth Century.* New York: Harper, 1965.

———. "The Economics of the Coming Spaceship Earth." In Jarrett, H., ed., *Environmental Quality in a Growing Economy*, pp. 3–14. Baltimore: Johns Hopkins University Press, 1966.

Bowett, Derek. *The Law of the Sea.* Dobbs Ferry, N.Y.: Oceana, 1967.

Bradley, Michael E., and Clark, M. Gardner. "Supervision and Efficiency in Socialized Agriculture." *Soviet Studies* 23 (1972): 465–73.

Braudel, Fernand. *The Mediterranean.* 2 vols. New York: Harper and Row, 1972.

Braybrooke, David, and Lindblom, Charles. *A Strategy of Decision.* New York: Free Press, 1970.

Brook, E. M., and Grilli, Enzo. "Commodity Price Stabilization and the Developing World." *Finance and Development* 14 (1977), 8–11.

Brown, E. D. *The Legal Regime of Hydrospace.* London: Stevens, 1971.

Brown, Lester R. *World without Borders.* New York: Vintage, 1972.

———. *By Bread Alone.* New York: Praeger, 1974.

———. *In the Human Interest.* New York: Norton, 1974.

———. *World Population Trend: Signs of Hope, Signs of Stress.* Washington, D.C.: Worldwatch Paper No. 8, 1976.

Brown, Peter G., ed. *Food Policy: The Responsibility of the United States in the Life and Death Choices.* New York: Free Press, 1977.

Brown, Seyom; Cornell, Nina W.; Fabian, Larry L.; and Weiss, Edith B. *Regimes for the Ocean, Outer Space, and Weather.* Washington, D.C.: Brookings Institution, 1977.

Brubaker, Sterling. *To Live on Earth.* New York: Mentor, 1972.

———. *In Command of Tomorrow.* Baltimore: Johns Hopkins University Press, 1975.

Burke, William T. "Some Thoughts on Fisheries and a New Conference on the Law of the Sea." In Rothchild, Brian J., ed., *World Fisheries Policy:*

Multidisciplinary Views, pp. 52–73. Seattle: University of Washington Press, 1972.

Burns, Scott. *The Household Economy*. Boston: Beacon Press, 1975.

Bush, Keith. "The U.S.S.R.'s Third Major Grain Purchase." *Radio Liberty Research*, 28 July 1975.

Butler, William E. "Pollution Control and the Soviet Arctic." *International and Comparative Law Quarterly* 21 (1972): 557–60.

Caldwell, John C. "Toward a Restatement of Demographic Transition Theory." *Population and Development Review* 2 (1976): 321–66.

Caldwell, Lynton K. *In Defense of Earth: International Protection of the Biosphere*. Bloomington: University of Indiana Press, 1972.

————. *Man and His Environment: Policy and Administration*. New York: Harper, 1975.

Cardoso, Fernando Henrique. "Dependency and Development in Latin America." *New Left Review* 74 (1972):

Carter, Luther. "Soil Erosion." *Science* 196 (1977): 409–11.

Carter, Vernon Gill, and Dale, Tom. *Topsoil and Civilization*. Rev. ed. Norman: University of Oklahoma Press, 1974.

Catton, William R. "Human Ecology and Social Policy." Unpublished paper, 1977.

Chamberlain, Neil W. *Beyond Malthus: Population and Power*. Englewood Cliffs, N.J.: Prentice-Hall, 1970.

Chen, Pi-chao. "China: Population Program at the Grassroots." In Brown, Harrison; Holdren, John P.; Sweezy, Alan; and West, Barbara, eds., *Population: Perspective 1973*, pp. 79–95. San Francisco: Freeman, Cooper, 1973.

Choucri, Nazli. *Global Energy Interdependence*. Cambridge, Mass.: MIT Center for International Studies, 1974.

————. "Forecasting in International Relations: Problems and Prospects." *International Interactions* 1 (1974): 63–86.

————, and North, R. C. *Nations in Conflict: National Growth and International Violence*. San Francisco: W. H. Freeman, 1975.

Christy, Francis T., Jr. "Disparate Fisheries: Problems for the Law of the Sea Conference and Beyond." *Ocean Development and International Law* 1 (1974): 337–53.

Clark, Grenville, and Sohn, Lewis B. *World Peace through World Law*. Cambridge, Mass.: Harvard University Press, 1966.

Clark, Wilson. *Energy for Survival*. New York: Doubleday, 1974.

Claude, Inis. *Swords into Plowshares*. 3rd ed. rev. New York: Random House, 1964.

Clinton, Richard L., ed. *Population and Politics: New Directions in Political Science Research*. Lexington, Mass.: D. C. Heath, 1973

————. "Politics and Survival." *World Affairs* 138 (1975): 108–27.

————. "Hacia una teoría del ecodesarrollo: concepto clave para ubicar el papel de las políticas de población en el proceso de desarrollo." *Comercio Exterior* (Mexico) 26 (1976): 64–76.

————. "Ecodevelopment." *World Affairs* 140 (1977): 111–26.

Coale, Ansley J. "The Demographic Transition." In International Union for the Scientific Study of Population, *International Population Conference*, 1 (1974): 53–72.

———. "The History of the Human Population." *Scientific American* 231 (1974): 40–51.

Cobb, R. W., and Elder, C. *International Community: A Regional and Global Study*. New York: Holt, Rinehart, and Winston, 1970.

Cole, H. S. D.; Freeman, Christopher; Jahoda, Marie; and Pavitt, K. L. R. *Models of Doom*. New York: Universe Books, 1973.

Commoner, Barry. *The Closing Circle*. New York: Bantam Books, 1972.

Connelly, Philip, and Perlman, Robert. *The Politics of Scarcity: Resource Conflicts in International Relations*. London: Oxford University Press, 1975.

Cooper, Richard N. *The Economics of Interdependence*. New York: McGraw-Hill, 1968.

Copithorne, L. "International Corporate Transfer Prices and Government Policy." *Canadian Journal of Economics* 4 (August 1971): 324–41.

Cornelius, Wayne A. "Urbanization and Political Demand Making: Political Participation among the Migrant Poor in Latin American Cities." *American Political Science Review* 68 (1974): 1125–46.

Crosson, Pierre R. "Institutional Obstacles to Expansion of World Food Production." *Science* 188 (1975): 523.

Crowe, Beryl L. "The Tragedy of the Commons Revisited." *Science* 166 (1969): 1103–07.

Csonka, P. L. "Space Colonization: An Invitation to Disaster?" *Futurist*, 11 (1977): 285–90.

Currie, Lauchlin. *Accelerating Development: The Necessity and the Means*. New York: McGraw-Hill, 1966.

Daly, Herman E., ed. *Toward a Steady-State Economy*. San Francisco: W. H. Freeman, 1973.

D'Amato, Anthony, and Hargrove, John L. *Environment and the Law of the Sea*. Washington, D.C.: American Society of International Law, 1974.

Danzig, Aaron. "A Funny Thing Happened to the Common Heritage on the Way to the Sea." *San Diego Law Review* 12 (1975): 655–64.

de Almedia, Miguel A. Ozorio. "The Confrontation between Problems of Development and Environment." *International Conciliation* 586 (1972): 37–56.

Debanne, Joseph C. "Evolution of the OPEC Leadership and the New Economic Order." Working Paper 75-18, Department of Management Sciences of the University of Ottawa (May 1975).

Deevey, Edward, Jr. "Pleistocene Family Planning." In Lee, Richard B., and Devore, Irven, eds., *Man the Hunter*, pp. 248–49. Chicago: Aldine, 1968.

De Jouvenel, Bertrand. "Political Science and Prevision." *American Political Science Review* 59 (1965): 29–38.

———. *The Art of Conjecture*. New York: Basic Books, 1967.

Demontribal, T. "For a New World Economic Order." *Foreign Affairs* 54 (1975), 61–78.

De Rougemont, Denis. "Choice of Power and Power to Choose." *Development Forum* 5 (1977): 1–2.

Desmond, Annabelle. "How Many People Have Ever Lived on Earth?" *Population Bulletin* 18 (1962): 1–19.

Deutsch, Karl. "Social Mobilization and Political Development." *American Political Science Review* 55 (1961): 493–514.

Doran, Charles. *Myth, Oil, and Politics: An Introduction to the Political Economy of Petroleum*. New York: Free Press, 1977.

Dunn, Frederick L. "Epidemiological Factors: Health and Disease in Hunter-Gatherers." In Lee, Richard B., and Devore, Irven, eds., *Man the Hunter*, pp. 221–28. Chicago: Aldine, 1968.

Eaton, Joseph W., and Mayer, Albert J. *Man's Capacity to Reproduce: The Demography of a Unique Population*. Glenco, Ill.: Free Press, 1954.

Eckhardt, William. *Compassion: Toward a Science of Value*. Oakville, Ont.: Canadian Peace Research Institute, 1972.

Eckholm, Eric P. *Losing Ground: Environmental Stress and World Food Prospects*. New York: Norton, 1976.

Edelman, Murray. *The Symbolic Uses of Politics*. Urbana, Ill.: University of Illinois Press, 1964.

Editors of the *Humanist*, "The Humanist Manifesto II." *Humanist* 33 (1973): 4–9.

Ehrlich, Paul. *The Population Bomb*. New York: Ballantine, 1968.

_____, and Ehrlich, Anne H. *Population, Resources, Environment: Issues in Human Ecology*. 2d ed. San Francisco: Freeman, 1972.

Eisenstadt, S. N. *Tradition, Change, and Modernity*. New York: John Wiley, 1973.

Ellul, Jacques. *The Technological Society*. New York: Vintage, 1967.

Enders, Thomas Ostrom. "North-South Dialogue: Towards One World System or Several?" Ottawa: United States Information Service, Information Release 76–35 (November 1976).

Engler, Robert. *The Brotherhood of Oil: Energy and the Public Interest*. Chicago: University of Chicago Press, 1977.

Enloe, Cynthia. *The Politics of Pollution in Comparative Perspective*. New York: David McKay, 1975.

Etzioni, Amitai. "The Epigenesis of Political Communities at the International Level." *American Journal of Sociology* 63 (1963): 407–21.

Falk, Richard A. *This Endangered Planet: Prospects and Proposals for Human Survival*. New York: Random House, 1972.

_____. *A Study of Future Worlds*. New York: Free Press, 1975.

Farnsworth, Clyde. "Multinational Corporations Turning Away from Third World Lands." *New York Times*, 16 October 1976, pp. 27, 29.

Fatemi, Nasrollah S. *Oil Diplomacy: Powderkeg in Iran*. New York: Whittier Books, 1954.

Feinberg, Gerald. *The Prometheus Project: Mankind's Search for Long-Range Goals*. New York: Doubleday-Anchor, 1969.

Fessler, Loren. "China: Development of Population Policy." In Brown, Harrison; Holdren, John P.; Sweezy, Alan; and West, Barbara, eds., *Population: Perspective 1973*, pp. 58–78. San Francisco: Freeman, Cooper, 1973.

Finch, E. R. "Energy-Ecospace." Paper presented to the International Astronautical Federation, 1976.

Ford Foundation Energy Policy Project. *A Time to Choose*. Cambridge, Mass.: Ballinger, 1974.

Forster, Malcolm J. "The Prevention of Oil Pollution Act 1971." *International and Comparative Law Quarterly* 21 (1972): 771–74.

Frank, Andre Gunder. *Capitalism and Underdevelopment in Latin America*. New York: Monthly Review Press, 1967.

Frejka, Tomas. *The Future of Population Growth: Alternative Paths to Equilibrium*. New York: The Population Council, 1973.

Friedheim, Robert L. "International Organization and the Uses of the Ocean." In Jordan, Robert S., ed., *Multinational Cooperation*, pp. 223–81. New York: Oxford University Press, 1972.

———, and Durch, William J. "The International Seabed Resources Agency Negotiations and the New International Economic Order." Paper presented to the American Political Science Association, 1976.

Friedman, John. *Retracking America: A Theory of Societal Planning*. New York: Doubleday, 1973.

Furtado, Celso. "The Concept of External Dependence in the Study of Underdevelopment." In Wilber, Charles K., ed., *The Political Economy of Development and Underdevelopment*, pp. 118–23. New York: Random House, 1973.

Gallagher, Charles F., "Japan and the World Food Problem." *Fieldstaff Reports* [East Asia Series] 22 (June 1975).

Galtung, Johan. "Violence, Peace, and Peace Research." *Journal of Peace Research* 6 (1969): 167–91.

———. "Peace Research: Past Experiences and Future Perspectives." *Bulletin of Peace Proposals* 4 (1972): 101–2.

———. "Measuring World Development." *Alternatives* 1 (1975): 523–55.

Garvey, Gerald, and Garvey, Lou Ann, eds. *International Resource Flows*. Lexington, Mass.: Lexington Books, 1977.

George, Susan. *How the Other Half Dies: The Real Reasons for World Food Hunger*. Montclair, N.J.: Allanheld, Osum, 1977.

Georgescu-Roegen, Nicholas, "The Entropy Law and the Economic Problem." In Daly, Herman E., ed., *Toward a Steady-State Economy*, pp. 37–49. San Francisco: W. H. Freeman, 1973.

———. *The Entropy Law and the Economic Process*. Cambridge: Harvard University Press, 1974.

Giddings, J. Calvin. "World Population, Human Disaster, and Nuclear Holocaust." *Bulletin of the Atomic Scientists* 29 (1973): 21–25, 45–50.

Gilpin, Robert. *US Power and the Multinational Corporation*. New York: Basic Books, 1975.

Girvan, N. "MNC's and Dependent Underdevelopment in Mineral Export Economics." *Social and Economic Studies* 29 (1970): 490–526.

Glazer, J. H. "Law-Making and Human Settlement at the Lagrangian Points of Trans-National Space." *Columbia Journal of Transnational Law*, forthcoming.

Goldie, L. F. E. "Development of an International Environmental Law—an Appraisal." In Hargrove, John L., ed., *Law, Institutions, and the Global Environment*, pp. 104–65. Dobbs Ferry, N.Y.: Oceana, 1972.

Goldman, Marshall I. *Ecology and Economics: Controlling Pollution in the 1970's.* Englewood Cliffs, N.J.: Prentice-Hall, 1972.

Goldsmith, Edward; Allen, Robert; Allaby, Michael; Davoll, John; Lawrence, Sam. *Blueprint for Survival*. Boston: Houghton Mifflin, 1972.

————. "Is Science a Religion?" *Ecologist* 5 (1975): 50–62.

Goulet, Denis. *The Cruel Choice: A New Concept in the Theory of Development.* New York: Atheneum, 1971.

————. *The Uncertain Promise: Value Conflicts in Technological Transfer.* New York: IDOC, 1977.

Guetzkow, Harold, et al. *Simulation in International Relations: Developments for Research and Teaching.* Englewood Cliffs, N.J.: Prentice-Hall, 1963.

Haas, Ernst. *Tangle of Hopes: American Commitments and World Order.* Englewood Cliffs, N.J.: Prentice-Hall, 1969.

Halpern, Manfred. *The Politics of Social Change in the Middle East and North Africa.* Princeton, N.J.: Princeton University Press, 1963.

Hammond, A. L.; Metz, W. D.; and Maugh, T. H., II. *Energy and the Future.* Washington, D.C.: American Association for the Advancement of Science, 1973.

Handler, Philip. "On the State of Man." *Bioscience* 25 (1975): 425–32.

Hardin, Garrett. "The Tragedy of the Commons." *Science* 162 (1968): 1243–48.

————. *Exploring New Ethics for Survival: The Voyage of the Spaceship "Beagle."* Baltimore: Penguin Books, 1973.

————. "Living on a Lifeboat." *Bioscience* 24 (1974): 561–68.

————. "Carrying Capacity as an Ethical Concept." *Soundings* 59 (1976): 120–37.

————. *The Limits of Altruism: An Ecologist's View of Survival.* Bloomington: Indiana University Press, 1977.

————, and Baden, John, eds. *Managing the Commons.* San Francisco: W. H. Freeman, 1977.

Hargrove, John L., ed. *Law, Institutions, and the Global Environment.* Dobbs, Ferry, N.Y.: Oceana, 1972.

Harmon, David. "An Optimistic View of Agriculture's Future." *New York Times*, 31 January 1976.

Harmon, Willis. *An Incomplete Guide to the Future.* San Francisco: San Francisco Book Co., 1976.

Harrison, Selig S. *China, Oil, and Asia: Conflict Ahead?* New York: Columbia University Press, 1977.

Hartshorn, J. E. *Oil Companies and Governments: An Account of the International Oil Industry in Its Political Environment.* London: Farber and Farber, 1962.

Hayes, Denis. *Rays of Hope.* New York: W. W. Norton, 1977.

Heilbroner, Robert. *An Inquiry into the Human Prospect.* New York: W. W. Norton, 1974.

————. "Second Thoughts on the Human Prospect." *Challenge* 3 (1975): 21–28.

Helleiner, G. K. "Canada and the New International Economic Order." *Canadian Public Policy* 2 (1976): 451–65.

Helmer, Olaf. *Social Technology*. New York: Basic Books, 1966.

Henkin, Louis. "Arctic Anti-Pollution: Does Canada Make—or Break—International Law?" *American Journal of International Law* 65 (1971): 131–36.

Heppenheimer, T., and Hopkins, M. "Initial Space Colonization: Concepts and R&D Aims," *Aeronautics and Astronautics* 14 (1976): 58–64, 72.

Herz, John. *International Politics in the Atomic Age*. New York: Columbia University Press, 1959.

Hinds, S. W. "Relation of Medical Triage to World Famine: A History." In Lucas, George, and Ogletree, T. R., eds., *Lifeboat Ethics: The Moral Dilemmas of Hunger*, pp. 29–51. New York: Harper & Row, 1976.

Hirsch, Fred. *The Social Limits to Growth*. Cambridge: Harvard University Press, 1976.

Hirst, David. *Oil and Public Opinion in the Middle East*. London: Farber and Farber, 1966.

Hogerton, J. F. "The Arrival of Nuclear Power." *Scientific American* 218 (1968): 21–31.

Hostetler, John Andrew. *Hutterite Society*. Baltimore: Johns Hopkins University Press, 1974.

Howe, James W., and Sewell, John W. "Triage and Other Challenges to Helping the Poor Countries Develop." In Howe, James W., ed., *The U.S. and World Development: Agenda for Action—1975*, pp.55–71. New York: Praeger, 1975.

Hughes, J. Donald. *Ecology in Ancient Civilizations*. Albuquerque: University of New Mexico Press, 1975.

Humpstone, Charles Cheney. "Pollution, Precedent and Prospect." *Foreign Affairs* 50 (1972): 325–38.

Huntington, Samuel P. "Political Development and Political Decay." *World Politics* 17 (1965): 386–430.

————. "The Democratic Distemper." *Public Interest* 41 (1975): 9–38.

Hyams, Edward. *Soil and Civilization*. New York: Harper Colophon, 1976.

Issawi, Charles, and Yeganeh, Mohammed. *The Economics of Middle Eastern Oil*. New York: Praeger, 1962.

Jacoby, Neil H. *Multinational Oil: A Study in Industrial Dynamics*. New York: Macmillan, 1974.

James, Bernard. *The Death of Progress*. New York: Alfred A. Knopf, 1973.

Jamgotch, Nish, ed. *Thinking the Thinkable: Investment in Human Survival*. Washington, D.C.: University Press of America, 1978.

"Japan's Economy in Transition." *Business Week*, 7 July 1975, pp. 44–50.

Johnson, Barbara. "A Review of Fisheries Proposals Made at the Caracas Session of LOS III." *Ocean Management* 2 (1975): 285–314.

Johnson, K. "Canadian Report Urges Domestic Comsat." *Aviation Week and Space Technology* 86 (27 March 1967): 69–71.

Johnson, Warren A.; Stoltzfus, Victor; Craumer, Peter. "Energy Conservation in Amish Agriculture." *Science* 198 (1977): 373–78.

Johnston, Douglas M. *The International Law of Fisheries: A Framework for Policy-Oriented Inquiries*. New Haven: Yale University Press, 1965.

Jones, T. E. "Current Prospects of Sustainable Energy Growth." In Laszlo, Ervin, and Bierman, J., eds., *Goals in a Global Community*. New York: Pergamon Press, 1977.

Joskow, Paul L. "The International Nuclear Industry Today." *Foreign Affairs* 54 (1976): 788–803.

Kahn, Herman; Brown, William; and Martel, Leon. *The Next 200 Years*. New York: William Morrow, 1976.

Kapp, Karl William. *The Social Costs of Private Enterprise*. Cambridge: Harvard University Press, 1950.

Kash, D. E. *The Politics of Space Cooperation*. Lafayette, Ind.: Purdue University Press, 1967.

Kateb, George. *Utopia and Its Enemies*. New York: Schocken, 1971.

Kelley, Donald R., ed. *The Energy Crisis and the Environment: An International Perspective*. New York: Praeger, 1977.

———; Stunkel, Kenneth R., and Wescott, Richard R. *The Economic Superpowers and the Environment: The United States, the Soviet Union, and Japan*. San Francisco: Freeman, 1976.

Kennard, H. P., comp. and ed. *The Russian Yearbook*. London: Eyre and Spottiswood, 1914.

Kent, George. "Dominance in Fishing." *Journal of Peace Research* 13 (1976): 35–47.

———. "Fisheries and the Law of the Sea." *Ocean Management*, forthcoming.

Keohane, Robert O., and Nye, Joseph S. *Power and Interdependence*. Boston: Little, Brown, 1977.

Kerr, Malcom H. "The Arabs and Israelis: Perceptual Dimensions to Their Dilemma." In Beling, Willard A., ed., *The Middle East: Quest for an American Policy*, pp. 3–31. Albany: State University of New York Press, 1973.

Keyfitz, Nathan. "World Resources and the World Middle Class." *Scientific American* 235 (1976): 28–35.

Kindelberg, Charles P. "U.S. Foreign Economic Policy, 1776–1976." *Foreign Affairs* 55 (1977): 395–417.

Kneese, Allen V. "The Political Economy of Pollution." *Papers and Proceedings of the Eighty-Third Annual Meeting of the American Economic Association*. *American Economic Review* 61 (1971): 153–66.

———, and Schultz, Charles. *Pollution, Prices, and Public Policy*. Washington, D.C.: Brookings Institution, 1975.

Kocher, James E. *Rural Development, Income Distribution, and Fertility Decline*. New York: Population Council, 1972.

Kravis, I. B. "International Commodity Agreements to Promote Aid and Efficiency: The Case of Coffee." *Canadian Journal of Economics* 1 (1968): 295–317.

Krueger, Robert B. *The United States and International Oil*. New York: Praeger, 1975.

Kuhn, Thomas S. *The Structure of Scientific Revolutions*. Chicago: University of Chicago Press, 1974.

Kury, Channing. "The Fisheries Proposals: An Assessment." *San Diego Law Review* 12 (1975): 644–54.

Ladejinsky, Wolf. "Ironies of India's Green Revolution." *Foreign Affairs* 48 (1970): 758–68.

Laird, Roy D. "Soviet Goals for 1965 and the Problems of Agriculture." In Shaffer, Harry G., ed., *The Soviet Economy*. New York: Appleton-Century-Crofts, 1963.

———. "Prospects for Soviet Agriculture." *Problems of Communism* 20 (1971): 31–40.

Lall, S. "Transfer-Pricing by Multinational Manufacturing Firms." *Oxford Bulletin of Economics and Statistics*, 1973.

Laporte, Todd R., ed. *Organized Social Complexity*. Princeton, N.J.: Princeton University Press, 1975.

Lappé, Frances M., and Collins, Joseph. *Food First: Beyond the Myth of Food Scarcity*. New York: Houghton Mifflin, 1977.

Laszlo, Ervin, et al. *Goals for Mankind: A Report to the Club of Rome on the New Horizons of Global Community*. New York: E. P. Dutton, 1977.

Lay, S. Houston, and Taubenfeld, H. J. *The Law Relating to Activities of Man in Space*. Chicago: University of Chicago Press, 1970.

———; Churchill, Robin; and Nordquist, Myron, comps. and eds. *New Directions in the Law of the Sea*. 3 vols. Dobbs Ferry, N.Y.: Oceana, 1973.

Leakey, Richard E. "New Fossil Evidence for the Evolution of Man." *Social Biology* 19 (1972): 99–114.

Lee, Richard B. "What Hunters Do for a Living; or, How to Make Out on Scarce Resources." In Lee, Richard B., and De Vore, Irven, eds., *Man the Hunter*, pp. 30–48. Chicago: Aldine, 1968.

Leipziger, Danny M., and Mudge, James. *Seabed Mineral Resources and the Economic Interests of Developing Countries*. Cambridge, Mass.: Ballinger, 1976.

Leiss, William. *The Domination of Nature*. Boston: Beacon Press, 1974.

Lenczowski, George. *The Middle East in World Affairs*. 3d ed. Ithaca, N.Y.: Cornell University Press, 1964.

Leontieff, Wassily. *The Future of the World Economy*. New York: Oxford University Press, 1976.

Leopold, Aldo. *A Sand County Almanac*. New York: Ballantine Books, 1973.

Levine, M. S. "Some Approaches to the Conceptualization and Analysis of Change in the International System." Paper presented to the annual meeting of the International Studies Association, St. Louis, 1974.

Levy, Marion. *Modernization and the Structure of Societies*. Princeton, N.J.: Princeton University Press, 1966.

Lewis, C. S. *The Abolition of Man*. New York: Macmillan, 1970.

Lindsey, Robert. "Hard Times in Copper Country." *New York Times*, 12 December 1976, pp. 1, 9.

Liska, George. *Nations in Alliance: The Limits of Interdependence*. Baltimore: Johns Hopkins University Press, 1952.

Livingston, Dennis. "Science, Technology, and International Law." In Falk, Richard A., and Black, Cyril, eds., *The Future of the International Legal Order*.

Vol. 4, *The Structure of the International Environment*, pp. 68–123. Princeton, N.J.: Princeton University Press, 1972.

Lockeretz, William, et al. *A Comparison of the Production, Economic Returns, and Energy Intensiveness of Corn Belt Farms That Do and Do Not Use Inorganic Fertilizers and Pesticides*. St. Louis: Center for the Study of the Biology of Natural Systems, 1975.

Longrigg, Stephen H. *Oil in the Middle East: Its Discovery and Development*. 3d ed. London: Oxford University Press, 1968.

Lovins, Amory B. "Energy Strategy: The Road Not Taken?" *Foreign Affairs* 55 (1976): 65–96.

———. *Soft Energy Paths*. Cambridge, Mass: Ballinger, 1977.

Lucas, George R. *Triage in Medicine and Society*. Houston: Institute of Religion, 1975.

———, and Ogletree, T. W., eds. *Lifeboat Ethics: The Moral Dilemmas of Hunger*. New York: Harper and Row, 1976.

McConnell, Grant. *Private Power and American Democracy*. New York: Knopf, 1966.

McIntyre, L. *The Incredible Incas*. Washington, D.C.: National Geographic Society, 1975.

McNicoll, Geoffrey. "Community-Level Population Policy: An Exploration." *Population and Development Review* 1 (1975): 1–22.

Makdashi, Zuhayr. *The International Politics of Natural Resources*. Ithaca, N.Y.: Cornell University Press, 1976.

Mankind 2000 and the Union of International Associations, *Yearbook of World Problems and Human Potential*. Brussels, 1976.

Marsden, Ralph W., ed. *Politics, Minerals, and Survival*. Madison: University of Wisconsin Press, 1974.

Maslow, Abraham H. *Toward a Psychology of Being*. Princeton, N.J.: Van Norstrand, 1962.

Mead, Margaret. "The Future: Prefigurative Cultures and Unknown Children." In Toffler, Alvin, ed., *The Futurists*, pp. 27–50. New York: Random House, 1972.

Meadows, Dennis L. *Dynamics of Growth in a Finite World*. New York: John Wiley, 1974.

———; and Randers, Jørgen. "Adding the Time Dimension to Environmental Policy." *International Organization* 26 (1972): 213–33.

Meadows, Donnella H.; Meadows, Dennis L.; Randers, Jørgen; and Behrens, William H. *The Limits to Growth*. New York: Signet, 1972.

Meiselman, D. I., and Laffer, A. B., eds. *The Phenomenon of Worldwide Inflation*. Washington, D.C.: American Institute for Public Policy Research, 1975.

Melville, Herman. "A Canticle." In *The Battle Pieces of Herman Melville*. New York: Thomas Yoseloff, 1963.

Mendlovitz, Saul H., ed. *On the Creation of a Just World Order: Preferred Worlds for the 1990's*. New York: Free Press, 1975.

Mesarovic, Mihajlo, and Pestel, Eduard. *Mankind at the Turning Point*. New York: E. P. Dutton, 1974.

Metlay, Daniel. "On Studying the Future Behavior of Complex Systems." In Laporte, Todd R., ed., *Organized Social Complexity*. Princeton, N.J.: Princeton University Press, 1975.

Michels, Roberto. *Political Parties*. New York: Free Press, 1966.

Mikesell, Raymond F. *Nonfuel Minerals: U.S. Investment Policies Abroad*. Beverly Hills, Calif.: Sage, 1975.

Milbrath, Lester, and Inscho, Frederick R. *The Politics of Environmental Policy*. Beverly Hills, Calif.: Sage, 1975.

Miles, Rufus E. *Awakening from the American Dream: The Social and Political Limits to Growth*. New York: Universe, 1976.

Miller, G. Tyler, Jr. *Living in the Environment: Concepts, Problems, and Alternatives*. Belmont, Calif.: Wadsworth, 1975.

Mische, Gerald, and Mische, Patricia. *Toward a Human World Order: Beyond the National Security Straitjacket*. New York: Paulist Press, 1977.

Mitrany, David. *A Working Peace System*. Chicago: University of Chicago Press, 1946.

Modelski, George. *Principles of World Politics*. New York: Free Press, 1972.

Moore, John Norton. "Foreign Policy and Fidelity to Law: The Anatomy of a Treaty Violation." *American Journal of International Law* 70 (1976): 802–808.

Moran, Theodore H. "The Theory of International Exploitation in Large Natural Resource Investment." In Rosen, S., and Kurth, J., eds., *Testing Theories of Economic Imperialism*, pp. 163–81. Lexington, Mass.: D. C. Heath, 1974.

———. *Multinational Corporations and the Politics of Dependence*. Princeton, N.J.: Princeton University Press, 1974.

Morgan, Edward P. "Stockholm: The Clean (But Impossible) Dream." *Foreign Policy* 8 (1972): 149–55.

Morris, David, and Hess, Karl. *Neighborhood Power*. Boston: Beacon Press, 1975.

Mosley, Leonard. *Power Play: Oil in the Middle East*. Baltimore: Penguin, 1973.

Mostert, Noel. *Supership*. New York: Warner, 1974.

Muir, Ramsay. *The Interdependent World and Its Problems*. Boston: Houghton Mifflin, 1933.

Mumford, Lewis. *The Myth of the Machine: The Pentagon of Power*. New York: Harcourt Brace Jovanovich, 1970.

———. *The Myth of the Machine: Technics and Human Development*. New York: Harcourt Brace Jovanovich, 1970.

Myrdal, Gunnar. *The Challenge of World Poverty: A World Anti-Poverty Program in Outline*. New York: Pantheon Books, 1970.

Nicholls, Yvonne I. *Source Book: Emergence of Proposals for Recompensing Developing Countries for Maintaining Environmental Quality*. Morges, Switzerland: International Union for Conservation of Nature and Natural Resources, 1973.

North, Robert C., and Choucri, Nazli. *Nations in Conflict*. San Francisco: W. H. Freeman, 1975.

Nove, Alex. "Soviet Agriculture Marks Time." In Shaffer, Harry G., ed., *The Soviet Economy*. New York: Appleton-Century-Crofts, 1963.

————. "Will Russia Ever Feed Itself?" *New York Times Magazine*, 1 February 1976.

Odell, Peter R. *Oil and World Power*. 4th ed. London: Penguin, 1975.

Odum, Eugene. *Fundamentals of Ecology*. 3d ed. Philadelphia: W. B. Saunders, 1971.

————. "The Emergence of Ecology as a New Integrative Discipline." *Science* 195 (1977): 1289–92.

Odum, Howard T. *Environment, Power, and Society*. New York: Wiley-Interscience, 1971.

Olson, Mancur, and Landsberg, Hans H., eds. *The No-Growth Society*. New York: Norton, 1973.

O'Neill, G. K. "The Colonization of Space." *Physics Today* 27 (September 1974): 32–40.

————. "Space Colonies and Energy Supply to the Earth." *Science* 190 (1975): 943–47.

————. *New York Times Magazine*. 18 January 1976, pp. 10–11, 27–29.

————. *The High Frontier*. New York: Morrow, 1977.

Ophuls, William. "The Scarcity Society." *Harpers Magazine*, April 1974.

————. *Ecology and the Politics of Scarcity*. San Francisco: Freeman, 1977.

Orleans, Leo A. *Every Fifth Child: The Population of China*. Stanford, Calif.: Stanford University Press, 1972.

Orr, David W. "Modernization and Conflict: The Second Image Implications of Scarcity." *International Studies Quarterly* 21 (1977): 593–618.

Osgood, Robert E., et al. *Toward a National Ocean Policy: 1976 and Beyond*. Washington, D.C.: Government Printing Office, 1976.

Osofsky, Stephen. "The Soviet Grain Problem in Perspective." *Russian Review* 32 (1973): 52–57.

Paddock, William, and Paddock, Paul. *Famine—1975! America's Decision: Who Will Survive?* Boston: Little, Brown, 1967.

————. *Time of Famines: America and the World Food Crisis*. Boston: Little, Brown, 1976.

Page, Talbot. *Conservation and Economic Efficiency*. Baltimore: Johns Hopkins University Press, 1977.

Page, William. "Mining and Development: Are They Compatible in South America?" *Resources Policy* 2 (December 1976): 235–46.

Palumbo, Dennis J. "Organization Theory and Political Science." In Greenstein, Fred, and Polsby, Nelson, eds., *Handbook of Political Science*, vol. 2. Reading, Mass.: Addison-Wesley, 1975.

Pardo, Arvid. *The Common Heritage: Selected Papers on Ocean and World Order, 1967–1974*. Occasional Paper no. 3. Malta: International Ocean Institute, 1975.

————, and Borgese, Elisabeth Mann. *The New International Economic Order and the Law of the Sea*. Malta: International Ocean Institute, 1976.

Parsons, Talcott, and Shils, Edward. *Toward a General Theory of Action*. New York: Harper, 1962.

Pateman, Carol. *Participation and Democratic Theory*. Cambridge: Cambridge University Press, 1970.

Patterson, W. *Nuclear Power*. Baltimore: Penguin Books, 1976.

Pavitt, Keith. "Technology, International Competition, and Economic Growth: Some Lessons and Perspectives." *World Politics* 25 (1973): 183–205.

Peare, David, and Richard, Grace. "Stabilising Secondary Materials Markets." *Resources Policy* 2 (1976): 118–27.

Piper, Don C. "Foreign Policy Outputs and International Law." *Policy Studies Journal* 3 (1974): 132–37.

_____. "The Cuban Missile Crisis and International Law: Precipitous Decline or Unilateral Development." *World Affairs* 138 (1975): 26–31.

Pirages, Dennis C., ed. *The Sustainable Society: Implications for Limited Growth*. New York: Praeger, 1977.

_____, ed. *International Politics of Scarcity*. Special Issue of *International Studies Quarterly* 21 (1977).

_____, and Ehrlich, Paul. *Ark II*. San Francisco: Freeman, 1974.

Poleman, Thomas T. "World Food: A Perspective." *Science* 188 (1975): 511.

Polgar, Steven. "Population History and Population Policies from an Anthropological Perspective." *Current Anthropology* 13 (1972): 203–11, 263–67.

Pontecorvo, Guilio, ed. *Fisheries Conflict in the North Atlantic: Problems of Management and Jurisdiction*. Cambridge, Mass.: Ballinger, 1974.

Principles for a Global Fisheries Management Regime, Washington, D.C.: American Society of International Law, 1974.

Quarles, John. *Cleaning Up America*. Boston: Houghton Mifflin, 1976.

Rainwater, Lee. "Equity, Income, Inequality, and the Steady State." In Pirages, Dennis C., ed., *The Sustainable Society*, pp. 262–73. New York: Praeger, 1977.

Raup, Philip M. "Some Consequences of Data Deficiencies in Soviet Agriculture." In Treml, Vladimir G., and Hardt, John P., eds., *Soviet Economic Statistics*. Durham, N.C.: Duke University Press, 1972.

Renshaw, Edward F. *The End of Progress: Adjusting to a No-Growth Economy*. North Scituate, Mass.: Duxbury, 1976.

Rich, William. *Smaller Families through Social and Economic Progress*. Washington, D.C.: Overseas Development Council, 1973.

Robinson, G. S. "Space Law." *Technology Review* 80 (1977): 59–64.

Rogers, Carl. *On Personal Power*. New York: Delacorte Press, 1977.

Rogers, Christopher. "Agreement about Commodity Agreements?" *Resources Policy* 2 (1976): 97–105.

Rogers, William. Statement in U.S. Department of State *Current Policy* Series, no. 16 (November 1976), p. 7.

Rohn, P. H. *World Treaty Index*. Santa Barbara, Calif.: ABC-Clio, 1974.

Roper, L. D. *Where Have All the Metals Gone?* Blacksburg, Va.: University Publications, 1976.

Rosecrance, Richard N. *Action and Reaction in World Politics*. Boston: Little, Brown, 1963.

Rosenbaum, Walter A. *The Politics of Environmental Concern*. 2d ed. New York: Praeger, 1977.

Roszak, Theodore. "The Monster and the Titan: Science, Knowledge, and Gnosis." *Daedalus* 103 (1974): 17–32.

————. *Where the Wasteland Ends*. New York: Anchor, 1972.

Russell, Jeremy. *Energy as a Factor in Soviet Foreign Policy*. Lexington, Mass.: Lexington Books, 1976.

Russett, Bruce. "The Ecology of Future International Relations." *International Studies Quarterly* 11 (1967): 12–31.

————. "Transactions, Community, and International Political Integration." *Journal of Common Market Studies* 9 (1971): 143–50.

Sachs, Ignacy. "Ambiente y estilos de desarrollo." *Comercio Exterior* (Mexico) 24 (1974): 360–68.

Sahlins, Marshall D. "Notes on the Original Affluent Society." In Lee, Richard B., and De Vore, Irven, eds., *Man the Hunter*, pp. 85–89. Chicago: Aldine, 1968.

Sayegh, Kamal S. *Oil and Arab Regional Development*. New York: Praeger, 1968.

Schinke, Eberhard. "Soviet Agricultural Statistics." In Treml, Vladimir G., and Hardt, John P., eds., *Soviet Economic Statistics*. Durham, N.C.: Duke University Press, 1972.

Schlesinger, Arthur, Jr. "Origins of the Cold War." *Foreign Affairs* 46 (1967): 22–32.

Schmid, Herman. "Peace Research and Politics." *Journal of Peace Research*. 5 (1968): 217–32.

Schneider-Sawris, Shadia. *The Concept of Compensation in the Field of Trade and the Environment*. Morges, Switzerland: International Union for Conservation of Nature and Natural Resources, 1973.

Scholars, Leonardo. *Resources and Decisions*. North Scituate, Mass.: Duxbury, 1975.

Schon, Donald. *Beyond the Stable State*. New York: W. W. Norton, 1971.

Schoultz, Lars. "Urbanization and Political Change in Latin America." *Midwest Journal of Political Science* 16 (1972): 367–87.

Schumacher, E. F. *Small Is Beautiful: Economics As If People Mattered*. New York: Harper & Row, 1973.

Scott, Andrew M. "The Global System and the Implications of Interaction." *International Interactions* 1 (1974): 229–36.

Segre, D. V., and Adler, J. H. "The Ecology of Terrorism." *Survival* 15 (1973): 178–83.

Sewell, James P. *Functionalism and World Politics*. Princeton, N.J.: Princeton University Press, 1966.

Shaw, Edward S. *Financial Deepening in Economic Development*. New York: Oxford University Press, 1973.

Shulman, Paul R. "Non-incremental Policy Making: Notes toward an Alternative Paradigm." *American Political Science Review* 69 (1975): 1354–70.

Shyam, Manjula. "Rights of the Coastal States to Fisheries Resources in the Economic Zone: An Empirical Analysis of State Preferences." *Ocean Management* 3 (1976): 1–30.

Singh, Shamsher. "The International Dialogue on Commodities." *Resources Policy* 2 (1976): 87–96.

Sivard, Ruth L. *World Military and Social Expenditures—1977*. Leesburg, Va.: WMSE Publications, 1977.

Skolnikoff, E. B. *The International Imperatives of Technology*. Institute of International Studies Research Series, no. 16. University of California, Berkeley, 1972.

Slater, Philip. *The Pursuit of Loneliness: American Culture at the Breaking Point*. Boston: Beacon Press, 1970.

Slouka, Zdenek. *International Custom and the Continental Shelf*. The Hague: Martinus Nijhoff, 1969.

———. "International Environmental Controls in the Scientific Age." In Hargrove, John L., ed., *Law, Institutions, and the Global Environment*. Dobbs Ferry, N.Y.: Oceana, 1972.

Smith, Courtland L. "Fishing Success in a Regulated Commons." *Ocean Development and International Law* 1 (1974): 369–81.

Smoker, Paul. "Social Research for Social Anticipation." *American Behavioral Scientist* 12 (1969): 7–13.

Soroos, Marvin S. "Behavioral Science, Forecasting, and the Design of Alternative Future Worlds." *International Interactions* 1 (1974): 269–72.

———. "A Methodological Overview of the Process of Designing Alternative Future Worlds." In Beres, Louis R., and Targ, Harry R., eds., *Planning Alternative World Futures: Values, Methods, and Models*. New York: Praeger, 1975.

———. "Adding an Intergenerational Dimension to Conceptions of Peace." *Journal of Peace Research* 13 (1976): 173–83.

Spengler, Joseph J. *Population and America's Future*. San Francisco: Freeman, 1975.

Sprout, Harold, and Sprout, Margaret. *The Ecological Perspective on Human Affairs*. Princeton, N.J.: Princeton University Press, 1965.

———. *Toward a Politics of the Planet Earth*. New York: Van Nostrand, Reinhold, 1971.

———. *Multiple Vulnerabilities: The Context of Environmental Repair and Protection*. Princeton, N.J.: Center for International Studies, 1974.

Stavrianos, L. S. *The Promise of the Coming Dark Age*. San Francisco: W. H. Freeman, 1976.

Steinhart, J. S., and Steinhart, C. E. "Energy Use in the U.S. Food System." *Science* 184 (1974): 307–15.

Steinhoff, E. A., ed. *Organizing Space Activities for World Needs*. New York: Pergamon Press, 1971.

Sterling, Richard W. *Macropolitics: International Relations in a Global Society*. New York: Alfred A. Knopf, 1974.

Stern, Paul C., and Kirkpatrick, Eileeen M. "Energy Behavior." *Environment* 19 (1977): 10–15.

Stone, Christopher D. *Should Trees Have Standing? Toward Legal Rights for Natural Objects*. Los Altos, Calif.: William Kaufmann, 1974.

Stretton, Hugh. *Capitalism, Socialism, and the Environment*. Cambridge: Cambridge University Press, 1976.

Strong, Maurice F. "One Year after Stockholm: An Ecological Approach to Management." *Foreign Affairs* 51 (1973): 690–707.

Study of Critical Environmental Problems. *Man's Impact on the Global Environment.* Cambridge, Mass.: MIT Press, 1970.

Sundquist, James L. *Dispersing Population.* Washington D.C.: Brookings Institution, 1975.

Sweeny, Richard J., et al. "Market Failure, the Common-Pool Problem, and Ocean Resource Exploitation." *Journal of Law and Economics* 17 (1974): 179–92.

Syzliowicz, Joseph H., and O'Neill, Bard E., eds. *The Energy Crisis and U.S. Foreign Policy.* New York: Praeger, 1975.

Taubenfeld, Howard J., ed. *Space and Society.* Dobbs Ferry, N.Y.: Oceana, 1964.

Teclaff, Ludwik A., and Utton, Albert E., eds. *International Environmental Law.* New York: Praeger, 1974.

Teitlebaum, Michael S. "Relevance of Demographic Transition Theory for Developing Countries." *Science* 181 (1975): 420–25.

Thayer, Frederick C. *An End to Hierarchy! An End to Competition! Organizing the Politics and Economics of Survival.* New York: Franklin Watts, 1973.

Tien, H. Yuan. *China's Population Struggle: Demographic Decisions of the People's Republic.* Columbus: Ohio State University Press, 1973.

Tilton, John E. "The Choice of Trading Partners: An Analysis of International Trade in Aluminum, Copper, Lead, Manganese, Tin, and Zinc." *Yale Economic Essays* 6 (1966): 419–74.

_____. *The Future of Nonfuel Minerals.* Washington, D.C.: Brookings Institution, 1977.

Tinbergen, Jan; Dolman, Antony J.; and van Ettinger, Jan, eds. *Reshaping the International Order: A Report to the Club of Rome.* New York: E. P. Dutton, 1976.

Tocqueville, Alexis de. *Democracy in America.* New York: Doubleday, 1969.

Todd, John. "Pioneering for the 21st Century." Unpublished manuscript, 1975.

Toffler, Alvin, ed. *Learning for Tomorrow: The Role of the Future in Education.* New York: Random House, 1974.

Tucker, Robert W. "Oil: The Issue of American Intervention." *Commentary* 59 (1975): 21–31.

Turnbull, Colin. "Population Control Factors: Infanticide, Disease, Nutrition, and Food Supply." In Lee, Richard B., and Devore, Irven, eds., *Man the Hunter*, pp. 243–45. Chicago: Aldine, 1968.

Utton, Albert E. "The Arctic Waters Pollution Prevention Act and the Right of Self-Protection." In Teclaff, Ludwik A., and Utton, Albert E., eds., *International Environmental Law*, pp. 140–53. New York: Praeger, 1974.

Vajk, J. P. "The Impact of Space Colonization on World Dynamics." *Technological Forecasting and Social Change* 9 (1976): 361–99.

_____. "An Open Door for a Closed World." Mimeographed. Pleasanton, Calif.: Science Applications, 1976.

Varnon, Bension, and Takeuchi, Kenji. "Developing Countries and Nonfuel Minerals." *Foreign Affairs* 51 (1974): 690–707.

Vernon, Raymond, ed. *The Oil Crisis.* New York: Norton, 1976.

Volin, Lazar. "Agricultural Organization." In Bergson, Abram, ed., *Soviet Economic Growth*. Evanston: Row, Peterson, 1953.

Wade, Nicholas. "Green Revolution (I): A Just Technology Often Unjust in Use." *Science* 186 (1974): 1093–96.

———. "Green Revolution (II): Problems of Adapting a Western Technology." *Science* 186 (1974): 1186–92.

Wadekin, Karl-Eugen. "Soviet Agricultural Statistics: Summary and Assessment." In Treml, Vladimir G., and Hardt, John P., eds., *Soviet Economic Statistics*. Durham, N.C.: Duke University Press, 1972.

Wald, George. "America's My Home. Not My Business, My Home." *Bulletin of the Atomic Scientists* 25 (1969): 29–31.

Walsh, Don, ed. *The Law of the Sea: Issues in Ocean Resource Management*. New York: Praeger, 1977.

Walsh, John. "U.S. Agribusiness and Agricultural Trends." *Science* 188 (1975): 531.

Walter, Ingo. *International Economics of Pollution*. New York: John Wiley and Sons, 1975.

Walters, Harry. "Difficult Issues Underlying Food Problems." *Science* 188 (1975): 528.

Wang, Kung-Ping. *Mineral Resources and Basic Industries in the Peoples' Republic of China*. Boulder, Colo.: Westview Press, 1977.

Ward, Barbara. *Spaceship Earth*. New York: Columbia University Press, 1966.

———. *The Home of Man*. New York: Norton, 1976.

———, and Dubos, René. *Only One Earth: The Care and Maintenance of a Small Planet*. New York: Norton, 1972.

Washburn, Sherwood L. "Population Control Factors: Infanticide, Disease, Nutrition, and Food Supply." In Lee, Richard B., and De Vore, Irven, eds., *Man the Hunter*, pp. 243–45. Chicago: Aldine, 1968.

Waskow, Arthur I. "Towards a Democratic Futurism." In Toffler, Alvin, ed., *The Futurists*, pp. 85–95. New York: Random House. 1972.

Webb, R. E. *The Accident Hazards of Nuclear Power Plants*. Amherst: University of Massachusetts Press, 1976.

Weinberg, Alvin. "Social Institutions and Nuclear Energy." *Science* 177 (1972): 27–34.

Wenk, Edward. *The Politics of the Ocean*. Seattle: University of Washington Press, 1972.

White, I. L. *Decision-making for Space*. Lafayette, Ind.: Purdue University Press, 1970.

White, Lynn. "The Historical Roots of Our Ecological Crisis." *Science* 155 (1967): 1203–7.

Whiteman, Marjorie M. *Digest of International Law*. 15 vols. Washington, D.C.: Government Printing Office, 1963–73.

Willrich, Mason. *Energy and World Politics*. New York: Free Press, 1975.

Wilson, Harlan. "Complexity as a Theoretical Problem: Wider Perspectives in Political Theory." In Laporte, Todd R., ed., *Organized Social Complexity*. Princeton, N.J.: Princeton University Press, 1975.

Winberg, Alan R. "Power Diffusion through Raw Material Producer Associations in the Third World." *Journal of International and Comparative Public Policy* 1 (1977): 149–60.

Winner, Langdon. *Autonomous Technology.* Cambridge, Mass.: MIT Press, 1977.

Winski, Joseph M. "By 2000, Prevention of Starvation May Be Chief Global Concern." *Wall Street Journal,* 25 March 1976.

Wirsing, Robert G., ed. *International Relations and the Future of Ocean Space.* Columbia: University of South Carolina Press, 1974.

Wonder, Edward F. *Nuclear Fuel and American Foreign Policy: Multilaterization.* Boulder, Colo.: Westview Press, 1977.

Woodburn, James. "An Introduction to Hadza Ecology." In Lee, Richard B., and De Vore, Irven, eds., *Man the Hunter,* pp. 49–55. Chicago, Aldine, 1968.

———. "Population Control Factors: Infanticide, Disease, Nutrition, and Food Supply." In Lee, Richard B., and De Vore, Irven, eds., *Man the Hunter,* pp. 243–45. Chicago: Aldine, 1968.

Woodhouse, Edward J. "Re-visioning the Future of the Third World: An Ecological Perspective." *World Politics* 25 (1972): 1–33.

Yoshino, M. Y. "The Multinational Spread of Japanese Manufacturing Investments since World War II." *Business History Review* 48 (1974): 357–81.

Young, Oran. *Resource Management at the International Level: The Case of the North Pacific.* New York: Nichols, 1977.

Zartman, William. "Negotiations: Theory and Reality." *Journal of International Affairs* 9 (1975): 69–77.

Documents

Commission of the European Communities. *Information: The Convention of Lomé* (129/76/X/E), July 1977.

General Agreement on Tariffs and Trade. *Industrial Pollution Control and International Trade.* Studies in International Trade, July 1971.

International Coffee Organization. *International Coffee Agreement 1976.* London: International Coffee Organization, 1976.

International Institute for Environment and Development. *Multilateral Aid and the Environment.* Washington, D.C.: IIED, 1976.

United Nations. Center for Economic and Social Information. *Thorough Examination of U.N. Role in International Economic Co-operation Expected* (OPI/CES I Features ESA/146), 11 February 1975.

———. Center for Economic and Social Information, UNCTAD Information Unit. *An Integrated Programme for Commodities* (TD/B/C/1/166/ Supp. 1–5), 9 December 1974–14 January 1975.

———. Conference on Trade and Development. *Environmental Policies and Their Implications for Trade and Development: A Case Study,* prepared by V. Ranganathan (ST/MD/10), 18 November 1977.

———. Conference on Trade and Development. *Impact of Environmental Policies on Trade and Development, in Particular of the Developing Countries* (UNCTAD, TD/130), 13 March 1972.

———. Conference on Trade and Development. *The Impact of Environmental Issues on Development and International Economic Relations* (Research Memorandum no. 53), 29 April 1976.

———. Conference on Trade and Development. *Implications for the Trade and Investment of Developing Countries of United States Environmental Controls*, prepared by Charles Pearson (UNCTAD, TD/B/C.2/150/Add. 1/Rev. 1), 1973.

———. Conference on Trade and Development. *Social Evaluation and Pricing of Natural Resources: Main Issues* (internal document), 1975–76.

———. Conference on Trade and Development. Information Unit (TD/214; TD/215), 9 June 1976.

———. Economic and Social Council. *Official Records* (1730th meeting), 13 November 1970.

———. Economic and Social Council. *Summary Records* (E/C. 7/SR.60), 9 February 1973.

———. Economic and Social Council. *Economic Survey for Latin America, 1974* (E/CEPAL.982.Rev.1), October 1975.

———. Economic Commission for Latin America. *Statistical Yearbook for Latin America, 1973* (E/CEPAL/977/Add.1), 15 August 1974.

———. Environmental Program. *Ecodevelopment* (GC/80) 15 January 1976.

———. Environmental Program, Report of the Executive Director. *Environment and Development* (GC/76), 29 January 1976.

———. Food and Agriculture Organization. *A Contribution to Discussion of a New Economic Order with Reference to the Living Resources of the Ocean*, prepared by Sidney J. Holt. Rome, FAO, 1977.

———. General Assembly. *Official Records* (A/C. 2/S.R. 1730), 29 November 1971.

———. General Assembly, Conference on the Human Environment. *Report of the United Nations Conference on the Human Environment* (A/Conf. 48/14/ Rev. 1), 1972.

———. General Assembly, Conference on the Human Environment. *Development and Environment* (A/Conf. 48/10, Annex 1), December 1971.

———. General Assembly, Third Conference on the Sea. Supplements to the *Official Records*, 1975.

———. General Assembly, Conference on the Law of the Sea. *Informal Composite Negotiating Text* (A/Conf.62/WP.10/Corr.1 and 2), 15 July 1977.

———. Industrial Development Organization. *Report of the Expert Group Meeting on the Study of Synthetic versus Natural Products* (ID/WG./188/3 and Corr.1), 8 November 1974.

———. International Bank for Reconstruction and Development. *Opportunities for OPEC-type Action in Agricultural Commodities*. (Commodity Paper no. 1), March 1973.

United Nations Office at Geneva. Information Service, Special Projects Section. 9th Geneva Graduate Study Programme, Human Environment, Working Group III, 5 August 1971.

———. Office of Public Information. *Charter of Economic Duties and Rights of States (OPI/542-75-38308), February 1975, p. 2.*

United States. Agency for International Development. Environmental Impact Statement on the AID Pest Management Program. Washington, D.C.: Government Printing Office, 1977.

————. Congress, House, Committee on Science and Technology, Subcommittee on Space Science and Applications. *Hearing on International Space Law* (testimony by C. Q. Christol). 94th Cong., 2d sess., 28 July 1976, pp. 2–16.

————. Congress, Senate, Committee on Aeronautical and Space Sciences. *Hearing on Space Shuttle Payloads* (testimony by P. E. Glaser). 93rd Cong., 1st sess., 31 October 1973, pp. 32–62.

————. Congress, Senate, Committee on Aeronautical and Space Sciences, Subcommittee on Aerospace Technology and National Needs. *Solar Power from Satellites* (testimony by P. E. Glaser). 94th Cong., 2d sess., 19 and 20 January 1976.

————. Congress, Senate, Committee on Foreign Relations. *Multinational Corporations in Brazil and Mexico: Structural Sources of Economic and Noneconomic Power*, prepared by Richard Newfarmer and Willard Mueller. Washington, D.C.: Government Printing Office, 1975.

————. Congress, Senate, Committee on Finance. *Oil Company Profitability.* 93d Cong., 2d sess., 12 February 1974.

————. Council on Environmental Quality. *Energy and the Environment— Electric Power.* Washington, D.C.: Government Printing Office, 1973.

————. Council on Environmental Quality. *The President's Environmental Program—1977.* Washington, D.C.: Government Printing Office, 1977.

————. Department of Agriculture. *The World Food Studies and Prospects to 1985.* Washington, D.C.: Government Printing Office, 1974.

————. Department of Commerce. *Statistical Abstract of the United States.* Washington, D.C.: Government Printing Office, 1974.

————. Department of Commerce. *The Effects of Pollution Abatement on International Trade—III.* April 1975.

————. Department of State, Bureau of Public Affairs. *International Collusive Action in World Markets for Nonfuel Metals*, prepared by Raymond S. Mikesell. Office of Media Services, Special Report no. 4, September 1974.

————. Information Service. Press Release HE 24 (72), 16 June 1972.

————. National Marine Fisheries Service. *Fisheries Management under Extended Jurisdiction: A Study of Principles and Policies.* Washington, D.C.: Government Printing Office, 1975.

————. National Aeronautics and Space Administration, Office of Aeronautics and Space Technology. *Space Manufacturing from Nonterrestrial Materials.* Ames Research Center, 1976.

————. National Aeronautics and Space Administration, Scientific and Technical Information Office. *Space Settlements: A Design Study* (NASA SP-413). Washington, D.C.: Government Printing Office, 1977.

World Bank. *Environment and Development.* June 1975.

Contributors

William Behrens is a resource specialist and a coauthor of *The Limits to Growth*.

Richard L. Clinton, associate professor of political science and associate dean of the College of Liberal Arts at Oregon State University, is the author of several articles on the political dimensions of world population dynamics and the editor of *Politics of Population* (with R. Kenneth Godwin) and *Population and Politics: New Directions in Political Science Research*.

Charles F. Doran is associate professor of political science at Rice University. He is the author of *The Politics of Assimilation: Hegemony and Its Aftermath* and *Myth, Oil, and Politics: An Introduction to the Political Economy of Petroleum*. His articles have appeared in the *Journal of Conflict Resolution*, *International Studies Quarterly*, and *Environmental Affairs*.

Stuart Hill is a graduate student in the Department of Political Science at The University of North Carolina at Chapel Hill. His primary research interests concern environmental policy.

Ole R. Holsti, George V. Allen Professor of Political Science at Duke University, is the author of *Crisis, Escalation, and War* and *Content Analysis for the Social Sciences and the Humanities*. He has been an associate editor of the *International Studies Quarterly*, the *Journal of Conflict Resolution*, and the *Western Political Quarterly*.

Lawrence Juda, affiliated with the Department of Geography and Marine Affairs at the University of Rhode Island, is the author of *Ocean Space Rights: Developing a U.S. Policy.*

George Kent, professor of political science at the University of Hawaii at Manoa, has authored numerous articles on international politics.

David W. Orr is assistant professor of political science at The University of North Carolina at Chapel Hill. He has authored or coauthored articles appearing in *Alternatives, International Interactions, Human Ecology,* the *International Studies Quarterly, Science and Public Policy, Polity,* and the *Western Political Quarterly.*

Don C. Piper, professor of political science at the University of Maryland, is the author of the *International Law of the Great Lakes: A Study of Canadian-U.S. Cooperation* and numerous other scholarly articles on international law.

Jørgen Randers is one of the coauthors of *The Limits to Growth* and related works on growth dynamics. He is presently the head of the Resource Policy Group in Oslo and is completing a study of long-term strategies for the use of Scandinavian forests.

Jack D. Salmon is associate professor of political science at the University of West Florida. He is the author of many articles dealing with the social and ecological aspects of technological developments.

Andrew M. Scott is professor of political science at The University of North Carolina at Chapel Hill. He is the author of numerous works on international affairs, including *The Revolution in Statecraft: Informal Penetration* and *The Functioning of the International System.* His current research involves the development of indicators for monitoring the international system.

Thomas J. Sloan is assistant professor of political science at Kansas State University. His articles have appeared in the *Papers* of the Peace Science Society (international) and the *Review of Peace Science.* He is the coauthor of *Dimensions of Interaction: A Source Book for the Study of the Behavior of 31 Nations from 1948 to 1973.*

Marvin S. Soroos is associate professor of political science at North Carolina State University at Raleigh. His articles have appeared in *International Interactions*, the *Review of Peace Science*, the *Journal of Peace Research*, *Peace Research Reviews*, and *International Studies Quarterly*.

James Larry Taulbee is associate professor of political science at Emory University. He is the author of many scholarly papers and articles on international affairs and law appearing in U.S. and international journals.

Alan R. Winberg, a senior economist with the Canadian National Energy Board, was formerly assistant professor at the Institute for International Cooperation at Ottawa University. He has published widely on the politics and economics of raw material producers' associations.

Index